Lecture Notes in Economics and Mathematical Systems 568

Founding Editors:

M. Beckmann
H. P. Künzi

Managing Editors:

Prof. Dr. G. Fandel
Fachbereich Wirtschaftswissenschaften
Fernuniversität Hagen
Feithstr. 140/AVZ II, 58084 Hagen, Germany

Prof. Dr. W. Trockel
Institut für Mathematische Wirtschaftsforschung (IMW)
Universität Bielefeld
Universitätsstr. 25, 33615 Bielefeld, Germany

Editorial Board:

A. Basile, A. Drexl, H. Dawid, K. Inderfurth, W. Kürsten, U. Schittko

Marco Caliendo

Microeconometric Evaluation of Labour Market Policies

Author

Dr. Marco Caliendo
DIW Berlin
Department of Public Economics
Königin-Luise-Str. 5
14195 Berlin
Germany
mcaliendo@diw.de

ISSN 0075-8442
ISBN-10 3-540-28707-8 Springer Berlin Heidelberg New York
ISBN-13 978-3-540-28707-0 Springer Berlin Heidelberg New York

This work is subject to copyright. All rights are reserved, whether the whole or part of the material is concerned, specifically the rights of translation, reprinting, re-use of illustrations, recitation, broadcasting, reproduction on microfilms or in any other way, and storage in data banks. Duplication of this publication or parts thereof is permitted only under the provisions of the German Copyright Law of September 9, 1965, in its current version, and permission for use must always be obtained from Springer-Verlag. Violations are liable for prosecution under the German Copyright Law.

Springer is a part of Springer Science+Business Media

springer.com

© Springer-Verlag Berlin Heidelberg 2006
Printed in Germany

The use of general descriptive names, registered names, trademarks, etc. in this publication does not imply, even in the absence of a specific statement, that such names are exempt from the relevant protective laws and regulations and therefore free for general use.

Typesetting: Camera ready by author
Cover design: *Erich Kirchner*, Heidelberg

Printed on acid-free paper   42/3153/DK   5 4 3 2 1 0

To Carolin, Henri and my parents

Preface

This study was accepted as a doctoral thesis by the Department of Economics of the Johann Wolfgang Goethe-University in Frankfurt/Main. It was undertaken within the research project 'The Effects of Job Creation and Structural Adjustment Schemes on the Participating Individuals', which was conducted by the Institute of Statistics and Econometrics (Empirical Economic Research) in cooperation with the Institute for Employment Research in Nuremberg.

I have to thank numerous people. First of all my thesis supervisor, Prof. Dr. Reinhard Hujer, for initiating this thesis and providing me with a great scientific environment. I owe the data I used to his persistent lobbying to promote and anchor evaluation research in Germany. I am also very grateful to Prof. Dr. Roland Eisen who did not hesitate to act as the second thesis supervisor. Thanks also to Christian Brinkmann and his team at the Institute for Employment Research (Institut für Arbeitsmarkt- und Berufsforschung) for valuable help with the datasets.

I have also benefited from continual discussions with my colleagues Stephan L.(!) Thomsen, Dubravko Radic, Paulo Rodrigues, Sandra Vuletic and Christopher Zeiss. A warm thanks goes also to Birgit Kreiner and all our current and former student research assistants.

I would also like to thank my parents for their love and support throughout my life. They gave me great opportunities and this thesis is also written for them. Last but not least I would like to thank my wife Carolin for her unlimited support and patience while I was writing this thesis. She has also done the proof-reading which probably was not too much fun. Her love and encouragement are great sources of strength and I could not have finished this thesis without her. I hope that I can give something back when she finishes her own thesis.

Frankfurt, October 2005 *Marco Caliendo*

Contents

Abbreviations XIII

Symbols XV

Introduction 1

Part I Microeconometric Evaluation Methods

1 Introduction in Programme Evaluation 9
  1.1 Introduction 9
  1.2 The Evaluation Framework 11
    1.2.1 Potential Outcome Approach and the Fundamental Evaluation Problem 11
    1.2.2 Parameters of Interest and Selection Bias 13
    1.2.3 Linking the Potential-Outcome-Framework to Textbook Econometrics 15
    1.2.4 Homogeneous vs. Heterogeneous Treatment Effects 16
  1.3 How Do Randomised Experiments Solve the Evaluation Problem? 17
    1.3.1 Possible Problems with Randomised Experiments 18
  1.4 Evaluation Estimators 19
    1.4.1 Three Commonly Used Evaluation Estimators 21
    1.4.2 Alternative Evaluation Estimators 25
  1.5 The Principle of Unconfoundedness 30
    1.5.1 The Basic Idea of Matching Under Unconfoundedness .. 30
    1.5.2 How Does Matching Solve the Selection Problem? 32
    1.5.3 Redefining Selection Bias 33
    1.5.4 How Do Matching and Regression Under Unconfoundedness Differ? 35
  1.6 Summary - Which Estimator to Choose? 38

2 The Evaluation of Policy Interventions with Matching Estimators 43
- 2.1 Introduction 43
- 2.2 The Balancing Property of the Propensity Score 45
- 2.3 Alternative Matching Estimators 46
  - 2.3.1 Nearest-Neighbour-Matching 47
  - 2.3.2 Caliper and Radius Matching 48
  - 2.3.3 Stratification and Interval Matching 49
  - 2.3.4 Kernel and Local Polynomial Matching 50
  - 2.3.5 Weighting on the Propensity Score 53
- 2.4 Matching on Covariates 54
  - 2.4.1 Simple Matching Estimator 55
- 2.5 Combination of Matching with Other Methods 56
  - 2.5.1 Conditional DID or DID Matching Estimator 57
  - 2.5.2 Regression-Adjusted Matching Estimators 58
  - 2.5.3 Bias-Corrected Matching Estimator 58
- 2.6 Efficiency and Large-Sample Properties of Matching Estimators 59
  - 2.6.1 Estimating the Variance for Treatment Effects 62
- 2.7 Which Matching Estimator to Choose? 65

3 Some Practical Guidance for the Implementation of Propensity Score Matching Estimators 71
- 3.1 Introduction 71
- 3.2 The Implementation of Matching Estimators 73
  - 3.2.1 Estimating the Propensity Score 73
  - 3.2.2 Assessing the Matching Quality 78
  - 3.2.3 Overlap and Common Support 80
  - 3.2.4 Choice-Based Sampling 83
  - 3.2.5 When to Compare and Locking-in Effects 83
- 3.3 Sensitivity Analysis with Rosenbaum Bounds 84
- 3.4 More Practical Issues 87
  - 3.4.1 Programme Heterogeneity 87
  - 3.4.2 Sequential Matching Estimators 89
  - 3.4.3 Choosing the Right Control Group - Random Programme Starts 91
- 3.5 Conclusion 93

Part II The Evaluation of Job Creation Schemes in Germany

4 The German Labour Market and Active Labour Market Policies - A Brief Overview 99
- 4.1 Introduction 99
- 4.2 Institutional Setup and Instruments 101
  - 4.2.1 The German Labour Market - Some Stylised Facts 101

| | | 4.2.2 | Labour Market Policies .... 103 |
| | | 4.2.3 | Job Creation Schemes.............................. 111 |

	4.3	Previous Empirical Studies 113
		4.3.1	Microeconometric Evaluations of Job Creation Schemes 113
		4.3.2	Macroeconomic Evaluations 115
	4.4	Dataset Used in our Analysis 119
	4.5	Outline of the Empirical Analysis.......................... 124

5 Microeconometric Evaluation of Job Creation Schemes - Part I: Individual and Regional Heterogeneity 127

5.1 Introduction 127
5.2 Groups of Analysis and Selected Descriptives 129
    5.2.1 Groups of Analysis 129
    5.2.2 Selected Descriptives for the Four Main Groups 131
    5.2.3 Selected Descriptives for the Regional Clusters 133
5.3 Implementation of the Matching Estimator 134
    5.3.1 Plausibility of CIA 134
    5.3.2 Estimating the Propensity Score 135
    5.3.3 Choosing the Matching Algorithm 138
    5.3.4 Common Support 141
    5.3.5 Matching Quality 143
5.4 Results... 147
    5.4.1 Results for the Main Groups 148
    5.4.2 Results for the Selected Sub-Groups 149
    5.4.3 Results for the Regional Clusters 155
    5.4.4 Sensitivity of the Results to Unobserved Heterogeneity . 156
5.5 Conclusion 158

6 Microeconometric Evaluation of Job Creation Schemes - Part II: Programme Heterogeneity 161

6.1 Introduction 161
6.2 Groups of Analysis and Selected Descriptives 162
    6.2.1 Groups of Analysis 162
    6.2.2 Selected Descriptives............................... 166
6.3 Implementation of the Propensity Score Matching 168
    6.3.1 Propensity Score Estimation 168
    6.3.2 Matching Quality and Common Support 170
6.4 Results... 172
    6.4.1 Results for the Five Sectors 173
    6.4.2 Results for the Sectors and Types of Promotion 175
    6.4.3 Results for the Sectors and Providers 178
6.5 Conclusions... 181

7 Conclusions and Outlook 183

XII   Contents

A   Additional Material to Chapter 4 189

B   Additional Material to Chapter 5 193

C   Additional Material to Chapter 6 219

List of Tables 239

List of Figures 243

References 245

Abbreviations

AFG	Arbeitsförderungsgesetz
ALMP	Active labour market policies
ATE	(Population) average treatment effect
ATT	(Population) average treatment effect on the treated
ATU	(Population) average treatment effect on the untreated
BAE	Before-after estimator
BewA	Bewerberangebotsdatei
CIA	Conditional independence assumption
CM	Caliper matching
DID	Difference-in-differences
EGQ	Eingliederungsquote
ESR	Employment statistics register
FEA	Federal employment agency
GSOEP	German socioeconomic panel
FIML	Full information maximum likelihood
IIA	Independence of irrelevant alternatives assumption
IQR	Interquartile range
IV	Instrumental variables
JCS	Job creation schemes
JPTA	Job training partnership act
KM	Kernel matching
LATE	Local average treatment effect
LIML	Limited information maximum likelihood
LLM	Local linear matching
LMM	Labour market monitor
RDD	Regression discontinuity design
MAT	Matching
MH	Mantel and Haenszel
MSB	Mean standardised bias
MSE	Mean squared error
MTE	Marginal treatment effects

Abbreviations (continued)

NN	Nearest neighbour
NSW	National supported work programme
OLS	Ordinary least squares
PLMP	Passive labour market policies
PS	Propensity score
PSM	Propensity score matching
RAM	Regression adjusted matching estimator
Reg	Regression
RRM	Roy-Rubin-model
SAS	Structural adjustment schemes
SATE	Average treatment effect for the sample at hand
SATT	Average treatment effect on the treated for the sample at hand
SB	Standardized bias
SDCIA	Strong dynamic conditional independence assumption
SGB	Sozialgesetzbuch
SM	Simple matching estimator
STM	Stratification matching
STD	Standard deviation
SUTVA	Stable unit-treatment value assumption
VBQ	Verbleibsquote
VT	Vocational training
WDCIA	Weak dynamic conditional independence assumption
WG	Weighting on propensity score estimator

Symbols

A_i	Set of potential matching partners for treated individual i
α_{N_0}	Bandwidth parameter
$b(X)$	Balancing score
$B(X)$	Bias and bias components B_1, B_2, B_3
$\overline{B}_{S_X(S_P)}$	Mean selection bias defined over X ($P(X)$)
$\beta_{1(0)}$	Regression coefficients in the treatment (comparison) group
β_k	Regression coefficient of the k-th covariate
$C(P_i)$	Neighborhood of treated individual i in terms of propensity score
d	Distance metric
D_i	Treatment indicator for individual i
$D_{it(it')}$	Treatment indicator for individual i at time period t (t')
$D^{(u)}$	Treatment indicator if treated at time u
δ	Tolerance level
Δ_i	Treatment effect for individual i
Δ_{it}	Treatment effect for individual i at time period t
Δ_q	Treatment effect in stratum q
Δ_{ATE}	Population average treatment effect
Δ_{ATT}	Population average treatment effect for the treated
Δ_{ATU}	Population average treatment effect for the untreated
Δ^{ml}	Effect of treatment m compared with treatment l on participants in treatment m
$E[(.)]$	Expectation operator
ϵ	Caliper (maximum tolerance level)
$F[(.)]$	Distribution function
$\phi(.)$	Density of a normal distribution
$\Phi(.)$	Distribution function of a normal distribution
$g_t^1(X_i)$	Relationship between potential outcome ($D_i = 1$) at time period t and observables
$g_t^0(X_i)$	Relationship between potential outcome ($D_i = 0$) at time period t and observables

Symbols (continued)

G_{ij}	Kernel function
γ_k	Coefficient of the k-th covariate in propensity score estimation
γ	Effect of unobserved characteristics u_i on participation decision
$I_{1(0)}$	Set of indices in the treatment (comparison) group
IN_i	Index of benefits from participating in a programme for individual i
J_{is}	Indicator for individual i being in stratum s
$J_M(i)$	Set of matched indices from the counterfactual group for individual i
K	Number of covariates, with $k = 1, ..., K$
$K_M(i)$	Number of times individual i is used as matching partner
L	Number of mutually different and exclusive treatments
$\ell_m(i)$	Index of nearest neighbor m for individual i
M	Number of nearest neighbors, with $m = 1, ..., M$
N	Set of individuals, with $i = 1, ..., N$
$N_{1(0)}$	Number of individuals in the treatment (comparison) group
$N_{1(0)s}$	Number of individuals in the treatment (comparison) group in stratum s
N_s	Total number of individuals in stratum s
$O(.)$	At most of order $(.)$
p	Polynomial order
$P(.)$	Probability operator
$P(X_i)$	Propensity score value for individual i $(= P_i)$
$P^{l\|ml}$	Probability of receiving treatment l given X and a choice between l and m
P_X	Proportion of the density of X given $D = 1$ in the common support
$\pi_{it(it')}$	Effect of selection on unobservables for individual i at time period t (t')
q	Percentage trimming level
Q_{MH}	Mantel-Haenszel test-statistic
R	Binary randomisation indicator
ρ	Correlation coefficient
ϱ	Rank of nearest neighbors
S	Number of blocks (stratums), with s=1,...,S
$S_{1(0)X}$	Support of X in the treatment (comparison) group
S_X	Region of overlap (common support) based on X
S_P	Region of overlap (common support) based on $P(X)$
Σ_X	Variance-covariance matrix
$\sigma^2_{1(0)}(X)$	Conditional outcome-variance in the treatment (comparison) group given X
t	Post-treatment period, with $t = u, u+1, ..., T$
t'	Pre-treatment period, with $t' = 0, 1, ..., u-1$

Symbols (continued)

$U^{1(0)}$	Unobservable characteristics for treated (untreated) individuals
u_i	Unobserved characteristics for individual i
U	Discrete (unemployment) duration until treatment start, with $u = 1,...,U^{Max}$
V	Unobserved variables influencing assignment into treatment
$V_{1(0)}(X)$	Variance of X in the treatment (comparison) group
W	Weighting matrix
$W(i,j)$	Weight for untreated individual j for constructing $Y_i(0)$ of treated individual i
X	Observed covariates (regressors)
x_{ik}	k-th element of the K-dimensional covariates vector X for individual i
$\overline{X}_{1[1M]}$	Sample average of X in the treatment group before [after] matching
$\overline{X}_{0[0M]}$	Sample average of X in the comparison group before [after] matching
Y_i	Observed outcome for individual i
$Y_{it(it')}$	Observed outcome for individual i at time period t (t')
Y_i^1	Potential outcome of individual i given $D_i = 1$
Y_i^0	Potential outcome of individual i given $D_i = 0$
Y_{it}^1	Potential outcome of individual i at time period t given $D_i = 1$
Y_{it}^0	Potential outcome of individual i at time period t given $D_i = 0$
$Y_t^{1(u)}$	Potential outcome over time t if treated at u
$Y_t^{0(u)}$	Potential outcome over time t if not treated at u
Y_{1s}	Number of successful participants in stratum s
Y_{0s}	Number of successful non-participants in stratum s
Y_s	Total number of successful individuals in stratum s
Z	Observed variables influencing assignment into treatment
Z^*	Instrumental variable

Introduction

Most OECD countries have been plagued by high and persistent unemployment since the early 1970s. During the last decade there has been a growing interest in active labour market policies (ALMP) as a means of fighting this unacceptable situation. This is easy to understand in view of the disillusionment with more aggregate policies. The traditional demand stimulation has been discredited because it faces the risk of increasing inflation with only small effects on employment. Furthermore supply-side structural reforms aimed to remove various labour market rigidities are difficult to implement or appear to produce results rather slowly. As Calmfors (1994) notes, ALMP are regarded by many as the deus ex machina that will solve the unemployment problem by providing a more efficient outcome on the labour market. As they also equip individuals with higher skills and therefore lower their risk of poverty they are capable of meeting efficiency and equity goals at the same time (OECD, 1991).

Alongside with the general tendency to deregulate markets and to promote work incentives, it has become a common theme in the political debate, that governments should shift the balance of public spending on labour market policies away from passive income support towards more active measures designed to get the unemployed back into work. Whereas the goal of passive labour market policies (PLMP) is mainly to bridge the income shortage caused by unemployment, ALMP are intended to fight the structural problems of the labour market and to enhance the re-employment probability of (long-term) unemployed, respectively to avoid people drifting off into this group.[1] Especially Anglo-Saxon policy makers favour the idea of tying the right of welfare to the duty of work; welfare then becomes 'workfare' (Card, 2000). Hence, it is no wonder that it has become standard for international bodies

---

[1] The OECD (1993) provides some standardised categories and sub-categories for labour market policies. The main categories for PLMP are unemployment compensation and early retirements. ALMP include public employment services and administration, labour market training, youth measures, subsidised employment and measures for the disabled.

like the OECD (1994) or the European Commission (2000) to recommend an expansion of ALMP. Table 1 compares the spending on ALMP and PLMP for some selected European countries in 1985 and 2002, showing the growing importance of ALMP. Whereas in 1985 only 0.88% of the gross domestic product (GDP) have been dedicated to active measures, the share rose to 1.01% in 2002. The spending for PLMP dropped from 2.00% to 1.43% in that time period. However, only Italy, Sweden and the Netherlands spent more money an ALMP than on PLMP in 2002. One obvious reason for the limited success in switching resources into active measures is the rising trend of unemployment in many countries. As unemployment benefits are entitlement programmes, i.e. rising unemployment automatically increases public spending on passive income support, most of the active labour market programmes are discretionary in nature and therefore easier disposable in a situation of tight budgets (Martin, 1998).

Table 1: Spending on Active and Passive Labour Market Policies for Selected European Countries

	Spending on (as a percentage of GDP)			
	ALMP		PLMP	
	1985[1]	2002[2]	1985[1]	2002[2]
Austria	0.27	0.53	0.93	1.24
Belgium	1.31	1.25	3.37	2.40
Denmark	1.12	1.58	3.82	3.04
Finland	0.90	1.01	1.31	2.06
France	0.66	1.25	2.37	1.81
Germany	0.80	1.18	1.42	2.13
Greece	0.17	0.46	0.35	0.47
Ireland	1.52	1.14	3.52	0.70
Italy	–	0.57	1.33	0.63
Netherlands	1.16	1.85	3.49	1.72
Portugal	0.35	0.61	0.35	0.90
Spain	0.33	0.87	2.81	1.55
Sweden	2.10	1.40	0.87	1.05
United Kingdom	0.75	0.37	2.12	0.37
Average	0.88	1.01	2.00	1.43

– No information available.
[1] Data for Denmark and Portugal from 1986.
[2] Data for Denmark from 2000, for Greece from 1998, for Ireland from 2001, for Portugal from 2000.

Source: OECD Employment Outlook, various issues.

Table 1 also makes clear, that active labour market policies absorb significant shares of national resources, which are than unavailable for alternative programmes or private expenditure. Germany is no exception and spent over

90 bn Euro on various active programmes from 2000 to 2003. In an era of tight government budgets and a growing disbelief regarding the positive effects of ALMP, evaluation of these policies becomes imperative.[2] The ideal evaluation process can be looked at as a series of three steps (Fay, 1996): First, the impacts of the programme on the individual should be estimated (MICROECONOMETRIC EVALUATION). Second, it should be examined if the impacts are large enough to yield net social gains (MACROECONOMIC EVALUATION). Third, it should be answered if this is the best outcome that could have been achieved for the money spent (COST-BENEFIT ANALYSIS).

The main question of MICROECONOMETRIC EVALUATIONS is whether outcome of an individual is affected by the participation in an ALMP programme. Empirical microeconometric evaluation is conducted with individual data, has to solve the fundamental evaluation problem and address the possible occurrence of selection bias. These problems arise, because we would like to know the difference between the value of the participant's outcome in the actual situation and the value of the outcome had he not participated in the programme. Since we never observe both states (participation and non-participation) for the same individual at the same time, one of the states is counterfactual. Therefore finding an adequate control group is necessary to make a comparison possible. Experimental evaluation does so by assigning individuals randomly to the group of participants and non-participants. In that case, both groups differ only with respect to participation and the differences in the outcomes can be taken as treatment effects. However, experimental data is scarce and in most cases researchers will have to rely on non-experimental (or observational) data. That is, one observes the outcome of participants with treatment and the outcome of non-participants without treatment. Since both groups usually differ in more aspects than just participation, taking simply the difference between their outcomes after treatment will lead to selection bias. The objective of non-experimental evaluation methods is to use the available data to restore the comparability of both groups by design.

In MACROECONOMIC EVALUATION STUDIES we want to know if a positive effect on the individual level leads also to positive effects on the aggregate level. This need not be the case if e.g. deadweight losses or substitution effects occur (see e.g. Layard, Nickell, and Jackman (1991) or OECD (1993)).[3] Another problem might be that ALMP crowd out regular employment. This can be seen as a generalisation of the so called displacement effect. This ef-

---

[2] Hujer and Caliendo (2001) and Hagen and Steiner (2000) provide an overview of evaluation studies for ALMP in Germany, Calmfors, Forslund, and Hemström (2002) summarise the findings for Sweden, and Martin and Grubb (2001) sum up evaluations for several OECD countries.

[3] If the outcome of the programme is not different from what would have happened in its absence, we talk about a deadweight loss. A common example is the hiring from the target group that would have occurred also without the programme. If a worker is taken on by a firm in a subsidised job instead of an unsubsidised worker who would have been hired otherwise, we talk about a substitution effect.

fect typically refers to displacement in the product market, e.g. if firms with subsidised workers are able to increase output, but displace (reduce) output among firms who do not have subsidised workers. Calmfors (1994) also stresses the importance of tax effects in the sense that programmes have to be financed by taxes which distort the choices of both participants and non-participants. Most macroeconomic evaluations of ALMP are based on panel data models, since a single time series for one country or region usually does not provide enough observations. Between these studies, two major strands can be distinguished. First, authors like e.g. Forslund and Krueger (1994) or Calmfors and Skedinger (1995) use variation in programme scale across regional units (jurisdictions) combined with data at the regional level to estimate the effects. Second, authors like Jackman, Pissarides, and Savouri (1990), Layard, Nickell, and Jackman (1991) or OECD (1993) use variation in programme scale across different countries even though such an analysis might suffer from the heterogeneous policy measures between the countries.

Finally, a COST-BENEFIT ANALYSIS helps determining if the best possible outcome is achieved for the money spent. The aim of cost-benefit analysis is an efficient allocation of scarce resources and is similar to commercial profitability calculations conducted by private businesses (see Boardman, Greenberg, Vining, and Weimer (2001) for an introduction).

However, evaluation in most countries focuses on the first step, namely the microeconometric evaluation, and so will we in this book.[4] Thereby, the aim of this book is twofold: In the first part of the book we are going to introduce and discuss several microeconometric evaluation methods. Our focus will be on the matching approach which has become increasingly popular for the evaluation of ALMP in recent years. We will use these methods in the second part of the book to evaluate the employment effects for the participating individuals of one major German ALMP programme, namely job creation schemes. The remainder of this book is organised as follows:

We are going to introduce a suitable framework for microeconometric evaluation analysis in chapter 1, where we also discuss several evaluation strategies for non-experimental data. We will show that each evaluation strategy imposes different identifying assumptions and hence works only if these assumptions are met. A major distinction between the strategies can be made regarding the assumed source of selection bias. We will present both methods that assume that selection is on observable characteristics (e.g. matching and regression) as well as methods that assume that selection is on unobservable characteristics (e.g. instrumental variable methods or selection models). The overall goal of this chapter is to give guidance to researchers on which evaluation strategy to choose. Thereby we discuss the data needed for their implementation, the inherent identifying assumptions and the advantages and

---

[4] See Caliendo, Hagen, and Hujer (2004) for an overview of several evaluation approaches on the macroeconomic level based on regional data, and Hujer, Caliendo, and Radic (2004) for a brief introduction in cost-benefit analysis.

disadvantages of each estimator. Additionally, we also assess their capability of dealing with effect heterogeneity. Whereas the older evaluation literature typically assumed that the programme effect is the same for everyone, a lot of progress has been made in recent years to introduce models that allow effects to differ between sub-populations (e.g. young and old or skilled and unskilled participants). Clearly, identifying effect heterogeneity is an obvious opportunity to improve the efficiency of programmes in the future.

In chapter 2 we will concentrate on one specific evaluation approach, which is based on the selection on observables assumption, namely matching. The basic idea of matching is to find for each participant a non-participant who is similar in all relevant characteristics. Several alternative matching estimators (e.g. Nearest-Neighbour and Kernel Matching) will be discussed and we will spend some time on efficiency issues concerning the estimation. We will also show how matching can be combined with other evaluation strategies to allow for selection on unobservables, too. In the conclusion to this chapter we will give guidance on how to choose between different matching approaches.

Since exact matching on all relevant characteristics can become unfeasible (if there are too many), we will also introduce one approach which is known as propensity score matching in chapter 3. Instead of matching on all covariates, we match on one score only (e.g. the participation probability) with this approach. Once the researcher has decided to use propensity score matching, he is confronted with a lot of questions regarding its implementation, e.g. concerning the model and variable choice for the participation probability as well as common support and matching quality issues and a possible sensitivity of the results with respect to 'hidden bias'. The goal of this chapter is to give some guidance for the practical implementation of propensity score matching.

Equipped with this knowledge, we are going to analyse the employment effects of job creation schemes (JCS) for the participating individuals in Germany in part II of the book. JCS are a wage-subsidy programme for unemployed and 'hard-to-place' individuals whose last chance for stabilising and qualifying for later re-integration into regular employment is participation in these schemes. After vocational training, JCS have for a long time been the second most important ALMP programme in Germany in terms of spending and the number of participants, even though their importance is currently decreasing. They can be promoted only if they support activities which are of value for the society and additional in nature. Hence, they are mainly implemented by public or non-commercial institutions.

We will introduce the institutional setup of labour market policies in Germany in chapter 4. JCS have often been criticised because they lack explicit qualificational elements and might involve 'stigma effects'. Such 'stigma effects' arise if programmes are targeted at people with 'disadvantages' and a possible employer takes participation in such schemes as a negative signal concerning the expected productivity or motivation of participants. However, it can also be argued that they are a reasonable opportunity for individuals who are not able to re-integrate themselves into the first labour market or who do not fit the criteria for other programmes, e.g. long-term unemployed or other 'hard-to-place' individuals. The absence of suitable data has hampered evaluation efforts for a long time. The earlier evaluation studies of JCS mainly concentrated on the East German labour market and were based on survey data. The relatively small groups of participants did not allow to take adequately account of effect heterogeneity. Hence, drawing policy relevant conclusions for West Germany and specific sub-groups was problematic. However, with the introduction of a new legislation for labour market policies in 1998, things have changed. Maybe the most important change from an evaluator's point of view was the legal anchoring of a mandatory output evaluation for all ALMP measures. As a consequence, new administrative datasets have been made accessible for scientific research and allow us to use a very informative dataset containing all entries in JCS from February 2000 and a control group of non-participants who were eligible to participate in February 2000 but did not do so. Additionally, we have information on regular employment of these individuals until December 2002.

This allows us to answer the policy relevant question, whether unemployed should join a JCS in February 2000 to enhance their employment prospects or not, in chapters 5 and 6. A major topic in these chapters will be the possible occurrence of effect heterogeneity. Identifying potential sources of effect heterogeneity can help to improve programmes in the future. Throughout the analysis, effects will be estimated separately for men and women in West and East Germany, since previous empirical findings have emphasised the importance of this differentiation. Additionally, chapter 5 focusses on group-specific and regional differences in treatment effects. To account for group-specific influences, we estimate the effects separately for specific problem groups of the labour market, like long-term unemployed, individuals with placement restrictions and persons without work experience or professional training. To account for regional differences in the effects, we will estimate the effects in the different labour market clusters as defined by the Federal Employment Agency (FEA). The emphasis of chapter 6 is different. Here, we focus on programme specific differences like the economic sector in which the JCS is started (e.g. AGRICULTURE vs. OFFICE AND SERVICES), the provider (PUBLIC or NON-COMMERCIAL institutions) and the type of promotion (REGULAR and ENFORCED) an individual receives.

Taking chapters 5 and 6 together should allow us to make a conclusive judgement of the employment effects of JCS for the participating individuals. We will try to use these conclusions to give some recommendations for the usage of JCS in the future.

Part I

Microeconometric Evaluation Methods

1

Introduction in Programme Evaluation

1.1 Introduction

The aim of this chapter is to give an introduction into microeconometric evaluation. Empirical microeconometric evaluation is conducted with individual data. The main question is if the outcome variable of interest for an individual is affected by the participation in an ALMP programme or not. Relevant outcome variables can be for example the future employment probability or the future earnings. In any case, we would like to know the difference between the value of the participant's outcome in the actual situation and the value of the outcome if he had not participated in the programme. The fundamental evaluation problem arises because we never observe both states (participation and non-participation) for the same individual at the same time, i.e. one of the states is counterfactual. Therefore finding an adequate control group is necessary to make a comparison possible.[1] This is not an easy task because participants in programmes usually differ in more aspects than just participation from non-participants. Taking simply the difference between their outcomes after treatment will not reveal the true treatment impact, i.e. will lead to a selection bias.

Depending on the data at hand, different evaluation strategies can be thought of. Whenever feasible, experimental evaluation will provide the most compelling evidence in most cases. The basic idea of this approach is to assign individuals randomly to the participant's and the control group. Both groups then differ only with respect to participation and the differences in the outcomes can be taken as treatment effects. Although this approach seems to be very appealing in providing a simple solution to the fundamental evaluation problem, there are also some problems associated with it which we will

---

[1] The terms control group and comparison group will be used interchangeably throughout the book. Either way the group consists of individuals who did not receive treatment.

discuss later on. More importantly, in most European countries experimental data are not available and therefore, the evaluator must choose among non-experimental evaluation estimators.

Whereas in the early stages of treatment evaluation, some analysts like LaLonde (1986) or Ashenfelter and Card (1985) viewed social experiments as the only valid evaluation method, a lot of methodological progress has been made to develop and justify non-experimental evaluation estimators which are based on econometric and statistical methods to solve the fundamental evaluation problem (see e.g. Heckman and Robb (1985b), Heckman and Hotz (1989) or Heckman, LaLonde, and Smith (1999)). They belong now to the standard toolbox of evaluation research. In non-experimental or observational studies, the data are not derived in a process that is completely under the control of the researcher. Instead one has to rely on information how individuals actually performed after the intervention. That is, we observe the outcome with treatment for participants and the outcome without treatment for non-participants. The objective of observational studies is to use this information to restore the comparability of both groups by design. To do so, more or less plausible identification assumptions have to be imposed. We will show that different strategies invoke different identifying assumptions and also require different kinds of data for their implementation.

The different estimators can be classified with respect to two dimensions. The first dimension is the required data for their implementation, where we can distinguish between longitudinal and cross-sectional methods. The second dimension concerns the handling of selection bias, where two categories arise. The first category contains approaches that rely on the so-called unconfoundedness or selection on observables assumption which we will present in section 1.5. The basic idea here is, that based on some observed characteristics the potential outcomes are independent of the assignment to treatment. In that case, the control group with similar characteristics can be used to construct the missing counterfactual outcome. We will present and compare two strategies in this category, namely matching and regression analysis. Clearly, the performance of these estimators depends on the data at hand. For their justification we need a rich dataset that contains all variables that jointly influence the participation decision and the outcome variable.

If one believes that the available data is not rich enough to justify the selection on observables assumption, he has to rely on the second category of estimators which explicitly allows selection on unobservables, too. The methods of instrumental variables and selection models will be presented for that situation. With selection models one tries to model the selection decision completely whereas IV methods focus on finding an instrument which determines participation but does not influence the outcome.

The main part of the conclusions to this chapter will deal with the question on how to choose between different evaluation estimators and what (data) requirements are necessary for their implementation. By doing so, we hope to give some advice for future evaluation analysis. An important topic which has become a major focus in evaluation research in the last years are heterogeneous treatment effects. Whereas the older literature on evaluation typically assumed that the impact of a programme is the same for anyone, substantial conceptual progress has been made in recent years to introduce models in which the impact of a programme differs across individuals. If programme impacts are heterogeneous, negative average effects must not apply for all strata of the population (Manski, 1997 and 2000). Therefore, abandoning the 'common effect' assumption of treatment effects and identifying the individuals that benefit from the programmes is an obvious opportunity to improve their future efficiency. Hence, each estimation method that we will present in the following has to be considered with respect to its ability to deal with the occurrence of heterogeneous treatment effects.

This chapter is organised as follows: First, we are going to introduce the evaluation framework in section 1.2 which will serve as a basis for the subsequent discussion. We are especially going to present the potential outcome approach, discuss parameters of interest, selection bias on observable and on unobservable characteristics as well as the heterogeneity of treatment effects. In section 1.3 we are going to show how randomised experiments solve selection bias and which problems might occur with this approach. Section 1.4 will present some basic evaluation strategies and two strategies - selection models and instrumental variable methods - that address the problem of selection on unobservable factors. In contrast to that, section 1.5 will be concerned with introducing the principle of unconfoundedness or selection on observable characteristics. Two estimators exploiting this idea - matching and regression analysis - are introduced and compared. Finally, section 1.6 concludes by comparing the presented estimators, their underlying assumptions and data requirements as well as their ability to handle heterogeneous treatment effects.

1.2 The Evaluation Framework

1.2.1 Potential Outcome Approach and the Fundamental Evaluation Problem

Inference about the impact of a treatment on the outcome of an individual involves speculation about how this individual would have performed in the labour market, had he not received the treatment.[2] The framework serving as a guideline for the empirical analysis of this problem is the potential outcome approach, variously attributed to Fisher (1935), Neyman (1935), Roy (1951),

---

[2] This is clearly different from asking whether there is an empirical association between treatment and the outcome (Lechner, 2000a). See Holland (1986) for an extensive discussion of concepts of causality in statistics, econometrics and other fields.

Quandt (1972, 1988) or Rubin (1974), but most often it is just called the Roy-Rubin-model (RRM).

The main pillars of this model are individuals, treatment (participating in a programme or not) and potential outcomes, that are also called responses.[3] In the basic model there are two potential outcomes (Y^1, Y^0) for each individual, where Y^1 indicates a situation with treatment and Y^0 without, i.e. the individual belongs to the comparison group. To complete the notation we additionally denote variables that are unaffected by treatments - called attributes by Holland (1986) - by X. Attributes are exogenous in the sense that their potential values for different treatment states coincide. Furthermore we define a binary assignment indicator D, indicating whether an individual actually received treatment $(D = 1)$, or not $(D = 0)$.

The treatment effect for each individual i is then defined as the difference between his potential outcomes:

(1.1) $$\Delta_i = Y_i^1 - Y_i^0.$$

The fundamental problem of evaluating this individual treatment effect arises because the observed outcome for each individual is given by:

(1.2) $$Y_i = D_i Y_i^1 + (1 - D_i) Y_i^0.$$

This means that for those individuals who participated in treatment we observe Y^1 and for those who did not participate we observe Y^0. Unfortunately, we can never observe Y^1 and Y^0 for the same individual simultaneously and therefore we cannot estimate (1.1) directly. The unobservable component in (1.1) is called the counterfactual outcome, so that for an individual who participated in the treatment Y^0 is the counterfactual outcome, and for another one who did not participate it is Y^1.

The concentration on a single individual requires that the effect of the intervention on each individual is not affected by the participation decision of any other individual, i.e. the treatment effect Δ_i for each person is independent of the treatment of other individuals. In statistical literature this is referred to as the stable unit treatment value assumption (SUTVA)[4] and guarantees that average treatment effects can be estimated independently of the size and composition of the treatment population. In particular, potential outcomes of an individual depend on his own participation only and not on the treatment status of other individuals. Furthermore, whether an individual participates or not does not depend on participation decisions of other individuals. The latter requirement excludes peer-effects, whereas the first one excludes cross-effects or general equilibrium effects (Sianesi, 2004). Even though its validity

---

[3] It should be clear, that this framework is not restricted to the evaluation of labour market programmes. It applies for every situation where one group, e.g. individuals, firms or other entities, receive some form of treatment and others do not. We will present several examples from diverse fields in chapter 2

[4] See Rubin (1980) or Holland (1986) for a further discussion of this concept.

facilitates a manageable formal setup, in practical applications it is frequently questionable whether it holds.[5]

1.2.2 Parameters of Interest and Selection Bias

Since there will never be an opportunity to estimate individual effects in (1.1) with confidence, we have to concentrate on population averages of gains from treatment. Two parameters are most frequently estimated in the literature. The first one is the (population) average treatment effect (ATE), which is simply the difference of the expected outcomes after participation and non-participation:

$$(1.3) \qquad \Delta_{ATE} = E(\Delta) = E(Y^1) - E(Y^0).$$

This parameter answers the question which would be the outcome if individuals in the population were randomly assigned to treatment. Heckman (1997) notes, that this estimate might not be of relevance to policy makers because it includes the effect on persons for whom the programme was never intended. For example, if a programme is specifically targeted at individuals with low family income, there is little interest in the effect of such a programme for a millionaire. Hence, estimating ATE is usually not policy relevant, because interest centers on the effects of programmes on the intended recipients. Therefore, the most prominent evaluation parameter is the so called average treatment effect on the treated (ATT), which focusses explicitly on the effects on those for whom the programme is actually intended. It is given by:

$$(1.4) \qquad \Delta_{ATT} = E(\Delta \mid D = 1) = E(Y^1 \mid D = 1) - E(Y^0 \mid D = 1).$$

The expected value of ATT is defined as the difference between expected outcome values with and without treatment for those who actually participated in treatment. In the sense that this parameter focuses directly on actual treatment participants, it determines the realised gross gain from the programme and can be compared with its costs, helping to decide whether the programme is successful or not (Heckman, LaLonde, and Smith, 1999). Heckman and Robb (1985b) and Heckman, Ichimura, and Todd (1997) argue that the subpopulation of participants is often of more interest than the total population if a narrowly targeted programme is examined.

---

[5] Looking at the immense amounts spent on ALMP in Germany (for details see chapter 4) and the large scale of the programmes, spill-over effects on non-participants are very likely. If we look at the typical small-scale U.S. programmes on the other hand, the occurrence of such effects is less likely. Therefore the microeconometric approach is partial-analytic and should only be seen as one-step to a complete evaluation.

1 Introduction in Programme Evaluation

Given equation (1.4), the problem of selection bias can be straightforwardly seen. Remember that the second term on the right hand side of equation (1.4) is unobservable as it describes the hypothetical outcome without treatment for those individuals who received treatment. If the condition

$$(1.5) \qquad E(Y^0 \mid D = 1) = E(Y^0 \mid D = 0)$$

holds, we can use the non-participants as an adequate control group. This identifying assumption is likely to hold only in randomised experiments and we will discuss this point further in section 1.3. With non-experimental data, equation (1.5) will usually not hold, i.e.

$$(1.6) \qquad E(Y^0 \mid D = 1) \neq E(Y^0 \mid D = 0).$$

Consequently, estimating ATT by the difference in sub-population means of participants $E(Y^1 \mid D = 1)$ and non-participants $E(Y^0 \mid D = 0)$ will therefore lead to a selection bias, since

$$(1.7) \qquad \begin{aligned} E(Y^1 \mid D = 1) - E(Y^0 \mid D = 0) &= E(Y^1 - Y^0 \mid D = 1) \\ &+ \{E(Y^0 \mid D = 1) - E(Y^0 \mid D = 0)\}. \end{aligned}$$

The second last term in (1.7) is the actual average treatment effect on the treated, whereas the term in squared brackets is the selection bias. Selection bias arises because participants and non-participants are selected groups that would have different outcomes, even in absence of the programme. The selection bias might arise from observable factors like age or skill differences. A good example is a situation where the programme group consists of unskilled individuals and we would compare their mean outcome with the mean outcome of a group of skilled individuals. Clearly, we would expect different potential outcomes even in the absence of treatment. Additionally, unobservable factors like motivation might also play a role in determining the participation decision. If, for example, highly motivated individuals are more likely to participate and are also more likely to have a higher outcome without treatment, we would again have a selection bias. We will discuss the problem of selection bias caused by observable and/or unobservable factors in more detail in subsection (1.2.3).

Before we do so, let us introduce another parameter one might think of - the average treatment effect on the untreated (ATU):

$$(1.8) \qquad \Delta_{ATU} = E(\Delta \mid D = 0) = E(Y^1 \mid D = 0) - E(Y^0 \mid D = 0).$$

The treatment effect for those individuals who actually did not participate in the programme is typically an interesting measure for decisions about extending some treatment to a group that was formerly excluded from treatment.

The most interesting parameter to estimate depends on the specific policy context and the specific question asked. Heckman, LaLonde, and Smith (1999) discuss further parameters, like the proportion of participants who benefit from the programme or the distribution of gains at selected base state values. For most evaluation studies, however, the focus lies on ATT and therefore we will focus on this parameter, too. For distributions of programme impacts, the interested reader is referred to Heckman, Smith, and Clements (1997).

1.2.3 Linking the Potential-Outcome-Framework to Textbook Econometrics

For the further discussion it will be helpful to relate the potential-outcome-framework to familiar econometric notation. To do so, we follow Blundell and Costa Dias (2002) and define the following outcome equations:

$$(1.9) \quad \begin{aligned} Y_{it}^1 &= g_t^1(X_i) + U_{it}^1 \\ Y_{it}^0 &= g_t^0(X_i) + U_{it}^0, \end{aligned}$$

where the subscripts i and t identify the individual and the time period, respectively. The functions g^0 and g^1 represent the relationship between potential outcomes and the set of observable characteristics. U^0 and U^1 are error terms which have zero mean and are assumed to be uncorrelated with regressors X. For the familiar case of linear regression, the g functions specialise to $g^1(X) = X\beta_1$, and $g^0(X) = X\beta_0$.

Heckman and Robb (1985a) note that the decision to participate in treatment may be determined by a prospective trainee, by a programme administrator, or both. Whatever the specific content of the rule, it can be described in terms of an index function framework. Let IN_i be an index of benefits to the relevant decision-maker from participating in the programme. It is a function of observed (Z_i) and unobserved (V_i) variables. Therefore:

$$(1.10) \quad IN_i = f(Z_i) + V_i.$$

In terms of this function,

$$\begin{aligned} D_i &= 1 \quad \text{if } IN_i > 0 \text{ and} \\ &= 0 \quad \text{otherwise}. \end{aligned}$$

Under this specification and the further assumption that treatment takes place in period k, one can define the individual-specific treatment effect for any X_i as:

$$(1.11) \quad \Delta_{it}(X_i) = Y_{it}^1 - Y_{it}^0 = [g_t^1(X_i) - g_t^0(X_i)] + [U_{it}^1 - U_{it}^0] \quad \text{with } t > k.$$

The different parameters of interest measured in the post-treatment period $t > k$ are then defined as:

$$(1.12) \quad \Delta_{ATE} = E(\Delta_{it} \mid X = X_i),$$
$$(1.13) \quad \Delta_{ATT} = E(\Delta_{it} \mid X = X_i, D_i = 1),$$
$$(1.14) \quad \Delta_{ATU} = E(\Delta_{it} \mid X = X_i, D_i = 0).$$

As already mentioned except in case of randomised experiments, the assignment process to treatment is most probably not random. Consequently, the assignment process will lead to non-zero correlation between enrollment (D_i) and the outcome's error term (U^1, U^0). This may occur because of stochastic dependence between (U^1, U^0) and V_i in (1.10) or because of stochastic dependence between (U^1, U^0) and Z_i. In the former case we have selection on unobservables, whereas in the latter case selection on observables is prevalent (Heckman and Robb, 1985b). We will present different methods that are able to deal with selection on observable and/or unobservable factors later on from subsection 1.4 onwards and in chapter 2.

1.2.4 Homogeneous vs. Heterogeneous Treatment Effects

The specification in subsection 1.2.3 allows us to consider the problem of homogeneous and heterogeneous treatment effects in a common and intuitive way. The older literature on evaluation typically assumes that the impact of a programme is the same for anyone - that is, that the impacts are homogeneous. In this case, $\Delta_i = \Delta$ for all i. Smith (2000a) notes that this assumption is unlikely to hold in a literal sense, but may be a reasonable approximation in some contexts. In recent years, substantial conceptual progress has been made to introduce models in which the impact of a programme differs across individuals. Three basic possibilities for effect variation can be distinguished (Smith, 2000a):

1. In the simplest case, there is no variation and this is the 'common effect' model already mentioned.
2. In a slightly more general world, the programme impact varies across persons, but, prior to the programme neither the participant nor programme administrators have any information about the person-specific component of the impact.
3. Finally, in the most general world, the impact varies across persons and either the person or the programme staff or both have some information about it before participation (and act on it).

Let us now consider what happens to the already defined parameters of interest under these assumptions. In the 'common effect' model where we assume the effect to be constant across individuals we get

$$(1.15) \qquad \Delta_t = \Delta_{it}(X_i) = g_t^1(X_i) - g_t^0(X_i) \qquad \text{with } t > k$$

for any i. This implies that g^1 and g^0 are two parallel curves that differ only in the level and, furthermore, that participation-specific error terms are not affected by the treatment status. The outcome equations stated in equation (1.9) can therefore be re-written as (Blundell and Costa Dias, 2002):

$$(1.16) \qquad Y_{it} = g_t^0(X_i) + \Delta_t D_{it} + U_i.$$

However, if the treatment impact varies across individuals this may come systematically through the observables' component or be part of the unobservables. In this case we re-write outcome equation (1.9) as

$$\begin{aligned}
Y_{it} &= D_{it}Y_{it}^1 + (1 - D_{it})Y_{it}^0 \\
&= D_{it}[g_t^1(X_i) + U_{it}^1] + (1 - D_{it})[g_t^0(X_i) + U_{it}^0] \\
&= g_t^0(X_i) + D_{it}[g_t^1(X_i) - g_t^0(X_i) + U_{it}^1 - U_{it}^0] + U_{it}^0 \\
&= g_t^0(X_i) + \Delta_{it}(X_i)D_{it} + U_{it}^0 \\
&= g_t^0(X_i) + \Delta_t(X_i)D_{it} + [U_{it}^0 + D_{it}(U_{it}^1 - U_{it}^0)],
\end{aligned}$$
(1.17)

where

(1.18) $$\Delta_t(X_i) = E[\Delta_{it}(X_i)] = g_t^1(X_i) - g_t^0(X_i)$$

is the expected treatment effect at time t for individuals characterised by X_i (Blundell and Costa Dias, 2002). The distinction between homogeneous and heterogeneous treatment effects is crucial for the following discussion and the actual evaluation in chapters 5 and 6. If programme impacts are heterogeneous, negative average effects must not apply for all strata of the population (Manski, 1997 and 2000). As Heckman, LaLonde, and Smith (1999) mention, negative mean impact results could be acceptable if most participants gain from the programme. Therefore, as mentioned already, abandoning the 'common effect' assumption of treatment effects and identifying the individuals that benefit from the programmes provides some scope to improve their future efficiency. Hence, we will assess for each each estimation method that we will present in the following, its capability to deal with heterogeneous treatment effects.

1.3 How Do Randomised Experiments Solve the Evaluation Problem?

To show how randomisation solves the evaluation problem we follow Heckman, Ichimura, and Todd (1997) and consider a situation where randomisation occurs among people who have applied to a programme and been provisionally accepted. To complete the notation we introduce a binary randomisation indicator $R \in \{0, 1\}$. $R = 1$ if an eligible provisionally-accepted applicant is randomised into the programme, and $R = 0$ otherwise. For the moment we assume that if $R = 1$, individuals accept admission into the programme and receive services and if $R = 0$, they do not obtain programme services (also not through other sources). We can write the observed outcome for the entire population ($D = 1$) as:

(1.19) $$Y = D[RY^1 + (1 - R)Y^0] + (1 - D)Y^0,$$

so

(1.20)
$$E(Y \mid X, D = 1, R = 1) = E(Y^1 \mid X, D = 1)$$
$$= g^1(X) + E(U^1 \mid X, D = 1),$$

and

(1.21)
$$E(Y \mid X, D = 1, R = 0) = E(Y^0 \mid X, D = 1)$$
$$= g^0(X) + E(U^0 \mid X, D = 1).$$

Randomised-out controls can be used to estimate equation (1.21) and with data on programme participants equation (1.20) can be consistently estimated. Subtracting (1.21) from (1.20) leads to (Heckman, Ichimura, and Todd, 1997):

(1.22)
$$E(Y \mid X, D = 1, R = 1) - E(Y \mid X, D = 1, R = 0)$$
$$= g^1(X) - g^0(X) + E(U^1 - U^0 \mid X, D = 1)$$
$$= E(\Delta \mid X, D = 1).$$

1.3.1 Possible Problems with Randomised Experiments

Equation 1.22 shows that we get an unbiased estimate of $E(\Delta)$, i.e. the randomly generated group of non-participants can be used as an adequate control group to consistently estimate the counterfactual term $E(Y^1 \mid D = 0)$ and thus the causal treatment effect $E(\Delta \mid D = 1)$. Although this approach seems to be very appealing in providing a simple solution to the fundamental evaluation problem, there are also some problems associated with it. Besides relatively high costs and ethical issues concerning the use of experiments, in practice, a randomised experiment may suffer from similar problems that affect behavioural studies. Bijwaard and Ridder (2004) investigate the problem of non-compliance to the assigned intervention, that is, when members of the treatment sample drop out of the programme and members of the control group participate. If the non-compliance is selective, i.e. correlated with the outcome variable, the difference of the average outcomes is a biased estimate of the effect of the intervention, and correction methods have to be applied, too. Further methodological problems might arise, like a substitution or a randomisation bias. A randomisation bias occurs when random assignment causes the types of persons participating in a programme to differ from the type that would participate in the programme as it normally operates, leading to an unrepresentative sample. We talk about a substitution bias, if members of an experimental control group gain access to close substitutes for the experimental treatment (Heckman and Smith, 1995). These considerations make clear that the use of experiments may be problematic. Smith (2000b) notes that social experiments have become the method of choice in America. The most famous among them is the National Job Training Partnership Act which had a major influence regarding the view on non-experimental studies. However, in

Europe social experiments have not received a similar acceptance, although recently some test experiments have been conducted. The most important one is the RESTART experiment in Britain (see Dolton and O'Neill (1996)), but also in Germany some experiments, though on a small scale, have been conducted, see e.g. Dann, Kirchmann, Sperman, and Volkert (2001). For an extensive discussion of the pros and cons of social experiments the interested reader should refer to Burtless (1995), Burtless and Orr (1986) and Heckman and Smith (1995).

1.4 Evaluation Estimators

The discussion in subsections 1.2.2 and 1.2.3 has made clear that the problem of selection bias is a severe one and cannot be solved with more data, since the fundamental evaluation problem will not disappear. Figure 1.1 highlights the problem once again.

Fig. 1.1: Relationship between Hypothetical (Counterfactual) Population and Observed Data

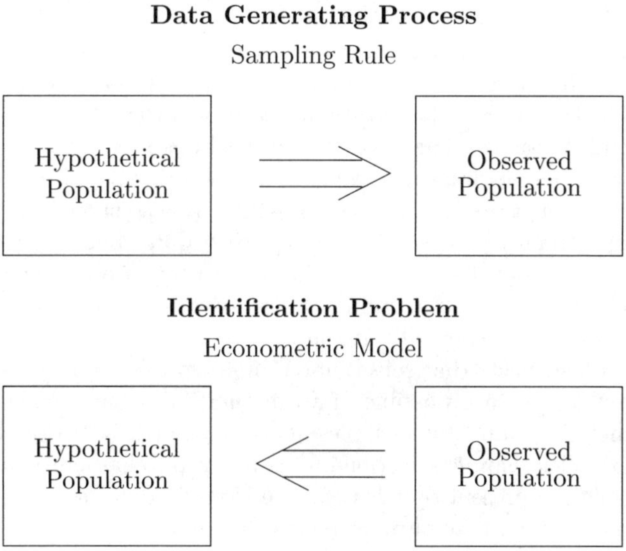

Data Generating Process

Sampling Rule

Hypothetical Population $\longrightarrow$ Observed Population

Identification Problem

Econometric Model

Hypothetical Population $\longleftarrow$ Observed Population

Source: Heckman (2001)

We have a distorted representation of a true population in a sample as a consequence of a sampling rule. This is the essence of the selection problem (Heckman, 2001). The identification problem is to recover features of a hypothetical population from an observed sample. If the sample is selected by any other rule than random sampling, we get a description of the population distribution of characteristics that does not describe the true population distribution properly.[6] And this is true no matter how big the sample size is (Heckman, 2001). Hence, we have to use some econometric model and/or identifying assumptions to draw inference about the hypothetical population based on the observed population. In the evaluation framework this means that we e.g. have to draw inference about the potential outcome of participants without treatment $E(Y^0|D=1)$ from the observed outcome of non-participants $E(Y^0|D=0)$.

In the following subsections we will present several different evaluation approaches. Each approach invokes different identifying assumptions to construct the required counterfactual outcome. Therefore, each estimator is only consistent in a certain restrictive environment. As Heckman, LaLonde, and Smith (1999) note, all estimators would identify the same parameter only if there is no selection bias at all.

We will start with three basic evaluation principles, namely the before-after, cross-section and the difference-in-differences estimator. They are still widely used and therefore we will discuss their properties and inherent identifying assumptions. Except the before-after estimator, all estimators make some comparisons of treated and untreated individuals. For the moment we will not discuss the construction of a valid comparison group any further and just assume that untreated individuals do not participate in the programme at all. We will discuss this topic in more detail in subsection 3.4.3. After having introduced the three basic estimators we will turn to more 'sophisticated' evaluation approaches. The main part of this book is concerned with matching estimators. These estimators are based on the principle of unconfoundedness which will be presented in section 1.5, where we also show how matching and regression estimators exploit it and how they differ between each other. For matching estimators to work, selection has to be on observable factors only, i.e. all relevant factors that influence the selection process and the outcome variable should be observed.[7] If the researcher is not convinced that this is the case and suspects that selection on unobservable factors plays a role, too, different strategies are possible. Two methods will be discussed in this section, namely instrumental variables and econometric selection models. These models explicitly handle selection on unobservable characteristics. Finally, we are also going to present the idea of regression-discontinuity design, which can be seen as a special case of instrumental variables.

---

[6] Distorting selection rules may arise from observable or unobservable factors, such as discussed in subsection 1.2.3.

[7] Later on in section 2.5 we will also discuss how matching estimators can be combined with other estimators to handle the problem of selection on unobservables, too.

1.4.1 Three Commonly Used Evaluation Estimators

Before-After Estimator

The most obvious and still widely used evaluation strategy is the before-after estimator (BAE). The basic idea is that the observable outcome in the pre-treatment period t' represents a valid description of the unobservable counterfactual outcome of participants without treatment in the post-treatment period t. The central identifying assumption of the before-after estimator can be stated as:

(1.23) $$E(Y_{t'}^0 \mid D = 1) = E(Y_t^0 \mid D = 1).$$

Given this identifying assumption, the following estimator of ATT can be derived:

(1.24) $$\Delta_{ATT}^{BAE} = E[(Y_t^1 \mid D = 1) - (Y_{t'}^0 \mid D = 1)].$$

The validity of (1.23) depends on a set of implicit assumptions. First of all, the pre-exposure potential outcome without treatment should not be affected by treatment. This may be invalid if individuals have to behave in a certain way in order to get into the programme or behave differently in anticipation of a future treatment participation. Secondly, no time-variant effects should influence potential outcomes from one period to the other. If there are changes in the overall state of the economy or changes in the lifecycle position of a cohort of participants, assumption (1.23) may be violated (Heckman, LaLonde, and Smith, 1999). A good example where this might be the case is the so-called Ashenfelter's dip (Ashenfelter, 1978). That is a situation where shortly before the participation in an ALMP programme the employment situation of future participants deteriorates. Ashenfelter found this 'dip' whilst evaluating the effects of treatment on earnings, but later research demonstrated that this dip can be observed on employment probabilities for participants, too (see e.g. Bergemann, Fitzenberger, and Speckesser (2001)). If the dip is transitory and only experienced by participants, assumption (1.23) will not hold. By contrast, permanent dips are not problematic, as they affect the employment probability before and after the treatment in the same way.

Figure 1.2 illustrates Ashenfelter's dip. Assume that an individual participates in a programme in period t and experiences a transitory dip in the pre-treatment period $t-1$, e.g. the employment probability is lowered as the individual is not actively seeking work, because he knows that he will participate in a programme in the next period. There are no economy-wide time-varying effects that influence the employment probability of the individual. After the programme took place, the employment probability might take many values. For the sake of simplicity we consider two cases. Case A assumes that there has been a positive treatment effect on the employment

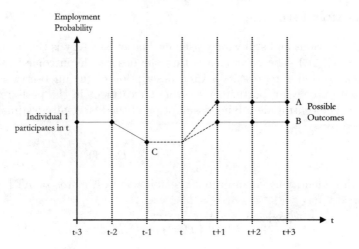

Fig. 1.2: Ashenfelter's Dip

probability (vertical difference between A and B). As the BAE compares the employment probability of the individual in period $t+1$ and $t-1$ (vertical difference between point A and C), it would overestimate the true treatment effect because it would attribute the restoring of the transitory dip completely to the programme. In a second example, we assume that there has been no treatment effect at all (B). In period $t+1$ the employment probability is restored to its original value before the dip took place in $t-1$. Again the BAE attributes this restoring completely to the programme and would estimate a positive treatment effect (vertical difference between point B and C). Clearly, the problem of Ashenfelter's dip could be avoided, if a time period is chosen as a reference level, before the dip took place, e.g. period $t-2$. However, in an empirical application it will not be easy to determine when the dip has started and to choose the right period.

A major advantage of the BAE is that it does not require information on non-participants. All that is needed is longitudinal data on outcomes of participants before and after the programme took place.[8] As the employment status of participants is known in nearly all of the ALMP programmes in Germany, the BAE does not impose any major problems regarding the data availability, which might explain why it is still widely used.[9]

---

[8] The BAE might also work with repeated cross-sectional data from the same population, not necessarily containing information on the same individuals. See Heckman and Robb (1985b) or Heckman, LaLonde, and Smith (1999) for details.

[9] Note that being unemployed is one of the entry conditions for many ALMP programmes in Germany.

Cross-Section Estimator

Instead of comparing participants at two different time periods, the cross-section estimator (CSE) compares participants and non-participants at the same time (after the programme took place), i.e. the population average of the observed outcome of non-participants replaces the population average of the unobservable outcome of participants. This is useful if no longitudinal information on participants is available or macroeconomic conditions shift substantially over time (Schmidt, 1999). The identifying assumption of the cross-section estimator can be stated formally as:

(1.25) $$E(Y_t^0 \mid D = 1) = E(Y_t^0 \mid D = 0),$$

that is persons who participate in the programme have on average the same non-treatment outcome as those who do not participate. Heckman, LaLonde, and Smith (1999) note that conditioning on observable characteristics makes the validity of the CSE more likely to hold. If the distribution of X characteristics is different between treatment and control group, conditioning on X may eliminate systematic differences in the outcomes.[10] Conditioning on observable characteristics X leads to the following identifying assumption:

(1.26) $$E(Y_t^0 \mid X, D = 1) = E(Y_t^0 \mid X, D = 0).$$

If this assumption is valid, the following estimator of ATT can be derived:

(1.27) $$\Delta_{ATT}^{CSE} = E[(Y_t^1 \mid X, D = 1) - (Y_t^0 \mid X, D = 0)].$$

Schmidt (1999) notes that for assumption (1.26) to be valid, selection into treatment has to be statistically independent of its effects given X (exogenous selection), that is, no unobservable factor should lead individual workers to participate. A good example where this is violated is given if motivation plays a role in determining the desire to participate and the non-treatment outcomes. In this case, even in the absence of any treatment effect a higher average outcome in the participating group compared to the non-participating group is obtained. Ashenfelter's dip is not problematic for the cross-section estimator, as we compare only participants and non-participants after the programme took place. Moreover, as long as economy-wide shocks and individuals' lifecycle patterns operate identically for the treatment and the control group, the cross-section estimator is not vulnerable to those problems that plague the BAE (Heckman, LaLonde, and Smith, 1999).

---

[10] On the other hand, if differences in the treatment and the control group are due to unobservable characteristics, conditioning may accentuate rather than eliminate differences in the no-programme state between both groups (Heckman, LaLonde, and Smith, 1999).

Difference-in-Differences Estimator

It has been claimed that controlling for selection on observables may not be sufficient since remaining unobservable differences may still lead to a biased estimation of treatment effects. These differences may arise from differences in benefits which individuals expect from programme participation that might influence their decision to participate. Furthermore, some groups might exhibit bad labour market prospects or differences in motivation. These features are unobservable to a researcher and might cause a selection bias.

To account for selection on unobservables, Heckman, LaLonde, and Smith (1999) suggest econometric selection models and difference-in-differences (DID) estimators. The DID estimator requires access to longitudinal data and can be seen as an extension to the classical BAE. Whereas BAE compares outcomes of participants after they participate in the programme with their outcomes before they participate, the DID estimator eliminates common time trends by subtracting the before-after change in non-participant outcomes from the before-after change for participant outcomes.

The DID-estimator forms simple averages over the group of participants and non-participants, that is, changes in the outcome variable Y for treated individuals are contrasted with the corresponding changes for non-treated individuals (Heckman, Ichimura, Smith, and Todd, 1998):

(1.28) $$\Delta^{DID} = [Y_t^1 - Y_{t'}^0 \mid D = 1] - [Y_t^0 - Y_{t'}^0 \mid D = 0].$$

The identifying assumption of this method is:

(1.29) $$E(Y_t^0 - Y_{t'}^0 \mid D = 1) = E(Y_t^0 - Y_{t'}^0 \mid D = 0).$$

The DID estimator is based on the assumption of time-invariant linear selection effects. The critical identifying assumption of this method is that biases are the same on average in different time periods before and after the period of participation in the programme, so that differencing the differences between participants and non-participants eliminates the bias (Heckman, Ichimura, Smith, and Todd, 1998).[11] To make this point clear, we give an example by denoting the outcome for an individual i at time t as:

(1.30) $$Y_{it} = \pi_{it} + D_{it} \cdot Y_{it}^1 + (1 - D_{it}) \cdot Y_{it}^0,$$

where π_{it} captures the effects of selection on unobservables. The validity of the DID estimator relies crucially on the assumption:

(1.31) $$\pi_{it} = \pi_{it'}.$$

Only if the selection effect is time-invariant it will be cancelled out and an unbiased estimate results. The differencing leads to:

---

[11] To increase the likelihood for that to be true, one could condition additionally once again on certain characteristics X.

(1.32)
$$\begin{aligned}Y_{it} - Y_{it'} =\ &[D_{it} \cdot Y^1_{it} + (1-D_{it}) \cdot Y^0_{it}] \\ &- [D_{it'} \cdot Y^1_{it'} + (1-D_{it'}) \cdot Y^0_{it'}] \\ &+ [\pi_{it} - \pi_{it'}].\end{aligned}$$

If (1.31) is fulfilled, the last term in the expression can be cancelled out, leading to an unbiased estimate. The DID approach does not require that the bias vanishes completely, but that it remains constant (Heckman, Ichimura, Smith, and Todd, 1998).[12] Ashenfelter's dip is definitely a problem for the DID estimator. If the 'dip' is transitory and the dip is eventually restored even in the absence of participation in the programme, the bias will not average out. To allow a more detailed discussion, Blundell and Costa Dias (2002) further decompose π_{it} in three parts: an individual-specific fixed effect, a common macroeconomic effect and a temporary individual-specific effect. Clearly, for the DID to be unbiased it is, as mentioned above, sufficient that selection into treatment is independent from the temporary individual-specific effect, since the other two effects vanish in the sequential differences. They also discuss the case where the macroeconomic effect has a differential impact across the group of participants and non-participants. This may happen, when both groups differ on unobserved characteristics which make them react differently to macroeconomic shocks. To overcome this problem they propose a differential trend adjusted DID estimators (Blundell and Costa Dias, 2002).

1.4.2 Alternative Evaluation Estimators

Instrumental Variables

We have shown in the last subsection that the DID estimator is able to handle selection on the basis of unobserved characteristics. An alternative strategy is the method of instrumental variables (IV). The basic idea of this identification strategy is to find a variable which determines treatment participation but does not influence the outcome equation. The instrumental variable affects the observed outcome only indirectly through the participation decision and hence causal effects can be identified through a variation in this instrumental variable. Since we will not use this identification strategy in our empirical analysis (the reason for that will become clear very soon), we restrict the presentation to the basic ideas. IV methods are extensively discussed in Imbens and Angrist (1994) and Angrist, Imbens, and Rubin (1996) among others.

In terms of the discussion in subsection 1.2.3, IV requires the existence of at least one regressor to the decision rule, Z^*, that satisfies the following three conditions (Blundell and Costa Dias, 2000):

---

[12] This is an important distinction compared to the methods assuming selection on observables which we will present later on in section 1.5.

1. Z^* determines programme participation. For that to be true, it has to have a non-zero coefficient in the decision rule in equation 1.10.
2. We can find a transformation, s, such that $s(Z^*)$ is uncorrelated with the error terms (U^1, V) and (U^0, V), given the exogenous variables X.
3. Z^* is not completely determined by X.

The variable Z^* is then called the instrument. In providing variation that is correlated with the participation decision but does not affect potential outcomes from treatment directly, it can be used as a source of exogenous variation to approximate randomised trials. Under these conditions, either the standard IV procedure may be applied - that is replacing the treatment indicator by $s(Z^*)$ and running a regression - or Z^* and X can be used to predict the treatment indicator, building a new variable $\hat{d}$ which is used in the regression instead of d (Blundell and Costa Dias, 2000). For a binary instrument $Z^* \in \{0, 1\}$, we can write the IV estimator as:

$$(1.33) \qquad \Delta^{IV} = \frac{E(Y|X, Z^* = 1) - E(Y|X, Z^* = 0)}{P(D = 1|X, Z^* = 1) - P(D = 1|X, Z^* = 0)}.$$

Clearly, a major problem with this estimator is to find a good instrument. In the treatment evaluation problem it is hard to think of variables that satisfy all three above mentioned assumptions. The difficulty lies mainly in the simultaneous requirement that the variable has to predict participation but does not influence the outcome equation. Bound, Jaeger, and Baker (1995) additionally point out arising problems when using 'weak instruments'. In this situation the instrumental variable is only weakly correlated with the participation indicator and therefore leads to inefficiency and possibly also inconsistency of the IV estimates. As pointed out by Blundell and Costa Dias (2000), a second drawback arises when considering the heterogeneous treatment framework. Recall that the error term from equation (1.17) in subsection 1.2.4 is given by $[U_{it}^0 + D_{it}(U_{it}^1 - U_{it}^0)]$. Clearly, even if Z^* is uncorrelated with U_{it}, the same cannot be true by definition for $U_{it}^0 + D_{it}(U_{it}^1 - U_{it}^0)$ since Z^* determines d_i by assumption. The violation of this assumption invalidates the application of IV methodology in a heterogeneous framework (Blundell and Costa Dias, 2000). However, in this situation it might still be possible to provide a potentially interesting parameter of the IV estimation - called local average treatment effect (LATE) by Imbens and Angrist (1994). The basic idea of LATE is as follows (see e.g. Blundell, Dearden, and Sianesi (2005)): Suppose that we have a single discrete instrument $\widetilde{Z} \in \{0, 1\}$, e.g. a discrete change in the regulation of unemployment benefits that is positively correlated with the treatment indicator D. In the population there will be four sub-groups of individuals: The ones who will not participate in the treatment under any circumstances, i.e. whatever value the instrument has ('never-takers'), those who always choose to participate ('always-takers') and those who change their behaviour due to a change in the value of the instrument. The last group consists of 'defiers', who change their treatment status in a perverse way and 'compliers' who change their status in line with the instrument. The group of 'compliers' is of particular interest, because this group consists of people who are in the treatment group ($D = 1$) after the rule change ($Z = 1$) and in the control group ($D = 0$) before ($Z = 0$). Additionally to those assumptions already made, we further have to assume that the instrument has the same directional effect on all those whose behaviour it changes. This assumption rules out the co-existence of defiers and compliers and is known as 'monotonicity assumption' (Imbens and Angrist, 1994). Usually it is assumed that $D_i(\widetilde{Z}_i = 1, X_i) \geq D_i(\widetilde{Z}_i = 0, X_i)$. In this case the IV estimator is given by:

$$(1.34) \quad \Delta^{IV}_{LATE} = \frac{E(Y_i|X_i, \widetilde{Z}_i = 1) - E(Y_i|X_i, \widetilde{Z}_i = 0)}{P(D_i = 1|X_i, \widetilde{Z}_i = 1) - P(D_i = 1|X_i, \widetilde{Z}_i = 0)}.$$

This estimator identifies the treatment effect for those individuals (with characteristics X) who are induced to change behaviour because of a change in the instrument. It should be clear that each instrument implies its own LATE, and LATEs for two different instruments may differ substantially depending on the impacts realised by the persons each instrument induces to participate (Hui and Smith, 2002). Hence, LATE should not be confused with ATE or ATT. If LATE should be the parameter of interest depends on the relevant policy question asked.[13]

These are also the major reasons why we do not use this identification strategy for the empirical analysis in chapters 5 and 6, where we inter alia estimate the effects of job creation schemes in Germany on the participating individuals. It is hard to think of variables in our dataset that influence only the participation decision but not the outcome variable. Additionally, the restriction to homogenous treatment effects seems not appropriate since we expect quite different effects for sub-groups of the population.

Regression Discontinuity Design

The regression-discontinuity design (RDD) can be seen as a particular type of instrumental variable identification strategy. It uses discontinuities in the selection process to identify causal effects. In this model, treatment depends on some observed variable, Z, according to a known, deterministic rule, such as $D = 1$ if $Z > \overline{Z}$ and $D = 0$ otherwise (Heckman, LaLonde, and Smith, 1999). As in the above mentioned IV framework we have a variable Z that has direct impact on Y as well as an indirect impact on Y through D. This indirect

---

[13] For continuous instruments Heckman and Vytlacil (2001) define marginal treatment effects (MTE). This is the effect on the person just indifferent to participate at his current value of the instrument. They also show that all common treatment effects, e.g. ATE and ATT, can be written as particular integrals of such MTEs. Presenting their work is beyond the scope of this chapter.

impact is the causal effect we would like to identify. Frölich (2002) notes that this effect is identified if the direct and indirect impacts of Z on Y can be separated. A good example is given by Angrist and Lavy (1999). They estimate the effects of the size of school classes on test scores of pupils. The discontinuity stems from a rule that classes with more than 40 pupils have to be divided in two, such that in each class remain on average 20.5 pupils. The treatment in this case is the fact of being in a class which has been divided due to reaching the maximum size of 41 pupils. Clearly, in this example class size affects the test scores of the pupils directly but also indirectly through D. Other examples are given by Hahn, Todd, and Van der Klaauw (1999), who analyse the effect of antidiscrimination laws of minority workers by exploiting the fact that only firms with more than 15 employees are subject to these laws. Barnow, Cain, and Goldberger (1980) consider a hypothetical enrichment programme for disadvantaged children, where children with a family income below a cut-off level receive the programme and all others do not. Whenever such deterministic rules are in place, RDD might be a possibility to estimate causal effects.

There are several things to note about RDD (see e.g. Heckman, LaLonde, and Smith (1999)). First, it is assumed that selection is on observable characteristics only. Second, it should be clear that there is no common support for participants and non-participants making matching impossible.[14] Hence, RDD takes over when there is selection on observables (here: the deterministic rule) but the overlapping support condition required for matching breaks down (with a certain Z you either belong to the participant or the non-participant group). Finally, the selection rule is assumed to be deterministic and known and that variation in the relevant variable Z is exogenous (Hahn, Todd, and Van der Klaauw, 2001).

Econometric Selection Models

This method is also known as the Heckman selection estimator (Heckman, 1978). It is more robust than the IV method but also more demanding in the sense that it imposes more assumptions about the structure of the model. Two main assumptions are required (Blundell and Costa Dias, 2000):

1. There has to be one additional regressor in the decision rule which has a non-zero coefficient and which is independent of the error term V.
2. Additionally, the joint density of the distribution of the errors U_{it} and V_i has to be known or can be estimated.

The basic idea of this estimator is to control directly for the part of the error term in the outcome equation that is correlated with the participation

---

[14] The significance of that will become clear very soon, after we have presented the identifying assumptions for the matching estimators in section 1.5.

dummy variable. It can be seen as a two-step-procedure. First, the part of the error term U_{it} that is correlated with D_i is estimated. Second, this term is then included in the outcome equation and the effect of the programme is estimated. By construction, the remains of the error term in the outcome equation are not correlated with the participation decision any more (Blundell and Costa Dias, 2000). To explain this estimator, we re-write the outcome equation in (1.16) in linear terms as $Y_i = X_i\beta_0 + \alpha D_i + U_i$, where we have dropped the time subscript for convenience. If we assume the popular special case where U_i and V_i are assumed to follow a joint normal distribution, we may write the conditional outcome expectations as:

$$E(Y_i|D_i = 1) = \beta + \alpha + \rho \frac{\phi(Z_i\gamma)}{\Phi(Z_i\gamma)}$$

and

$$E(Y_i|D_i = 0) = \beta - \rho \frac{\phi(Z_i\gamma)}{1 - \Phi(Z_i\gamma)}.$$

The new regressor includes the part of the error term that is correlated with the decision process in the outcome equation, allowing us to separate the true impact of the treatment from the selection process. Thus it is possible to identify α as outlined above, by replacing γ with $\hat{\gamma}$ and running a least-squares regression on the conditional outcome expectations (Blundell and Costa Dias, 2000). Blundell and Costa Dias (2000) also show that this approach is capable of identifying ATT if effects are assumed to be heterogeneous.[15] The Heckman selection estimator is not without critique. Puhani (2000) summarises this critique which rests mainly on the two following points: First, if there are no exclusion restrictions, i.e. variables that influence the selection process but not the outcome equation (other than indirectly), the models are identified only by assumptions about functional form and error distributions. This may lead to large standard errors and results that are very sensitive to the particular distributional assumptions invoked. Second, based on findings from several Monte Carlo studies, he concludes that the classical two-step-procedure might be inefficient as it is only a limited information maximum likelihood (LIML) method. Instead, the usage of full information maximum likelihood (FIML) methods are proposed, which make use of the full information set at once by estimating the participation and outcome equation jointly.[16]

The first point of the criticism is very closely related to the problem of finding a good instrument as described for the IV method. In fact, in a recent paper Vytlacil (2002) shows that the identifying assumptions for the selection model are equivalent to those invoked by Imbens and Angrist (1994) in the linear instrumental variables context.

---

[15] However, ATE is not identified.
[16] The main reason why LIML was preferred to FIML were restrictions in computing power.

1.5 The Principle of Unconfoundedness

One major strand of evaluation literature focusses on the estimation of treatment effects under the assumption that the treatment satisfies some form of exogeneity. Different versions of this assumption are referred to as unconfoundedness (Rosenbaum and Rubin, 1983), selection on observables (Heckman and Robb, 1985b, see also section 1.2.3) or conditional independence assumption (CIA, Lechner, 1999). We will use these terms throughout the book interchangeably. This assumption implies that systematic differences in outcomes between treated and comparison individuals with same values for covariates are attributable to treatment. Imbens (2004) gives an extensive overview of estimating average treatment effects under unconfoundedness.

Basically, there are two methods using this exogeneity assumption: Matching and regression. We will show that matching is a more flexible way of estimating treatment effects and that regression estimates do not exploit the richness of this identifying assumption. Since matching algorithms and estimators are the main topic of the next section, we will restrict the discussion here to presenting the basic ideas of matching and regression under unconfoundedness and to comparing both approaches.

1.5.1 The Basic Idea of Matching Under Unconfoundedness

The method is based on the identifying assumption that conditional on some covariates X, the outcome Y is independent of D. In the notation of Dawid (1979), it assumes that:

Assumption 1 *Unconfoundedness:*

$$Y^0, Y^1 \amalg D \mid X,$$

where $\amalg$ denotes independence. X are called covariates or pre-determined variables that are not influenced by the treatment. If assumption 1 is true, then

$$F(Y^0 \mid X, D = 1) = F(Y^0 \mid X, D = 0)$$

and

$$F(Y^1 \mid X, D = 1) = F(Y^1 \mid X, D = 0).$$

The first line means that conditional on X, non-participant outcomes have the same distribution that participants would have experienced if they had not participated in the programme. The second line implies that participant outcomes have the same distribution that non-participants would have experienced had they participated (Heckman, Ichimura, and Todd, 1997). Similar to randomisation in a classical experiment, matching balances the distributions of all relevant, pre-treatment characteristics X in the treatment and comparison group.[17] Thus it achieves independence between the potential outcomes and the assignment to treatment. Hence, if the mean exists,

$$E(Y^0 \mid X, D = 1) = E(Y^0 \mid X, D = 0) = E(Y^0 \mid X)$$
$$\text{and}$$
$$E(Y^1 \mid X, D = 1) = E(Y^1 \mid X, D = 0) = E(Y^1 \mid X)$$

and the missing counterfactual means can be constructed from the outcomes of non-participants and participants. In order for both sides of the equations to be well defined simultaneously for all X, it is usually additionally assumed that

Assumption 2 *Overlap:*

$$0 < Pr(D = 1 \mid X) < 1,$$

for all X.

This implies that the support of X is equal in both groups, i.e. $S = \text{Support}(X|D = 1) = \text{Support}(X|D = 0)$.[18] Assumption 2 prevents X from being a perfect predictor in the sense that we can find for each participant a counterpart in the non-treated population and vice versa. If there are regions where the support of X does not overlap for the treated and non-treated individuals, matching has to be performed over the common support region only.[19] The estimated effects have then to be redefined as the mean treatment effect for those individuals falling within the common support (Blundell, Dearden, and Sianesi, 2005). Rosenbaum and Rubin (1983) called assumptions 1 and 2 together 'strong ignorability'. Under 'strong ignorability' ATE in (1.3) and ATT in (1.4) can be defined for all values of X. Heckman, Ichimura, and Todd (1998) demonstrate that the ignorability or unconfoundedness conditions are overly strong. All that is needed for estimation of (1.3) and (1.4) is mean-independence:

Assumption 3 *Mean Independence:*

---

[17] If we say relevant we mean all those covariates that influence the assignment to treatment as well as the potential outcomes.

[18] The support is a statistical term meaning the set of values for which a density function is non-zero, i.e. the set of values of a variable that one observes with positive probability (Hui and Smith, 2002).

[19] We will discuss this issue in more detail in subsections 1.5.3 and 3.2.3.

$$E(Y^0 \mid X, D = 1) = E(Y^0 \mid X, D = 0)$$
$$\text{and}$$
$$E(Y^1 \mid X, D = 1) = E(Y^1 \mid X, D = 0).$$

However, Lechner (2002b) argues that assumption 1 has the virtue of identifying mean effects for all transformations of the outcome variables. The reason is that the weaker assumption of mean independence is intrinsically tied to functional form assumptions, making an identification of average effects on transformations of the original outcome impossible (Imbens, 2004). Furthermore, it will be difficult to argue why conditional mean independence should hold and assumption 1 might still be violated in empirical studies.

If we are interested in estimating the average treatment effect on the treated only, we can weaken the unconfoundedness assumption in a different direction. In that case one needs only to assume:

Assumption 4 *Unconfoundedness for Controls:*

$$Y^0 \amalg D \mid X,$$

and the weaker overlap assumption:

Assumption 5 *Weak Overlap:*

$$P(D = 1 \mid X) < 1.$$

These assumptions are sufficient for identification of (1.4), because the moments of the distribution of Y^1 for the treated are directly estimable.

1.5.2 How Does Matching Solve the Selection Problem?

Hence, the basic idea behind matching is to approximate the counterfactual outcome of one group with the observed outcome of other individuals with similar (identical) covariate values. If the 'strong ignorability' condition holds, one can generate marginal distributions of the counterfactuals

$$F_0(Y_0 \mid D = 1, X) \quad \text{and} \quad F_1(Y_1 \mid D = 0, X).$$

Heckman, Ichimura, and Todd (1998) point out, however, that we cannot estimate the joint distribution of $(Y^0, Y^1), F(y_0, y_1 \mid D, X)$, without making further assumptions about the structure of outcome and participation equations. Heckman, Smith, and Clements (1997) and Heckman and Smith (1998) consider the identification and estimation of distribution of impacts. Since we are interested in mean effects only, we do not present their results here.

Under the above stated assumptions - either assumptions 1 and 2 or 4 and 5 - the mean impact of treatment on the treated can be written as:

1.5 The Principle of Unconfoundedness

$$\begin{aligned}\Delta^{MAT}_{ATT} &= E(Y^1 - Y^0|X, D = 1) \\ &= E(Y^1|X, D = 1) - E_X[E(Y^0|X, D = 1)|D = 1] \\ &= E(Y^1|X, D = 1) - E_X[E(Y^0|X, D = 0)|D = 1],\end{aligned}$$

where the first term can be estimated from the treatment group and the second term from the mean outcomes of the matched comparison group. The outer expectation is taken over the distribution of X in the treated population.

The method of matching can also be used to estimate ATT at some points $X = x$, where x is a particular realisation of X:

$$\begin{aligned}ATT(X = x) &= E(\Delta \mid X = x, D = 1) \\ &= E(Y^1 \mid X = x, D = 1) - E(Y^0 \mid X = x, D = 1).\end{aligned}$$

This parameter measures the mean treatment effect for persons who were randomly drawn from the treated population given a specific realisation of certain characteristics X, e.g. if X is the educational level, one could define the expected impact for those with university degree. This feature of the estimator will be used repeatedly in our empirical analysis, since we want to estimate the effects of job creation schemes for certain sub-groups of the participating population.

Additionally, an averaged version of this effect focusses on a subset S of the support of X given $D = 1$ (see e.g. Heckman, Ichimura, Smith, and Todd (1998):

$$(1.35) \qquad M(S) = \frac{\int_S E(\Delta|X = x, D = 1)dF(X|D = 1)}{\int_S dF(X|D = 1)}.$$

We have shown in section 1.3 that randomisation guarantees that the support for the comparison group equals the support for programme participants. To give an example, let us reconsider the case where our matching variable X is the educational level. A randomised experiment would guarantee that we find approximately the same number of individuals with university degree within both treatment and control group. However, this needs not to be true with non-experimental data and, hence, a major limitation of non-experimental methods is that they do not guarantee equal support for both groups. The inability to find for programme participants comparable individuals in the control group is a major source of selection bias (Heckman, Ichimura, and Todd, 1997). We are going to discuss this problem in more detail in the next subsection.

1.5.3 Redefining Selection Bias

To see the possibilities matching offers to solve the problem of selection bias it is helpful to use a re-definition of the classical form of selection bias, introduced by Heckman, Ichimura, Smith, and Todd (1996) and Heckman, Ichimura, Smith, and Todd (1998). We have assumed so far that selection bias arises if the observed outcome of non-participants differs from the hypothetical outcome of participants if they had not been treated, that is:

(1.36) $$B(X) = E(Y^0 \mid X, D = 1) - E(Y^0 \mid X, D = 0).$$

The selection bias measure $B(X)$ is rigourously defined only over the set of X values which are common to both populations, $D = 1$ and $D = 0$. Heckman, Ichimura, Smith, and Todd (1998) use experimental data to decompose the conventional measure into three parts. First, they note that the support of X in the treated population is given by $S_{1X} = \text{Support}(X \mid D = 1)$ and might differ from the support of X in the control group which is given by $S_{0X} = \text{Support}(X \mid D = 0)$. Using the X distribution of participants, Heckman, Ichimura, Smith, and Todd (1996) define the mean selection bias $\overline{B}_{S_X}$ as

(1.37) $$\overline{B}_{S_X} = \frac{\int_{S_X} B(X) dF(X \mid D = 1)}{\int_{S_X} dF(X \mid D = 1)},$$

where $S_X = S_{1X} \cap S_{0X}$ is the set of X in the common support and $F(X|D = 1)$ is the conditional density of X given $D = 1$.[20] Given that, we can re-write equation (1.36) as:

(1.38)
$$B = \int_{S_{1X}} E(Y^0|D = 1, X) dF(X|D = 1) - \int_{S_{0X}} E(Y^0|D = 0, X) dF(X|D = 0).$$

Further decomposition yields to:

(1.39) $$B = B_1 + B_2 + B_3,$$

where

$$B_1 = \int_{S_{1X} \setminus S_X} E(Y^0|D = 1, X) dF(X|D = 1)$$
$$- \int_{S_{0X} \setminus S_X} E(Y^0|D = 0, X) dF(X|D = 0),$$

$$B_2 = \int_{S_X} E(Y^0|X, D = 0)[dF(X|D = 1) - dF(X|D = 0)],$$

and

$$B_3 = P_X \overline{B}_{S_X}.$$

$P_X = \int_{S_X} dF(X|D = 1)$ is the proportion of the density of X given $D = 1$ in the overlap set S_X, $S_{1X} \setminus S_X$ is the support of X given $D = 1$ that is not in

---

[20] One can also define the mean selection bias based on the propensity score $P(D = 1|X) = P(X)$, i.e. $\overline{B}_{S_P}$. In that case $P(X)$ replaces X in 1.37.

the overlap set S_X and $S_{0X} \setminus S_X$ is the support of X given $D = 0$ that is not in the overlap set S_X (Heckman, Ichimura, Smith, and Todd, 1996).

Term B_1 in equation (1.39) arises from the failure to find counterparts to $E(Y^0|D = 1, X)$ in the set $S_{0X} \setminus S_X$ and the failure to find counterparts to $E(Y^0|D = 0, X)$ in the set $S_{1X} \setminus S_X$. That is, for some treated individuals we do not find adequate matching partners from the comparison group and vice versa. The second term B_2 in (1.39) arises from the differential weighting of $E(Y^0|D = 0, X)$ by the densities for X given $D = 1$ and $D = 0$ within the overlap set. This can be seen as a mis-weighting over the common support S_X. In other words, B_2 occurs because of differences in the distribution of X over the common support between both groups. Only the last term B_3 arises from selection bias precisely defined and is due to failure of the conditional independence assumption either if not all relevant observable covariates have been included in the estimation and/or selection into treatment occurs because of unobservable characteristics (Heckman, Ichimura, Smith, and Todd, 1998).

Matching methods that impose the condition of (pointwise) common support eliminate two of three sources of bias. Clearly, imposing the common support condition eliminates B_1. The bias due to different density weighting is eliminated because matching effectively re-weights the non-participant data. Finally $P_X \bar{B}_{S_X}$ is the only component of (1.39) that is not eliminated by matching (Heckman, Ichimura, Smith, and Todd, 1998).

1.5.4 How Do Matching and Regression Under Unconfoundedness Differ?

Both, matching and regression, rely on the assumption of unconfoundedness. However, there are some key differences of both approaches which we will discuss in this subsection. One key difference is that matching, due to its non-parametric nature, avoids functional form assumptions implicit in linear regression models. Basically, linear regression makes the additional assumption that simply conditioning linearly on X suffices to eliminate selection bias. We have already introduced the linear regression notation in subsection 1.2.3, let us reconsider the main points. For notational convenience we drop the individual subscript i and the time subscript t. Hence, the potential outcomes in a linear regression framework can be written as $Y^1 = X\beta_1 + U^1$ and $Y^0 = X\beta_0 + U^0$ and ATT under regression is given by:

$$(1.40) \quad \Delta_{ATT}^{Reg} = E(Y^1 - Y^0 | X, D = 1) = X(\beta_1 - \beta_0) + E(U^1 - U^0 | X, D = 1).$$

The identifying assumption needed to justify regression under unconfoundedness is analogue to assumption 4 and can be re-written as:

Assumption 6 *Unconfoundedness in Regression:*

$$U^0, U^1 \amalg D \mid X,$$

In the matching framework, the goal is to set the bias $B(X) = 0$ which basically only requires that the mean of the error terms in the treatment group given a covariate cell X equals the corresponding mean in the control group, that is $B(X) = E(U^1|X, D = 1) - E(U^0|X, D = 0) = 0$. Basically, this means that it is possible to match on variables that are correlated with the error term in the outcome equation (Hui and Smith, 2002). In the regression framework, however, we need to eliminate the dependence between (U^0, U^1) and X, that is $E(U^1|X, D = 1) = E(U^0|X, D = 0) = 0$ (Heckman, Ichimura, Smith, and Todd, 1998).

Dehejia and Wahba (1999) and Smith and Todd (2005) directly compare the results of matching and regression estimates constructed with the same X and show that avoiding functional form assumptions can be important to reduce bias. Of course, as Smith (2000a) notes, the difference between both approaches fades with the inclusion of a sufficient number of higher-order and interaction terms in the regression. However, not only is such an inclusion not very common in practice, it is also not straightforward to choose these terms.

Moreover, whereas matching estimators do rely on the common support assumption, regression estimators do not. Matching ensures that comparisons between treated and control individuals are only calculated over the region of common support. For instance, if we have a treated individual with a high participation probability and cannot find any similar non-treated observations, the treated individual is dropped from the analysis. In that case, the treatment effect has to be re-defined (over the common support region). In contrast, standard regression approaches will produce estimates even in the absence of similar comparison units since the linear functional form assumption fills in for the missing data. The regression identifies the untreated outcome model in the region of the data where the untreated observations lie and then projects it out into the region of the data where the treated units lie, thereby implicitly estimating the counterfactual (Smith, 2004).

Figure 1.3 highlights the problem. The horizontal axis represents the matching variable, e.g. the educational level, the vertical axis represents the outcome. The two clouds of data represent participants and non-participants.

Region B in the center of the figure is the region of common support. In this region we can find treated individuals and individuals from the comparison group with similar values of X. However, the support condition fails in regions A and C. Region C includes treated observations only, so we cannot find untreated individuals with similar values of X in region C. No matching estimate can be constructed in this region. In regression analysis this would not be a problem. With the functional form assumption we would use the data on non-treated observations in regions A and B to construct the conditional mean outcome without treatment in region C. Similar problems occur in region A where we have control individuals only. When estimating ATT, matching ignores these individuals, as they are not required to construct the counterfactual for any of the treated individuals. In linear regression analy-

Fig. 1.3: Common Support in Matching and Regression Analysis

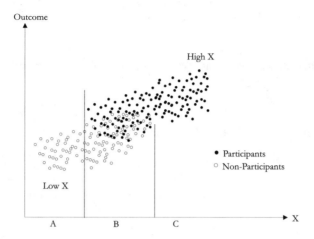

sis, however, they are used to estimate the relationship between X and the outcome.

Another key difference between regression and matching is the way both approaches handle heterogeneous treatment effects. As Lechner (2002b) notes, the non-parametric matching approach leaves the individual causal effect unrestricted and allows individual effect heterogeneity in the population. This is not true for the regression approach which will not recover ATT, although, at times it might provide a close approximation as shown by Angrist (1998). Blundell, Dearden, and Sianesi (2005) show straightforward why this is the case. Both, matching and regression, produce weighted regressions of the covariate-specific treatment effect $E(Y^1 - Y^0|X)$, but the estimators differ in the attached weights. Matching weights the X−heterogeneous effects according to the proportion of treated at each value of X, that is, proportionally to the propensity score at X, $P(D = 1|X) = P(X)$. By contrast, simple regression analysis weights the X−heterogeneous effects proportionally to the variance of treatment status at X, that is proportional to $P(X) \cdot [1 - P(X)]$. So, regression analysis will not recover ATT with heterogeneous effects, even though it will provide a close approximation if there is either no large heterogeneity in treatment impacts (varying with X), or if the values of the propensity score are smaller than 0.5.

Finally, another point worth mentioning is the scale of the outcome variable. In standard parametric regression, the scale of the outcome variable has to be borne in mind from the beginning of the estimation procedure either using e.g. linear or probability regression models. In the matching approach the construction of the matched sample is severed from the scale of the outcome variable. Only when calculating differences in means one has to account for the scale. If the outcome variable of interest is a duration variable (e.g. unemployment duration), a simple mean comparison is not appropriate among other things due to the right-censoring problem. A comparison in this case has to be done using methods such as a non-parametric Kaplan-Meier-estimator or a discrete hazard model. It is straightforward to combine matching with such approaches, see Hujer and Wellner (2000a) for an empirical application.

1.6 Summary - Which Estimator to Choose?

We have presented several different evaluation strategies in this chapter. The final question to be answered is: Which strategy to choose when evaluating labour market programmes? When feasible, an experimental evaluation will provide the most compelling evidence on the effectiveness of labour market programmes (Smith, 2004), even though some restrictions might apply as discussed in subsection 1.3.1. However, in most European countries experimental data are not available and therefore the evaluator must choose among the presented non-experimental evaluation estimators. Unfortunately, there is no 'one' answer to this question because there is no 'magic bullet' that will solve the evaluation problem in any case. As described above, different strategies invoke different identifying assumptions and also require different kinds of data for their implementation. When those assumptions hold, a given estimator will provide consistent estimates of certain parameters of interest (Smith, 2004). The literature provides a lot of guidance for making the right choice. Most of this guidance comes from papers that use experimental datasets to benchmark the performance of alternative evaluation estimators. That is, in a first step the experimental impacts are estimated and then used as a benchmark for different non-experimental evaluation strategies. The literature includes the studies by LaLonde (1986), Fraker and Maynard (1987), Heckman and Hotz (1989), Heckman, Ichimura, and Todd (1997), Heckman, Ichimura, Smith, and Todd (1998) and Dehejia and Wahba (1999, 2002) among others. Several Monte-Carlo simulations have also been done like in Heckman, LaLonde, and Smith (1999), Augurzky and Schmidt (2000a) or Hujer, Caliendo, and Radic (2001b).

The different estimators can be classified with respect to two dimensions. The first dimension is the required data for their implementation. We can distinguish between longitudinal and cross-sectional methods. The before-after and the difference-in-differences estimator presented in subsection 1.4.1 require access to longitudinal data. In the former case we need information on participants before and after the programme took place, in the latter case we additionally need information on non-participants (before and after the programme took place). Both estimation strategies can be seen as 'basic' evaluation estimators. They are relatively easy to implement as they do not

1.6 Summary - Which Estimator to Choose?

require any econometric methodology and in their simplest version also no covariates. The main identifying assumption is that the selection is based on permanent differences. Heckman and Smith (1999) show that when individuals select into treatment based on transitory labour market shocks (as it will be the case for most labour market programmes), longitudinal estimators like the BAE or the DID perform quite poorly. The cross-section estimator (see subsection 1.4.1) and all other estimators presented, including matching and regression (see section 1.5) as well as IV and selection models (see subsection 1.4.2), require only cross-sectional information for the group of participants and non-participants. Even though longitudinal information might help to justify the unconfoundedness assumption and also allows to combine e.g. matching with DID estimators.[21]

The second dimension concerns the handling of selection bias. The estimators can be classified in two broad categories. The first category consists of estimators that assume that selection is on observable characteristics, i.e. that we have enough information to credibly invoke the conditional independence or unconfoundedness assumption. We have presented two estimators for this context: Matching and linear regression analysis. Clearly the performance of these estimators depends on the quality of the data at hand. The results from the experimental studies mentioned above show that to justify the selection on observables strategy, rich data on observable determinants of participation and outcomes is required. If such data is not available, i.e. if we suspect that selection is on unobservables, too, we have to turn to the second category of estimators. For that case we have presented the instrumental variable approach and standard selection models.

Let us review the main points made in this chapter and concentrate on the relevant identifying assumptions and the ability of different estimators to deal with effect heterogeneity. We start with the two evaluation approaches that deal with selection on observables.

Clearly, the most crucial point for these estimators is that the identifying conditional independence assumption is in general a very strong one. Both, matching and linear regression, depend on this crucial assumption and thus both are only as good as the used control variables X. Blundell, Dearden, and Sianesi (2005) argue that the plausibility of such an assumption should always be discussed on a case-by-case basis, thereby taking account of the informational richness of the data and a detailed understanding of the institutional set-up by which selection into treatment takes place. When we discuss the matching estimator in more detail in chapters 2 and 3, we will also present several tests which might help to justify (or rule out) the CIA. Assuming for the moment that the CIA holds, let us compare both approaches. Three major differences can be established.

---

[21] We will come back to this issue in section 2.5, where we discuss extensions of the matching estimator.

First, matching is non- or semi-parametric.[22] No functional form assumption for the outcome equation is required for implementation, whereas in standard regression usually a linear functional form is assumed. With this functional form assumption, even if we have the correct covariates, we can still get biased estimates if we assume the incorrect functional form, e.g. by failing to include needed higher order or interaction terms (Hui and Smith, 2002). However, if the linear functional form restriction implicit in regression analysis in fact holds for the data, then failing to impose it reduces the efficiency of estimates. In other words, if the outcome equation is linear, imposing linearity will lead to smaller standard errors on impact estimates (Hui and Smith, 2002). An additional advantage of matching is that one can match on variables that are correlated with the error term in the outcome equation, because matching only assumes that the mean of the error term is the same for participants and non-participants.

Second, matching relies on the common support requirement, whereas regression does not. In contrast to randomised experiments, the common support requirement may be in some situations quite restrictive as noted by Blundell, Dearden, and Sianesi (2005). Randomisation generates a comparison group for each X in the treated population. Hence, ATT can be estimated over the entire support of the treated. Matching estimators on the other hand might not always succeed in finding comparable non-treated observations for each participant. If the common support condition fails for some regions of X, the estimated treatment effect has to be redefined for those treated falling within the common support region (Blundell, Dearden, and Sianesi, 2005). Even though this is clearly a drawback when compared to randomised experiments, it can be seen as an advantage compared to standard regression methods. In standard regression approaches we can produce estimates even in the absence of similar comparison units. The functional form assumption fills in for the missing data and extrapolates outside the common support. Clearly, this is not a desired feature in most cases. Finally, if treatment effects are heterogeneous, we have shown that matching is a better way to recover ATT.

So, if selection is on observables only, both, matching and regression, can be used. Since regression analysis ignores the common support problem, imposes a functional form for the outcome equation, and is not as capable as matching in handling effect heterogeneity, matching should be preferred. However, if the common support is not a problem for given data, and the outcome equation is indeed linear, both approaches coincide, with regression analysis providing more efficient estimates.

Let us now turn to estimators that take into account selection on unobservables, too. We have presented two strategies. Whereas selection models try to model the selection process completely, IV methods focus on searching

---

[22] We will discuss the distinction between non- and semi-parametric in more detail in chapter 2.

1.6 Summary - Which Estimator to Choose?

a source of independent variation affecting the participation decision (but not the outcome).

So, the first requirement of IV estimation is the ability to find a suitable and credible instrument. This is not an easy task, since in most cases variables are likely to influence the selection into a labour market programme and the labour market outcome simultaneously. While the literature on IV was traditionally centered around the question of finding good instruments, the recent literature focusses on two other concerns. The first one is instrument strength. If we have weak instruments, i.e. the instrument is only weakly connected to the participation decision, we might get biased estimates (Bound, Jaeger, and Baker, 1995). Thus, for applied research more attention should be drawn to the importance of instruments in predicting the endogenous variable (Hui and Smith, 2002). If a valid instrument is available, we can use it to estimate ATT in a world of homogeneous effects. However, in a heterogeneous effect world, IV estimation breaks down and this is the second concern discussed recently. What is left to be estimated in a heterogeneous effect world is LATE, i.e. the effect for those individuals who are induced to participate by a change in the instrument. Our discussion of LATE has made clear that the IV estimate will typically vary with the choice of the instrument (Blundell, Dearden, and Sianesi, 2005). As Hui and Smith (2002) note, each different instrument implies its own LATE, and LATEs for two different instruments may substantially differ, depending on the impacts realised by the persons each instrument induces to participate. So, instead of ATT, which is generally the parameter of interest, we get LATE. If this parameter is of political interest depends on the question asked (and the local sub-population examined).

Estimating ATT in a heterogeneous effect world is not a problem for the second type of estimators we discussed for the selection on unobservables situation, namely selection models. Selection models are general enough to allow for heterogeneous effects. Björklund and Moffit (1987) were the first who discussed this extension. However, this flexibility comes at a price. In contrast to IV, the selection model approach requires a full specification of the assignment rule (Blundell, Dearden, and Sianesi, 2005) and makes stronger assumptions. In general, selection models do not rest on an exclusion restriction as they can be identified through functional form restrictions. Technically, the Heckman (1979) model is identified solely based on a joint normality assumption. However, extensive experience in the literature indicates that these estimators perform poorly in absence of such an exclusion restriction. Hence, in practice an exclusion restriction is required to ensure the stability of the model and therefore data requirements are identical to IV estimation. As Heckman and Robb (1985b) note, the selection estimator makes stronger assumptions than the IV estimator. Hence, if the common effect assumption is plausible in a given context, the IV estimator should be preferred (Smith, 2004).

Figure 1.4 summarises the main findings. Let us conclude this section with a somewhat obvious quote from Smith (2000a): 'Better data helps a lot!'. The discussion in this chapter has shown that each non-experimental

Fig. 1.4: Alternative Evaluation Estimators

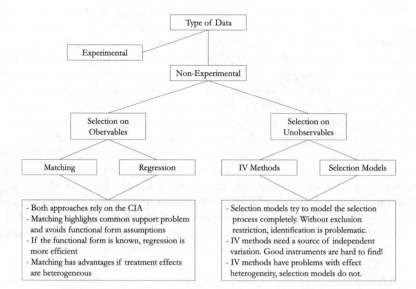

estimation strategy relies on identifying assumptions and has to be justified case-by-case. In an ideal world, the evaluator is already involved at early stages of the programme design and has influence on the data collected for later evaluation. In that case, one can make sure to collect those data needed to justify either the unconfoundedness assumption or to create an instrument (exclusion restriction) that allows to use IV methods or selection models. In that context, Heckman, Ichimura, Smith, and Todd (1998) demonstrate the importance to draw comparison group members from the same local labour market. They also show that using outcomes measured in different ways for treated and untreated units, e.g. administrative data for participants and survey data for non-participants, can lead to outcome differences that are due to measurement errors.

If the evaluator is instead faced with an ongoing programme, he carefully has to assess which identification strategy works for the situation at hand, taking the design of the programme, the selection process, and the available data into account. With matching one tries to construct a 'comparable' control group, selection models try to model the selection decision completely and IV methods focus on finding a good instrument. As Smith (2004) notes, matching methods make no sense without rich data, IV methods make no sense without a good instrument, and finally, longitudinal methods make no sense when selection into treatment depends on transitory rather than permanent shocks.

2

The Evaluation of Policy Interventions with Matching Estimators

2.1 Introduction

The matching approach originated from the statistical literature and shows a close link to the experimental context.[1] The basic idea underlying this approach is to find in a large group of non-participants those individuals who are similar to the participants in all relevant pre-treatment characteristics. That being done, differences in outcomes of this well selected and thus adequate control group and of the participants can then be attributed to the programme. Matching has become a popular method especially when evaluating labour market policies, but examples for usage of the matching method can be found in very diverse fields of study. It applies for all situations where we have a treatment, a group of treated individuals and a group of non-treated individuals. The nature of treatment may be very diverse. For example, Perkins, Tu, Underhill, Zhou, and Murray (2000) discuss the usage of matching in pharmacoepidemiologic research. Hitt and Frei (2002) analyse the effect of online banking on the profitability of customers. Davies and Kim (2003) compare the effect on the percentage bid-ask spread of Canadian firms being interlisted on an US-Exchange, whereas Hujer and Radic (2005) analyse the effects of subsidies on the innovation activities of firms in Germany. Brand and Halaby (2003) analyse the effect of elite college attendance on career outcomes, while Ham, Li, and Reagan (2003) study the effect of a migration decision on the wage growth of young men. Bryson (2002) analyse the effect of union membership on wages of employees and Behrman, Cheng, and Todd (2004) apply matching methods to estimate the impact of preschool programmes on cognitive, psycho-social and anthropometric outcomes of children.

This is only a short listing which could be easily augmented. It should merely point out the popularity of matching in diverse fields of research.

---

[1] See Rubin (1974), (1977), (1979), Rosenbaum and Rubin (1983), (1985a), (1985b) or Lechner (1998)).

Of course, matching is first of all plagued by the same problem as all non-experimental estimators, which means that the condition in equation (1.5) cannot be expected to hold when treatment assignment is not random. However, following Rubin (1977), treatment assignment may be random given a set of covariates. The construction of a valid control group via matching is based on the identifying assumption that conditional on all relevant pre-training covariates X, potential outcomes are independent of treatment assignment. We have already discussed this assumption, known as unconfoundedness or conditional independence assumption (CIA), in section 1.5. Similar to randomisation in a classical experiment, the role of matching is to balance the distributions of all relevant pre-treatment characteristics X in the treatment and control group, and thus to achieve independence between potential outcomes and assignment into treatment, resulting in an unbiased estimate. We have also shown that matching represents an important extension of standard regression approaches as it does not impose functional forms on the outcome equations, highlights the common support problem, and allows for heterogeneous treatment effects (see our discussion in subsection 1.5.4).

Conditioning on all relevant covariates is, however, limited in case of a high dimensional vector X. For instance, if X contains n covariates which are all dichotomous, the number of possible matches will be 2^n. In this case exact matching on X (cell matching) is in practice not possible, because an increase in the number of variables increases the number of matching cells exponentially. In the dataset underlying our further analyses in chapters 5 and 6 we have approximately 38 discrete and 6 continuous variables. This gives us a possible number of over 278 million cells and makes the use of exact covariate matching impossible.

To deal with this dimensionality problem, Rosenbaum and Rubin (1983) suggest the use of balancing scores $b(X)$, i.e. functions of the relevant observed covariates X such that the conditional distribution of X given $b(X)$ is independent of assignment into treatment. We will discuss their results in the following section. One possible balancing score is the propensity score, i.e. the probability of participating in a programme given observed characteristics X. Matching procedures based on this balancing score are known as propensity score matching (PSM) and will be the focus of this chapter. Whereas exact (or cell) matching is completely non-parametric, propensity score matching is semi-parametric as it combines a parametric model for estimation of the participation probability with a non-parametric comparison of the outcomes.[2]

Even though propensity score matching was developed in the early 1980s (Rosenbaum and Rubin, 1983) and has its roots in a conceptual framework which dates back even further, its use in labour market policy evaluation was established in the late 1990s only. Especially the work of Dehejia and Wahba

---

[2] Note that Hirano, Imbens, and Ridder (2003) suggest a non-parametric series estimator for the propensity score which makes propensity score matching completely non-parametric.

(1999, 2002) can be seen as a milestone. They re-analysed a sub-set of the data from the LaLonde (1986) study and showed that PSM performs very well in reducing the bias in observational study.[3] Their work has subsequently been criticised (e.g. by Smith and Todd (2005)) and further clarifications regarding the necessary assumptions required for PSM have been put forward.

This chapter is organised as follows: First, we will present the balancing property of the propensity score that justifies propensity score matching. Following that we will present several matching algorithms that have been suggested in the literature, e.g. nearest-neighbour and kernel matching. We will also discuss very briefly matching on covariates and alternative distance metrics which can be used in this case, before we discuss several extensions of matching when combined with other methods in section 2.5. The large-sample properties of matching estimators are the topic of section 2.6, where we also discuss the estimation of variances of treatment effects. Finally, in section 2.7 we try to give some recommendations for which matching estimator to choose in certain situations.

2.2 The Balancing Property of the Propensity Score

To deal with the above mentioned dimensionality problem, Rosenbaum and Rubin (1983) suggest the use of balancing scores $b(X)$, i.e. functions of the relevant observed covariates X such that the conditional distribution of X given $b(X)$ is independent of assignment into treatment, that is

(2.1) $$X \amalg D | b(X)$$

holds. For participants and non-participants with identical balancing scores, the distributions of the covariates X are the same, i.e. they are balanced across both groups. The propensity score $P(X)$, i.e. the probability of participating in a programme is one possible balancing score. It summarises the information of the observed covariates X into a single index function. The propensity score can be seen as the coarsest balancing score, whereas X is the finest balancing score (Rosenbaum and Rubin, 1983). The authors also show that if treatment assignment is strongly ignorable given X, it is also strongly ignorable given any balancing score. The conditional independence or unconfoundedness assumption, which we presented in section 1.5, then extends to the use of the propensity score:

Lemma 1 *Unconfoundedness given the Propensity Score:*

$$Y^1, Y^0 \amalg D | X \Rightarrow Y^1, Y^0 \amalg D | P(X).$$

---

[3] We will come back to the LaLonde study in section 2.7.

To prove lemma 1, it is sufficient to show that

$$P[D=1|Y^0,Y^1,P(X)] = P[D=1|P(X)] = P(X),$$

which implies independence of (Y^0,Y^1) and D conditional on $P(X)$ (see Rosenbaum and Rubin (1983) or Imbens (2004)). We start with:

$$\begin{aligned}P(D=1|Y^0,Y^1,P(X)) &= E[D=1|Y^0,Y^1,P(X)]\\ &= E[E[D|Y^0,Y^1,P(X),X]|Y^0,Y^1,P(X)]\\ &= E[E[D|Y^0,Y^1,X]|Y^0,Y^1,P(X)]\\ &= E[E[D|X]|Y^0,Y^1,P(X)]\\ &= E[P(X)|Y^0,Y^1,P(X)] = P(X),\end{aligned}$$

where the last equality follows from unconfoundedness. It can also be shown that:

$$\begin{aligned}P(D=1|P(X)) &= E[D=1|P(X)]\\ &= E[E[D=1|X]|P(X)]\\ &= E[P(X)|P(X)] = P(X).\end{aligned}$$

It follows that

$$E(Y^0|P(X),D=1) = E(Y^0|P(X),D=0) = E(Y^0|P(X)).$$

As a consequence from lemma 1 we can re-write the crucial term in the mean treatment effect in equation (1.4) as:

$$E(Y^0|D=1) = E_{P(X)}[E(Y^0|P(X),D=0|D=1].$$

The outer expectation is taken over the propensity score distribution in the treated population, replaces the missing counterfactual outcome and solves the fundamental evaluation problem. Clearly, this finding explains a lot of the popularity of PSM, since conditioning on one single index function is relatively easy to implement. It is the starting point for our further discussion.

2.3 Alternative Matching Estimators

Several matching procedures have been suggested and we will review them in this section. A good overview can be found in Heckman, Ichimura, Smith, and Todd (1998), Smith and Todd (2005) and Imbens (2004). To introduce them, a more general notation is needed: Let I_0, and I_1 denote the set of indices for non-participants and participants. We estimate the effect of treatment for each treated observation $i \in I_1$ in the treatment group, by contrasting his outcome with treatment with a weighted average of control group observations $j \in I_0$ in the following way:

$$(2.2) \qquad \Delta^{MAT} = \frac{1}{N_1} \sum_{i \in I_1} [Y_i^1 - \sum_{j \in I_0} W_{N_0}(i,j) Y_j^0],$$

where N_0 is the number of observations in the control group I_0 and N_1 is the number of observations in the treatment group I_1. Matching estimators differ in the weights attached to the members of the comparison group (Heckman, Ichimura, Smith, and Todd, 1998), where $W_{N_0}(i,j)$ is the weight placed on the j-th individual from the comparison group in constructing the counterfactual for the i-th individual of the treatment group. The weights always satisfy $\sum_j W_{N_0}(i,j) = 1, \forall i$, that is the total weight of all controls sums up to one for each treated individual. Define a neighbourhood $C(P_i)$ for each i in the participant sample and denote as neighbours for i those non-participants $j \in I_0$ for whom $P_j \in C(P_i)$. Individuals matched to i are those people in the set A_i where $A_i = \{j \in I_0 | P_j \in C(P_i)\}$. The matching estimators discussed in the following differ in how the neighbourhood is defined and the weights are constructed (Smith and Todd, 2005).

2.3.1 Nearest-Neighbour-Matching

The most popular matching estimator is nearest neighbour (NN) matching. It sets

$$(2.3) \qquad C^{NN}(P_i) = \min_j \|P_i - P_j\|, j \in N_0,$$

where $\|(.)\|$ is either based on comparing the index function or obtained through a distance metric, as will be discussed in section 2.4. Doing so, the non-participant with a value of P_j that is closest to P_i is selected as the match, therefore:

$$(2.4) \qquad W_{N_0}^{NN}(i,j) = \begin{cases} 1 \text{ if } \|P_i - P_j\| = \min_j \|P_i - P_j\| \\ 0 \text{ otherwise} \end{cases}.$$

Several variants of NN matching are proposed, e.g. NN matching 'with replacement' and 'without replacement'. In the former case, a non-participating individual can be used more than once as a match, whereas in the latter case it is considered only once. Matching with replacement involves a trade-off between bias and variance. If we allow replacement, the average quality of matching will increase and the bias will decrease. This is of particular interest with data where the propensity score distribution is very different in the treatment and the control group. For example, if we have a lot of treated individuals with high propensity scores but only few comparison individuals with high propensity scores, we get bad matches as some of the high-score participants will get matched to low-score non-participants. This can be overcome by allowing replacement, which in turn reduces the number of distinct non-participants used to construct the counterfactual outcome and thereby increases the variance of the estimator (Smith and Todd, 2005). Another problem which is related to NN matching without replacement is that the estimates depend on the order in which observations get matched. Hence, when using this approach it should be ensured that ordering is randomly done.

It is also suggested to use more than one nearest neighbour ('oversampling'). This form of matching involves a trade-off between variance and bias, too. It trades reduced variance, resulting from using more information to construct the counterfactual for each participant, with increased bias that results from on average poorer matches (see e.g. Smith (1997)). When using oversampling, one has to decide how many matching partners m should be chosen for each individual i and which weight should be assigned to them. One possibility is to use uniform weights, that is all the m control individuals within set A_i receive the weight $\frac{1}{m}$, whereas all other individuals from the control group receive the weight zero:

$$(2.5) \qquad W^{NN0_1}(i,j) = \begin{cases} \dfrac{1}{m} & \text{if } j \in A_i \\ 0 & \text{else} \end{cases}.$$

Another possibility is to use triangular weights like suggested by Davies and Kim (2004). To do so, the m individuals within set A_i have to be ranked, where $\varrho = 1$ is the closest neighbour, $\varrho = 2$ is the next closest neighbour and so on. The weights can then be written as:

$$(2.6) \qquad W^{NN0_2}(i,j) = \begin{cases} \dfrac{2(m-\varrho+1)}{m(m+1)} & \text{if } j \in A_i \\ 0 & \text{else} \end{cases}.$$

A clear advantage of this approach is that more similar control individuals get a higher weight.

2.3.2 Caliper and Radius Matching

NN matching faces the risk of bad matches, if the closest neighbour is far away. This can be avoided by imposing a tolerance level on the maximum distance $\|P_i - P_j\|$ allowed. This form of matching, known as caliper matching (Cochrane and Rubin, 1973), imposes the condition:

$$(2.7) \qquad \|P_i - P_j\| < \epsilon, j \in N_0,$$

where ϵ is a pre-specified level of tolerance. The weights for caliper matching (CM) are given by:

$$(2.8) \quad W^{CM}(i,j) = \begin{cases} 1 \text{ if } \|P_i - P_j\| = \min_j \|P_i - P_j\| \wedge \|P_i - P_j\| < \epsilon \\ 0 \text{ else} \end{cases}.$$

Treated observations for whom no matches within the neighbourhood $C(P_i) = \{P_j | \|P_i - P_j\| < \epsilon\}$ can be found are excluded from the analysis. Hence, caliper matching is one form of imposing a common support condition. As Smith and Todd (2005) note, a possible drawback of caliper matching is that it is difficult to know a priori what choice for the tolerance level is reasonable.

Dehejia and Wahba (2002) suggest a variant of caliper matching which we will call radius matching. The basic idea of this variant is to use not only the nearest neighbour within each caliper but all of the comparison members within the caliper. A benefit of this approach is that it uses only as many comparison units as are available within the caliper and therefore allows for usage of extra (fewer) units when good matches are (not) available. Hence, it shares the attractive feature of oversampling mentioned above, but avoids the risk of bad matches.

2.3.3 Stratification and Interval Matching

The idea of stratification matching (STM) is to partition the common support of P into a set of intervals and to calculate the impact within each interval by taking the mean difference in outcomes between treated and control observations. This method is also known as interval matching, blocking and subclassification (Rosenbaum and Rubin, 1983).

To implement STM, the (estimated) propensity score is used to divide the full sample into M blocks of units of approximately equal probability of treatment. Let J_{is} be an indicator for unit i being in block s. One way of implementing this is to divide the unit interval into S blocks with boundary values equal to $\frac{s}{S}$ for $s = 1, ..., S-1$, so that (Imbens, 2004):

$$(2.9) \quad J_{is} = 1\left\{\frac{(s-1)}{S} < P(X_i) \leq \frac{s}{S}\right\}.$$

Within each block there are N_{1s} treated and N_{0s} untreated individuals, where $N_{1s} = \sum_i 1\{D_i = 1, J_{is} = 1\}$ and $N_{0s} = \sum_i 1\{D_i = 0, J_{is} = 1\}$. Hence, given these sub-groups, the average treatment effect within each block can be estimated as if random assignment was held:

$$(2.10) \quad \Delta_s^{STM} = \frac{1}{N_{1s}} \sum_{i=1}^{N} J_{is} D_i Y_i - \frac{1}{N_{0s}} \sum_{i=1}^{N} J_{is}(1 - D_i) Y_i.$$

The overall average treatment effect is then estimated as:

$$\Delta_{ATE}^{STM} = \sum_{s=1}^{S} \Delta_s^{STM} \cdot \frac{N_{1s} + N_{0s}}{N}. \quad (2.11)$$

Basically, the effects in each block are weighted by the number of individuals in each block (relative to the full sample). For ATT, one will weight the within-block average treatment effects by the number of treated units:

$$\Delta_{ATT}^{STM} = \sum_{s=1}^{S} \Delta_s^{STM} \cdot \frac{N_{1s}}{N_1}. \quad (2.12)$$

Clearly, one question to be answered is how many blocks should be used in empirical analysis. Cochrane and Chambers (1965) shows that five subclasses are often enough to remove 95% of the bias associated with one single covariate. Since, as Imbens (2004) notes, all bias under unconfoundedness is associated with the propensity score, this suggests that under normality the use of five blocks removes most of the bias associated with all covariates. In a recent application Aakvik (2001) chooses ad-hoc twelve sub-groups. One way to justify the choice of s is to check the balance of the propensity score (or the covariates) within each block. Most of the algorithms can be described in the following way: First, check if within a block the propensity score is balanced. If not, the blocks are too large and need to be split. If, conditional on the propensity score being balanced, the covariates are unbalanced, the specification of the propensity score is not adequate and has to be re-specified, e.g. through the addition of higher-order terms or interactions (Dehejia and Wahba, 1999). We will come back to this point in subsection 3.2.1 when we discuss the propensity score estimation.

2.3.4 Kernel and Local Polynomial Matching

The matching estimators discussed so far have in common that only a few observations from the comparison group are used to construct the counterfactual outcome of a treated individual. Kernel matching (KM) and local linear matching (LLM) are non-parametric matching estimators that use all units in the control group to construct a match for each programme participant. Thus, one major advantage of these approaches is the lower variance which is achieved because more information is used for constructing counterfactual outcomes. A drawback of these methods is that possibly observations are used that are very bad matches. Hence, the proper imposition of the common support condition is of major importance for KM and LLM. Heckman, Ichimura, and Todd (1998) derive the asymptotic distribution of these estimators and Heckman, Ichimura, and Todd (1997) present an application.

It is worth noting that if weights from a symmetric, nonnegative, unimodal kernel are used, then the average places higher weight on persons close in terms of P_i and lower weight on more distant observations. Kernel matching sets $A_i = I_0$ and uses the following weights:

$$W_{N_0}^{KM}(i,j) = \frac{G_{ij}}{\sum_{k \in I_0} G_{ik}}, \tag{2.13}$$

where $G_{ik} = G[(P_i - P_k)/a_{N_0}]$ is a kernel that downweights distant observations from P_i and a_{N_0} is a bandwidth parameter (Heckman, Ichimura, Smith, and Todd, 1998).[4]

However, before applying kernel matching, assumptions have to be made regarding the choice of the kernel function and the bandwidth parameter a_{N_0}. The choice of the kernel appears to be relatively unimportant in practice (DiNardo and Tobias, 2001). Table 2.1 summarises some possible kernel functions.

Table 2.1: Kernel Functions

Kernel	$\kappa(x) = \kappa(\frac{X_j - X_i}{h})$	Support
Rectangular	$\frac{1}{2}$	$\|x\| \leq 1$
Epanechnikov	$\frac{3}{4\sqrt{5}}(1 - \frac{1}{5}x^2)$	$\|x\| \leq \sqrt{5}$
Biweight or "Quadratic"	$\frac{15}{16}(1 - x^2)^2$	$\|x\| \leq 1$
Triangular	$1 - \|x\|$	$\|x\| \leq 1$
Normal or "Gaussian"	$\frac{1}{\sqrt{2\pi}} \cdot e^{-0.5x^2}$	$-\infty < x < \infty$

Source: DiNardo and Tobias (2001)

What is seen as more important in the non-parametric literature is the choice of the bandwidth parameter a_{N_0}. Silverman (1986) and Pagan and Ullah (1999) note that there is little to choose between various kernel functions, whereas results more depend on a_{N_0} with the following trade-off arising: High values of a_{N_0} yield a smoother estimated density function, therefore leading to a better fit and a decreasing variance between the estimated and the true underlying density function. On the other hand, underlying features may be smoothed away by a large a_{N_0} leading to a biased estimate. The choice of a_{N_0} is therefore a compromise between a small variance and an unbiased estimate of the true density function. A standard way for choosing a_{N_0} is the following 'rule of thumb' proposed by Silverman (1986): Given the true underlying

---

[4] a_{N_0} satisfies $\lim_{N_0 \to \infty} a_{N_0} = 0$. See Heckman, Ichimura, and Todd (1998) for precise conditions on the rate of convergence needed for consistency and asymptotic normality of the kernel matching estimator.

density function is distributed according to a Gaussian density function, an optimal a which minimises the mean squared error of the kernel estimate is given by $a_{N_0}^{opt} = 0.9 \cdot A \cdot n^{-1/5}$ with $A = \min(\text{STD},\text{IQR}/1.34)$, where STD is the standard deviation and IQR is the interquartile range of the sample. Clearly, in empirical applications the choice of the bandwidth is not straightforward. Optimal bandwidth choice for matching estimators has only recently become a topic in the matching literature. Frölich (2004b) discusses this problem and derives a mean squared error approximation for matching estimators and analyses its usefulness for bandwidth selection. It turns out that conventional cross-validation is a promising method for bandwidth selection.[5]

A generalised version of KM is local linear matching. LLM has some advantages like a faster rate of convergence near boundary points, and greater robustness to different data design densities (Heckman, Ichimura, and Todd, 1997). LLM uses the weight:

(2.14)
$$W^{LLM}(i,j) = \frac{G_{ij} \sum_{k \in I_0} G_{ik}(P_k - P_i)^2 - [G_{ij}(P_j - P_i)][\sum_{k \in I_0} G_{ik}(P_k - P_i)]}{\sum_{j \in I_0} G_{ij} \sum_{k \in I_0} G_{ij}(P_k - P_i)^2 - (\sum_{k \in I_0} G_{ik}(P_k - P_i))^2}.$$

As Smith and Todd (2005) note, kernel matching can be seen as a weighted regression of Y_j^0 on an intercept with weights given by the kernel weights $W(i,j)$. The weights depend on the distance between each control unit and the participant observation for which the counterfactual is estimated. The estimated intercept provides an estimate of the counterfactual mean. The difference between kernel matching and local linear matching is that the latter includes in addition to the intercept a linear term in P_i. This is an advantage whenever comparison group observations are distributed asymmetrically around the treated observation, e.g. at boundary points, or when there are gaps in the distribution of P. LLM is a special case of local polynomial matching which includes an intercept term of polynomial order p in P_i, e.g. $p = 2$ for local quadratic matching or $p = 3$ for local cubic matching.[6] Local linear estimation is known for its optimality properties (see e.g. Fan (1993)). In small samples, however, local linear regression often leads to a very rugged curve in regions of sparse data. To increase the reliability in such cases, Seifert and Gasser (1996, 2000) suggest to add a 'ridging' term, and based on this Frölich (2004b) develops a 'ridge matching' estimator which turns out to perform very well in simulation studies.[7]

---

[5] Presenting his results is beyond the scope of this chapter. We will come back to the cross-validation method in section 2.7.

[6] Since there are only very few empirical applications that make use of higher-order polynomials, we will not discuss this point further.

[7] See Frölich (2004b) for an extensive discussion.

2.3.5 Weighting on the Propensity Score

The basis for this estimator is the key insight of Rosenbaum and Rubin (1983) that under unconfoundedness treatment assignment and potential outcomes are independent conditional on a scalar function of covariates like the propensity score (as discussed in section 2.2). Thus, adjusting for the propensity score removes the bias associated with differences in observed covariates between both treated and control group. Hirano and Imbens (2002) suggest a straightforward way to implement this estimator by re-weighting treated and control observations to make them representative of the population of interest. This follows the Horowitz-Thompson (1952) estimators for stratified sampling. The starting point is the expectation (Imbens, 2004):

$$E\left[\frac{YD}{P(X)}\right] = E\left[\frac{Y^1 D}{P(X)}\right] = E\left[E\left[\frac{Y^1 D}{P(X)} \mid X\right]\right]$$
$$= E\left[\frac{P(X)E[Y^1 \mid X]}{P(X)}\right]$$
$$= E\left[Y^1\right].$$

Unconfoundedness is used in the second to last equality and can also be used to derive:

$$E\left[\frac{(1-D)Y}{1-P(X)}\right] = E[Y^0].$$

Hence we can write the average treatment effect as:

$$E\left[\frac{YD}{P(X)} - \frac{(1-D)Y}{1-P(X)}\right] = E[Y^1 - Y^0] = \Delta.$$

If the propensity score is known, the estimator can directly be implemented as the difference between a weighted average of the outcomes for the treated individuals and a weighted average of the outcomes for the non-participants (Imbens, 2004). However, a problem arises because the weights do not necessarily add up to one. As a solution, the weights can be normalised to unity.[8] The simple weighting estimator is then given by:

$$(2.15) \quad \Delta_{ATE}^{WG} = \sum_{i=1}^{N} \frac{D_i Y_i}{\hat{P}(X_i)} \Big/ \sum_{i=1}^{N} \frac{D_i}{\hat{P}(X_i)} - \sum_{i=1}^{N} \frac{(1-D_i)Y_i}{1-\hat{P}(X_i)} \Big/ \sum_{i=1}^{N} \frac{1-D_i}{1-\hat{P}(X_i)}.$$

To estimate ATT one should weight the contribution for unit i by the propensity score $P(X_i)$:

$$(2.16) \quad \Delta_{ATT}^{WG} = \left[\frac{1}{N_1}\sum_{i \in I_1} Y_i\right] - \left[\sum_{i \in I_0} Y_i \cdot \frac{\hat{P}(X_i)}{1-\hat{P}(X_i)} \Big/ \sum_{i \in I_0} \frac{\hat{P}(X_i)}{1-\hat{P}(X_i)}\right].$$

---

[8] Hirano, Imbens, and Ridder (2003) suggest to use a non-parametric series estimator for the propensity score and show that this estimator is asymptotically efficient. Since we do not use the weighting estimator in the empirical section, we do not discuss this any further.

2.4 Matching on Covariates

The alternative matching estimators we presented in section 2.3 are in principle also applicable to matching on covariates. Instead of minimising the difference in the propensity scores between treated and control observations, the basic idea here is to find for each treated individual i with characteristics X_i a control individual j with the same characteristics, such that:

$$(2.17) \quad X_i = X_j \Rightarrow g^0(X_i) = g^0(X_j) \quad \text{and} \quad g^1(X_i) = g^1(X_j).$$

This equation justifies exact matching (Zhao, 2004). If we additionally assume that g^0 and g^1 are continuous at X, that is
(2.18)
$$d(X_i, X_j) < \epsilon \Rightarrow d'(g^0(X_i), g^0(X_j)) < \delta \quad \text{and} \quad d'(g^1(X_i), g^1(X_j)) < \delta,$$

neighbourhood matching is justified when exact matching is infeasible, where d and d' are some metrics in the mathematical sense.[9]

Here the choice of the matching metrics becomes more important, since we condition on a possible high-dimensional matrix X instead of just a one-dimensional function of X. Several different distance metrics have been suggested in the literature. They have the general form:

$$(2.19) \quad d = (X_i - X_j)' W (X_i - X_j),$$

where W is a weighting matrix.

The most common choice is the Mahalanobis metric, which uses the inverse of the covariance matrix of the exogenous variables as a weight:

$$(2.20) \quad d^M = (X_i - X_j)' \Sigma_X^{-1} (X_i - X_j),$$

where Σ_X^{-1} is the inverse of the covariance matrix of the covariates.

Imbens (2004) shows that the Mahalanobis metric can have some less attractive implications and therefore suggests to use the metric introduced by Abadie and Imbens (2004):

$$(2.21) \quad d^{AI} = (X_i - X_j)' diag(\Sigma_X^{-1})(X_i - X_j),$$

which uses the diagonal matrix of the inverse of the covariate variances.[10] In a simulation study Zhao (2004) adds two alternative metrics which depend on

---

[9] Zhao (2004) shows that continuity of g^0 and g^1 is needed because the average treatment effect at x is $E[Y^1 - Y^0 | x] = g^1(x) - g^0(x) + E(u^1 - u^0 | x)$. If exact matching is infeasible and matching is done on some x' within a small neighbourhood of x, such that $d(x, x') < \delta$ but $x \neq x'$ then $E(Y^1 | x) - E(Y^0 | x') = g^1(x) - g^0(x')$. Only if g^0 is a continuous function of x this will converge to the true treatment effect at x.

[10] Imbens (2004) considers the case where one matches on two highly correlated covariates, X_1 and X_2, with equal variances. The variance-covariance matrix in

the correlation between covariates, treatment assignment and outcomes. The first one weights absolute differences in covariates by their coefficient in the propensity score estimation:

$$(2.22) \qquad d^{Z1} = \sum_{k=1}^{K} \|x_{ik} - x_{jk}\| \cdot \|\gamma_k\|,$$

where x_{ik} and x_{jk} are the kth elements of the K-dimensional vector X and γ_k is the relevant coefficient of the score estimation. The second metric from Zhao (2004) weights the absolute differences by the regression coefficients (β_k) of the (linear) outcome equation:

$$(2.23) \qquad d^{Z2} = \sum_{k=1}^{K} \|x_{ik} - x_{jk}\| \cdot \|\beta_k\|.$$

Zhao (2004) runs simulations to test his proposed metrics but finds no clear winner given his specific design. However, it seems quite promising to use outcomes in defining the metric.[11]

2.4.1 Simple Matching Estimator

To introduce the simple matching estimator (SM) from Abadie and Imbens (2004) we need some additional notation first (see also Imbens (2004) and Abadie, Drukker, Leber Herr, and Imbens (2004)). Given a sample $\{(Y_i, X_i, D_i)\}$, let $\ell_m(i)$ be the index ℓ of the unit in the control group that is

---

this example is: $\Sigma_X = \begin{pmatrix} 1 & 0.9 \\ 0.9 & 1 \end{pmatrix}$. He supposes that there is a treated unit i with $X_i = \{0,0\}$ and two control units j and k with $X_j = \{5,5\}$ $X_k = \{4,0\}$. The difference in covariates for the first match is the vector $(5,5)'$, the difference for the second match is $(4,0)'$. Using the Mahalanobis metric leads to $d_{i,j}^M = \begin{pmatrix} -5 & -5 \end{pmatrix} \begin{pmatrix} \frac{100}{19} & \frac{-90}{19} \\ \frac{-90}{19} & \frac{100}{19} \end{pmatrix} \begin{pmatrix} -5 \\ -5 \end{pmatrix} \simeq 26$ for individual j and to 84 for individual k.
Using the metric from Abadie and Imbens (2004) in equation (2.21), however, leads to a distance of 50 for a match between individual i and j, and a distance of 16 for a match between individuals i and k. So, the two different metrics would choose different matching partners, because the correlation between the covariates is interpreted very differently under both metrics. For considering which metric to choose, one has to carefully assess what match would be appropriate for the given case.

[11] Imbens (2004) notes that one problem arises when the regression function is mis-specified, because then this particular metric may not lead to a consistent estimator.

the mth closest to unit i in the treatment group. Especially, $\ell_1(i)$ is the nearest match for unit i, $\ell_2(i)$ is the second nearest match and so on. Let $J_M(i)$ denote the set of these indices for the first M matches for unit i which are used to construct the counterfactual outcomes, that is $J_M(i) = \{\ell_1(i), \ell_2(i), ..., \ell_M(i)\}$. The potential outcomes are then estimated as:

(2.24) $$\widehat{Y}_i^0 = \begin{cases} Y_i^0 \text{ if } D_i = 0 \\ \frac{1}{M} \sum_{j \in J_M(i)} Y_j^0 \text{ if } D_i = 1 \end{cases}.$$

and

(2.25) $$\widehat{Y}_i^1 = \begin{cases} \frac{1}{M} \sum_{j \in J_M(i)} Y_j^1 \text{ if } D_i = 0 \\ Y_i^1 \text{ if } D_i = 1 \end{cases}.$$

Additionally, $K_M(i)$ denotes the number of times an individual i is used as a matching partner given that M matches per individual are used. The ATE can then be estimated as:

(2.26) $$\Delta_{ATE}^{SM} = \frac{1}{N} \sum_{i=1}^{N} (\widehat{Y}_i(1) - \widehat{Y}_i(0)) = \frac{1}{N} \sum_{i=1}^{N} (2D_i - 1) \cdot (1 + \frac{K_M(i)}{M}) \cdot Y_i.$$

Alike, ATT is given by:

(2.27) $$\Delta_{ATT}^{SM} = \frac{1}{N_1} \sum_{i \in I_1} (Y_i - \widehat{Y}_i(0)) = \frac{1}{N_1} \sum_{i=1}^{N} (D_i - (1 - D_i) \cdot \frac{K_M(i)}{M}) \cdot Y_i.$$

2.5 Combination of Matching with Other Methods

So far we have presented several non-experimental strategies for estimating programme impacts. Imbens (2004) notes that one method alone is often sufficient to obtain consistent or even efficient estimates. However, combining some of these methods is a straightforward way to improve their performance by eliminating remaining bias and/or improving precision. We are going to present three extensions. First, we introduce an estimator which combines matching with the DID approach presented in subsection 1.4.1. By doing so, a possible bias due to time-invariant unobservables is eliminated. Second, we present a regression-adjusted matching estimator that combines matching with regression. This strategy is promising because matching alone does not directly address the correlation between the covariates and the outcome. Finally, the bias-corrected matching estimator is an extension to the SM estimator (discussed in subsection 2.4.1) and helps in situations where matching is not exact.

2.5.1 Conditional DID or DID Matching Estimator

The matching estimators described so far assume that after conditioning on a set of observable characteristics, mean outcomes are conditionally mean independent of programme participation. The conditional DID or DID matching estimator relaxes this assumption and allows for temporally invariant differences in outcomes between participants and non-participants. It compares the conditional before-after outcome of participants with those of non-participants. It was first defined by Heckman, Ichimura, Smith, and Todd (1998) and Heckman, Ichimura, and Todd (1997). Smith and Todd (2005) find that it is more robust than traditional cross-section matching estimators. This new estimator is a combination of the DID approach presented in subsection 1.4.1 and classical matching estimators. It extends the DID estimator by defining outcomes conditional on $P(X)$ and using semiparametric methods to construct the differences. Therefore it is superior to DID as it does not impose linear functional form restriction in estimating the conditional expectation of the outcome variable and it re-weights the observations according to the weighting function of the matching estimator (Smith and Todd, 2005). The DID propensity score matching estimator is based on the following identifying assumption:

$$(2.28) \qquad E(Y_t^0 - Y_{t'}^0 | P(X), D = 1) = E(Y_t^0 - Y_{t'}^0 | P(X), D = 0).$$

It also requires the common support condition to hold. If panel data on participants and non-participants are available, it can be implemented as:

$$(2.29) \qquad \Delta_{ATT}^{DDM} = \frac{1}{N_1} \sum_{i \in I_1 \cap S_P} \left[(Y_{it}^1 - Y_{it'}^0) - \sum_{j \in I_0 \cap S_P} W(i,j)(Y_{jt}^0 - Y_{jt'}^0) \right],$$

where S_P is the region of overlap in the propensity score distribution between participants and non-participants (see the discussion in section 1.5.3). The weights W depend on the choice of the particular matching estimator chosen (see section 2.3).[12] There are quite a few recent applications of this estimator evaluating German labour market policies. For example, Hujer, Caliendo, and Radic (2001a) evaluate the effects of wage subsidies on the labour demand in West Germany, and Bergemann, Fitzenberger, and Speckesser (2001) evaluate the employment effects of public sector sponsored training in East Germany.

---

[12] Smith and Todd (2005) present a variant of this estimator when repeated cross-section data are used instead of panel data. With repeated cross-section data the identity of future participants and non-participants may not be known in t', Blundell and Costa Dias (2000) suggest a solution for that case.

2.5.2 Regression-Adjusted Matching Estimators

The regression-adjusted matching estimator (developed by Heckman, Ichimura, Smith, and Todd (1998) and Heckman, Ichimura, and Todd (1997)) combines local linear matching on the propensity score with regression adjustment on covariates. By utilising information on the functional form of outcome equations and by incorporating exclusion restrictions across outcome and participation equation, it extends classical matching methods. To see how the estimator works, let us reconsider our findings from subsection 1.2.3. If we assume additive separability and linearity, the outcome Y^0 is given by: $Y^0 = X\beta_0 + U^0$.[13] In the first step using partially linear regression methods applied to the comparison group sample, the components of $E(Y^0|X, D=0) = X\beta_0 + E(U^0|X, D=0)$ are estimated. To do so, an exclusion restriction has to be imposed. To estimate the treatment effect, $X\hat{\beta}_0$ are removed from Y^1 and Y^0. The regression-adjusted matching (RAM) estimator of ATT is then defined as:

$$(2.30) \quad \Delta_{ATT}^{RAM} = \frac{1}{N_1} \sum_{i \in I_1 \cap S_P} \left[(Y_i^1 - X_i\hat{\beta}_0) - \sum_{j \in I_0 \cap S_P} W(i,j)(Y_j^0 - X_j\hat{\beta}_0) \right].$$

Heckman, Ichimura, and Todd (1998) present a proof of consistency and asymptotic normality of this estimator. Navarro-Lozano (2002) provides a nice example for an application and evaluates a popular training programme in Mexico.

2.5.3 Bias-Corrected Matching Estimator

The simple matching estimator (on covariates) which we presented in subsection 2.4.1 will be biased when the matching is not exact. Hence, it might be useful to remove some of this bias that remains after matching. A number of such corrections have been proposed, e.g. by Rubin (1973), we draw on Abadie and Imbens (2004) and the discussion in Imbens (2004). Recall the notation from subsection 2.4.1, where $\hat{Y}^0$ and $\hat{Y}^1$ are the observed or imputed outcomes for individual i and the closest match ℓ_i. The bias in their comparison arises because the covariates X_i and X_{i_ℓ} are not equal, even though they will be close as a result of matching. For each unit we can define:

$$(2.31) \quad \hat{X}_i^0 = \begin{cases} X_i & \text{if } D_i = 0 \\ X_{\ell_i} & \text{if } D_i = 1 \end{cases}.$$

---

[13] For notational convenience we drop the individual subscript i.

(2.32) $$\hat{X}_i^1 = \begin{cases} X_{\ell_i} \text{ if } D_i = 0 \\ X_i \text{ if } D_i = 1 \end{cases}.$$

With exact matching one has for each unit $\hat{X}_i^0 = \hat{X}_i^1$. If matching is not exact, there will be some discrepancies that lead to a potential bias. The difference $\hat{X}_i^0 - \hat{X}_i^1$ will therefore be used to reduce the bias of the simple matching estimator. In principle these corrections are taken to be linear in covariates, i.e. $\beta_0'(X_i - X_{\ell_i})$. Rubin (1973) proposed three correction methods that differ in the way β_0 is estimated. Imbens (2004) introduces the first correction by re-writing the matching estimator as the least squares estimator for the regression function:

(2.33) $$\hat{Y}_i^1 - \hat{Y}_i^0 = \Delta + u_i.$$

Incorporating the correction leads to the modified regression function

(2.34) $$\hat{Y}_i^1 - \hat{Y}_i^0 = \Delta + (\hat{X}_i^1 - \hat{X}_i^0)'\beta + u_i,$$

where Δ can be estimated by least squares. The second correction estimates the expected outcome Y^0 directly by estimating a linear regression of the form $Y_i = \alpha_0 + \beta_0'X_i + u_i$ for the control individuals only, and vice versa for Y^1 and the treated individuals (Imbens, 2004). Finally, the third method uses the same regression for the non-participants, but uses only those individuals that are used as matches. Even though this approach might be less efficient as it discards some of the comparison units, it has the advantage of using only the relevant matches. Abadie, Drukker, Leber Herr, and Imbens (2004) provide an implementation of this estimator in STATA and give some useful examples based on data from the LaLonde (1986) study.

2.6 Efficiency and Large-Sample Properties of Matching Estimators

The asymptotic properties of matching and weighting estimators have been studied e.g. by Hahn (1998), Heckman, Ichimura, and Todd (1998) and Abadie and Imbens (2004). Frölich (2004a) discusses the finite-sample properties of these estimators, Zhao (2004) concentrates on covariate and propensity score matching. The results from Hahn (1998) are a good starting point for the efficiency discussion. He derives the semi-parametric efficiency bounds for ATE and ATT under various assumptions. He especially takes into account cases where the propensity score is known and where it has to be estimated. Under the unconfoundedness assumption $(Y_i^0, Y_i^1 \amalg D_i | X_i)$ the asymptotic variance bounds for ATE and ATT are given by:

(2.35) $$Var_{ATE} = E\left[\frac{\sigma_1^2(X_i)}{P(X_i)} + \frac{\sigma_0^2(X_i)}{1-P(X_i)} + (E(Y_i^1|X_i) - E(Y_i^0|X_i) - \Delta_{ATE})^2\right],$$

and

$$(2.36) \quad Var^{PSunknown}_{ATT} = E\left[\frac{P(X_i)\sigma_1^2(X_i)}{E[P(X_i)]^2} + \frac{P(X_i)^2\sigma_0^2(X_i)}{E[P(X_i)]^2(1-P(X_i))} \right.$$
$$\left. + \frac{(E(Y_i^1|X_i) - E(Y_i^0|X_i) - \Delta_{ATT})^2 P(X_i)}{E[P(X_i)]^2}\right].$$

To examine the role of the propensity score in efficient estimation of Δ_{ATE} and Δ_{ATT}, Hahn (1998) considers the situation where the propensity score is known and $(Y_i^0, Y_i^1 \text{ II } D_i|X_i)$ is still valid. He shows that the propensity score does not play a role for the estimation of Δ_{ATE}, but plays some role for the estimation of Δ_{ATT}. The variance of Δ_{ATT} when the propensity score is known is given by:

$$(2.37) \quad Var^{PSknown}_{ATT} = E\left[\frac{P(X_i)\sigma_1^2(X_i)}{E[P(X_i)]^2} + \frac{P(X_i)^2\sigma_0^2(X_i)}{E[P(X_i)]^2(1-P(X_i))} \right.$$
$$\left. + \frac{(E(Y_i^1|X_i) - E(Y_i^0|X_i) - \Delta_{ATT})^2 P(X_i)^2}{E[P(X_i)]^2}\right].$$

Comparing (2.37) and (2.38) shows that knowledge of the propensity score reduces the variance bound by:

$$(2.38) \quad E\left[\frac{(E(Y_i^1|X_i) - E(Y_i^0|X_i) - \Delta_{ATT})^2 P(X_i)(1-P(X_i))}{E[P(X_i)]^2}\right].$$

Hahn (1998) argues that the reduction in the variance of ATT can be attributed to the 'dimension reduction' feature of the propensity score. However, recent work by Frölich (2004c) casts doubt on this explanation. He argues that the reason why knowledge of the propensity score affects the variance bounds is not the dimension reduction, but the information it provides for estimating the distribution function of the covariates in the treated population. If the propensity score is not known, the distribution $F_{X|D=1}$ is estimated by the empirical distribution function of X among treated individuals. In this case, the X values of control observations contain no information about $F_{X|D=1}$. When the propensity score is known, the control individuals become informative, because the distributions $F_{X|D=0}$ and $F_{X|D=1}$ are related trough the propensity score by Bayes' theorem: $\frac{P(X)}{1-(P(X))} = \frac{f_{X|D=1}P(D=1)}{f_{X|D=0}P(D=0)}$. The distribution function $F_{X|D=1}$ is used as a weighting function for ATT, and hence, its information reduces the variance. The variance of the ATE is unaffected, because it is obtained through weighting by the distribution of X in the full population.

There is an ongoing discussion in the literature on how the efficiency bounds are achieved and if the propensity score should be used for estimation of ATT and ATE or not. In the above cited paper Hahn (1998) shows that when using non-parametric series regression, adjusting for all covariates can

2.6 Efficiency and Large-Sample Properties of Matching Estimators

achieve the efficiency bound, whereas adjusting for the propensity score does not. Hirano, Imbens, and Ridder (2003) show that weighting with the inverse of a non-parametric estimate of the propensity score can achieve the efficiency bound, too.

Angrist and Hahn (2004) use the results from Hahn (1998) as a starting point for their analysis. As Hahn (1998) has shown that covariate matching is asymptotically efficient, whereas propensity score matching is not, they note that conventional asymptotic arguments would appear to offer no justification for anything other than full control for covariates in estimation of average treatment effects. However, they argue that conventional asymptotic results can be misleading and provide poor guidance for researchers who face a finite sample. They develop an alternative theory and propose a panel-style estimator which can provide finite-sample efficiency gains over covariate and propensity score matching.

Heckman, Ichimura, and Todd (1998) analyse large sample properties of local polynomial matching estimators for the estimation of ATT. They show that these estimators are $\sqrt{n}$-consistent and asymptotically normal distributed. This holds true when matching with respect to X, the known propensity score or the estimated propensity score. They conclude that none of the approaches dominates the others per se. In case of matching on the known propensity score, the asymptotic variance of Var_{ATT} is not necessarily smaller than that when matching on X.[14]

Abadie and Imbens (2004) analyse the asymptotic efficiency of n-nearest neighbours matching when n is fixed, i.e. when the number of neighbours does not grow with increasing sample size. They show that simple matching estimators (see subsection 2.4.1) include a conditional bias term of order $O(N^{-1/k})$, where k is the number of continuous covariates. The bias does not disappear if k equals 2 and will dominate the large sample variance if k is at least 3. Hence, these estimators do not reach the variance bound in (2.35) and (2.37) and are inefficient. Finally, they describe a bias-correction that removes the conditional bias asymptotically, making estimators $\sqrt{n}$-consistent (see section 2.5). Additionally, they suggest a new estimator for the variance that does not require consistent non-parametric estimation of unknown functions and will be presented in subsection 2.6.1. Imbens (2004) highlights some caveats of these results. First, it is important to make clear that only continuous covariates should be counted in dimension k, since with discrete covariates the matching will be exact in large samples. Second, if only treated individuals are matched and the number of potential controls is much larger than the number of treated individuals, it can be justified to ignore the bias by appealing to an

---

[14] Whereas matching on X involves k-dimensional non-parametric regression function estimation (where $k = 1, ..., K$ are the number of covariates), matching on $P(X)$ only involves one-dimensional non-parametric regression function estimation. Thus from the perspective of bias, matching on $P(X)$ is preferable, since it allows $\sqrt{n}$-consistent estimation of Δ_{ATT} for a wider class of models (Heckman, Ichimura, and Todd, 1998).

asymptotic sequence where the number of potential controls increases faster than the number of treated individuals.

Frölich (2002) notes that the analysis of asymptotic properties of matching estimators imply no firm recommendations on which estimator to use in practice. Even though not all of the estimators achieve the semi-parametric efficiency bounds, this does not mean that these should be discarded in practice, i.e. in finite samples (Imbens, 2004). The discussion has shown that propensity score matching implies no advantage over matching on X per se. However, for practical purposes it might be useful since inference for average treatment effects is often less sensitive to mis-specification of the propensity score than to mis-specification of the conditional expectations of the potential outcomes (Imbens, 2000). There is only limited literature on the small-sample properties of matching and weighting estimators and we will review this literature in section 2.7.

2.6.1 Estimating the Variance for Treatment Effects

There are a number of ways to estimate the variance of average treatment effects as displayed in equations (2.35) and (2.37). One is by 'brute force' (Imbens, 2004), that is estimating the five components of the variance $\sigma_0^2(x)$, $\sigma_1^2(x)$, $E(Y^1|X)$, $E(Y^0|X)$ and $P(X)$ using kernel methods or series. Even though this is consistently possible and hence the asymptotic variance will be consistent, too, Imbens (2004) notes that this might be an additional computational burden.[15] Hence, practical alternatives are called for and we are going to present three of them. Two of them, bootstrapping and the variance approximation by Lechner (2001), are very common in the literature. Additionally, we are going to present a new method from Abadie and Imbens (2004) that is based on the distinction between average treatment effects and sample average treatment effects.

Testing the statistical significance of treatment effects and computing their standard errors is not a straightforward thing to do. The problem is that the estimated variance of the treatment effect should also include the variance due to the estimation of the propensity score, the imputation of the common support and possibly also the order in which the treated individuals are matched.[16] These estimation steps add variation beyond the normal sampling variation (see the discussion in Heckman, Ichimura, and Todd (1998)).

---

[15] If one estimates the average treatment effects using only the two regression functions, estimating the conditional variances and the propensity score in order to estimate Var_{ATT} or Var_{ATE} is burdensome. If one estimates the effects with weighting on the estimated propensity score, additionally the first two moments of the conditional outcome distributions have to be estimated (Imbens, 2004).

[16] This matters only when matching is done without replacement as discussed in subsection 2.3.1.

2.6 Efficiency and Large-Sample Properties of Matching Estimators

For example, in the case of NN matching with one nearest neighbour, treating the matched observations as given will understate the standard errors (Smith, 2000a).

Bootstrapping:

One way to deal with this problem is to use bootstrapping as suggested e.g. by Lechner (2002b). This method is a popular way to estimate standard errors in case analytical estimates are biased or unavailable.[17] Even though Imbens (2004) notes that there is little formal evidence to justify bootstrapping, it is widely applied, see e.g. Black and Smith (2004) or Sianesi (2004). Each bootstrap draw includes the re-estimation of the results, including the first steps of the estimation (propensity score, common support, etc.). Repeating the bootstrapping N times leads to N bootstrap samples and in our case N estimated average treatment effects. The distribution of these means approximate the sampling distribution (and thus the standard error) of the population mean. Clearly, one practical problem arises because bootstrapping is very time-consuming and might therefore not be feasible in some cases.

Variance Approximation by Lechner:

An alternative is suggested by Lechner (2001) and e.g. applied by Hujer, Caliendo, and Thomsen (2004). For the estimated ATT by NN-matching the following formula applies:

$$(2.39) \quad Var(\hat{\Delta}_{ATT}) = \frac{1}{N_1} Var(Y^1 \mid D = 1) + \frac{(\Sigma_{j \in I_0}(w_j)^2)}{(N_1)^2} \cdot Var(Y^0 \mid D = 0),$$

where N_1 is the number of matched treated individuals. w_j is the number of times control j has been used, i.e. this takes into account that matching is performed with replacement. If no unit is matched more than once, the formula coincides with the 'usual' variance formula. By using this formula to estimate the variance of the treatment effect at time t, we assume independent observations and fixed weights. Furthermore we assume homoscedasticity of the variances of the outcome variables within treatment and control group and that the outcome variances do not depend on the estimated propensity score. This approach can be justified by results from Lechner (2002b) who finds little differences between bootstrapped variances and the variances calculated with (2.39).

Variance Estimators by Abadie and Imbens:

To introduce this variance estimator, some additional notation is needed. Imbens (2004) explicitly distinguishes average treatment effects like given in

---
[17] See Brownstone and Valletta (2001) for a discussion of bootstrapping methods.

subsection 1.2.2 from sample average treatment effects. The latter estimators focus on the average treatment effects in the specific sample rather than in the population at large. Hence, the sample-average treatment effect (SATE) is given by:

$$(2.40) \qquad \Delta_{SATE} = \frac{1}{N} \sum_{i=1}^{N} [Y_i^1 - Y_i^0].$$

In this case the appropriate variance is given by:

$$(2.41) \qquad Var^{\Delta_{SATE}} = E\left[\frac{\sigma_1^2(X)}{P(X)} + \frac{\sigma_0^2(X)}{1 - P(X)}\right].$$

The sample-average treatment effect for the treated (SATT) is given by:

$$(2.42) \qquad \Delta_{SATT} = \frac{1}{N_1} \sum_{i \in I_1} [Y_i^1 - Y_i^0].$$

Abadie and Imbens (2004) derived a matching variance estimator that does not require additional non-parametric estimation. The basic idea is that even though the asymptotic variance depends on the conditional variances $\sigma_1^2(X)$ and $\sigma_0^2(X)$, one actually need not to estimate this variance consistently at all values of the covariates. Instead only the average of this variance over the distribution weighted by the inverse of $P(X)$ and $1 - P(X)$ is needed. The variance of $SATE$ can then estimated by:

$$(2.43) \qquad Var^{SATE} = \frac{1}{N} \sum_{i=1}^{N} \left(1 + \frac{K_M(i)}{M}\right)^2 \hat{\sigma}_{D_i}^2(X_i),$$

where M is the number of matches and $K_M(i)$ is the number of times unit i is used as a match. The variance of the SATT is calculated by:

$$(2.44) \qquad Var^{SATT} = \frac{1}{N} \sum_{i=1}^{N} \left(D_i - (1 - D_i) \cdot \frac{K_M(i)}{M}\right)^2 \hat{\sigma}_{D_i}^2(X_i).$$

It should be noted, that the estimation of the conditional variances requires estimation of conditional outcome variances $\sigma_D^2(X_i)$. Abadie and Imbens (2004) offer two options: With the first option one assumes that the treatment effect is constant for all individuals i and that $\sigma_D^2(X_i)$ does not vary with X or D. This is the assumption of homoscedasticity, whereas heteroscedasticity is allowed in the section option, where it is explicitly allowed that $\sigma_D^2(X_i)$ differ in D and X.[18]

---

[18] See Abadie and Imbens (2004) and Abadie, Drukker, Leber Herr, and Imbens (2004) for details about the derivation of the relevant formulas and some easy implementable examples.

2.7 Which Matching Estimator to Choose?

Now that we have presented several different matching methods, it is time to pose the question how one should select and justify a particular approach. Figure 2.1 depicts the different estimators and the inherent choices to be made when they are used.

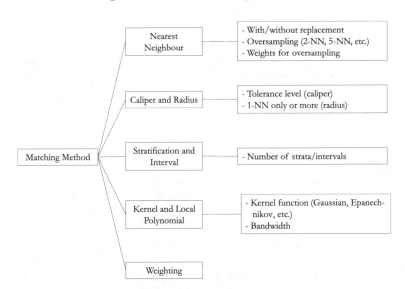

Fig. 2.1: Different Matching Estimators

Clearly, asymptotically all approaches should yield the same results, because with growing sample size they all become closer to comparing only exact matches (Smith, 2000a). However, in small samples the choice of the matching approach can be important (Heckman, Ichimura, and Todd, 1997). All matching estimators contrast the outcome of a treated individual with the outcome of comparison group members. The presented estimators differ not only in the way the neighbourhood for each treated individual is defined and the common support problem is handled, but also with respect to the weights given to these neighbours. Usually a trade-off between bias and variance arises. We start this section by reviewing the main findings for each estimator in terms of bias and variance. Following that, we will present the results of some simulation studies that try to assess the performance of the various techniques in settings where the assumptions are known to hold. We will also very briefly present some results from studies that use randomised experiments as a yardstick to assess the capability of different estimators (see Imbens (2004) for an extensive overview of simulation studies and results from experiments).

Table 2.2: Trade-Offs in Terms of Bias and Efficiency

Decision	Bias	Variance
Nearest neighbour matching:		
multiple neighbours / single neighbour	(+)/(-)	(-)/(+)
with caliper / without caliper	(-)/(+)	(+)/(-)
Use of control individuals:		
with replacement / without replacement	(-)/(+)	(+)/(-)
Choosing method:		
NN-matching / Radius-matching	(-)/(+)	(+)/(-)
KM or LLM / NN-methods	(+)/(-)	(-)/(+)
Bandwidth choice with KM:		
small / large	(-)/(+)	(+)/(-)

KM: Kernel Matching, LLM: Local Linear Matching
NN: Nearest Neighbour
Increase: (+), Decrease: (-)

Let us start with the trade-off between bias and variance arising from different matching methods, summarised in table 2.2. With NN matching as discussed in subsection 2.3.1, two decisions have to be made. First, regarding the number of nearest neighbours to be used and second, if matching should be with or without replacement. Using more than one nearest neighbour ('oversampling') trades reduced variance, resulting from using more information to construct the counterfactual outcome for each participant, with increased bias that results from on average poorer matches. Allowing replacement will increase the average quality of matching but also the variance of the estimates since less information is used to construct the counterfactual outcome. Imposing a caliper works in the same direction. Bad matches are avoided and hence the matching quality rises. However, if fewer matches can be performed, the variance of the estimates increases. Since pair matching matches only a single observation to each observation of the other population, it may have a rather high variance (Frölich, 2004b).[19] With KM or LLM all control units are used to construct the counterfactual and hence the variance will decrease.[20] In turn, the bias increases. Choosing the bandwidth parameter in KM also trades bias with variance. Large values of the bandwidth yield a smoother estimated density function therefore leading to a better fit and a decreasing variance.

---

[19] Abadie and Imbens (2004) show that pair-matching is inefficient and may not even be $\sqrt{n}$-consistent.

[20] Heckman, Ichimura, and Todd (1997) and Heckman, Ichimura, and Todd (1998) proposed local polynomial matching and showed its $\sqrt{n}$-consistency and asymptotic normality.

On the other hand, underlying features may be smoothed away leading to a higher bias.

Evidence from Experimental Data

Imbens (2004) gives an extensive overview of these studies. Their basic idea is the following: Given a randomised experiment, the true (unbiased) treatment effect can be estimated without further assumptions. Then, one can use non-experimental control groups and methods, and attempt to replicate the experimental results. If the experimental results can be replicated, the methods and assumptions are plausible. The first and most prominent study is the one by LaLonde (1986). He used experimental data on an American labour market programme (National Supported Work Programme) in combination with non-experimental control group data from two panels to create non-experimental estimates of the average treatment effect. He concluded that the methods (including regression, selection models and DID) were not able to replicate the experimental results. Following that a lot of researchers used this data for further investigation. Heckman and Hotz (1989) develop some formal tests which would have eliminated many of the critical LaLonde estimates. Dehejia and Wahba (1999) use matching methods and find that for the subsample of the LaLonde data they used, these methods replicated the experimental more accurately. Smith and Todd (2005) cast doubt on the results from Dehejia and Wahba (1999) and show for other subsamples that matching is not able to replicate the experimental results.[21]

Heckman, Ichimura, and Todd (1997, 1998) as well as Heckman, Ichimura, Smith, and Todd (1998) study another programme, the national Job Training Partnership Act (JPTA). There aim is to reveal the nature of biases associated with different estimators. They are particularly concerned with justifying the unconfoundedness assumption and find that detailed information on earnings histories helps a lot. Additionally, control individuals should be located in the same local labour market as treated individuals and the data should stem from the same sources.

Clearly, the different covariates used and estimators applied makes it somewhat difficult to compare the results in these studies (Imbens, 2004). However, some valuable guidance can be perceived from these experimental studies. An interesting alternative to this approach (comparing experimental results with non-experimental estimators) is possible when two non-treated groups are available. Heckman, Ichimura, Smith, and Todd (1998) analyse the JPTA data and use two control groups who both are not subject to treatment and try to model the outcome in the first group with data from the second one. Hence, if experimental data is not available, this might be a valuable alternative to test the validity of different approaches and/or datasets.

---

[21] There is still an ongoing discussion as to the validity of the Dehejia and Wahba (1999) results. See Dehejia (2005) for an additional reply.

Evidence from Simulation Studies

A different way to assess the capabilities and limitations of evaluation estimators is to run simulation studies. In the matching context these are predominantly used to explore the large- and small-sample properties of matching estimators. We have already discussed the large-sample properties of different matching estimators in section 2.6. The discussion there has also made clear that conventional asymptotic theory on matching estimators may provide poor guidance for researchers who have to deal with small samples (Angrist and Hahn, 2004). Unfortunately, there are relatively few studies focussing on the small-sample properties of matching estimators, but the literature is growing.

Frölich (2004a, 2004b) discusses the finite-sample properties of matching estimators. Ridge matching (some special form of kernel matching as discussed in subsection 2.3.4) turned out to be superior to all other estimators, followed by kernel matching.[22] Local linear matching is susceptible to regions of sparse data and sensitive to the bandwidth choice. Frölich (2004b) discusses the optimal bandwidth choice and derives a mean squared error approximation for matching estimators. It turns out that conventional cross-validation is a promising method for bandwidth selection. The weighting estimator he analyses is sensitive to trimming and its relative performance worsens with increasing sample size. Weighting without trimming fails completely. Frölich (2004b) notes that further usage of the weighting estimator would require the development of an appropriate method for estimating the optimal trimming level.

Zhao (2004) compares the performance of propensity score matching methods with covariate matching estimators. Three conclusions are worth noting. First, when correlations between covariates and the participation indicator are high, propensity score matching is a good choice. Second, despite the fact that PS matching can overcome the small-cell (or empty-cell) problem when the sample size is small, it does not perform well compared with other matching estimators if the sample size is too small. One reason is that in small samples the variance dominates the bias. Finally, he finds that the Mahalanobis metric is relatively robust under different settings (also compared to his suggested metrics).

Abadie and Imbens (2004) study the performance of the bias-corrected matching estimator presented in subsection 2.5.3 using a data-generating process inspired by the LaLonde (1986) study. Their study finds that matching estimators, and in particular the bias-adjusted ones, perform better than linear and quadratic regression estimators.

---

[22] Zhao (2004) questions the results of Frölich (2004a) as his simulations include only one covariate. He notes that when the number of covariates increases, neither the bias of his suggested local linear estimator nor that of the matching estimators vanish fast enough. Hence it is unclear, whether the increase of the number of covariates will affect his results.

Angrist and Hahn (2004) present a panel framework for estimating average treatment effects and suggest that in many practical relevant cases, covariate matching is less efficient than propensity score matching. More precisely, they show that full control for covariates is dominated by propensity score matching when cell sizes are small, the explanatory power of the covariates conditional on the propensity score is low, and/or the probability of treatment is close to 0 or 1.

Summing up, the results from these simulation studies are somewhat inconclusive and as Imbens (2004) notes more work in this direction is required. He suggests for future research to closely model the data-generating process on actual datasets, to ensure that the results have practical relevance. Additionally, it is important to learn which features of the data-generating process are important for the properties of the various estimators.

So what advice can be given at this moment to researchers facing the problem of choosing a matching estimator? It should be clear by now that there is no clear winner for all situations and that the choice of the estimator crucially depends on the situation at hand. The performance of different matching estimators varies case-by-case and depends largely on the data structure at hand (Zhao, 2000). To give an example, if there are only a few control observations, it makes no sense to match without replacement. On the other hand, if there are a lot of comparable non-treated individuals it might be worth using more than one nearest neighbour (either by oversampling or kernel matching) to gain more precision in estimates. Pragmatically, it seems sensible to try a number of approaches. Should they give similar results, the choice may be unimportant. Should the results differ, further investigation may be needed in order to reveal more about the source of the disparity (Bryson, Dorsett, and Purdon, 2002). Black and Smith (2004) suggest to use a least squares leave-one-out validation mechanism to choose among different matching estimators.[23] Finally, it might also be beneficial to combine matching with other methods as presented in section 2.5, e.g. to take time-invariant unobservable factors into account or to exploit the relation between covariates and outcomes.

---

[23] The basic idea of leave-one-out validation is to drop the jth observation in the comparison group and use the remaining $N_0 - 1$ observations in the comparison group to form an estimate of Y_j^0, denoted by $\hat{Y}_{j,-j}^0$. The associated forecast error is than given by $\epsilon_{j,-j} = Y_{j,-j}^0 - \hat{Y}_{j,-j}^0$. Repeating the process for the remaining N_0-1 observations allows comparisons of the mean squared error (MSE) or root MSE of the forecasts associated with different matching estimators - or bandwidths when selecting a bandwidth - to guide the choice of estimator or bandwidth (Smith and Todd, 2005).

3

Some Practical Guidance for the Implementation of Propensity Score Matching Estimators

3.1 Introduction

In the previous chapter we have presented several different matching estimators. We have also discussed their advantages and disadvantages when used in large and finite samples and we have given some guidance to decide which matching algorithm to choose. It has become clear that exact covariate matching is unfeasible in case of a high dimensional vector of covariates and that propensity score matching (PSM) is a good alternative for such situations.

Once the researcher has decided to use PSM, he is confronted with a lot of questions regarding its implementation. To begin with, a first decision has to be made concerning the estimation of the propensity score. One has not only to decide about the probability model to be used for estimation, but also about the variables which should be included in this model. Following that one has to determine how to check the overlap between treatment and control group and how to implement the common support requirement (see the discussion in section 1.5). Based on these findings and on the trade-offs in terms of bias and efficiency (see section 2.7), one has to decide which matching estimator to choose, e.g. nearest-neighbour or kernel matching. Subsequently, one has to test the matching quality, estimate standard errors and the treatment effects. Additionally, it might be the case that the researcher wants to test the sensitivity of his results with respect to 'hidden bias'. 'Hidden bias' might arise if treatment and control group differ on unobserved variables which simultaneously affect assignment into treatment and the outcome variable. In that case, individuals who look similar in terms of observed covariates may have very different probabilities of receiving treatment. Since it is not possible to estimate the magnitude of 'hidden bias' with non-experimental data, we address this problem with a bounding approach suggested by Rosenbaum (2002). Figure 3.1 summarises the necessary steps when implementing PSM. Some of the steps (e.g. the decision between covariate and propensity score matching and the choice of the matching algorithm) have been already discussed in chapter

2. The aim of this chapter is to discuss the remaining implementation issues and give some guidance to researchers who want to use PSM for evaluation purposes, and are confronted with the above mentioned decisions. The chapter is organised as follows. In section 3.2 we will focus on the implementation of PSM estimators. We will start with the estimation of the propensity score (subsection 3.2.1), before we discuss how to assess the matching quality in subsection 3.2.2. Overlap and common support will be the topics of subsection 3.2.3. After that we present the problem of choice-based sampling and discuss the question when to measure programme effects. Section 3.3 will be concerned with the sensitivity of the estimates with respect to 'hidden bias'.

Fig. 3.1: Implementing Propensity Score Matching[1]

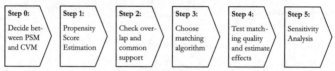

[1] CVM = Covariate Matching, PSM = Propensity Score Matching

Section 3.4 deals with more practical issues, like programme heterogeneity (3.4.1), multiple participation of individuals (3.4.2) and the choice of the right control group (3.4.3). Programme heterogeneity may become an issue when evaluating ALMP of countries which do not have only one homogeneous programme, but a variety of different ones, e.g. job creation schemes, vocational training and rehabilitation programmes. It should also be regarded when evaluating one programme with varying characteristics. This is important for our empirical analysis in chapter 6 where we analyse the effects of job creation schemes, which can be operated in very different sectors like AGRICULTURE, CONSTRUCTION & INDUSTRY or OFFICE & SERVICES. It is very likely that the effects differ depending on these sectoral differences and hence, programme heterogeneity has to be considered. Multiple participation has to be taken into account if it can be assumed that individuals participate more than once in (possibly different) programmes in the time span under consideration. In that case we have to move from the static framework to a dynamic one. Finally, choosing the right control group has become an important topic in the last years. One can either choose to define the control group as persons who never participate in the analysed programme or who do not participate until a certain point in time. Finally, section 3.5 concludes by outlining the arising issues when implementing PSM and highlighting our answers once again.

3.2 The Implementation of Matching Estimators

3.2.1 Estimating the Propensity Score

When estimating the propensity score, two choices have to be made. The first one concerns the model to be used for the estimation, and the second one the variables to be included in this model. We will start with the model choice before we discuss which variables to include in the model.

Model Choice:

Little advice is available regarding which functional form to use (see e.g. the discussion in Smith (1997)). In principle any discrete choice model can be used. Preference for logit or probit models (compared to linear probability models) derives from the well-known shortcomings of the linear probability model, especially the unlikeliness of the functional form when the response variable is highly skewed and predictions that are outside the 0-1 bounds of probabilities. However, when the purpose of a model is classification rather than estimation of structural coefficients, it is less clear that these criticisms apply (Smith, 1997). For the binary treatment case, where we estimate the probability of participation vs. non-participation, logit and probit models usually yield similar results. Hence, the choice is not too critical, even though the logit distribution has more density mass in the bounds. However, when leaving the binary treatment case, as we will do later on in subsection 3.4.1, where we are going to present an extension to the multiple treatment case, the choice of the model becomes more important. The multiple treatment case constitutes of more than two alternatives, e.g. when an individual is faced with the choice to participate in job-creation schemes, vocational training or wage subsidy programmes or do not participate at all. For that case it is well known that the multinomial logit is based on stronger assumptions than the multinomial probit model, making the latter one the preferable option.[1] However, since the multinomial probit is computational more burdensome, a practical alternative is to estimate a series of binomial models like suggested by Lechner (2001). Bryson, Dorsett, and Purdon (2002) note that there are two shortcomings regarding this approach. First, as the number of options increases, the number of models to be estimated increases disproportionately (for L options we need $0.5(L(L-1))$ models). Second, in each model only two options at a time are considered and consequently the choice is conditional on being in one of the two selected groups. On the other hand, Lechner (2001) compares

---

[1] Especially the 'independence from irrelevant alternatives' assumption (IIA) is critical. It basically states that the odds ratio between two alternatives are independent of other alternatives. This assumption is convenient for estimation but not appealing from an economic or behavioural point of view (for details see e.g. Greene (2003)).

the performance of the multinomial probit approach and the series estimation and finds little difference in their relative performance. He suggests that the latter approach may be more robust since a mis-specification in one of the series will not compromise all others as would be the case in the multinomial probit model.

Variable Choice:

More advice is available regarding the inclusion (or exclusion) of covariates in the propensity score model. The matching strategy builds on the conditional independence assumption (as discussed in section 1.5), requiring that the outcome variable(s) must be independent of treatment conditional on the propensity score. Hence, implementing matching requires choosing a set of variables X that credibly satisfy this condition. Heckman, Ichimura, and Todd (1997) show that omitting important variables can seriously increase bias in resulting estimates. Only variables that influence simultaneously the participation decision and the outcome variable should be included. Hence, economic theory, a sound knowledge of previous research and also information about the institutional settings should guide the researcher in building up the model (see e.g. Smith and Todd (2005) or Sianesi (2004)). It should also be clear that only variables that are unaffected by participation (or the anticipation of it) should be included in the model. To ensure this, variables should either be fixed over time or measured before participation. In the latter case, it must be guaranteed that the variable has not been influenced by the anticipation of participation (see the Ashenfelter's dip example in subsection 1.4.1). Economic theory gives some guidance on which variables to choose. The accumulated evidence in the evaluation literature points out that the labour market history of individuals is a crucial variable to be included in the estimation. Heckman and Smith (1999) examine data from a major social experiment in the United States and find that it is rather unemployment dynamics than earnings or employment dynamics that drive participation in programmes. Heckman, LaLonde, and Smith (1999) additionally emphasise the importance of drawing treated and comparison people from the same local labour market and administering them the same questionnaire. The latter problem is of less importance when using administrative data for both groups, even though it might still be the case that participants and non-participants data stems from different sources.[2] The better and more informative the data are, the easier it is to credibly justify the CIA and the matching procedure. However, it should also be clear that 'too good' data is not helpful either. If $P(X) = 0$ or $P(X) = 1$ for some values of X, then we cannot use matching conditional on those X values to estimate a treatment effect, because persons with such characteristics either always or never receive treatment. Hence,

---

[2] In our empirical application in chapters 5 and 6 we make sure to use information for participants and non-participants from the same data source only.

the common support condition $0 < P(X) < 1$ fails and matches cannot be performed. Some randomness is needed that guarantees that persons with identical characteristics can be observed in both states (Heckman, Ichimura, and Todd, 1998).

In cases of uncertainty of the proper specification, sometimes the question may arise if it is better to include too many rather than too few variables. Bryson, Dorsett, and Purdon (2002) note that there are two reasons why over-parameterised models should be avoided. First, it may be the case that including extraneous variables in the participation model exacerbate the support problem. Second, although the inclusion of non-significant variables will not bias the estimates or make them inconsistent, it can increase their variance.

The results from Augurzky and Schmidt (2000b) point in the same direction. They run a simulation study to investigate propensity score matching when selection intro treatment is remarkably strong, and treated and non-treated individuals differ considerably in their observable characteristics. In their setup, explanatory variables in the selection equation are partitioned into two sets. The first set includes variables that strongly influence the participation and the outcome equation, whereas the second set does not (or only weakly) influence the outcome equation. Including the full set of covariates in small samples might cause problems in terms of higher variance, since either some treated have to be discarded from the analysis or control units have to be used more than once. They show that matching on an inconsistent estimate of the propensity score (i.e. the one without the second set of covariates) produces better estimation results of the average treatment effect.

On the other hand, Rubin and Thomas (1996) recommend against 'trimming' models in the name of parsimony. They argue that a variable should only be excluded from analysis if there is consensus that the variable is either unrelated to the outcome or not a proper covariate. If there are doubts about these two points, they explicitly advise to include the relevant variables in the propensity score estimation.

By these criteria, there are both reasons for and against including all of the reasonable covariates available. Basically, the points made so far imply that the choice of variables should be based on economic theory and previous empirical findings. But clearly, there are also some formal (statistical) tests which can be used. Heckman, Ichimura, Smith, and Todd (1998) and Heckman and Smith (1999) discuss two strategies for the selection of variables to be used in estimating the propensity score.

Hit or Miss Method:

The first one is the 'hit or miss' method or prediction rate metric, where variables are chosen to maximise the within-sample correct prediction rates. This method classifies an observation as '1' if the estimated propensity score is larger than the sample proportion of persons taking treatment, i.e. $\hat{P}(X) > \overline{P}$. If $\hat{P}(X) \leq \overline{P}$ observations are classified as '0'. This method maximises the overall classification rate for the sample assuming that the costs for the misclassification are equal for the two groups (Heckman, Ichimura, and Todd, 1997).[3] But clearly, it has to be kept in mind that the main purpose of the propensity score estimation is not to predict selection into treatment as good as possible but to balance all covariates (Augurzky and Schmidt, 2000b).

Statistical Significance:

The second approach relies on statistical significance and is very common in textbook econometrics. To do so, one starts with a parsimonious specification of the model, e.g. a constant, the age and some regional information, and then 'tests up' by iteratively adding variables to the specification. A new variable is kept if it is statistically significant at conventional levels. If combined with the 'hit or miss' method, variables are kept if they are statistically significant and increase the prediction rates by a substantial amount (Heckman, Ichimura, Smith, and Todd, 1998).

Leave-one-out Cross-Validation:

Leave-one-out cross validation can also be used to choose the set of variables to be included in the propensity score. Black and Smith (2004) implement their model selection procedure by starting with a 'minimal' model containing only two variables. They subsequently add blocks of additional variables and compare the resulting mean squared errors. As a note of caution they note, that this amounts to choosing the propensity score model based on goodness-of-fit considerations, rather than based on theory and evidence about the set of variables related to the participation decision and the outcomes (Black and Smith, 2004). They also point out an interesting trade-off in finite samples between the plausibility of the CIA and the variance of the estimates. When using the full specification, bias arises from selecting a wide bandwidth in response to the weakness of the common support. In contrast to that, when matching on the minimal specification, common support is not a problem but the plausibility of the CIA is. This trade-off also affects the estimated standard errors, which are smaller for the minimal specification where the common support condition poses no problem.

Finally, checking the matching quality can also help to determine which variables should be included in the model. We will discuss this point later on in subsection 3.2.2.

---

[3] See e.g. Breiman, Friedman, Olsen, and Stone (1984) for theory and Heckman, Ichimura, Smith, and Todd (1998) or Smith and Todd (2005) for applications.

Overweighting some Variables:

Let us assume for the moment that we have found a satisfactory specification of the model. It may sometimes be felt that some variables play a specifically important role in determining participation and outcome (Bryson, Dorsett, and Purdon, 2002). As an example, one can think of the influence of gender and region in determining the wage of individuals. Let us take as given for the moment that men earn more than women and the wage level is higher in West Germany compared to East Germany. If we add dummy variables for gender and region in the propensity score estimation, it is still possible that women in East Germany are matched with men in West Germany, since the gender and region dummies are only a sub-set of all available variables.

There are basically two ways to put greater emphasis on specific variables. One can either find variables in the comparison group who are identical with respect to these variables, or carry out matching on sub-populations. The study from Puhani (1998) is a good example for the first approach. He evaluates the effects of ALMP in Poland and uses the propensity score as a 'partial' balancing score. In order to improve the comparability of treated and matched comparison persons, he matches exactly on the labour force state and the unemployment duration before entry into the programme. Lechner (2002b) does the same when evaluating labour market policies in Switzerland. Complementary to the propensity score, he exactly matches on sex, duration of unemployment and native language. Heckman, Ichimura, and Todd (1997) and Heckman, Ichimura, Smith, and Todd (1998) use the second strategy and implement matching separately for four demographic groups. That implies that the complete matching procedure (estimating the propensity score, checking the common support, etc.) has to be implemented separately for each group. We will use this approach in our application in chapters 5 and 6 as well, where we implement the matching procedures separately for men and women in West and East Germany.[4] This is analogous to insisting on a perfect match in terms of gender and region and then carrying out propensity score matching. This procedure is especially recommendable if one expects the effects to be heterogeneous between certain groups.

Alternatives to the Propensity Score:

Finally, it should also be noted that it is possible to match on a measure other than the propensity score, namely the underlying index of the score estimation. The advantage of this is that the index differentiates more between observations in the extremes of the distribution of the propensity score (Lechner, 2000a). This is useful if there is some concentration of observations

---

[4] When analysing the effects in certain sub-groups of the population, e.g. long-term unemployed, we carry out the matching procedure in the specific sub-group under consideration.

in the tails of the distribution. Additionally, in some recent papers the propensity score is estimated by duration models. This is of particular interest if the 'timing of events' plays a crucial role (see e.g. Brodaty, Crepon, and Fougere (2001), Sianesi (2004) or Hagen (2003a)).

3.2.2 Assessing the Matching Quality

Since we do not condition on all covariates but on the propensity score, it has to be checked if the matching procedure is able to balance the distribution of the relevant variables in both the control and treatment group. Several procedures to do so will be discussed in this subsection. These procedures can also, as already mentioned, help in determining which interactions and higher order terms to include for a given set of covariates X. The basic idea of all approaches is to compare the situation before and after matching and check if there remain any differences after conditioning on the propensity score. If there are differences, matching on the score was not (completely) successful and remedial measures have to be done, e.g. by including interaction-terms in the estimation of the propensity score. A helpful theorem in this context is suggested by Rosenbaum and Rubin (1983) and states that:

(3.1) $$X \amalg D | P(D=1|X).$$

This means that after conditioning on $P(D=1|X)$, additional conditioning on X should not provide new information about the treatment decision. Hence, if after conditioning on the propensity score there is still dependence on X, this suggests either mis-specification in the model used to estimate $P(D=1|X)$ or a failure of the CIA (Smith and Todd, 2005).[5]

Standardised Bias:

One suitable indicator to assess the distance in marginal distributions of the X-variables is the standardised bias (SB) suggested by Rosenbaum and Rubin (1985b). For each covariate X it is defined as the difference of sample means in the treated and matched control subsamples as a percentage of the square root of the average of sample variances in both groups. The standardised bias before matching is given by:

(3.2) $$SB_{before} = 100 \cdot \frac{(\overline{X}_1 - \overline{X}_0)}{\sqrt{0.5 \cdot (V_1(X) + V_0(X))}}.$$

The standardised bias after matching is given by:

---

[5] Smith and Todd (2005) note that this theorem holds for any X, including those that do not satisfy the CIA required to justify matching. As such, the theorem is not informative about which set of variables to include in X.

(3.3) $$SB_{after} = 100 \cdot \frac{(\overline{X}_{1M} - \overline{X}_{0M})}{\sqrt{0.5 \cdot (V_{1M}(X) + V_{0M}(X))}},$$

where X_1 (V_1) is the mean (variance) in the treated group before matching and X_0 (V_0) the analogue for the comparison group. X_{1M} (V_{1M}) and X_{0M} (V_{0M}) are the corresponding values for the matched samples. This is a common approach used in many evaluation studies, e.g. by Lechner (1999), Sianesi (2004) and Hujer, Caliendo, and Thomsen (2004). One possible problem with the standardised bias approach is that we do not have a clear indication for the success of the matching procedure, even though in most empirical studies a bias reduction below 3% or 5% is seen as sufficient.

t-Test:

A similar approach uses a two-sample t-test to check if there are significant differences in covariate means for both groups (Rosenbaum and Rubin, 1985b). Before matching differences are expected, but after matching the covariates should be balanced in both groups and hence no significant differences should be found. The t-test might be preferred if the evaluator is concerned with the statistical significance of the results. The shortcoming here is that the bias reduction before and after matching is not clearly visible.

Joint significance and Pseudo-R^2:

Additionally, Sianesi (2004) suggests to re-estimate the propensity score on the matched sample, that is only on participants and matched non-participants and compare the pseudo-R^2's before and after matching. The pseudo-R^2 indicates how well the regressors X explain the participation probability. After matching there should be no systematic differences in the distribution of covariates between both groups and therefore, the pseudo-R^2 should be fairly low. Furthermore, one can also perform an F-test on the joint significance of all regressors. The test should not be rejected before, and should be rejected after matching.

Stratification Test:

Finally, Dehejia and Wahba (1999, 2002) divide observations into strata based on the estimated propensity score, such that no statistically significant difference between the mean of the estimated propensity score in both treatment and control group remain. Then they use t-tests within each strata to test if the distribution of X-variables is the same between both groups (for the first and second moments). If there are remaining differences, they add higher-order and interaction terms in the propensity score specification, until such differences no longer emerge.

This makes clear that an assessment of matching quality can also be used to determine the propensity score specification. If the quality indicators are not satisfactory, one reason might be mis-specification of the propensity score model and hence it may be worth to take a step back, include e.g. interaction or higher-order terms in the score estimation and test the quality once again. If after re-specification the quality indicators are still not satisfactory, it may indicate a failure of the CIA (Smith and Todd, 2005) and alternative evaluation approaches should be considered (see our discussion in section 1.4.2).

3.2.3 Overlap and Common Support

Our discussion in sections 1.5.1 and 1.5.3 has shown that ATE and ATT are only defined in the region of common support. Hence, before assessing the matching quality, an important step to do is to check the overlap and the region of common support between treatment and comparison group. Several ways are suggested in the literature, the most straightforward way is a visual analysis of the density distribution of the propensity score in both groups. Lechner (2000b) argues that given that the support problem can be spotted by inspecting the propensity score distribution, there is no need to implement a complicated formal estimator. However, some formal guidelines might help the researcher to determine the region of common support more precisely. We will present two methods, where the first one is essentially based on comparing the minima and maxima of the propensity score in both groups and the second one is based on estimating the density distribution in both groups. Implementing the common support condition ensures that any combination of characteristics observed in the treated group can also be observed among the comparison group (Bryson, Dorsett, and Purdon, 2002). For ATT it is sufficient to ensure the existence of potential matches in the control group. For ATE it is also required that the combinations of characteristics in the comparison group may also be observed in the treatment group (Bryson, Dorsett, and Purdon, 2002).

Minima and Maxima comparison:

The basic criterion of this approach is to delete all observations whose propensity score is smaller than the minimum and larger than the maximum in the opposite group. To give an example let us assume for a moment that the propensity score lies within the interval $[0.07, 0.94]$ in the treatment group and within $[0.04, 0.89]$ in the control group. Hence, with the 'minima and maxima criterion', the common support is given by $[0.07, 0.89]$. Observations which lie outside this region are discarded from analysis. Clearly a two-sided test is only necessary if the parameter of interest is ATE; for ATT it is sufficient to ensure that for each participant a close non-participant can be found.

3.2 The Implementation of Matching Estimators

It should also be clear that the common support condition is in some ways more important for the implementation of kernel matching than it is for the implementation of nearest-neighbour matching. That is, because with kernel matching all non-treated observations are used to estimate the missing counterfactual outcome, whereas with NN-matching only the closest neighbour is used. Hence, NN-matching (with the additional imposition of a maximum allowed caliper) handles the common support problem pretty well. There are some problems associated with the 'minima and maxima comparison', e.g. if there are observations at the bounds which are discarded even though they are very close to the bounds. Another problem arises if there are areas within the common support interval where there is only limited overlap between both groups, e.g. if in the region $[0.51, 0.55]$ only treated observations can be found. Additionally problems arise, if the density in the tails of the distribution are very thin, for example when there is a substantial distance from the smallest maximum to the second smallest element. Therefore, Lechner (2002b) suggests to check the sensitivity of the results when the minima and maxima are replaced by the 10th smallest and 10th largest observation.

Trimming to Determine the Common Support:

A different way to overcome these possible problems is suggested by Smith and Todd (2005). They use a trimming procedure to determine the common support region and define the region of common support as those values of P that have positive density within both the $D = 1$ and $D = 0$ distributions, that is:

$$(3.4) \quad \hat{S}_P = \{P : \hat{f}(P|D=1) > 0 \quad \text{and} \quad \hat{f}(P|D=0) > 0\},$$

where $\hat{f}(P|D = 1) > 0$ and $\hat{f}(P|D = 0) > 0$ are non-parametric density estimators. Any P points for which the estimated density is exactly zero are excluded. Additionally - to ensure that the densities are strictly positive - they require that the densities exceed zero by a threshold amount q. So not only the P points for which the estimated density is exactly zero, but also an additional q percent of the remaining P points for which the estimated density is positive but very low are excluded:[6]

$$(3.5) \quad \hat{S}_{Pq} = \{Pq : \hat{f}(P|D=1) > q \quad \text{and} \quad \hat{f}(P|D=0) > q\}.$$

Figure 3.2 gives a hypothetical example and clarifies the differences between both approaches. In the first example the propensity score distribution

---

[6] For details on how to estimate the cut-off trimming level see Smith and Todd (2005). Galdo (2004) notes that the determination of the smoothing parameter is critical here. If the distribution is skewed to the right for participants and skewed to the left for non-participants, assuming a normal distribution may be very misleading.

Fig. 3.2: The Common Support Problem

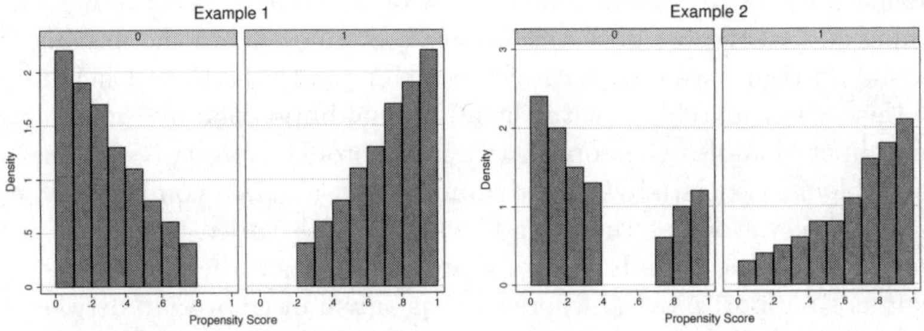

The left side in each example refers to non-participants (D=0), the right side to participants (D=1).

Source: Hypothetical Example

is highly skewed to the left (right) for participants (non-participants). Even though this is an extreme example, researchers are confronted with similar distributions in practice, too. With the 'minima and maxima comparison' we would exclude any observations lying outside the region of common support given by $[0.2, 0.8]$. Depending on the chosen trimming level q, we would maybe also exclude control observations in the interval $[0.7, 0.8]$ and treated observations in the interval $[0.2, 0.3]$ with the trimming approach since the densities are relatively low there. However, no large differences between both approaches would emerge. In the second example we do not find any control individuals in the region $[0.4, 0.7]$. The 'minima and maxima comparison' fails in that situation, since minima and maxima in both groups are equal at 0.01 and 0.99. Hence, no observations would be excluded based on this criterion making the estimation of treatment effects in the region $[0.4, 0.7]$ questionable. The trimming method on the other hand would explicitly exclude treated observations in that propensity score range and would therefore deliver more reliable results. Hence, the choice of the method depends on the data situation at hand and before making any decisions, a visual analysis is recommended.

Failure of the Common Support:

Once one has defined the region of common support, individuals that fall outside this region have to be disregarded and for these individuals the treatment effect cannot be estimated. Bryson, Dorsett, and Purdon (2002) note that when the proportion of lost individuals is small, this poses few problems. However, if the number is too large, there may be concerns whether the estimated effect on the remaining individuals can be viewed as representative. It may be instructive to inspect the characteristics of discarded individuals since those can provide important clues when interpreting the estimated treatment effects. Lechner (2000b) notes that both ignoring the support problem and estimating programme effects only within the common support may be misleading. He develops an approach that can be used to derive bounds for the true programme effect.[7]

3.2.4 Choice-Based Sampling

An additional problem arising in evaluation studies is that samples used are often choice-based (Smith and Todd, 2005). This is a situation where programme participants are oversampled relative to their frequency in the population of eligible persons. Even though this is not a problem in our applications in chapters 5 and 6, we discuss this point briefly and suggest one correction mechanism introduced by Heckman and Smith (1995). First of all, note that under choice-based sampling weights are required to consistently estimate the probability of programme participation. Heckman and Smith (1995) show that with weights unknown, matching methods can still be applied, because the odds ratio estimated using the incorrect weights (those that ignore the fact of choice-based samples) is a scalar multiple of the true odds ratio, which is itself a monotonic transformation of the propensity scores. Hence, matching can be done on the (mis-weighted) estimate of the odds ratio (or of the log odds ratio). Clearly, with single nearest-neighbour matching it does not matter whether matching is performed on the odds ratio or the estimated propensity score (with wrong weights), since ranking of the observations is identical and therefore the same neighbours will be selected. However, for methods that take account of the absolute distance between observations, e.g. kernel matching, it does matter.

3.2.5 When to Compare and Locking-in Effects

An important decision which has to be made in the empirical analysis is when to measure the effects. The major goal is to ensure that participants and non-participants are compared in the same economic environment and the same individual lifecycle position. One possible problem which has to be taken into account is the occurrence of locking-in effects. The literature is dominated by two approaches, either comparing the individuals from the begin of the programme or after the end of the programme. To give an example let us assume that a programme starts in January and ends in June. The latter of the two alternatives implies that the outcome of participants who re-enter the labour market in July is compared with matched non-participants in July.

---

[7] Since we do not have major common support problems in our empirical applications, we do not present his approach here.

There are two shortcomings to this approach. First, if the exits of participants are spread over a longer time period, it might be the case that very different economic situations are compared. Second, a further problem which arises with this approach is that it entails an endogeneity problem (Gerfin and Lechner (2002)), since the abortion of the programme may be caused by several factors which are usually not observed by the researcher.[8]

The above mentioned second approach is predominant in the recent evaluation literature (see e.g. Sianesi (2004) or Gerfin and Lechner (2002)) and measures the effects from the begin of the programme. One major argument to do so concerns the policy relevance. In the above example the policy-maker is faced with the decision to put an individual in January in a programme or not. He will be interested in the effect of his decision on the outcome of the participating individual in contrast with the situation if the individual would not have participated. Therefore comparing both outcomes from begin of the programme is a reasonable approach. What should be kept in mind, however, is the possible occurrence of locking-in effects for the group of participants. Since they are involved in the programme, they do not have the same time to search for a new job as non-participants. Following van Ours (2004), the net effect of a programme consists of two opposite effects. First, the increased employment probability through the programme and second, the reduced search intensity. Since both effects cannot be disentangled, we only observe the net effect and have to take this into account when interpreting the results. As to the fall in the search intensity, we should expect an initial negative effect from any kind of participation in a programme. However, a successful programme should overcompensate for this initial fall. So, if we are able to observe the outcome of the individuals for a reasonable time after begin/end of the programme, the occurrence of locking-in effects poses fewer problems but nevertheless has to be taken into account in the interpretation.

3.3 Sensitivity Analysis with Rosenbaum Bounds

The estimation of treatment effects with matching estimators is based on the conditional independence assumption (CIA). The CIA states, as discussed in section 1.5.1, that treatment participation and treatment outcomes are independent conditional on a set of observable characteristics X, i.e. $(Y^0, Y^1) \amalg D \mid X$. Hence, the distribution of covariates X in both groups is balanced and the treatment effect can simply be estimated by comparing the outcomes in both groups. If, however, both groups differ on unobserved variables which affect simultaneously assignment into treatment and the outcome variable, a 'hidden bias' might arise. It should be clear that matching

---

[8] It may be the case for example that the participant receives a job offer, refuses to participate because he thinks the programme is not enhancing his employment prospects or because lack of motivation. As long as the reasons for abortion are not identified, an endogeneity problem arises.

3.3 Sensitivity Analysis with Rosenbaum Bounds

estimators are not robust against this 'hidden bias'. Since it is not possible to estimate the magnitude of selection bias with non-experimental data, we address this problem with the bounding approach proposed by Rosenbaum (2002).

The basic question to be answered is, if inference about programme effects may be altered by unobserved factors. In other words, we want to determine how strongly an unmeasured variable must influence the selection process in order to undermine the implications of matching analysis. Two recent applications of this approach can be found in Aakvik (2001) and DiPrete and Gangl (2004).

The Model:

Let us assume that the participation probability is given by

$$(3.6) \qquad P(x_i) = P(D_i = 1 \mid x_i) = F(\beta x_i + \gamma u_i),$$

where x_i are the observed characteristics for individual i, u_i is the unobserved variable and γ is the effect of u_i on the participation decision. Clearly, if the study is free of hidden bias, γ will be zero and the participation probability will solely be determined by x_i. However, if there is hidden bias, two individuals with the same observed covariates x have differing chances of receiving treatment. Let us assume we have a matched pair of individuals i and j and further assume that F is the logistics distribution. The odds that individuals receive treatment are then given by $\frac{P(x_i)}{(1-P(x_i))}$ and $\frac{P(x_j)}{(1-P(x_j))}$, and the odds ratio is given by:

$$(3.7) \qquad \frac{\frac{P(x_i)}{1-P(x_i)}}{\frac{P(x_j)}{1-P(x_j)}} = \frac{P(x_i)(1-P(x_j))}{P(x_j)(1-P(x_i))} = \frac{\exp(\beta x_j + \gamma u_j)}{\exp(\beta x_i + \gamma u_i)} = exp[\gamma(u_i - u_j)].$$

If both units have identical observed covariates - as implied by the matching procedure - the x-vector is cancelled out. But still, both individuals differ in their odds of receiving treatment by a factor that involves the parameter γ and the difference in their unobserved covariates u. So, if there are either no differences in unobserved variables ($u_i = u_j$) or if unobserved variables have no influence on the probability of participating ($\gamma = 0$), the odds ratio is one, implying the absence of hidden or unobserved selection bias. It is now the task of sensitivity analysis to evaluate how inference about the programme effect is altered by changing the values of γ and $(u_i - u_j)$. We follow Aakvik (2001) and assume for the sake of simplicity that the unobserved covariate is a dummy variable with $u_i \in \{0, 1\}$. A good example is the case where motivation plays a role for the participation decision and the outcome variable, and a person is either motivated ($u = 1$) or not ($u = 0$). Rosenbaum (2002) shows that (3.7) implies the following bounds on the odds-ratio that either of the two matched individuals will receive treatment:

$$(3.8) \qquad \frac{1}{e^\gamma} \leq \frac{P(x_i)(1-P(x_j))}{P(x_j)(1-P(x_i))} \leq e^\gamma.$$

Both matched individuals have the same probability of participating only if $e^\gamma = 1$. If $e^\gamma = 2$, then individuals who appear to be similar (in terms of x) could differ in their odds of receiving the treatment by as much as a factor of 2. In this sense, e^γ is a measure of the degree of departure from a study that is free of hidden bias (Rosenbaum, 2002).

The Test-Statistic:

Aakvik (2001) suggests to use the Mantel and Haenszel (MH, 1959) test statistic. To do so, some additional notation is needed. We observe the outcome y some time after treatment for both participants and non-participants. If y is unaffected by different treatment assignments, treatment d is said to have no effect. If y is different for different assignments, then the treatment has some positive (or negative) effect. To be significant, the treatment effect has to cross some test statistic $t(d, y)$. The MH non-parametric test compares the successful number of persons in the treatment group against the same expected number given the treatment effect is zero. Aakvik (2001) notes that the MH test can be used to test for no treatment effect both within different strata of the sample and as a weighted average between strata. Under the null-hypothesis the distribution of y is hypergeometric. We notate N_{1s} and N_{0s} as the numbers of treated and non-treated individuals in stratum s, where $N_s = N_{0s} + N_{1s}$. Y_{1s} is the number of successful participants, Y_{0s} is the number of successful non-participants, and Y_s is the number of total successes in stratum s. The test-statistic $Q_{MH} = (Y_{1s} - E(Y_{1s})/Var(Y_{1s}))$ follows the chi-square distribution with one degree of freedom and is given by:

$$(3.9) \qquad Q_{MH} = \frac{U^2}{Var(U)} = \frac{[\sum_{s=1}^{S}(Y_{1s} - \frac{N_{1s}Y_s}{N_s})]^2}{\sum_{s=1}^{S} \frac{N_{1s}N_{0s}Y_s(N_s - Y_s)}{N_s^2(N_s - 1)}}.$$

To use such a test-statistic, we first have to make treatment and control group as equal as possible since this test is based on random sampling. Since this is done by our matching procedure, we can proceed to discuss the possible influences of $e^\gamma > 1$. For fixed $e^\gamma > 1$ and $u \in \{0,1\}$, Rosenbaum (2002) shows that the test-statistic Q_{MH} can be bounded by two known distributions. As noted already, if $e^\gamma = 1$ the bounds are equal to the 'base' scenario of no hidden bias. With increasing e^γ, the bounds move apart reflecting uncertainty about the test-statistics in the presence of unobserved selection bias. Two scenarios can be thought of. Let Q_{MH}^+ be the test-statistic given that we have overestimated the treatment effect and Q_{MH}^- the case where we have underestimated the treatment effect. The two bounds are then given by:

$$(3.10) \qquad Q_{MH}^+ = \frac{[\sum_{s=1}^{S}(Y_{1s} - \widetilde{E}_s^+)]^2}{\sum_{s=1}^{S} Var(\widetilde{E}_s^+)}$$

and

(3.11) $$Q_{MH}^- = \frac{[\sum_{s=1}^{S}(Y_{1s} - \widetilde{E}_s^-)]^2}{\sum_{s=1}^{S} Var(\widetilde{E}_s^-)},$$

where $\widetilde{E}_s$ and $Var(\widetilde{E}_s)$ are the large sample approximations to the expectation and variance of the number of successful participants when u is binary and for given γ. The large sample approximation of $\widetilde{E}_s^+$ is the unique root of the following quadratic equation:

(3.12) $$\widetilde{E}_s^2(e^\gamma - 1) - \widetilde{E}_s[(e^\gamma - 1) + (N_{1s} + Y_s) + N_s] + e^\gamma Y_s N_{1s},$$

with the addition of $max(0, Y_s + N_{1s} - N_s \leq \widetilde{E}_s \leq min(Y_s, N_{1s}))$ to decide which root to use. $\widetilde{E}_s^-$ is determined by replacing e^γ by $\frac{1}{e^\gamma}$. The large sample approximation of the variance is given by:

(3.13) $$Var(\widetilde{E}_s) = (\frac{1}{\widetilde{E}_s} + \frac{1}{Y_s - \widetilde{E}_s} + \frac{1}{N_{1s} - \widetilde{E}_s} + \frac{1}{N_s - Y_s - N_{1s} - \widetilde{E}_s})^{-1}.$$

We will use this approach in chapter 5 to test the sensitivity of our results with respect to 'hidden bias'.

3.4 More Practical Issues

3.4.1 Programme Heterogeneity

When evaluating active labour market policies of countries, researchers are usually not confronted with only one homogeneous programme but with a variety of different ones, e.g. wage subsidies, training programmes or job creation schemes (JCS). Even when looking at one specific programme, like in our case JCS, subparts of the programme may be very heterogeneous regarding the type of occupation, intensity, duration, etc. To account for programme heterogeneity, the standard evaluation framework has been extended by Imbens (2000) and Lechner (2001). The multiple treatment framework considers the case of $(L+1)$ mutually different and exclusive treatments instead of just two. For every individual only one component of the $L+1$ different outcomes $\{Y^0, Y^1, ..., Y^L\}$ can be observed, leaving L as counterfactuals. Participation in treatment l is indicated by $D \in \{0, 1, ..., L\}$.

The interest lies in the causal effect of one treatment relative to another treatment on an outcome variable. Even though Lechner (2001) defines several interesting parameters, we will focus on ATT.[9] In the multiple-treatment

---

[9] Other parameters of interest are e.g. the average treatment effect of treatment m relative to treatment l for persons randomly drawn from the population or randomly drawn from participants in either m or l.

notation, that effect is defined as a pair-wise comparison of the effects of the treatments m and l for an individual randomly drawn from the group of participants in m only:

(3.14) $\Delta^{ml}_{ATT} = E(Y^m - Y^l \mid D = m) = E(Y^m \mid D = m) - E(Y^l \mid D = m)$.

It is worth noting that this treatment effect is not symmetric if the participants in m and l differ in a non-random fashion which is related to the outcomes. In the presented framework, the causal treatment effect is generally not identified, as discussed in subsection 1.2.2. To overcome the counterfactual situation, the conditional independence assumption (see section 1.5) can also be used in the heterogeneous treatment case. Imbens (2000) and Lechner (2001) consider identification under CIA in the multiple treatment framework and formalise it in the following way:

(3.15) $\qquad Y^0, Y^1, ..., Y^L \amalg D \mid X = x, \forall x \in \chi.$[10]

That is, all potential treatment outcomes are independent of the assignment mechanism for any given value of a vector of attributes, X, in an attribute space, χ (Lechner, 2002a). As discussed earlier for this assumption to be fulfilled, the researcher has to observe all characteristics that jointly influence the participation decision as well as the outcomes and therefore its plausibility depends on the dataset at hand.

We have also discussed that conditioning on all relevant covariates is, however, limited in case of a high dimensional vector X (see section 2.2). Lechner (2001) shows that a generalisation of the balancing score property holds for the case of multiple treatments as well:

(3.16) $Y^0, Y^1, ..., Y^L \amalg D \mid X = x$
$\qquad \rightarrow Y^0, Y^1, ..., Y^L \amalg D \mid b(X) = b(x), \forall x \in \chi.$[11]

Given that, ATT (here: effect of treatment m compared with treatment l on the participants in treatment m) can be written as (Lechner, 2002a):

(3.17) $\qquad \Delta^{ml}_{ATT} = E(Y^m \mid D = m)$
$\qquad\qquad - E_{P^{l|ml}}[E\{Y^l \mid P^{l|ml}(X), D = l\} \mid D = m],$

where: $P^{l|ml}(x) = P^{l|ml}(D = l \mid S \in \{l, m\}, X = x) = \dfrac{P^l(x)}{P^l(x) + P^m(x)}.$

The marginal probability of treatment l conditional on X is denoted as $P(D = l \mid X = x) = P^l(x)$. Δ^{ml}_{ATT} is identified and the dimension of the estimation problem is reduced to one. It is interesting to note that if $P^{l|ml}$ is modelled directly, no information from sub-samples other than those containing participants in m and l is needed for the identification of (3.18). In

---

[10] This identifying assumption is termed 'strong unconfoundness' by Imbens (2000).

this case, we are basically back in the binary treatment framework. Since the choice probabilities in (3.18) will not be known a-priori, they have to be replaced by an estimate, e.g. a probit model. If all values of m and l are of interest, the whole sample is needed for identification. In that case either the binary conditional probabilities can be estimated or a structural approach can be used where a complete choice problem is formulated in one model and estimated on the full sample, e.g. with a multinomial probit model. We have discussed the (dis-)advantages of the multinomial modelling in comparison to discrete estimation of binomial models already in subsection 3.2.1.

3.4.2 Sequential Matching Estimators

What we have discussed so far is basically a static evaluation framework where an individual can participate in one programme (or not). A recent extension of this framework considers the case, where individuals can participate in subsequent treatments. Lechner and Miquel (2002) discuss identifying assumptions for so-called sequential matching estimators. These estimators mimic the matching estimators described above but allow to estimate effects in a dynamic causal model. Lechner (2004) suggests estimation procedures based on these identifying assumptions, runs a Monte Carlo study, and applies them to Swiss data. We briefly discuss the principle ideas of these dynamic approaches in the following, the interested reader is referred to Lechner and Miquel (2002) and Lechner (2004).

Let us first of all make clear in which case a dynamic evaluation problem arises. Assume that we are in a two-periods-world where an individual has the possibility to participate e.g. in a training programme. In the first period the individual participates or not. The outcome in the second period will be influenced by the participation decision from the first period. In the second period the individual can again participate in a programme or not, where the participation decision not only depends on the covariates X but also on the participation decision from the first period and the related (intermediate) outcome. Hence, a dynamic selection problem arises. Most empirical work about dynamic selection problems ignores intermediate outcomes and treats the sequence participation as being determined from the start. Lechner (2004) points out that in such a process there is no role for intermediate outcomes to determine selection. Mainly, problems are circumvented by either estimating the effect of the first programme only (see e.g. Gerfin and Lechner (2002)) or applying the static framework subsequently as in Bergemann, Fitzenberger, and Speckesser (2001). Even though these are reasonable approaches, they do not explicitly allow for causal effects of dynamic sequences. This is the starting point for the work by Lechner and Miquel (2002) and Lechner (2004).

The basic points of their framework can be made clear in a three-periods-two-treatments model. We follow the discussion in Lechner (2004) and present the needed additional notation in the following. First, we introduce a time index $t \in \{0, 1, 2\}$ and extend the treatment indicator D by this time index, that is $D = (D_0, D_1, D_2)$. It is further assumed that in period 0 everybody is in the same treatment state $D_0 = 0$, whereas from the second period on D_t can take two values. Realisations of D_t are denoted by $d_t \in \{0, 1\}$. So in period 1 an individual is observed in exactly one of these two treatments $(0, 1)$, whereas in period 2 an individual participates in one of four possible treatment sequences $\{(0,0), (1,0), (0,1), (1,1)\}$. Additionally, the history of variables up to period t are denoted by a bar below a variable, e.g. $\underline{d}_2 = (d_1, d_2)$. The potential outcomes are indexed by treatments and the time period, i.e. $Y^{\underline{d}_t} = (Y_0^{d_t}, Y_1^{d_t}, Y_2^{d_t})$. The observed outcomes are given by the following equation:

$$(3.18) \quad Y_t = D_1 Y_t^1 + (1 - D_1) Y_t^0 = D_1 D_2 Y_t^{1,1} + D_1 (1 - D_2) Y_t^{1,0} \\ + (1 - D_1) D_2 Y_t^{0,1} + (1 - D_1)(1 - D_2) Y_t^{0,0}.$$

As in the static model, variables that influence treatment selection and potential outcomes are called attributes and are denoted by X. An important distinction has to be made regarding the exogeneity of these variables. Whereas in the static model exogeneity is assumed, in the dynamic model the X-variables in later periods can be influenced by treatment realisations. Hence, there are potential values of these variables as well: $X^{d_t} = (X_0^{d_t}, X_1^{d_t}, X_2^{d_t})$, where e.g. $X_1^{d_1}$ may contain $Y_1^{d_1}$ or functions of it. This is an interesting feature and highlights the dynamics of the model once again.

Since causal effects of length 1 can be estimated in the static framework, the interest lies in the estimation of mean effects of a sequence of treatments defined up to period 2 compared to another sequence of the same length, e.g. participating in both periods versus participating only in the first. Two identifying assumptions are considered: Weak and strong dynamic conditional independence assumptions (henceforth called WDCIA and SDCIA). Let us begin with the WDCIA.

Assumption 7 *Weak dynamic conditional independence assumption (WDCIA):*

a) $Y_2^{0,0}, Y_2^{1,0}, Y_2^{0,1}, Y_2^{1,1} \amalg D_2 \mid D_1 = d_1, \underline{X}_1 = \underline{x}_1$;

b) $Y_2^{0,0}, Y_2^{1,0}, Y_2^{0,1}, Y_2^{1,1} \amalg D_1 \mid X_0 = x_0$;

c) $0 < P(D_1 = 1 \mid X_0 = x_0) > 1$,
$0 < P(D_2 = 1 \mid \underline{X}_1 = \underline{x}_1, D_1 = d_1) > 1; \forall \underline{x}_1 \in \underline{\chi}_1, \forall d_1 : d_1 \in \{0, 1\}$.

The first line states that conditional on the previous treatment (d_1), observable outcomes and confounding variables, potential outcomes are independent of selection in period 2. The second line implies that conditional on some exogenous variables X_0, potential outcomes are independent of assignments in period 1. The last line is the usual common support restriction. It can be shown that under WDCIA pair-wise comparisons of all sequences are identified (see Lechner and Miquel (2002)). This is however only true for those individuals defined by their treatment status in period 1. To identify the effects of two different sequences defined for a sub-population given by treatment status in both periods, additional assumptions are required:

Assumption 8 *Strong dynamic conditional independence assumption (SD-CIA):*

a) $Y_2^{0,0}, Y_2^{1,0}, Y_2^{0,1}, Y_2^{1,1} \amalg D_2 \mid \underline{D}_1 = \underline{d}_1, \underline{X}_1 = \underline{x}_1;$

b) $Y_2^{0,0}, Y_2^{1,0}, Y_2^{0,1}, Y_2^{1,1}, (Y_2^{0,0}, X_1), (Y_2^{1,0}, X_1),$
$(Y_2^{0,1}, X_1), (Y_2^{1,1}, X_1) \amalg D_1 \mid X_0 = x_0;$

c) $0 < P(D_2 = 1 \mid \underline{X}_1 = \underline{x}_1, D_1 = d_1) > 1,$
$0 < P(D_1 = 1 \mid X_0 = x_0) > 1; \forall \underline{x}_1 \in \underline{\chi}_1, \forall d_1 : d_1 \in \{0,1\}.$

The SDCIA states that conditional on X_0, knowing S_1 does not help to predict the potential outcomes given a value of the observed X_1. This assumption allows for outcomes of previous treatments (predetermined endogenous variables) to appear in the conditioning set and identifies all relevant effects.

The sequential matching framework is a powerful tool and is applicable for situations where individuals can participate more than once in a programme and where it is possible to identify treatment sequences. It allows intermediate outcomes to play a role in the participation decision for sequential participation and thus allows estimation in a dynamic context. To our knowledge Lechner (2004) is the only application so far and hence, practical experiences with this identifying strategy are rather limited.

3.4.3 Choosing the Right Control Group - Random Programme Starts

Another important topic in applied evaluation research is to choose an appropriate control group. In the 'usual' evaluation setup for matching estimators, we have a group of participants and a group of non-participants. Both groups are usually observed from a certain starting point t to an end point T. The researcher does not have any information outside this limited time interval. Controls are defined as those individuals who did not participate in any programme in $[t, T]$, whereas participants are those individuals who took part in a programme for a certain interval τ in $[t, T]$.[12]

In a series of papers, Sianesi (2001, 2004) casts doubt if this standard approach is appropriate. She suggests a solution which is based on a re-definition

---

[12] Controls may also be defined as those individuals who did not participate at the programme under consideration but may have participated in another programme.

of the comparison group. Instead of defining controls as those who never participate, she defines controls as those who did not participate until a certain time period. Fredriksson and Johansson (2004) formalise her approach and argue that the standard way of defining a control group might lead to biased results, because the CIA might be violated. The reason for this is that in the standard approach the treatment indicator itself is defined conditional on future outcomes. In fact, in the Swedish context it can be argued that an unemployed individual will join a programme at some time, provided his unemployment spell is long enough (Sianesi, 2004). Hence, if the reason for non-participation is that the individual has found a job before a participation in the programme was offered or considered, it leads to negatively biased effects. To overcome this problem Sianesi (2004) defines non-participation in a different way. We will present her basic ideas in the following.

Joining versus Waiting:

The key choice faced by the unemployed in this framework is not whether to participate at all, but whether to participate in a programme or not *now*. In the latter case, the individual searches longer in open unemployment. The corresponding parameter of interest in this setting is then defined as the effect of joining a programme now in contrast to waiting longer. Let us introduce some additional notation: $U = 1, 2, ..., u, ..., U_{Max}$ denotes the unemployment duration since registration. The population of interest at time u are those still openly unemployed after u months. Treatment receipt in u is denoted by $D^{(u)} = 1$. The comparison group consists of all persons who do not join at least up to u, denoted by $D^{(u)} = 0$. The outcome of interest is defined over time t and is given by $Y_t^{(u)}$. The potential outcome if an individual joins in u is denoted by $Y_t^{1(u)}$ and if he does not join at least up to u by $Y_t^{0(u)}$. For each point of elapsed unemployment duration the parameter of interest is:

$$(3.19) \quad \Delta_u^t = E(Y_t^{1(u)} - Y_t^{0(u)}|D^{(u)} = 1) = E(Y_t^{1(u)}|D^{(u)} = 1)$$
$$-E(Y_t^{0(u)}|D^{(u)} = 1), \quad \text{for} \quad t = u, u+1, \ldots, T.$$

This is the average impact at time t, for those joining a programme in their u^{th} month of unemployment compared to waiting longer in open unemployment. Sianesi (2004) notes that the treatment effects are based on a comparison of individuals who have reached the same elapsed duration of unemployment. Measurement starts at time u, the start of the programme and therefore possible locking-in effects might encounter (see also subsection 3.2.5). The second term on the right hand side is unidentified and the CIA needed in that case is given by:

$$(3.20) \quad Y_t^{0(u)} \amalg D^{(u)}|X = x \quad \text{for} \quad t = u, u+1, \ldots, T,$$

which means that given a set of observed characteristics X, the counterfactual distribution of $Y_t^{0(u)}$ for individuals joining in u is the same as for those not joining in u and waiting longer. The estimated treatment effect is then the effect for those who participate in a programme at some time in their unemployment spell instead of waiting longer. Even though this is not a standard evaluation parameter of interest, it still shows whether a programme was effective or not. In a recent paper, Steiger (2004) compares the sensitivity of the effects of Swiss labour market policy with respect to the definition of the non-participant group. The first definition (no participation at all) leads to negative effects of almost all programmes when compared to non-participation. However, based on the second definition (not participated until now) non-participation loses its superiority compared to other programmes. This makes clear that further research in this direction is fruitful for evaluating labour market policies. Clearly, using this approach implies access to a dataset where subsequent programme entries into one (or more) programmes can be identified. In our empirical application in chapters 5 and 6 we have data on participants who joined the programme in the same month (February 2000) making this approach unfeasible. However, we use a slightly different version and ask if an individual should join a job creation scheme in February 2000 or not.

3.5 Conclusion

The aim of this chapter was to give some guidance for the implementation of propensity score matching. Basically five implementation steps have to be considered when using PSM (as depicted in figure 3.1). The discussion has made clear, that the researcher faces a lot of decisions during the implementation and that it is not always an easy task to give recommendations for a certain approach. Table 3.1 summarises the main findings of this chapter and also highlights the parts of this book where information for each implementation step can be found.

The first step of implementation is the estimation of the propensity score. We have shown, that the choice of the underlying model is relatively unproblematic in the binary case as logit and probit models usually yield similar results. Since the logit model has more density mass in the probability bounds, the choice depends on the data at hand. For the multiple treatment case one should either use a multinomial probit model or a series of binary probits (logits). After having decided about which model to be used, the next question concerns the variables to be included in the model. We have argued that the decision should be based on economic theory and previous empirical findings, and we have also presented several statistical strategies which may help to determine the choice. If it is felt that some variables play a specifically important role in determining participation and outcomes, one can use an 'overweighting' strategy, for example by carrying out matching on sub-populations.

Table 3.1: Implementation of Propensity Score Matching

Step	Decisions, Questions and Solutions	Chapter
1. Estimation of Propensity Score		
Model Choice:	→ Unproblematic in the binary treatment case (logit or probit)	3.2.1/3.4.1
	→ In the multiple treatment case multinomial probit or series of binomial models should be preferred	3.2.1/3.4.1
Variable Choice:	→ Variables should not be not influenced by participation (or anticipation) and must satisfy CIA	1.5/3.2.1
→ Economic Issues	→ Choose variables by economic theory and previous empirical evidence	3.2.1
→ Statistical Issues:	→ 'Hit or miss'-method, stepwise augmentation, leave-one-out cross validation	3.2.1
→ Key Variables:	→ 'Overweighting' by matching on sub-populations or insisting on perfect match	3.2.1
2. Check Overlap and Common Support		
Common Support	→ Treatment effects can be estimated only over the CS region!	3.2.3
→ Tests:	→ Visual analysis of propensity score distributions	3.2.3
→ Implementation:	→ 'Minima and maxima comparison' or 'trimming' method	3.2.3
	→ Alternative: Caliper matching	2.3.2
3. Choice Among Alternative Matching Algorithms		
Matching Algorithms	→ The choice (e.g. nearest-neighbour matching with or without replacement, caliper or kernel matching) depends on the sample size, the available number of treated/control observations and the distribution of the estimated PS → Trade-off between bias and efficiency!	2.3/2.7
4.1 Assessing the Matching Quality		
Balancing Property	→ Is the matching procedure able to balance the distribution of relevant covariates?	3.2.2
→ Tests:	→ Standardised bias, t-test, stratification test, joint significance and Pseudo-R^2	3.2.2
	→ If matching was not successful go back to step 1 and include higher-order terms, interaction variables or different covariates	← Step 1
	After that, if matching is still not successful → Reconsider identifying assumption and consider alternatives	← 1.4.2
4.2 Calculation of Treatment Effects		
→ Standard Errors:	→ Calculate standard errors by bootstrapping or variance approximations	2.6.1
→ When to Compare:	→ Compare from begin of the programme to avoid endogeneity problems!	3.2.5
	→ Pay attention to the possible occurrence of locking-in effects!	3.2.5
5. Sensitivity Analysis		
→ Hidden Bias:	→ Test the sensitivity of the estimated treatment effects with respect to unobserved covariates	3.3
	→ Calculate Rosenbaum-bounds. If results are very sensitive reconsider identifying assumption and consider alternatives	← 1.4.2

CS: Common Support, SB: Standardised Bias, PS: Propensity Score, CIA: Conditional Independence Assumption

The discussion has also emphasised that treatment effects can only be estimated in the region of common support. To identify this region we recommend to start with a visual analysis of the propensity score distributions in the treatment and comparison group. Based on that, different strategies can be applied to implement the common support condition, e.g. by 'minima and maxima comparison' or 'trimming'. The first approach faces some problems if there are observations discarded which are close to the bounds and if the density in the tails of the distribution are very thin. Hence, the trimming method may be a better alternative, where we require the density at each propensity score value in both groups to be over a certain threshold level. A practical alternative is to use caliper matching which ensures that the propensity score difference between treated and matched control observations does not exceed a certain caliper.

The third implementation step, namely the choice between different matching algorithms, has been already extensively discussed in section 2.7, such that we can directly come to step 4, the assessment of the matching quality. The main goal of the matching procedure is to balance the distribution of covariates in the treatment and control group. Since we do not condition on all covariates but on the propensity score, we have to check if matching is able to do so. We have presented several procedures, including standardised bias, t-tests, stratification, joint significance and pseudo-R^2. If the quality indicators are not satisfactory, one should go back to step 1 of the implementation procedure and include higher-order or interaction terms of the existing covariates or choose different covariates (if available). If, after that, the matching quality is still not acccptable, one has to reconsider the validity of the identifying assumption and possibly consider alternatives. However, if the matching quality is satisfactory one can move on to estimate the treatment effects. The estimation of standard errors should either be done by bootstrapping methods or the variance approximation as discussed in section 2.6.1. Another important decision is when to measure the effects. We argue that it is preferable to measure the effects from the beginning of the programme. This ensures not only that possible endogeneity problems are circumvented but also answers the policy-relevant question if an individual should participate in a certain programme at a certain time or not. Clearly, what has to be kept in mind for the interpretation is the possible occurrence of locking-in-effects. Finally, a last step of matching analysis is to test the sensitivity of the results with respect to 'hidden bias'. We have presented an approach (Rosenbaum bounds) that allows the researcher to determine how strongly an unmeasured variable must influence the selection process in order to undermine the implications of matching analysis. If the results are sensitive and if the researcher has doubts about the CIA he should reconsider to use alternative identifying assumptions.

Let us briefly also mention the further practical issues we have presented in section 3.4. Programme heterogeneity may become an issue, when evaluating a variety of heterogenous programmes and should also be regarded when evaluating one programme with varying characteristics (as will be the case in our application in chapter 6). Multiple participation has to be taken into account when it can be assumed that individuals participate more than once in (possibly different) programmes in the time span under consideration, which will not be a topic for us since we concentrate on the first participation only. And finally, we have also presented the discussion about the choice of the right control group.

To conclude, we have discussed several issues surrounding the implementation of PSM. We hope to give some guidance for researchers who believe that their data is strong enough to credibly justify the CIA and who want to use PSM. We will use most of the tests in our empirical analysis in chapter 5.

Part II

The Evaluation of Job Creation Schemes in Germany

4

The German Labour Market and Active Labour Market Policies - A Brief Overview

4.1 Introduction

The German labour market is plagued by persistently high unemployment in combination with a clearly separated situation on the labour markets in West and East Germany. After a slight recovery at the end of the 1990s, unemployment rates have risen again to 9.3% in West and 20.1% in East Germany in the year 2003. The Federal Employment Agency ('Bundesagentur für Arbeit', FEA) spends substantial amounts of the fiscal budget to overcome this unemployment problem. A particular emphasis in recent years has been laid on active labour market policies (ALMP), as the spendings of 12.3 bn Euro in West Germany and 8.9 bn Euro in East Germany reflect. The main purpose of ALMP is the permanent integration of unemployed persons into regular employment, i.e. to balance labour demand and supply. Unemployment should be circumvented by an efficient filling of vacancies and the increase of the individual employment chances by upgrading worker's human capital or worker's employability. ALMP were first introduced in Germany in the late 1960s. Since then, the set of programmes has been gradually adjusted to important changes on the labour market, like the oil price shocks during the 1970s or the growth of the labour market after the German Re-Unification. The general tendency to use more activating elements of labour market policies in the 1990s has led to a major reform step which cumulated in the introduction of the Social Code III in 1998 as the legal basis for ALMP. Within that reform, new instruments were introduced, competencies were decentralised and a more flexible allocation of funds has been made possible. Maybe the most important change from an evaluator's point of view was the legal anchoring of a mandatory output evaluation for all ALMP measures. As a consequence, new administrative datasets have been made accessible for scientific research. Evaluation of labour market policies before that was mainly based on survey data like the German Socio Economic Panel (GSOEP) or the Labour Market Monitors of East Germany and Sachsen-Anhalt. Clearly, the main problem with these datasets was the relatively small number of observations which did not allow to properly take into account effect heterogeneity, e.g. due to individual characteristics like the previous unemployment duration, different skill levels or the age. As we will show later on, this is not a problem for our analysis, since the administrative data we use allows to draw on large groups of participants and examine several sources of effect heterogeneity.

In conjunction with the introduction of the Social Code III, the importance of ALMP rose significantly. The share of ALMP in per cent of the total spending of the FEA rose from 21.7% in 1997 to 30.6% in 2000 in West Germany and from 37.8% to 40.0% in East Germany. Shifting resources from passive labour market policies (PLMP) to ALMP in East Germany was less successful, since unemployment benefits are entitlement programmes, where a rising unemployment automatically increases public spending on passive income support. The unemployment rate dropped from 11.0% in 1997 to 8.0% in 2001 in West Germany, whereas the decrease in East Germany was much lower from 19.5% (1997) to 18.8% (2001). However, following this satisfactory development, the situation worsened again at the begin of the new century, bringing the unemployment rate back to very high levels.

Due to this disappointing situation, the reform process on the German labour market is still ongoing. More reforms, which have become to be known as the 'Hartz-reforms', are implemented gradually (see Bundesministerium für Wirtschaft und Arbeit (2003)).[1] Whereas the change from AFG to the Social Code III was mainly characterised by an emphasis on ALMP, the new reforms also tackle the second pillar of labour market policies, namely the unemployment benefits. The tendency is to gradually limit access to unemployment benefits and to lower their level. Since we focus in our empirical analysis on the time period from 2000 until 2002, we are not going to discuss the current reforms here. A good overview of the most relevant issues can be found in Hagen and Spermann (2004).

The aim of this chapter is to present the institutional setup and the most relevant instruments of ALMP for the time period under consideration in our empirical analysis (section 4.2). The focus will lie on job creation schemes since these are the programmes which will be evaluated in chapters 5 and 6. In section 4.3 we will present the previous empirical studies on the effects of JCS both on the micro- and macroeconomic level. Following that we introduce the dataset used for our analysis in section 4.4. Finally, section 4.5 outlines the further steps of our empirical analysis.

---

[1] Peter Hartz was the chairman of a commission initiated by the Federal Government to provide suggestions for the reduction of unemployment and the reorganisation of the Federal Employment Office (which has been renamed to Federal Employment Agency). The title of the commissions report is 'Modern Services on the Labour Market' (Bundesministerium für Wirtschaft und Arbeit, 2003).

4.2 Institutional Setup and Instruments

4.2.1 The German Labour Market - Some Stylised Facts

A persistent unemployment rate in connection with high expenses for labour market policies characterises the German labour market of the last two decades. However, talking of 'the' German labour market might be misleading due to the special situation of the re-unified Germany after 1990. As a legacy of the former countries, the regional labour markets in West and East Germany differ substantially. From 1990 until 1993 the East German labour market was characterised by an enormous employment reduction from about 9.75 million jobs down to 6.25 million. The sudden exposure to a western-style economical environment and the loss of the main trading partners in the East led to a sharp reduction in production which changed the relative prices dramatically. Due to political pressure to reduce the disparity in living standards between both parts of Germany and to avoid massive migration from the East to the West, the growth rate of gross earnings was pushed above which was considered economically to be the market-clearing level. Besides the structural crisis, problems also arose through difficulties in the adoption of the new economical and behavioural situation. As a consequence, the stock of unemployed increased. However, because of a massive deployment of active labour market and social policy measures, a strong migration and a high number of commuters to the western part, there were only about 1.15 million workers openly unemployed on yearly average. In the years between 1993 and 1995, after this 'Re-Unification-Shock', the eastern labour market was stabilised and recovered slightly. This was mainly driven by a higher demand in the construction business. Since 1996, however, the situation is declining again. While the number of jobs has decreased in the following years, the stock of unemployed has risen up to 1.37 million. Although these figures represent the persistent problems of the eastern labour market, there were also some positive developments, like a good progress in setting-up a more competitive economic environment and modernising the economy. The transformation is processing still, and a quick convergence cannot be expected.

While the eastern labour market suffered from the Re-Unification, the western labour market boomed. The labour force rose both by the immigrants from the eastern part and abroad. Together with a strong increase of employment between 1989 and 1992, the number of unemployed was reduced to 1.80 million. In the years from 1993 to 1997, the West German labour market was affected by an economic slowdown, a delayed effect of the global recession determined by the oil-price shock during and after the Gulf War. In contrast to the eastern part, typical attributes of the economy and the labour market in the western part are a strong export-dependence due to production of superior industrial goods and an expanding services sector. In these years unemployment rose heavily up to 3.02 million on yearly average. In the end of the 1990s the West German labour market recovered. Between 1997 and 2000 the number of unemployed decreased again but was still persistent on a level around 2.5 million.

Table 4.1: Some Key Figures of the German Labour Market, 1997-2003

Germany	1997	1998	1999	2000	2001	2002	2003
Employed persons[1] (in million)	37.19	37.54	37.94	38.75	38.91	38.67	38.25
Employees subject to social security	27.28	27.21	27.48	27.83	27.82	27.57	26.95
Unemployed persons	4.38	4.28	4.10	3.89	3.85	4.06	4.38
Unemployment Rate[2]	12.7	12.3	11.7	10.7	10.3	10.8	11.6
New vacancies	3.28	3.83	4.04	4.10	3.77	2.80	2.47
West-Germany							
Employed persons[1]	30.81	31.12	31.51	32.37	31.52	31.40	31.09
Employees subject to social security	22.10	22.07	22.39	22.85	22.27	22.18	21.73
Unemployed persons	3.02	2.90	2.76	2.53	2.32	2.50	2.75
Unemployment Rate[2]	11.00	10.50	9.90	8.70	8.00	8.50	9.30
New vacancies	2.43	2.69	2.97	3.12	2.74	2.06	1.83
East-Germany							
Employed persons[1]	6.38	6.42	6.44	6.38	7.40	7.27	7.16
Employees subject to social security	5.18	5.13	5.09	4.98	5.55	5.39	5.22
Unemployed persons	1.36	1.37	1.34	1.36	1.53	1.56	1.62
Unemployment Rate[2]	19.5	19.5	19.0	18.8	18.8	19.2	20.1
New Job Vacancies	0.85	1.14	1.08	0.98	1.02	0.74	0.64

[1] Employed persons are defined as employees plus self-employed plus unpaid family members.
[2] Measured in relation to the dependent labour force.
Source: Bundesanstalt für Arbeit, various issues.

Table 4.1 shows some key figures of the German labour market for the period 1997 until 2003. It can be seen that the unemployment rate fell from 12.7% in 1997 to 10.3% in 2001. This development was mainly driven by the situation in West Germany. In the first half of the year 2000, the German economy had the biggest upswing since the Re-Unification. Despite this, only the western labour market with its strong export-dependence profited. From 1997 to 2001 the unemployment rate in West Germany declined from 9.8% to 7.2%. The higher foreign demand did not affect the eastern part because of its minor importance in the export-sector. Furthermore, the continuing structural problems and a reduced demand in the construction sector were disturbing factors, allowing the unemployment rate to drop from 19.5% to 18.8% only.

Starting in the second half of the year 2000, the German economy experienced a new downswing. Consequently, unemployment rose again in both parts, bringing it back to 9.3% in West Germany and 20.1% in East Germany in 2003. The critical constitution of the labour market is also reflected by the number of new vacancies. Whereas in the boom period in 2000 nearly 4.1 million new jobs were available, the number dropped to 2.47 million in 2003. This is a reduction of nearly 40% and hit the western and the eastern labour market equally hard. New vacancies dropped in West Germany from 3.12 million (2000) by 41% to 1.83 million (2003) and in East Germany from 0.98 million to 0.64 million which corresponds to a decline of 35%. Hence, it is not surprising that the German government is currently revising its policy approach on the labour market once again. Based on the report of the 'Hartz-commission', some new laws ('Hartz III') have been enacted in 2003. Additionally to that, the government has also initiated a large evaluation project of all instruments of ALMP and the results should provide the basis for a new legislation in 2005/2006. Details about this project can be found in Hagen and Spermann (2004) or Fertig, Kluve, and Schmidt (2004).

4.2.2 Labour Market Policies

Labour market policies in Germany are organised by the FEA.[2] Since 1969 the legal basis for labour market policies was the work support act ('Arbeitsförderungsgesetz', AFG), which has been replaced by the new Social Code SGB III ('Sozialgesetzbuch III') in 1998. Changes have been made not only in the objectives, like a more intensive focus on problem groups of the labour market, but also in the institutional organisation of labour market policy, leading to decentralisation and more flexibility in the regional allocation of resources to different measures. As already mentioned, the reform process is currently still on-going with a bundle of new initiatives ('Hartz-reforms').

However, since the data we analyse in chapters 5 and 6 ranges from 2000 to 2002, we focus our discussion on the SGB III. To allow the reader an assessment of the changes, we discuss the AFG very briefly, too. A good overview of AFG's historical evolution can be found in Staat (1997). The main goals of the AFG have been: (a) securance of a high employment ratio, (b) avoidance of low-quality employment, (c) improvement of the structure of the labour force, (d) promotion of mobility, (e) social goals and (f) promotion of target groups.[3] The improvement of the labour force structure, i.e. the adjustment of the labour supply to the changing labour demand, has been the primary goal in the early years. It was aimed to accompany the continual growth of the economy, that changed the labour market conditions permanently, with a continuous adjustment of the labour force structure to fulfill the new requirements. In detail, a short supply of jobs with specific (high-level) skills as well as an excess supply of jobs requiring low skills only was to be avoided. These goals had to be revised quite soon. At the end of 1973, the sharp rising unemployment rate in connection with the first oil price shock drove attention to the fight against this development. This becomes clear when we look at the participation structure of ALMP. In the early 1970s, less than 15 per cent

---

[2] Within the process of the 'Hartz-reforms', the former 'Bundesanstalt für Arbeit' has been renamed to 'Bundesagentur für Arbeit'.

[3] See §§1,2 AFG for details.

of all participants had been unemployed before participation, whereas in the 1980s this was the case for almost 80 per cent.

After some innovations and amendments, the AFG has been replaced by the SGB III in 1998. A good overview of the most relevant reforms can be found in Fitzenberger and Speckesser (2000). Sell (1998) presents an extensive discussion of the new SGB III, regarding especially the self-responsibility of employees for their own labour market success. Fertig and Schmidt (2000) explain and classify the different measures of employment promotion and explicitly distinguish between non-discretionary and discretionary measures. The latter distinction is quite important since unemployment benefits are entitlement programmes, i.e. rising unemployment automatically increases public spending on passive income support, whereas most of the active labour market programmes are discretionary in nature and therefore easier disposable in a situation of tight budgets (Martin, 1998).[4] Brinkmann (1999) discusses aspects of decentralisation and regionalisation as well as the now mandatory output evaluations.

Whereas the AFG has been implemented under full employment conditions, the SGB III has been created in a rougher economic situation, where labour market policy is affected by narrower budget constraints. Some of the AFG's objectives, like the securance of a high employment ratio and the avoidance of low-quality employment, were dropped. The most important goal (§7,3 SGB III) is the (re-)integration of problem groups in the regular labour market whilst using the resources in an efficient way ('Grundsatz der Wirtschaftlichkeit und Sparsamkeit').

As the government sees itself in a promoting role only, the SGB III places particular emphasis on the fact that employees have to act on their own responsibility regarding their labour market success. This comes together with a tightening of the reasonableness-clause ('Zumutbarkeitsklausel'), which for example makes it harder for unemployed to turn down job offers.

---

[4] There are two kinds of unemployment compensation in Germany. The first kind are unemployment benefits (UB) that are paid dependent on the preceding duration of employment, the age and if the individual has children. To get UB, an individual must register unemployed at the local labour office, seek for a regular occupation and have worked in regular employment before. The UB amounts to 60% (67%) of the net-wage of the last occupation for unemployed without (with) children. The longest possible UB entitlement is 32 months. After expiration of the UB entitlement, unemployed can gain unemployment assistance (UA) if they are in need of further promotion. In analogy to the UB entitlement, the UA differs dependent on the existence of children. The amount of UA for persons without (with) children is 53% (57%) of the last net-wage. The UA is paid for one year at maximum, but can be prolonged by case-wise revision. For every following year the grants are paid on a p.a. 3% reduced, last net-income basis. Participation in a job creation scheme prolongs the entitlement for UB in the same way as regular employment.

Besides the change of the objectives, there have been organisational changes, too, increasing the flexibility of ALMP on a regional and local level. The local employment offices are now allowed to allocate their budgets relatively freely to different measures. According to §§71b, SGB IV, several categories of ALMP must be financed by one single budget item ('Eingliederungstitel'), which is then assigned to the regional employment office. The new feature of the SGB III is now that the employment offices are free to set their priorities on how much weight to assign to each programme. This leaves the decision of the mix of instruments free to the particular regional branch of the FEA (Brinkmann, 1999). This decentralisation allows an adjustment to the situation on the local labour markets. Furthermore, 10% of the budget can be used for 'free promotion' ('Freie Förderung', §10, SGB III), allowing a more individualised support. Each employment office has considerable flexibility to act with local focus, e.g. by implementing measures which are custom made for the situation on the local labour market. Another promising feature is the so-called 'Eingliederungsplan' to avoid long-term unemployment. Under this new plan, the local labour exchange and the unemployed have to establish which active measures or which action from the unemployed will help to avoid a drifting off into (long-term)unemployment within six months after the begin of the unemployment spell. Other interesting new measures, like the special programme to combat youth unemployment ('JUMP'), measures which are implemented in pathfinder regions and aim to promote the employment of low-qualified individuals or long-term unemployed ('CAST') as well as the reform law regarding the ALMP instruments ('JOB-AQTIV'), cannot be discussed here. For a comprehensive overview see Fitzenberger and Hujer (2002).

Another new point in the SGB III is the mandatory output evaluation. The employment offices are now required to draw up output evaluations ('Eingliederungsbilanzen', §11, SGB III), including most importantly the (un)employment status of each participant some time after completion of a programme. For example, the employment offices have to disclose the share of participants who are not registered as unemployed again six months after end of any programme ('Verbleibsquote', VBQ). Clearly, not being registered as unemployed does not necessarily mean that the individuals have found a regular job. Instead individuals could for example be in maternity leave or retirement. To overcome this problem, the employment offices are now additionally obliged to disclose the share of participants who are regularly employed six months after end of the programme ('Eingliederungsquote', EGQ). Clearly, these output evaluations are a step in the right direction but have two flaws. The first one relates to the fact, that the success of programmes is measured only once (six months after programme end) and therefore just pictures one point in time. This flaw is of minor importance, since it would be relatively unproblematic to extend the documentation to more months and thus give a more complete image of the effects. The second one, however, is far more important and relates to the fact that these output evaluations only measure the gross effects of programmes. That is, they do not solve the fundamental evaluation problem ('What would have happened to the participant if he had not participated?') and do not allow to draw any conclusions about the net effects of programmes. Hence, deriving policy relevant implications from these figures is problematic and they should rather be used as controlling indicators.[5] Net effects can only be estimated with microeconometric evaluations, where the outcome of participants is contrasted with the outcome of a defined control group who did not participate. In a recent paper, Caliendo and Jahn (2004) use the above mentioned information 'not registered as unemployed' as an outcome variable and estimate the net effects of JCS with matching estimators. They relate these net effects to the gross effects (VBQ) estimated by the FEA and show how large the gross effects would have to be in order to guarantee positive net effects. If this would be done for other measures, too, and if some stable relation between gross and net effects could be established, this might be a proper approach to allow policy relevant conclusions based on gross effects.

Table 4.2: Spending on Labour Market Policies (in bn Euro), 1997-2003

Germany	1997	1998	1999	2000	2001	2002	2003
Total Spending (in bn Euro)	69.17	68.09	69.17	64.40	65.78	71.52	73.68
Passive Labour Market Policies	45.76	43.62	41.51	37.80	38.77	44.12	47.34
in % of total spending	66.2	64.1	60.0	58.7	58.9	61.7	64.2
Active Labour Market Policies	19.15	20.15	23.16	22.01	22.32	22.40	21.20
in % of total spending	27.7	29.6	33.5	34.2	33.9	31.3	28.8
Relation PLMP:ALMP	2.39	2.17	1.79	1.72	1.74	1.97	2.23
West-Germany							
Total Spending (in bn Euro)	43.55	42.01	42.56	39.95	41.05	44.12	47.83
Passive Labour Market Policies	30.77	28.77	27.26	24.09	24.91	28.13	31.58
in % of total spending	70.7	68.5	64.0	60.3	60.7	63.7	66.0
Active Labour Market Policies	9.47	9.86	11.75	12.23	12.42	12.15	12.28
in % of total spending	21.7	23.5	27.6	30.6	30.3	27.5	25.7
Relation PLMP:ALMP	3.25	2.92	2.32	1.97	2.01	2.32	2.57
East-Germany							
Total Spending (in bn Euro)	25.61	26.08	26.61	24.45	24.72	27.40	25.86
Passive Labour Market Policies	14.99	14.86	14.25	13.71	13.86	16.00	15.76
in % of total spending	58.5	57.0	53.6	56.1	56.1	58.4	61.0
Active Labour Market Policies	9.68	10.28	11.41	9.77	9.89	10.25	8.92
in % of total spending	37.8	39.4	42.9	40.0	40.0	37.4	34.5
Relation PLMP:ALMP	1.55	1.44	1.25	1.40	1.40	1.56	1.77

Source: Bundesanstalt für Arbeit, various issues.

---

[5] For example to compare the results across different local employment offices and programmes.

Table 1 shows the spending on labour market policies in Germany from 1997 to 2003. Whereas in 1997 only 27.7% of the total spending have been dedicated to active measures, the share rose to 34.2% in 2000, before it started falling again, reaching a level of 28.8% in 2003. In West Germany, the share of ALMP rose from 21.7% to 30.6%, whereas the increase in East Germany was much less pronounced (from 37.8% in 1997 to 40% in 2000). It is quite informative to look at the relation between PLMP and ALMP in terms of spending. For example in the year 1997 the FEA spend 3.25 times more money on PLMP than on ALMP in West Germany. With the general tendency to use more activating elements, this number was reduced to 1.97 in 2000. In East Germany the relation remained relatively constant. Starting from 1.55 in 1997 it reached the lowest level of 1.25 in 1999 and the highest level of 1.77 in 2003. Clearly, the obvious reason for the limited success in switching resources into active measures is the constantly high unemployment rate in East Germany and the already mentioned fact that unemployment benefits are entitlement programmes. This is also one explanation for the falling share of ALMP after 2000, since unemployment rates started to rise again after 2001.

The most important active measures in the year 2000, which is the begin of our observation period in chapters 5 and 6, have been vocational training ('Förderung der beruflichen Weiterbildung', VT) with 6.81 bn Euro and subsidised employment, consisting of traditional job creation schemes ('Arbeitsbeschaffungsmaßnahmen', JCS) with 3.68 bn Euro and structural adjustment schemes ('Strukturanpassungsmaßnahmen', SAS) with 1.36 bn Euro. For the time period from 1991-1999, VT has clearly been the most important programme in West Germany. For East Germany this is true only up to 1993. From that time onwards the number of entries into job creation schemes and the newly created structural adjustment schemes outnumbered the entries into vocational training. As Kraus, Puhani, and Steiner (2000) note, JCS and SAS have not only been used as a means to keep people off the dole and to avoid social hardship associated with long-term unemployment, but also as an investment in the East German industrial infrastructure, such as the removal of environmental damages. Therefore it is easy to understand that these measures have been very important in East Germany. After a peak in 1994, the number of entries decreased due to policy changes and financial restrictions as did the entries into all important active labour market policies. However, the decline in the number of participants was not equally reflected in the development of expenditures on JCS and SAS. This is due to the fact that the programmes became more cost-intensive when large scale programmes, so called 'Mega-JCS' and 'Societies for Employment Promotion and Structural Development' ('ABS-Gesellschaften') were established (Kraus, Puhani, and Steiner, 2000). Figures 4.1 (West Germany) and 4.2 (East Germany) show the number of entries and the money spent on these measures for the time period from 1997 until 2003.

It gets clear that vocational training has been the predominantly used measure in West Germany. At the begin of our observation period in 2000,

Fig. 4.1: Entries in and Spending on Vocational Training and Subsidised Employment in West Germany, 1997-2003

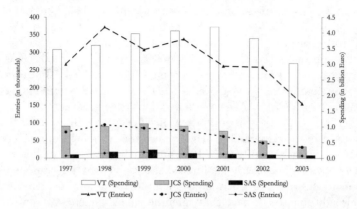

Fig. 4.2: Entries in and Spending on Vocational Training and Subsidised Employment in East Germany, 1997-2003

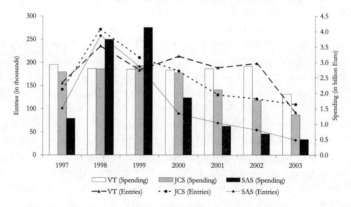

VT: Vocational Training, JCS: Job Creation Schemes, SAS: Structural Adjustment Schemes
SAS contain traditional SAS and SAS-East for private firms.
Source: Bundesagentur für Arbeit, various issues.

approximately 338,000 individuals started such a programme, whereas only 79,000 started a JCS and around 12,000 started a SAS. In East Germany on the other hand the mix of instruments is much more balanced. In 2000 around 214,000 individuals began a VT programme, 181,000 started a JCS and around 89,000 individuals joined in SAS. The regional variation can be seen as a direct outcome of the decentralisation introduced with the SGB III. Since the decision of the mix of instruments is free to the particular regional branch of the FEA, an adjustment to the situation on the local labour market is possible. Typically, in situations with great imbalances on the labour market, JCS and SAS are preferred to training measures, whereas in areas with

4.2 Institutional Setup and Instruments

low unemployment rates hardly any JCS or SAS are started. This can easily be seen from a comparison of figures A.1 and A.2 in appendix A. Figure A.1 shows the distribution of the job seeker rate in Germany in 1999.[6] It is a very severe problem in the East and the lowest rates can be found in the south. The extreme values concerning the job seeker rate are 4.24% in Freising (Southern Germany, to the North of Munich) and 33.0% in Sangershausen (Eastern Germany). Under the institutional structure of one country, very different labour market situations are visible. Even if only West Germany is regarded, there are high differences with 18.32% in Gelsenkirchen as the maximum value. These regional disparities provoke very different strategies of labour market policy. Figure A.2 gives the relation between people participating in job creation schemes to those involved in measures of vocational training. The comparison of both maps shows the logic behind the regional distribution of the measures, since vocational training is not very useful in areas where hardly any jobs are available. To enhance the comparability of the labour office districts, a project group of the FEA (Blien *et al.*, 2004) classified the 181 labour office districts into twelve types of districts with comparable labour market circumstances.[7] We will describe this in more detail in section 4.4 and use it as a starting point for our analysis of the effects of JCS with respect to regional variation in chapter 5.

Before we do so, we briefly discuss the most relevant measures. In principle, public vocational training under the AFG comprised three types of training measures, namely further training ('Fortbildung'), retraining ('Umschulung') and training to familiarise with a new occupation ('Einarbeitung').[8] The first two types have been summarised in one item (§§77-96, 153-159, 517 SGB III). The latter is now part of the employment subsidies and will not be discussed here.[9] The FEA pays the costs of the training measures and a subsistence allowance ('Unterhaltsgeld') to the participants, which amounts to 60 per cent (67 with one or more children) of the previous net income (equal to unemployment benefit). The main goals are to re-integrate unemployed by improving their skills and turn away the danger of unemployment for employees at risk.

Let us now turn to subsidised employment programmes, consisting of traditional job creation schemes and structural adjustment schemes. JCS is the more important programme in West and East Germany and the spending in 2000 sum up to 3.68 bn Euro (West: 1.02 bn Euro in West Germany and 2.66 bn in East Germany). JCS (§§260-271 SGB III) are normally only avail-

---

[6] The job seeker rate is defined as the unemployment rate extended by the rate of people participating in measures of ALMP.

[7] Please note that the labour office districts are nowadays called employment office districts. Both terms mean the same thing, i.e. the regional branch of the FEA. We will use them interchangeably throughout the book.

[8] See Hujer and Wellner (2000b) for an overview of vocational training under the AFG.

[9] See Hujer, Caliendo, and Radic (2001a) for an overview.

able to non-profit organisations. They should support activities which are of value for the society and additional in nature, that is without the subsidy they could not be executed. We will discuss them in more detail in the following subsection. Especially in East Germany, structural adjustment schemes (§§272-279 SGB III) play a prominent role, the spending amounting to 1.86 bn Euro in 2000. Their goal is, analogous to JCS, the integration into regular employment, but less severe eligibility criteria apply to participants, so not only unemployed but also individuals threatened by unemployment may participate. The SAS consist of a wage subsidy equal to the average amount of unemployment allowance or assistance (including contributions to the social security system) which is paid on the Federal territory. The subsidy is typically paid for a maximum period of 36 (48) months. In East Germany, the SAS may be implemented by public institutions and private companies ('SAM Ost für Wirtschaftsunternehmen', SAS-East), whereas in West Germany only the first is possible.[10] 43,600 individuals started a SAS in East Germany in the year 2000 and around 45,800 began a SAS-East.

Figures 4.1 and 4.2 also make clear, that the overall importance of the three mentioned measures (VT, JCS and SAS) is declining over the last years. The number of participants in VT dropped from 551,000 in 2000 to 246,000 in 2003. Entries in JCS surged from 260,000 to 141,000 and finally, also the declining importance of SAS gets clear by the fall from 101,000 to 40,000 entries. Instead, other measures of ALMP have become more important. A good example are employment integration subsidies ('Eingliederungszuschüsse', §§217-224 SGB III) with 181,768 entries in 2003. These subsidies are paid directly to the employer (private businesses) if an individual is employed who could not have been integrated in the labour market without the subsidy. The major difference between employment integration subsidies on the one hand and JCS and traditional SAS on the other hand is, that the former one is paid to private businesses. It is hoped that unemployed individuals who get a job with that subsidy have better chances to remain either in the receiving firm or in the first labour market in general. Clearly, these measures are also surrounded by some criticism since windfall gains and substitution effects cannot be ruled out. We will not discuss these measures here, since the focus of our empirical analysis are JCS. However, the interested reader is referred to Hujer and Caliendo (2003) and Caliendo and Hujer (2004a) for a most recent overview of other wage subsidy programmes. The authors also offer a threefold evaluation approach to account for substitution and displacement effects. A good overview of other measures, e.g. bridging allowance ('Überbrückungsgeld'), temporary work and mini-jobs, can be found in Hagen and Spermann (2004).

---

[10] Since January 1998, SAS-East could also be requested in West-Berlin.

4.2.3 Job Creation Schemes

After having described the general institutional setup of ALMP in Germany, it is now time to focus on JCS. These measures have been the second most important programme, regarding the expenses and the number of entries with a fiscal volume of 3.68 billion Euro and 260,079 newly promoted individuals at the begin of our observation period in 2000 (Bundesanstalt für Arbeit, 2002). JCS can be promoted if they support activities which are of value for the society and additional in nature.[11] Additional in nature means that the activities could not be executed without the subsidy. Furthermore individuals have to be employed whose last chance to stabilise and qualify for later reintegration into regular employment is participation in these schemes. Hence, JCS are primarily targeted at specific problem groups of the labour market, like long-term unemployed or persons without work experience or professional training. Measures with a predominantly commercial purpose have been excluded explicitly up to January 2002; now they can be accomplished with a special permission by the administration board of the local labour office. However, some special clauses to prevent substitution effects and windfall gains have to be regarded. Besides the social value and the additional benefit of the activities, participants in JCS in the private sector should be from special target groups of the labour market, e.g. young unemployed without professional training, and get educational supervision during occupation. Due to these special requirements, the majority of activities is conducted by public or non-commercial institutions.[12] Financial support for JCS is obtained as a wage subsidy to the implementing institution. JCS in the public sector are conducted by the administration departments of municipalities and towns, of administrative districts, of the Federal Authority, of churches and of universities. Non-commercial entities are mainly friendly societies, charities and non-profit enterprises. It is also quite interesting that JCS can be implemented in nine different economic sectors, like AGRICULTURE, CONSTRUCTION AND INDUSTRY or OFFICE AND SERVICES. The distinction between the implementing institution or provider of JCS and the sector in which they work will especially be important in chapter 6 where we test if there are different effects of JCS for different providers and different economic sectors. A further distinction can be made regarding the type of promotion, that is regular or enforced. In general, JCS should be co-financed measures where between 30% and 75% of the costs are subsidies by the FEA and the rest is paid by the provider and the subsidy is normally paid for 12 months. However, exceptions can be made in the direction of a higher subsidy-quota (up to 100%) and programmes can be extended up to 24 or even 36 months, if the JCS create the preconditions for permanent jobs, provide jobs for unemployed individuals with strong labour market disadvantages or improve social infrastructure or environment.

---

[11] See §§260-271 and 416 in the Social Code III (SGB III) for details.

[12] As our later analysis will show, JCS in private businesses are not relevant for our sample of participants.

Participants in JCS are allowed to do a practical training up to 40% of the time and a VT up to 20%, together no more than 50% of the programme duration. Priority should be given to projects which enhance the chances for permanent jobs, support structural improvement in social or environmental services or aim at the integration of extremely hard-to-place individuals.

The legal requirements for individuals to enter JCS are relaxed by the SGB III amendment (Job-Aqtiv-Gesetz) in January 2002. Before that time, potential participants had to be long-term unemployed (more than one year) or unemployed for at least six months within the last twelve months. Additionally they had to fulfil the conditions for the entitlement of unemployment compensation. In addition, the local placement officers were allowed to place up to five percent of the allocated individuals who do not meet these conditions ('Five-Percent-Quota'). Further exceptions are made for young unemployed (under 25 years) without professional training, short-term unemployed (with at least three months of unemployment) placed as tutors, and disabled who could be stabilised or qualified. With the 2002 amendment, all unemployed individuals can enter a JCS independent of the preceding unemployment duration, but with the restriction that JCS is the only opportunity for occupation. In addition, the 'Five-Percent-Quota' was augmented up to ten percent.

Participation in JCS results from placement by the local labour office caseworker. Unemployed individuals who cannot be integrated into regular employment or do not fit the conditions for another instrument of active labour market policy are offered a specific job in one measure where a place is available and which fits his characteristics. Clearly, this is an important point for the later analysis, when the question arises how to estimate the participation probabilities. Since the decision process is a binary one, i.e. taking the place in one specific programme or not, we will use a binary probability model, too. The responsible caseworker can cancel the treatment before the regular end if the participating individual can be placed in the first labour market. If an unemployed rejects the offer of a JCS or if a participant denies a career counselling by the placement officer, the labour office can stop the unemployment benefits for up to twelve weeks. However, due to legal restrictions the use of this penalty is negligible.

A final thing to note is, that within the 'Hartz-reforms' JCS are reformed, too. One major change is that JCS and SAS will be pooled to one homogenous instrument. Major goal will be to offer unemployed individuals (or individuals threatened by unemployment) an alternative if either the situation on the regional labour market or individual specific restraints do not allow an integration into regular employment. The 'old' rules of JCS will be the basis for the new instrument and the 'old' rules of SAS are repealed. Since these reforms do not fall into our observation period, we refrain from presenting them in detail. Caliendo and Hujer (2004b) provide an overview of the most relevant points.

4.3 Previous Empirical Studies

In this section we present the previous empirical evidence on the micro- and macroeconomic effects of job creation schemes in Germany. We will start with the microeconometric evaluation studies where the absence of suitable data has hampered evaluation efforts for a long time. The earlier evaluation studies of JCS mainly concentrated on the East German labour market and were based on survey data, either the labour market monitor of East Germany (LMM-East) or the one of Sachsen-Anhalt (LMM-SA). The relatively small groups of participants did not allow to take adequately account of effect heterogeneity. Hence, drawing policy relevant conclusions for West Germany and specific sub-groups was problematic. In succession of the introduction of the SGB III and the mandatory output evaluations, administrative data were made available for scientific research improving the data situation enormously. Caliendo, Hujer, and Thomsen (2003) and Hujer, Caliendo, and Thomsen (2004) were the first to use these rich data allowing to estimate effects for West Germany and specific sub-groups of the labour market, too. The problem in these studies was that the outcome variable was the unemployment status of individuals, permitting conclusions about the re-integration effects into regular employment.

The number of macroeconomic evaluation studies is rather small, too. The problem here is not so much missing data but the open methodological questions regarding the suitable framework of macroeconomic evaluation analysis (see Caliendo, Hagen, and Hujer (2004) for an overview). Clearly, most macroeconomic evaluation studies do not focus on one programme only but on the most important measures altogether. Hence, we will also present the macroeconomic effects of other programmes, e.g. for VT, in subsection 4.3.2. More extensive overviews regarding the microeconomic effects of other measures than JCS can be found in Hagen and Steiner (2000) and Hujer and Caliendo (2001).

4.3.1 Microeconometric Evaluations of Job Creation Schemes

Table 4.3 contains the few existing evaluation studies of microeconometric job creation schemes for East Germany and the study by Hujer, Caliendo, and Thomsen (2004). The array of evaluation methodologies is rather wide and we presented most of them in chapter 1.[13] The outcome variables considered include unemployment probabilities, transition rates to regular employment as well as (re)employment probabilities and (un)stable employment.

---

[13] The only approach we did not present are duration models. See van den Berg (2001) for a general introduction in duration models and Abbring and van den Berg (2003) for a more specific outline on the estimation of treatment effects with duration models.

Steiner and Kraus (1995) use a duration model and the transition rates from unemployment and JCS to regular employment to analyse the effects of JCS on the re-employment probability of participants. They use the first six waves of the LMM-East and cover the time period from November 1990 until November 1992. They find positive effects on the transition rates to regular employment only for men and only after the programme has ended. During the programme, the transition rates for participants and non-participants do not show considerable differences. After twelve months, the usual duration of JCS, the transition probability of participants increases strongly for a short period (at least for those participants who had a high probability of participating in a JCS). Additionally they find, that women with ex ante relatively good employment prospects are more likely to participate in a JCS than women with ex ante bad employment prospects. However, whereas for the latter group no significant effects could be established, the first group suffers from participation as the transition probabilities from JCS to regular employment are much lower than the transition probabilities from unemployment to regular employment. What has to be noted when interpreting these effects is, that JCS were not used target-specific during that time. Instead they were used to cushion the transition process after re-unification. Kraus, Puhani, and Steiner (2000) extend this study by additionally allowing for unobserved heterogeneity and by using the first eight waves of the LMM-East (November 1990 until November 1994). They additionally split the time period in two sub-samples (November 1990-August 1992 and September 1992-November 1994). They find clearly negative effects on the re-employment probabilities for the participants irrespective of gender and time period.

Hübler (1997) uses the same data (LMM-East, November 1990 until November 1994) and applies an array of evaluation methods, including matching and instrumental variables, to estimate the effects of job creation schemes (or public work programmes) on the employment status. JCS is only one of the programmes he analyses and he cannot find any positive effects for them. To be specific, JCS have at best no significant effect on the employment probability of participants and have in one specification negative effects.

The studies from Bergemann and Schultz (2000), Bergemann, Fitzenberger, Schultz, and Speckesser (2000) and Bergemann, Fitzenberger, and Speckesser (2001) are based on the LMM-Sachsen-Anhalt. Bergemann and Schultz (2000) analyse the effects of JCS on the re-employment chances of participants and use the LMM-SA waves from 1997 and 1998. Thereby they cover participation from 1990 until 1998. The fundamental evaluation problem is addressed by using a matched DID approach as described in subsection 2.5.1. To account for possible anticipation effects, they use a time span of seven to twelve months before programme begin in the DID estimation. The results show considerable locking-in effects during programme participation which vanish 18 months after programme end. Two years after programme end, participants have a significantly higher employment rate when compared to matched non-participants. For the sub-group of participants with an entry into JCS between 1990 and 1993, they find strong negative effects, indicating that the effects of JCS improved over time. Bergemann, Fitzenberger, Schultz, and Speckesser (2000) use the same data and additionally allow for multiple participation in JCS. They find that participation in JCS leads to more negative results in the beginning of the sample period and less negative results later on. Hence they confirm the finding that JCS gained more efficiency over time. However, the long run effects are at best insignificant.

The only study which finds clearly positive effects of public employment programmes is the one from Eichler and Lechner (2002). They use the LMM-SA and analyse the effects of JCS between April 1991 and September 1997. They only analyse participants who are aged between 22 and 52 years using a combined matching and difference-in-differences estimator. Their results indicate a substantially reduced unemployment risk for participants, especially for men. For women the effects are only significantly positive for a short period after programme end.

Drawing conclusions based on these studies is difficult even though the overall picture seems to be negative. There is only one study which finds clearly positive effects and the other results are mixed. The positive effects in the Eichler and Lechner (2002) study may be caused by their restriction of participants in a certain age group. Overall, all studies are based on rather small samples. Effect heterogeneity (e.g. caused by age or previous unemployment duration) is not considered. The studies from Caliendo, Hujer, and Thomsen (2003) and Hujer, Caliendo, and Thomsen (2004) overcome this problem by explicitly considering regional, group-specific and sectoral heterogeneity. Their analysis is based on the same data as our analysis in chapters 5 and 6. However, the outcome variable used only allows to evaluate the effects of JCS on the unemployment probability. They find that JCS mainly have negative effects, i.e. the unemployment rate among the participants is higher than among the non-participants two years after programmes have started. Two points restrict the interpretation of the results. First, the time period under consideration is relatively short and second, the used outcome variable does not allow to draw any conclusions about the re-integration effects into regular employment. Hence, we will use these results as a starting point and evaluate the effects of JCS with respect to re-integration into regular employment in chapters 5 and 6, where we are also able to use a longer time period after programme begin. We will outline the steps of our empirical analysis in section 4.5.

4.3.2 Macroeconomic Evaluations

Before we do so let us briefly discuss the results from the existing macroeconomic evaluations for West and East Germany which can also be found in table 4.4. They are all based on aggregated regional data coming either from the local labour office districts, planning regions or districts.

Table 4.3: Microeconometric Evaluations of Job Creation Schemes in East Germany

Authors	Data Period	No. of obs.	Programme	Evaluation Methodology	Outcome Variable	Results
Steiner and Kraus (1995)	LMM-East 1990-1992	T:582 C:2,179	Job creation schemes	Discrete hazard rate model (multinomial logit), different sub-groups	Transition rates to regular employment	Negative effects for women, positive effects for men after 12 months, only slight effects before
Kraus, Puhani, and Steiner (2000)	LMM-East 1990-1992 1992-1994	T:718 C:3,503	Public work programmes	Discrete hazard rate model with unobserved heterogeneity	Re-employment probabilities, (un)stable employment	Negative effects on re-employment probabilities
Hübler (1997)	LMM-East 1990-1994	T:varies N:2,886	Job creation schemes (public work programmes) and other programmes	Linear control functions, IV-estimator, random-effects estimator, matching approach	Employment opportunities	JCS (public work programmes) have no positive effects
Bergemann and Schultz (2000)	LMM-SA 1990-1993 1994-1998	T:431 C:3,450	Job creation schemes and other programmes	Conditional DID	Employment	Positive effects two years after programme end; strong negative effects for entries between 1990-1993
Bergemann, Fitzenberger, Schultz, and Speckesser (2000)	LMM-SA 1990-1998	T:615 C:3,137	Job creation schemes and training	Matching, 'conditional' DID regarding multiple participation	Employment	Long-run effects of JCS are at best insignificant
Eichler and Lechner (2002)	LMM-SA 1992-1997	T:1,299 C:16,334	Public employment programmes	Matching, 'conditional' DID	Unemployment probabilities	Unemployment risk for participants is reduced substantially
Hujer, Caliendo, and Thomsen (2004)	Administr. Data 2000-2002	T:11,151 C: 219,622	Job creation schemes	Matching	Unemployment probability	Mainly negative effects, i.e. participants are more likely to be unemployed two years after programme begin

LMM-SA: Labour Market Monitor Sachsen-Anhalt, LMM-East: Labour Market Monitor East Germany
DID: Difference-in-differences, T: Participants, C: Non-Participants estimation.

Table 4.4: Macroeconomic Evaluations of Labour Market Policies in Germany

Authors	Data Period	No. of obs.	Programme	Evaluation Methodology	Outcome Variable	Results
Büttner and Prey (1998)	PR of West Germany 1986-1993	N:74 (West)	Training programmes, public job creation	Disequilibrium approach, matching efficiency (static and dynamic), estimation with OLS, LSDV and 2SLS, controlling for endogeneity	Labour market mismatch	No significant effects of training programmes, job creation schemes reduce mismatch
Prey (1999) [extension of Büttner and Prey (1998)]	PR of West Germany 1986-1993	N:74 (West)	Training programmes, public job creation	As above, with additional control variables, separate estimation for men and women	Labour market mismatch	VT increases (decreases) the mismatch for women (men), JCS decreases the mismatch for men
Pannenberg and Schwarze (1998)	LLOD 1992-1994	N:35 (East)	Training programmes	Various approaches (OLS, FGLS and 2SLS with fixed and random effects)	Hourly (aggregate) wages	ALMPs have negative effects on regional wages
Steiner et al. (1998)	LLOD 1992-1997 (and sub-periods)	N:35 (East)	Vocational training	Pooled cross-section analysis, augmented matching function	Outflow of unemployment	No (very small) effects on the matching efficiency (in the short run)
Schmid, Speckesser and Hilbert (2000)	LLOD 1994-1997	N:142 (West)	Further training, retraining, public job creation and wage subsidies	Pooled cross-section analysis, fixed-effects model; augmented matching model	Long-term unemployment (LTU); unemployment outflows	JCS reduces only 'short' LTU (≤6 months), VT reduce LTU (not all significant), wage subsidies help only the 'very' long-term unemployed
Hagen and Steiner (2000)	LLOD 1990-1999 (and sub-periods)	N:142 (West) N:35 (East)	Vocational training; job-creation schemes, structural adjustment schemes	Augmented matching function, fixed-effects model	Inflow in / outflow of unemployment	Net-effects East: JCS and VT increase the unemployment rate, SAM reduces it slightly. West: All measures increase unemployment
Blien et al. (2002)	Employm. stat. districts	N:112	ALMP in general	Shift-share analysis	Regional employment	ALMP have positive impacts
Hujer, Caliendo, Zeiss (2005)	LLOD 1999-2001	N:141 (West) N:34 (East)	Vocational training, job creation schemes, structural adjustment schemes	Reduced form approach based on dynamic panel models	Job seeker rate	VT (SAS) reduces the JSR in West (East) Germany. No significant effects of JCS
Hujer and Zeiss (2003)	LLOD 1999-2003	N:141 (West)	Vocational training, job creation schemes	Augmented matching function, dynamic panel data model with GMM and ML	Matching efficiency	Vocational training does not affect the matching process, job creation schemes have a negative effect
Hagen (2003b)	LLOD 1998-2003	N:35 (East)	Vocational training, job creation schemes, structural adjustment schemes	Matching function, Beveridge curve, labour demand	Varies between approaches	Mainly negative effects of JCS, no effects of VT and SAS

OLS: Ordinary Least Squares, LSDV: Least Squares Dummy Variables, 2SLS: Two-Stage Least Squares, FGLS: Feasible Generalised Least Squares, GMM: Generalised Method of Moments, ML: Maximum-Likelihood
LLOD: Local labour office districts, PR: Planning regiors

Büttner and Prey (1998) use yearly data (1986 to 1993) from 74 planning regions of West Germany to evaluate the effects of training programmes and public sector job creation on the labour market efficiency. They use a disequilibrium approach and their results suggest that training programmes have no effect and job creation programmes have a significant positive effect on the matching efficiency, i.e. they reduce the mismatch. Prey (1999) extends this work by additionally controlling for the regional age structure and recipients of social assistance and running the estimation separately for men and women. She finds that VT increases (decreases) the mismatch for women (men), whereas JCS decreases the mismatch for men. Pannenberg and Schwarze (1998) use data from 35 local labour office districts to evaluate training programmes in East Germany. They use monthly data from 1992 to 1994 and find that the programmes have negative effects on the regional wages. Schmid, Speckesser, and Hilbert (2000) use yearly data from 142 local labour office districts to estimate the effects of further training, retraining, public sector job creation and wage subsidies on long-term unemployment and the unemployment outflow in the period 1994-1997. They find that job creation programmes reduce only 'short' long-term unemployment (6-24 months), whereas vocational training reduces long-term unemployment (> 24 months) and wage subsidies help only the 'very' long-term unemployed. Steiner, Wolf, Egeln, Almus, Schrumpf, and Feldotto (1998) examine the effects of vocational training on the labour market mismatch using the data from 35 local labour office districts in East Germany. They observe only very small effects on the matching efficiency which disappear in the long-run. Hagen and Steiner (2000) evaluate VT, JCS and SAS for East and West Germany using data from local labour office districts. The time period under consideration differs and ranges from 1990-1999. The estimated net-effects are not very promising as all measures increase unemployment in West Germany. Only SAS reduces the unemployment rate slightly in East Germany, whereas JCS and VT increase it, too. Blien et al. (2002) analyse the effects of ALMP on the development of regional employment in Eastern Germany and find positive impacts. They use detailed data from the employment statistics and the time span of 1993-99. Their regional units are 112 districts ('Landkreise/ kreisfreie Städte'). Their method is an econometric equivalent to conventional shift-share analysis (based on constrained regression), which is extended to include many determining variables. Hujer, Blien, Caliendo, and Zeiss (2005) use a dynamic panel approach to estimate the effects of JCS, SAS and VT on the regional job seeker rate in Germany. They analyse the time period from 1999 to 2001 and base their analysis on data from the local labour office districts. They start with an identification of the most important channels through which ALMP may influence the JSR and apply a 'reduced form approach' for the estimation. Their findings indicate that VT are able to reduce the JSR in West Germany and SAS do the same in East Germany. No significant effects for JCS are established. Hujer and Zeiss (2003) investigate the effects of job creation schemes and vocational training on the matching processes in West

Germany. Their analysis is based on regional data for local labour office districts for the period from 1999 to 2003. They base the analysis on a dynamic version of an augmented matching function and use dynamic panel data models; to be specific they apply a first-differences generalised method of moments and a transformed maximum likelihood estimator. The results indicate that vocational training does not significantly affect the matching process and that job creation schemes have a negative effect. Hagen (2003b) uses regional data for East Germany and the time period 1998 to 2003. He applies three different approaches to analyse the effects of VT, JCS and SAS. His results indicate negative effects of JCS on the matching efficiency when using the augmented matching function approach (VT and SAS are not significant). The augmented Beveridge curve approach does not indicate any long-term effects of ALMP on regional job-seekers rate. Finally, his labour demand estimation leads to crowding-out effects of JCS on regular employment.

Drawing conclusions from the macroeconomic studies is not an easy task. Not only that the data used in the analyses differ (between West and East Germany and local labour office districts and planning regions), but also the applied methods. The discussion in Caliendo, Hagen, and Hujer (2004) makes clear, that one precondition for the credibility of the results is that the study addresses the endogeneity problem of ALMP adequately. The studies from Hagen and Steiner (2000), Hagen (2003b) and Hujer, Blien, Caliendo, and Zeiss (2005) give good examples on how to deal with endogeneity in this context. Studies that fail to address (and solve) this problem are likely to achieve biased results and hence should not be considered any longer. Since our analysis in chapters 5 and 6 focusses on the microeconomic level, we will not discuss these topics any further.

4.4 Dataset Used in our Analysis

Data Sources

The data used for the empirical analysis contain information on all participants, who were placed in a JCS in February 2000, and a comparison group of non-participants, who were eligible for participation in January 2000, but did not enter those schemes in February. Information on non-participants and participants were merged from several datasets of the FEA. The central source for the information derived for the participants is a prototype version of the programme participants master dataset ('Maßnahmeteilnehmergrunddatei', MTG). This dataset merges information from the job-seekers data base ('Bewerberangebotsdatei', BewA), an adjusted version of this dataset for statistical purposes (ST4) and the particular information of subsidised employment programmes (ST11TN). Due to that, the MTG contains a large number of attributes to describe individual aspects and provides a reasonable basis for the construction of the comparison group. The included attributes can be split into four classes: socio-demographic and qualification information, labour market history and particular programme information.[14] The information for the comparison group is derived from the BewA with the additional information of the ST4. Therefore, almost all attributes in the analysis for the comparison as well as for the treatment group originate from the same datasets. Table 4.5 gives detailed information of the data sources and the included attributes. A selection of these attributes will later on be used to estimate the participation probability.[15] The special situation of the labour market in the capital city requires a separate evaluation of the effects of JCS. However, due to the small number of participants, interpretation of the results is aggravated and therefore we exclude participants in Berlin from our analysis. Our final sample consists of 11,151 participants and 219,622 non-participants.

Table 4.5: Data Sources and Attributes

	Data Source	Attributes
MTG[1]	BewA and ST4[2]	a) **Socio-demographic**: age, gender, marital status, number of children, nationality, health restrictions b) **Qualification**: graduation, professional training, occupational group, position in last occupation, work experience, appraisal of qualification by the placement officer c) **Labour market history**: duration of unemployment, duration of last occupation, number of job offers, occupational rehabilitation, programme participation before unemployment
	ST11TN[3]	d) **Programme**: institution that receives subsidy, activity sector, time of qualification and/or practical training during programme, begin and end of programme (payment of the subsidy), entry and leave of the participant, duration of programme

[1] Programme participants master data set (Maßnahmeteilnehmergrunddatei, MTG)
[2] Job-seekers data base (Bewerberangebotsdatei, BewA) and adjusted version for statistical purposes (ST4)
[3] Programme participants of subsidised employment data set (ST11TN)

---

[14] The final version of the MTG includes information on all ALMP programmes of the FEA.

[15] The value of good data is an essential building block for a valid evaluation. As for example Heckman, Ichimura, Smith, and Todd (1998) mention, having access to a geographically-matched comparison group administered the same questionnaire as programme participants matters in devising effective non-experimental estimators of programme impacts.

Regional Information

The information is completed by a characterisation of the regional labour market situation. The classification of the labour office districts was undertaken by a project group of the FEA (Blien et al., 2004) whose aim was to enhance the comparability of the labour office districts for a more efficient allocation of funds. The 181 labour office districts were split into twelve types of office districts with similar labour market conditions. The comparability of the office districts is build upon several labour market characteristics, where the most important criteria are the underemployment quota and the corrected population density. The underemployment quota is defined as the relation of the sum of unemployed individuals and participants in several ALMP programmes (including JCS, SAS and VT) to the sum of all employed persons and these participants. The corrected population density is used to improve the comparability of rural labour office districts with metropolitan and city areas. In addition to that, the vacancy quota describing the relation of all reported vacancies at the labour office in relation to the number of employed persons, the placement quota, that contains the number of placements in relation to the number of employed persons, and the quota of people who achieve maintenance allowance in relation to the underemployment quota are used. Furthermore, an indicator for the tertiarisation level built on the number of employed persons in agricultural occupations and an indicator for the seasonal unemployment are considered.

The twelve types of comparable labour office districts can be summarised into five types for strategic purposes. Since almost all labour office districts in East Germany belong to the first of these five strategic types, we use the finer classifications of three groups here. For West Germany we use the remaining four types for strategic purposes. Table 4.6 presents the classification which will be used in the following analysis, containing a short description of the clusters and the number of labour offices in each cluster. The first cluster (Ia) contains the five East German districts with the worst labour market condition. The situation is characterised by the highest underemployment, a population density below average and the slightest labour market dynamics. The 'typical' East German labour office districts are characterised by a high underemployment and minor labour market dynamics. These 23 office districts are pooled in cluster Ib. The five districts with the most promising labour market situation of East Germany belong to cluster Ic, even though the underemployment is still above average and the dynamics are only moderate here. Cluster II contains 21 labour office districts dominated by large cities. The regional labour market environment in these clusters can be described by an above average to high underemployment, a high population density, moderate labour market dynamics, a high number of welfare recipients and an above average tertiarisation of jobs. Except the labour office of Dresden, all districts in this cluster are in West Germany. The majority of West German labour office districts (63) belong to cluster III, which can be described by an average to above average underemployment, little labour market dynamics and a low population density. Additionally these districts have rural elements and mainly medium-sized industry. Cluster IV pools West German labour office districts with advantageous labour market prospects. These are ten big city districts with the highest labour market dynamics, an underemployment below average, a high tertiarisation of jobs, but also an above average number of welfare recipients. The last cluster (V) contains the 46 labour office districts with the best labour market situation. Underemployment and also the number of welfare recipients are the lowest in Germany.

Table 4.6: Classification of Labour Office Districts in Germany

Cluster	Description	Number of districts	Men	in %	Women	in %
Ia	East German labour office districts with worst labour market conditions	5	696	13.7	1,232	20.2
Ib	East German labour office districts with bad labour market conditions	23	1,829	36.1	3,234	53.1
Ic	East German labour office districts with high unemployment	5	324	6.4	490	8.1
II[1]	Labour office districts dominated by large cities	21	902	17.8	422	6.9
III	West German labour office districts with rural elements, medium-sized industry and average unemployment	63	820	16.2	418	6.9
IV	West German centers with good labour market prospects	10	184	3.6	81	1.3
V[2]	West German labour office districts with the best labour market prospects	47	309	6.1	210	3.5
Total Number of Participants			5,064	100 %	6,087	100%

Columns 4–7 header: Number of participants

[1] Labour office districts of Berlin belong to type II. Since we do not consider these districts in the empirical analysis, they are not enlisted here.
[2] Our dataset contains no information on participants in the labour office district of Donauwörth. Therefore, this district is excluded from the classification.

Table 4.6 also contains the number of participants in each cluster. It shows once again the disproportionate usage of JCS in East-Germany. Over 56% of the male and over 81% of the female participants are located in East-Germany. Predominantly in labour office districts from cluster Ib, which are characterised by a bad labour market situation, JCS are used. In West-Germany JCS are mainly used in labour office districts dominated by large cities (cluster II) and districts with rural elements, medium-sized industry and average unemployment (cluster III). In centers with good and best labour market conditions, the usage of JCS is very limited. The largest group of participants are women in East Germany with 5,035 observations followed by men in East Germany with 2,924 observations. Whereas more women than men participate in East Germany, the relation in West Germany is reverted. There we have 2,140 male and 1,052 female participants. The numbers also show that it will be possible to estimate the effect in specific sub-groups of the labour market, since we start with a large pool of observations. However, the discussion in chapters 5 and 6 will also make clear, that the number of observations in some of the sub-groups decreases rapidly (e.g. for women in West Germany). Hence, having access to a large group of participants is an invaluable asset to properly take into account effect heterogeneity in evaluation studies.

Outcome Variable

For the outcome variable we use information from the Employment Statistics Register ('Beschäftigtenstatistik', ESR), which includes information about the total population of all people who are registered in the social security system. These are all regular employed persons and participants of several ALMP programmes, but no self-employed or pensioners. To identify the spells of regular employment without further promotion, we complete the information on the outcome variable with the content of the final version of the MTG, since only regular employment is defined as a success. All kinds of subsidised employments or participations in ALMP are defined as a failure. We observe the labour market outcome for the treatment and comparison group until

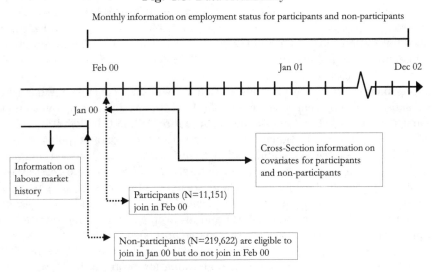

Fig. 4.3: Data Availability

December, 2002. Figure 4.3 summarises the structure of the data and its availability.

4.5 Outline of the Empirical Analysis

Having discussed the institutional setup of labour market policies in Germany in general and of JCS in particular brings us now to the actual evaluation analysis. In the following two chapters we will analyse the employment effects of JCS on the participating individuals. Other enacted purposes of JCS, like the relief of the stock of unemployed in regions with great imbalances of the labour market, are secondary only and will not be evaluated here. JCS have often been criticised because they lack explicit qualificational elements and might involve 'stigma effects'. Such 'stigma effects' arise if programmes are targeted at people with 'disadvantages' and a possible employer takes participation in such schemes as a negative signal concerning the expected productivity or motivation of participants. However, it can also be argued that they are a reasonable opportunity for individuals who are not able to re-integrate into the first labour market themselves or who do not fit the criteria for other programmes, e.g. long-term unemployed or other 'hard-to-place' individuals. The major goal of JCS is the (re-)integration of participants into regular unsubsidised employment. Our discussion in section 4.3 has shown that a broad evaluation of JCS has not been possible for a long time, since datasets have either not been available or been to small to draw policy relevant conclusions. However, with the introduction of the SGB III in 1998 things have changed and allow us now to use a very rich administrative dataset as described in section 4.4, containing all entries in JCS in February 2000 and a control group of non-participants who were eligible to participate in February 2000 but did not do so. This allows us to answer the policy relevant question, if unemployed individuals should join a JCS in February 2000 to enhance their employment prospects or not.

As mentioned in the previous section we will only consider regular (unsubsidised) employment as a success. All kinds of subsidised employments or participations in ALMP are defined as a failure. While this definition might conflict with the institutional setting, it reflects the economic point of view to measure the integration ability of JCS into regular (unsubsidised) employment. Since the dataset is an entry-dataset into JCS only, we restrict the analysis on the first participation and treat possible subsequent participations as an outcome of the first treatment. Given the available time period (three years after programme start) and an average programme duration of approximately one year, this is a reasonable approach.

Since we work with non-experimental data, we have to address possible selection bias and solve the fundamental evaluation problem. In chapter 1 we have outlined the potential outcome approach as a suitable framework for

4.5 Outline of the Empirical Analysis 125

such an analysis. Inference about the impact of JCS on the outcome of a participating individual involves speculation about how this individual would have performed had he not received JCS. Since we never observe the same individual at the same time with and without JCS, we have a counterfactual situation which has to be overcome. To do so, we have presented several different evaluation strategies that can be categorised according to their underlying identifying assumptions, i.e. selection on observables or unobservables. Due to the extensive set of available individual characteristics in our data in combination with information on the regional labour market situation, we believe that the conditional independence or unconfoundedness assumption (see section 1.5) can be justified and hence we will apply a matching estimator.

A major topic in the following two chapters will be the possible occurrence of effect heterogeneity. We have spend some time in the methodological chapters to show how different evaluation estimators deal with effect heterogeneity and it turned out, that the matching approach is a very flexible way to allow for heterogeneous treatment effects. Identifying potential sources of effect heterogeneity can help to improve programmes in the future. Throughout the analysis, effects will be estimated separately for men and women in West and East Germany, since previous empirical findings have emphasised the importance of this differentiation. Additionally, chapter 5 focusses on group-specific and regional differences in treatment effects. To account for group-specific influences we estimate the effects separately for specific sub-groups of the labour market, like long-term unemployed, individuals with placement restrictions and persons without work experience or professional degree. The discussion in 4.2.2 has also emphasised the importance of regional variation in the organisation of labour market policies. To account for regional differences in the effects we will estimate the effects in the different labour market clusters as defined in section 4.4. The emphasis of chapter 6 is different. Here, we will focus on programme specific differences like the sector in which the JCS is started (e.g. AGRICULTURE vs. OFFICE AND SERVICES), the provider (PUBLIC or NON-COMMERCIAL institutions) and the type of promotion (REGULAR and ENFORCED).

Taking chapters 5 and 6 together should allow us to draw a conclusive judgement of the employment effects of JCS for the participating individuals. We will try to use these conclusions to give some recommendations for the usage of JCS in the future.

5

Microeconometric Evaluation of Job Creation Schemes - Part I: Individual and Regional Heterogeneity

5.1 Introduction

In this chapter we evaluate the employment effects of JCS on the participating individuals in Germany. Given the very informative administrative dataset at hand described in section 4.4, we base the analysis on the conditional independence assumption. Basically, we presented in chapter 1 two approaches which use this assumption: matching and regression. Our decision to prefer matching is based on the discussion in subsection 1.5.4 where we have shown, that matching estimators have some favourable properties regarding common support issues and also provide a very flexible way to allow for heterogeneity in treatment effects. As outlined in section 4.5, we will focus in this chapter on individual (group-specific) and regional heterogeneity, whereas in the following chapter we will concentrate on programme (sectoral) heterogeneity. The importance of individual (group-specific), regional and sectoral heterogeneity for the evaluation of JCS in Germany has been well documented in previous empirical research. The studies of Caliendo, Hujer, and Thomsen (2003) and Hujer, Caliendo, and Thomsen (2004) examine the effects of JCS with respect to these three sources of heterogeneity and find large differences in the effects. Basically there are two shortcomings to these studies. The first one refers to the used outcome variable which allows only to monitor if the individual is registered unemployed or not. This is the same information used by the FEA to calculate the 'Verbleibsquote', but does not allow to draw conclusions about the re-integration success into regular (unsubsidised) employment. A second restriction relates to the relatively short observation period after programme start, namely two years. This chapter extends the previous analyses in four directions. First, we are able to evaluate the re-integration effects of JCS into regular (unsubsidised) employment. Second, we can monitor the employment status of participants and non-participants nearly three years after programme start. Third, we also test the sensitivity of the results with respect to various decisions which have to be made during the implementation of the matching estimator, like the choice of the matching algorithm or the estimation of the propensity scores. Finally, we also test if a possible occurrence of 'unobserved heterogeneity' or 'hidden bias' distorts interpretation of our results.

Previous empirical findings have shown that the effects of JCS differ with respect to region and gender. There are basically two ways to put greater emphasis on specific variables. One can either find variables in the comparison group who are identical with respect to these variables or carrying out matching on sub-populations (see subsection 3.2.1 for details). We choose the second approach and separate the analysis by these characteristics, i.e. we estimate the effects separately for men and women in West and East Germany. These four groups will be the 'main groups' of our analysis. Since it can certainly be assumed that the effects are not homogeneous for sub-populations of these main groups, we estimate group-specific effects, too. Thereby we will not only focus on groups defined by age and unemployment duration (as in Hujer, Caliendo, and Thomsen (2004)), but also on specific problem-groups with disadvantages on the labour market. To be specific, we estimate the effects for individuals without professional training or professional experience, with a high degree, with placement restrictions, for rehabilitation attendants and individuals with health restrictions.[1] This leaves us with eleven 'subgroups' for whom the effects are estimated separately. The situation on the regional labour market might be an additional source of effect heterogeneity. The effects of JCS might differ in regions with high underemployment when compared to prospering regions. To account for that, we additionally evaluate the programme effects with respect to regional differences by using the classification of similar and comparable labour office districts which has been described in section 4.4.

The remainder of this chapter is organised as follows. Since we have already presented the institutional background of ALMP in general and of JCS in specific in section 4.2, we will start with a presentation of the groups we want to analyse and show some selected descriptive statistics for them in section 5.2. The general framework for evaluation analysis has been discussed already in chapter 1, and in chapter 2 we have described matching estimators at length. Hence, section 5.3 of this chapter focusses on the actual implementation of the matching estimator. Since the number of covariates in our data makes the use of covariate matching unfeasible, we rely on propensity score matching. In particular we discuss the justification of the matching estimator (subsection 5.3.1), the estimation of the propensity scores (subsection 5.3.2) and the choice of the proper matching algorithm (subsection 5.3.3) for our situation. Section 5.3.4 deals with common support issues, whereas section

---

[1] Clearly, people with a high degree are not individuals with disadvantages on the labour market per se. Nonetheless, we estimate the effects for them, too, out of two reasons. First, they can be seen as the opposite of people without professional training. Second, it might be the case that those people who have a high degree and nevertheless participate in JCS are a special problem group.

5.3.5 discusses some quality indicators for the chosen matching algorithm. In section 5.4 we present the results for the main and sub-groups as well as for the regional clusters. Additionally we also test the sensitivity of our estimates with respect to unobserved heterogeneity. Section 5.5 concludes and gives some policy recommendations.

5.2 Groups of Analysis and Selected Descriptives

5.2.1 Groups of Analysis

The empirical analysis is based on a dataset merged from several administrative sources of the FEA and has been described already in section 4.4. It contains information on all participants who started a JCS in February 2000 and a group of individuals who were eligible for participation in January 2000, but did not enter those schemes in February 2000. Since all information (except the programme variables) originate from the same sources for participants and non-participants, the dataset provides a good basis for the construction of the comparison group. Our final sample consists of 11,151 participants and 219,622 non-participants. Previous empirical findings have shown that the effects of JCS differ with respect to region and gender. Thus, we separate our analysis by these aspects, i.e. we estimate the effects separately for men and women in West and East Germany, which are the four 'main groups' of our analysis. Table 5.1 shows that the largest groups are women (5,035) and men (2,924) in East Germany. In West Germany, 2,140 men and 1,052 women started a JCS in February 2000.

Due to the large number of observations in our sample, we are also able to analyse the programme effects for specific problem-groups of the labour market. We evaluate the effects separately for three age categories (younger than 25 years, between 25 and 50 years, and older than 50 years) and for different unemployment durations (up to 13 weeks, between 13 and 52 weeks, and for more than 52 weeks), as well as for persons without work experience, without professional training and for the counterfactual group of persons with a high educational degree (college and university graduates). Furthermore, we analyse the effects for rehabilitation attendants, and for individuals for whom the caseworkers have noted placement restraints due to health restrictions. In total we get eleven 'sub-groups' for whom the effects will be estimated separately in both regions and for both gender. Table 5.1 contains the observations in these groups, differentiated by participation status. What can be seen as most important is that nearly all groups contain a reasonable number of participants (> 100), allowing a proper estimation and interpretation of the effects. We exclude any groups with less than 100 observations from the analysis.

Table 5.1: Number of Observations in Main and Sub-Groups

	West Germany				East Germany[1]			
	Men		Women		Men		Women	
Groups	Part.	Non-Part.	Part.	Non-Part.	Part.	Non-Part.	Part.	Non-Part.
Total (Main group)	2,140	44,095	1,052	34,227	2,924	64,788	5,035	76,512
Age (in years)								
<25 years	458	4,102	182	2,443	240	8,743	148	4,864
25-50 years	1,337	23,560	709	19,732	1571	35,927	3,342	44,329
>50 years	345	16,433	161	12,052	1,113	20,118	1,545	27,319
Unemployment duration (in weeks)								
<13 weeks	558	12,198	237	7561	578	22,003	575	12,447
13-52 weeks	744	13,909	403	12,235	1,248	22,864	1,970	26,657
>52 weeks	838	17,988	412	14,431	1,098	19,921	2,490	37,408
Without professional experience	273	3,281	159	2,548	293	7,023	498	7945
Without professional training	1,340	21,659	476	17,093	837	14,966	1,121	19,776
With high degree	112	1,486	146	1,165	146	2,682	191	1,619
Rehabilitation attendant	111	2,763	44	1,063	218	4,849	156	3,520
With placement restrictions	354	9,516	148	5,993	394	10,470	376	9,121

[1] Observations from the labour office districts of Berlin are excluded.

Our discussion in section 4.2.2 has emphasised the importance of regional variation in the administration of programmes. We have shown that different labour market situations provoke very different policy strategies. To account for that, we will evaluate the programme effects with respect to regional differences, too, using the classification of similar and comparable labour office districts of the FEA as described in section 4.4 and table 4.6. We have seen that the largest number of observations can be found in cluster Ib, where 53.1% of all female and 36.1% of all male participants are located. The smallest number of participants is found in cluster IV, where only 3.6% of the male and 1.3% of the female participants can be found. We have discussed already that the twelve types of comparable labour office districts can be summarised into five types for strategic purposes. Since almost all labour office districts in East Germany belong to the first of these five strategic types, we use the finer classifications of three groups here. For West Germany we use the remaining four types for strategic purposes. This leaves us with seven clusters (Ia, Ib, Ic, II, III, IV, V) for which the effects will be estimated separately.

In the following two subsections we will discuss some selected descriptives for the 'main groups' and the participants in the regional clusters and will compare them with the characteristics for the relevant non-participants.

5.2.2 Selected Descriptives for the Four Main Groups

Table B.1 in the appendix shows selected descriptive statistics for the 'main groups', i.e. differentiated for men and women in West and East Germany and with respect to participation status. The variables are measured at the begin of the programme in February 2000. Whereas the numbers from table 5.1 have shown that more individuals participate in East Germany, the individual attributes show regional differences, too. In the following, we will describe the most important ones.

First of all, participants in West Germany are on average younger than non-participants. While participating men in West Germany are on average 37.2 years old at programme begin, the non-participants are on average 43.2 years old. The same proportion holds for women in West Germany, where the participants are 37.8 years and the non-participants 43.3 years. In contrast to that, participating men in East Germany are older (44.5 years vs. 41.7 years) than non-participants, whereas participating women in East Germany are approximately the same age (44 years) as their respective counterparts in the comparison group.

More explicit differences between participants and non-participants can be found in the number of (unsuccessful) placement propositions, which is much higher for participants in all groups. This can be seen as an indicator for a more problematic placement process of the participants. Participating men (women) in West Germany have on average 7.7 (6.9) placement propositions, whereas the corresponding number in the group of non-participants is only 3.6 (3.0). In East Germany we get a similar picture, where participating men (women) have on average 6.1 (5.4) placement propositions, whereas non-participating men (women) have 3.0 (2.8). However, concluding from these figures that allocation of individuals to JCS is target-oriented to specific problem groups of the labour market, is not straightforward. This becomes clear when looking at the variable placement restrictions. It indicates the reduced placement opportunities due to individual health restrictions noted by the local placement officers. It reflects the caseworker's assessment of the individual's situation and is often used to identify the need of an individual for further assistance. It is quite interesting to note, that the share of people with placement restrictions is higher in the group of non-participants independently of region and gender. Additionally, individuals in the treatment group have in general fewer health restrictions, which complements the above statement.

No large differences can be detected with respect to aspects like last contact to the job center, share of rehabilitation attendants and number of children. An interesting feature concerns the marital status. In East Germany married individuals are over-represented in the treatment group (Men: 54% vs. 48%, Women: 68% vs. 64%), whereas the situation in West Germany shows that only 35% (40%) of the participating males (females) are married. In the comparison group 52% of all males and 63% of all females are married.

Another interesting difference between East and West Germany becomes obvious regarding the qualification variables. In the Western part the majority of participants does not have a completed professional training (62% of the men, 45% of the women), whereas the numbers in East Germany are much lower. In East Germany only around 28% (22%) of the participating men (women) do not have a completed professional training. Within the regions and gender, no large differences emerge between participants and non-participants. One exception are men in West Germany, where the share of non-participants without professional training lies around 49% and is much lower compared to the share of participants. With respect to work experience, no significant differences can be found between participants and non-participants in East Germany - the share of people with work experience is around 90% - whereas in West Germany participating men (87%) and women (85%) have on average less work experience compared to their counterparts in the comparison group (men and women: 93%). Clearly, both points (qualification and work experience) have to be seen in conjunction with the age of participants which is lower in West Germany. Turning back to table 5.1 shows, that the share of participants below 25 years is 21.4% (17.3%) for men (women) in West Germany and only 8.2% (2.9%) for men (women) in East Germany. This may indicate a different purpose of JCS in both regions, where JCS are more target-oriented (e.g. for young unemployed without professional training) in West-Germany and also used to relief the tense situation on the labour market in East Germany. We will come back to that point in the next subsection when we discuss the situation in the regional clusters. Before we do so, let us briefly discuss the occupational group and the unemployment duration of individuals. It is quite interesting to see that there are nearly no differences between participants and non-participants in East Germany regarding their occupational group. Whereas women in East Germany come predominantly from service professions (68.6% of the participants and 70.3% of the non-participants), men have been mainly employed in manufacturing (52.4% / 52.8%). In West Germany the relations are more unbalanced. 52.1% of the participating men come from manufacturing, but only 47.7% of the non-participating men do so. Additionally, 79.6% of the female participants come from service professions and the corresponding share in the comparison groups is only 71.2%. The unemployment duration of individuals shows that the share of short-term unemployed individuals (less than 13 weeks) is rather high and equally distributed between participants and non-participants in West Germany. 26.1% (22.5%) of all male (female) participants are short-term unemployed, whereas in East Germany only 19.8% of the male and 11.4% of the female participants are unemployed less than 13 weeks. The share of long-term unemployed individuals (more than 52 weeks) is highest for participating women in East Germany with nearly 50%, even though also nearly 40% of the participants in West Germany are long-term unemployed, too.

5.2.3 Selected Descriptives for the Regional Clusters

As mentioned above we differentiate our analysis between seven regional clusters, which have been described in section 4.4. Tables B.2 (cluster Ia, Ib and Ic) and B.3 (cluster II-V) in appendix B present selected descriptives for participants and non-participants in these clusters. Starting with the results for the clusters in East Germany, some findings should be noted. First of all, it is quite interesting to note that the number of placement propositions varies considerably between the clusters. For example, participating men in cluster Ia (worst labour market conditions in East Germany) have on average 5.1 placement propositions, whereas participating men in cluster Ic (best labour market conditions in East Germany) have on average 7.2 propositions. For women in these clusters the same tendency emerges with 4.8 placement propositions in cluster Ia and 6.3 propositions in cluster Ic. Additionally, it becomes obvious that independently of gender, in districts with a bad labour market environment the average programme duration is longer than in districts with a better environment. Men and women in districts of cluster Ia remain in programmes on average for 336.4 and 345.2 days, whereas they remain only 295.2 and 304.9 day in cluster Ic. Considering the shares of participants without professional training shows, that in a better labour market environment a higher share of participants belong to this group. Taken together, this may be seen as an indication for different purposes in the implementation of programmes. In labour office districts, where the labour market has only the slightest dynamics and is also characterised by high underemployment, JCS are used to relieve this tense labour market situation. In regions with more dynamics, allocation to JCS is more likely to follow the postulations from the law and hence is more target-oriented to specific problem groups of the labour market. Turning to the results for clusters II to V in table B.3 shows that this finding does not hold for participants in the primarily West German districts. Here, the share of persons without professional training is higher in districts with worse opportunities. However, this may be caused by the fact that in regions with better labour market conditions and consequently lower unemployment other programmes (e.g. vocational training) are offered. Therefore, the share of participants without professional training is lower in those districts. Additionally, for cluster II to V it can also be seen that the share of short-term unemployed persons increases with the situation on the labour market. Whereas in cluster II approximately 22% (19%) of the participating and non-participating men (women) are short-term unemployed, the share of short-term unemployed in cluster V ranges from 24.8% (participating women) to nearly 40% (non-participating men). A last point to mention are the findings for persons without participation in ALMP programmes before the last unemployment. While the figures remain relatively constant for clusters II to V, we find a decreasing figure for cluster Ia to Ic. This indicates that especially in East Germany a repeated participation is more likely in districts with a better labour market situation. This corresponds to the expectation that there are more funds available for a smaller number of potential recipients.

5.3 Implementation of the Matching Estimator

Our discussion in chapter 1 and especially in section 1.6 has made clear, that there is no 'one' evaluation approach which should be preferred whenever using non-experimental data. As Smith (2004) notes, matching methods make no sense without rich data, IV methods make no sense without a good instrument and longitudinal methods make no sense when selection into treatment depends on transitory rather than permanent shocks. The different strategies invoke different identifying assumptions and when those assumptions hold, a given estimator will provide consistent estimates of certain parameters of interest (Smith, 2004). Therefore, every evaluation task requires a careful consideration of the available data. The matching estimator we like to apply is based on the CIA. Hence, we start the discussion with the plausibility of the CIA in our context. Once the decision to use matching is made, one also has to decide between covariate matching and propensity score matching. Since the number of covariates in the data makes the use of covariate matching unfeasible, we rely on propensity score matching. After having decided to use PSM, we are confronted with a lot of questions regarding its implementation (see the discussion in chapter 3 and especially section 3.2). We will consider the correct model and the choice of variables for the participation probability in subsection 5.3.2. Following that, we choose one matching algorithm to be used in the further analysis in subsection 5.3.3. Subsections 5.3.4 and 5.3.5 will be concerned with common support and matching quality issues.

5.3.1 Plausibility of CIA

Before starting with the estimation of the propensity scores, we have to consider briefly the plausibility of the CIA in our context. As already noted, for the CIA to be fulfilled we need to condition on all variables that jointly influence the participation decision and the outcome variable. The available dataset, described in section 4.4, contains a rich set of variables, which can be classified in four categories. The socio-demographic variables include age, marital status, number of children, nationality and health restrictions. The second category consists of qualification variables including professional training, occupational group, professional rank and work experience. In the third category we summarise career variables like duration of last employment and unemployment, number of placement propositions, last contact to job center, rehabilitation attendance, placement restrictions and previous labour market programmes. This category is most important since previous empirical studies have emphasised the importance of the labour market history. Finally, to take account of the regional labour market situation, the fourth category contains the regional clusters as described in table 4.6 in section 4.4. Additionally, all attributes in the analysis for the comparison as well as for the treatment group originate from the same datasets[2] and are measured at the same point in time. Given this informative dataset, we argue henceforth that the CIA can be justified in our case. To test the sensitivity of our estimates to this assumption, we present a bounding analysis in subsection 5.4.4, which is based on the discussion in section 3.3.

5.3.2 Estimating the Propensity Score

When estimating the propensity score, two choices have to be made. The first one concerns the model to be used for the estimation, and the second one the variables to be included in this model. We have presented an extensive discussion of these issues in subsection 3.2.1. As we face a binary decision (participation vs. non-participation), the choice of the model is less important, since logit and probit models usually yield similar results. However, we will use the logit model for estimation since the underlying distribution has more density mass in the probability bounds and reflects our data situation better.[3]

More advice is available regarding the inclusion (or exclusion) of covariates in the propensity score model. Only variables that simultaneously influence the participation decision and the outcome variable should be included. Hence, economic theory, a sound knowledge of previous research and also information about the institutional settings should guide the researcher in building up the model (see e.g. Smith and Todd (2005) or Sianesi (2004)). The accumulated evidence in the evaluation literature points out that the labour market history of individuals and the regional labour market environment are crucial variables to be included in the estimation (Heckman, LaLonde, and Smith, 1999). In cases of uncertainty of the proper specification, the question might arise if it is better to include too many rather than too few variables. We have presented both reasons for and against including all covariates available. To help choosing the relevant variables we have also presented some formal tests like the 'hit or miss' method and the pseudo-R^2. With the 'hit or miss' method or prediction rate metric (suggested by Heckman, Ichimura, Smith, and Todd (1998) and Heckman and Smith (1999)), variables are chosen to maximise the within-sample correct prediction rates.[4] The pseudo-R^2 indicates how well the regressors X explain the participation probability.

---

[2] Clearly, one exception is the programme information (provider, type of promotion, sector) which is available only for participants.

[3] This will get clear very soon when we present the propensity score distributions for participants and non-participants and discuss common support issues in section 5.3.4.

[4] As discussed in section 3.2.1 this method classifies an observation as '1' if the estimated propensity score is larger than the sample proportion of persons taking

Table 5.2: Hit-Rates and Pseudo-R^2 for Different Propensity Score Specifications [1]

Specification (Sets of Variables included)				West Germany				East Germany			
				Men		Women		Men		Women	
Socio-Demogr.[2]	Qualifica-tion[3]	Career[4]	Region[5]	Hit-Rate	R^2	Hit-Rate	R^2	Hit-Rate	R^2	Hit-Rate	R^2
x				55.20	0.036	64.51	0.050	44.46	0.014	54.47	0.019
	x			61.03	0.033	76.19	0.036	59.10	0.014	67.29	0.013
		x		73.21	0.106	79.45	0.130	76.64	0.106	72.70	0.097
			x	54.00	0.000	81.67	0.001	63.69	0.000	73.95	0.000
x	x			62.60	0.062	67.29	0.076	58.12	0.030	55.18	0.030
x		x		68.81	0.122	73.03	0.153	74.56	0.116	72.20	0.105
x			x	55.21	0.036	65.31	0.051	45.64	0.014	54.11	0.019
	x	x		69.74	0.123	78.09	0.153	75.36	0.110	72.61	0.106
	x		x	61.40	0.033	74.63	0.037	55.98	0.014	67.60	0.013
		x	x	72.62	0.106	77.01	0.133	76.26	0.106	72.81	0.098
x	x	x		70.65	0.138	75.53	0.174	74.28	0.122	72.18	0.113
x	x		x	62.61	0.062	67.26	0.077	57.94	0.030	55.28	0.030
x		x	x	68.97	0.123	73.23	0.157	74.51	0.117	72.12	0.106
	x	x	x	69.99	0.124	77.51	0.156	75.12	0.111	72.69	0.107
x	x	x	x	70.60	0.139	75.70	0.177	74.20	0.122	72.24	0.114

[1] *Hit-rates* are computed in the following way: If the estimated propensity score is larger than the sample proportion of persons taking treatment, i.e. $\hat{P}(X) > \overline{P}$, observations are classified as '1'. If $\hat{P}(X) \leq \overline{P}$ observations are classified as '0'.
[2] *Socio-demographic variables* include age, age^2, marital status, number of children, nationality (german=1) and health restrictions.
[3] *Qualification variables* include professional training, occupational group, professional rank and work experience.
[4] *Career variables* include duration of last employment and unemployment, number of placement propositions, last contact to job center, rehabilitation attendants, placement restrictions and previous labour market programmes.
[5] *Regional variables* consist of the seven clusters defined by the FEA and discussed in 5.2.3.

We have estimated both statistics for several propensity score specifications. We have started with base specifications, containing only the variables of one of the four above mentioned categories. Using this as a starting point, we added another category of variables. The results can be found in table 5.2. To give an example, the first line of table 5.2 shows the results for a model specification where only the socio-demographic variables are included. The results in line 5 are for a model with socio-demographic and qualificational variables. Testing all possible combinations of two and three categories and finally using all information gives us 15 specifications for the four main groups. One shortcoming of such statistical tests becomes obvious from the results. If we take for example the results for women in West Germany we see that the best hit-rate (81.7%) is achieved by only including the regional dummy variables. With the full specification we achieve only a hit-rate of 75.7%. Following that rule would mean that we should estimate the propensity score solely based on the model with regional dummy variables. This makes no economic sense since obviously important characteristics, e.g. age and qualification variables, would be excluded. It has to be kept in mind that the main purpose of the propensity score estimation is not to predict selection into treatment as well as possible but to balance all covariates (Augurzky and Schmidt, 2000b). The Pseudo-R^2 shows that the full specification does the best job in explaining the participation probability. For the other three groups the findings are similar. The full specification does the best job in terms of R^2. However, even though the hit-rates are above 70% for the full specification, there are some specifications with higher hit-rates.

Considering these findings and bearing in mind that we see no economic reasons for excluding sets of variables, we use the full specification for the estimation of the propensity scores. Table B.4 in the appendix contains the results of the propensity score estimation which will be used in the following. Looking at table B.4 clarifies that the influence of variables on the participation probability differs by regions and gender. The coefficients of the socio-demographic variables show that the participation probability of men in West Germany decreases with age, while in East Germany older men and women are more likely to participate. This indicates once again the slightly different purpose of the programmes in East and West Germany. Especially in East Germany, JCS function as a relief for the labour market and are used as a bridge to retirement. Furthermore, it has to be noted that persons of German nationality are more likely to participate than foreigners. This may be due to the fact that other measures of ALMP (e.g. language courses) are preferred for foreigners. The influence of marital status is also different in both parts. While in West Germany married persons are less likely to participate, in East Germany they are more likely to do so. Responsible for this difference might be

---

treatment, i.e. $\hat{P}(X) > \overline{P}$, and else as '0'. It maximises the overall classification rate for the sample assuming that the costs for the misclassification are equal for the two groups (Heckman, Ichimura, and Todd, 1997).

the labour market environment. If both spouses are unemployed, assignment of one partner may be more likely than for singles. Health restrictions also increase the individual participation probability independently of the region which indicates an allocation according to the definitions by law.

The coefficients for the qualification characteristics emphasise gender specific differences in the allocation. A higher qualification (compared to the reference category 'without completed professional training and common-school exam') increases the participation probability for women in both parts, while the effects for men are insignificant or negative. It can be assumed that it is for unemployed women with higher qualification harder than for higher qualified unemployed men to end their unemployment and so they are more likely to participate in JCS. Previous work experience reduces the participation probability for all groups. This was expected, since work experience is generally an important criterion for placement into regular employment. As unemployment duration is an eligibility criterion for participation, its influence is of major importance. We included unemployment duration in three categories (up to 13 weeks, between 13 weeks and one year, and more than one year). The participation probability increases with unemployment duration. The number of (unsuccessful) placement propositions is an indicator for bad labour market opportunities. A higher number of placement propositions corresponds to a higher participation probability, which indicates that allocation is done according to the law. A last interesting point to note is that placement restrictions annotated by the caseworker harm the participation probability. This is somewhat surprising, because JCS should also be offered to these groups. The coefficients for the regional context are in reference to the labour office districts with the best (in relation to the region) labour market environment. The coefficients are not significant for women in East Germany. For men in East Germany we find a significant negative effect for individuals from clusters Ib and Ic. Living in labour office districts belonging to cluster II, III and IV (II, III) reduces the participation probability for women (men) in West Germany (compared to cluster V). We will use the estimated propensity scores in the following to implement the matching estimator.

5.3.3 Choosing the Matching Algorithm

After having specified the propensity score model, the next choice to be made concerns the matching algorithm to be used. We have presented several different matching algorithms in section 2.3. Hence, we will not discuss them here any further. Clearly, all approaches should yield asymptotically the same results, because with growing sample size all of them become closer to comparing only exact matches (Smith, 2000a). However, in small samples the choice of the matching approach can be important (Heckman, Ichimura, and Todd, 1997). Usually a trade-off between bias and variance arises. First, one has to decide on how many non-treated individuals to match to a single treated individual. Nearest-neighbour (NN) matching only uses the participant and his closest neighbour. Therefore it minimises the bias but might also involve an efficiency loss, since a large number of close neigbours is disregarded. Kernel-based matching on the other hand uses more non-participants for each participant, thereby reducing the variance but possibly increasing the bias. Finally, using the same non-treated individual more than once (NN matching with replacement) can possibly improve the matching quality, but increases the variance. We do not use kernel matching here out of two interrelated reasons. First, the control group is extremely large (up to thirty times larger than the various treatment groups) making a use of all non-participants questionable (since large proportions of the non-participants will not be comparable to the participants). Second and more importantly, the computing time would be too high, as we use bootstrapping methods to estimate the standard errors. However, to see if the inclusion of more comparison units for the construction of the counterfactual outcome has influence on the estimated effects, we also use 'oversampling' methods. This form of matching involves a trade-off between variance and bias, too. It trades reduced variance, resulting from using more information to construct the counterfactual for each participant, with increased bias that results from on average poorer matches (Smith and Todd, 2005).

This brief discussion makes clear that even with NN matching several alternatives emerge. It seems reasonable to try a number of approaches and test the sensitivity of the results with respect to the algorithm choice. If they give similar results, the choice may be unimportant. Else, if the results differ, further investigation may be needed in order to reveal more about the source of the disparity (Bryson, Dorsett, and Purdon, 2002). We implement eleven matching algorithms, including NN matching without replacement (without caliper and with calipers of 0.01, 0.02 and 0.05) and NN matching with replacement with the same calipers. To see if the estimates differ when more neighbours are included, we additionally implement oversampling with 2, 5 and 10 nearest neighbours.[5]

Table 5.3 contains the results separately for the main groups for the last month of the observation period. Bold letters indicate significance at the 1%-level, italic letters refer to the 5%-level, standard errors are bootstrapped with 50 replications. The estimates illustrate two points: First of all, the results are not sensitive to the chosen matching algorithm. For men in West Germany the effects are insignificant and centered around zero. For men in East Germany the significant effects vary between -2.37% (5-NN-Matching) and -2.94% (NN with replacement). This means that the employment rate of men in East Germany, who started their JCS in February 2000, is in December 2002 on average between 2.37% and 2.94% lower when compared to matched non-participants. We will give an extensive interpretation of the results in the next section and

---

[5] We use the Stata module PSMATCH2 by Leuven and Sianesi (2003) for the estimation.

Table 5.3: The Effects in the Main Groups for Different Matching Algorithms[1,2]

West Germany	Men			Women		
Matching Algorithm	Effect	S.E.	Obs.[3]	Effect	S.E.	Obs.[3]
NN without replacement	-0.0005	0.0108	2,132	**0.0554**	0.0200	1,028
caliper 0.01	-0.0028	0.0137	2,119	*0.0451*	0.0213	975
caliper 0.02	-0.0019	0.0158	2,123	0.0459	0.0258	980
caliper 0.05	-0.0009	0.0128	2,131	*0.0479*	0.0223	1,002
NN with replacement	0.0061	0.0110	2,140	*0.0504*	0.0231	1,052
caliper 0.01	0.0042	0.0139	2,132	*0.0504*	0.0233	1,051
caliper 0.02	0.0056	0.0150	2,139	*0.0504*	0.0211	1,052
caliper 0.05	0.0061	0.0133	2,140	*0.0504*	0.0207	1,052
Oversampling						
2 NN	0.0023	0.0140	2,140	*0.0466*	0.0221	1,052
5 NN	0.0011	0.0106	2,140	**0.0529**	0.0161	1,052
10 NN	-0.0003	0.0100	2,140	**0.0610**	0.0180	1,052
East Germany	**Men**			**Women**		
Matching Algorithm	Effect	S.E.	Obs.[3]	Effect	S.E.	Obs.[3]
NN without replacement	**-0.0291**	0.0080	2,924	*-0.0135*	0.0075	5,032
caliper 0.01	**-0.0289**	0.0085	2,908	*-0.0137*	0.0070	5,026
caliper 0.02	**-0.0287**	0.0088	2,923	*-0.0135*	0.0064	5,027
caliper 0.05	**-0.0291**	0.0101	2,924	-0.0135	0.0076	5,027
NN with replacement	**-0.0294**	0.0112	2,924	**-0.0193**	0.0063	5,035
caliper 0.01	**-0.0294**	0.0086	2,924	**-0.0191**	0.0069	5,031
caliper 0.02	**-0.0294**	0.0092	2,924	**-0.0193**	0.0075	5,032
caliper 0.05	**-0.0294**	0.0105	2,924	*-0.0193*	0.0081	5,034
Oversampling						
2 NN	**-0.0250**	0.0090	2,924	-0.0128	0.0073	5,035
5 NN	**-0.0237**	0.0065	2,924	-0.0101	0.0055	5,035
10 NN	**-0.0249**	0.0076	2,924	**-0.0106**	0.0038	5,035

Bold letters indicate significance at the 1%-level, *italic* letters refer to the 5%-level. Standard errors are bootstrapped with 50 replications.
[1] Nearest Neighbour (NN) matching without replacement uses each non-participant only once, whereas with NN matching with replacement each non-participant can be used repeatedly. Caliper defines the maximal allowed difference in the propensity score of participants and matched non-participants.
[2] Matching is implemented with the Stata module PSMATCH2 by Leuven and Sianesi (2003).
[3] Obs. is the number of participants after matching.

restrict the discussion here to sensitivity issues. The significant effects for females in East Germany vary between -1.06% (10 NN) and -1.93% (NN with replacement). The only group for whom a somewhat higher variation in the effects is detected are women in West Germany, where the lowest estimated effect is 4.51% (NN without replacement and without caliper) and the highest estimated effect is 6.1% (10 NN). The second point to note is that the standard errors are (as expected) in general lower for the oversampling algorithms, even though the differences here are not very pronounced. Hence, the choice of the matching algorithm seems not to be a critical issue in our case, as the results show that the estimates are not sensitive to the algorithm choice. The improvement which comes from oversampling methods in terms of reduced variance is limited only. Hence, we decide to use NN matching for the further analysis. Since we have a very large sample of non-participants, the probability of finding good matches without using replacement is quite high. Therefore, to avoid an unnecessary inflation of the variance, we match without replacement. Finally, to ensure a good matching quality, we implement a caliper of 0.02. This is mostly driven by the finding for women in West Germany, where imposing this caliper reduces the number of treated observations by approximately 4.6% of the sample. In turn, this means that if we did not impose this caliper, the distance in the propensity scores would be higher than 0.02 for 4.6%. For the other groups, imposing the caliper does not have much influence. Henceforth, we use NN matching without replacement and a caliper of 0.02 for the analysis.

5.3.4 Common Support

Before assessing the matching quality, it is important to check the overlap or common support region for participants and non-participants. The most straightforward way is a visual analysis of the density distribution of the propensity score in both groups. The results can be found in figures B.1 to B.4 in appendix B. The left hand side of each graph shows the propensity score distribution for the non-participants, the right hand side refers to the participants in each group. Taking for instance the results for men in West Germany (figure B.1), it can be seen that the distribution for non-participants is highly skewed to the left in nearly all of the sub-groups. Problems arise, when the distributions in both groups do not overlap. A good example are short-term unemployed men in West Germany, where quite a large amount of observations in the treatment group has a propensity score over 0.5 and nearly none of the comparison individuals can be found in this region.

There are several ways of imposing the common support condition, e.g. by 'minima and maxima comparison' or 'trimming', and we presented them in subsection 3.2.3. We impose the 'minima and maxima condition' and additionally implement NN matching with a caliper of 0.02. As mentioned above, this implies that comparison individuals are only matched if their propensity score does not differ from the propensity score of the treated individuals by more than 0.02. Treated individuals who fall outside the common support region have to be disregarded and for these individuals the treatment effect cannot be estimated. Bryson, Dorsett, and Purdon (2002) note that if the proportion of lost individuals is small, this poses few problems. However, if the number is too large, there may be concerns whether the estimated effect on the remaining individuals can be viewed as representative.

Table 5.4: Number of Treated Individuals Lost Due to Common Support Requirement[1,2]

West Germany	Men			Women		
	Before Matching	After	Lost in %	Before Matching	After	Lost in %
Total	2140	2123	0.79	1052	980	6.84
Age (in years)						
<25	458	434	5.24	182	162	10.99
25-50	1337	1328	0.67	709	663	6.49
>50	345	344	0.29	161	150	6.83
Duration of unemployment						
< 13 weeks	558	440	21.15	237	189	20.25
13-52 weeks	744	720	3.23	403	365	9.43
> 52 weeks	838	835	0.36	412	400	2.91
Without professional experience	273	247	9.52	159	128	19.50
Without professional training	1340	1296	3.28	476	447	6.09
With high degree	112	96	14.29	146	120	17.81
Rehabilitation attendant	111	100	9.91	44	35	20.45
With placement restrictions	354	326	7.91	148	117	20.95
East Germany	**Men**			**Women**		
	Before Matching	After	Lost in %	Before Matching	After	Lost in %
Total	2924	2923	0.03	5035	5027	0.16
Age (in years)						
<25	240	229	4.58	148	144	2.70
25-50	1571	1570	0.06	3342	3335	0.21
>50	1113	1074	3.50	1545	1481	4.14
Duration of unemployment						
< 13 weeks	578	467	19.20	575	431	25.04
13-52 weeks	1248	1230	1.44	1970	1963	0.36
> 52 weeks	1098	1098	0.00	2490	2490	0.00
Without professional experience	293	289	1.37	498	489	1.81
Without professional training	837	835	0.24	1121	1116	0.45
With high degree	146	136	6.85	191	164	14.14
Rehabilitation attendant	218	215	1.38	156	148	5.13
With placement restrictions	394	371	5.84	376	362	3.72

[1] We used the minima-maxima restriction as common support condition.
[2] Results refer to a NN matching without replacement and a caliper of 0.02.

Table 5.4 contains the number of treated individuals lost in each of the sub-groups. It can be seen that the number of lost individuals is fairly low for three of the main groups. For men in West Germany we lose 0.79% of the observations, for men (0.03%) and women (0.16%) in East Germany the proportion is even smaller. However, for women in West Germany we cannot find similar non-participants for around 6.84% of the treated population and have to discard these individuals. Figure B.2 makes very clear that the overlap between participating and non-participating women in West Germany is fairly limited in the sub-groups, too. As a consequence, we there lose up to 20.95% of the treated population (for women with placement restrictions). Hence, the interpretation of the effects has to take this into account.

For the rest of the sub-groups the share of lost individuals is acceptable. However, two sub-groups are problematic for both gender and regions. The first is the group of short-term unemployed persons (less than 13 weeks unemployed). For this specific sub-group we lose 21.15% of the participating men in West Germany, 19.20% of men and 25.04% of women in East Germany. This means that we are not able to find short-term unemployed individuals in the comparison group that have similar propensity scores as the treated individuals. For women in East Germany this gets very clear when looking at figure B.4 for the short-term unemployed. Whereas the density of observations for the non-participants is very low above 0.2, participants can be found even at scores close to 1. As already said, this is a common finding for short-term unemployed persons and can also be found for individuals with high degree. For this sub-group the share of lost individuals is 6.85% (14.14%) for men (women) in East Germany and 14.29% (17.81%) for men (women) in West Germany. Hence, the interpretation of the results for these sub-groups has to be made carefully. Overall, we note that the share of lost individuals is rather small in East Germany, higher for men in West Germany and highest for women in West Germany.

5.3.5 Matching Quality

Since we do not condition on all covariates but on the propensity score, we have to check the ability of the matching procedure to balance the relevant covariates. We do so by comparing the absolute bias between the respective participating and non-participating groups before and after matching took place. One suitable indicator to assess the distance in the marginal distributions of the X-variables is the standardised bias (SB) suggested by Rosenbaum and Rubin (1985b) and described in subsection 3.2.2.

Matching Quality for the Main Groups

To abbreviate the documentation, we calculated the means of the SB before and after matching for the four main groups (Table 5.5) as an unweighted average of all variables (mean standardised bias, MSB). The results for each variable can be found in table B.5 in appendix B. The overall bias before matching lies between 10.9% for women in East Germany and 15.36% for women in West Germany. A significant reduction can be achieved for all groups so that the bias after matching is 2.5% (3.1%) for men (women) in West Germany and 1.8% (1.6%) for men (women) in East Germany. Clearly, this is an enormous reduction and shows that the matching procedure is able to balance the characteristics in the treatment and the matched control group.[6]

Table 5.5: Some Quality Indicators

	West Germany		East Germany	
	Men	Women	Men	Women
Before Matching				
Pseudo R^2	0.1389	0.1775	0.1225	0.1144
F-Test[1]	2,406.8	1,679.4	2,951.3	4,323.3
Mean of standardised bias[2]	14.62	16.08	12.01	10.83
After Matching				
Pseudo-R^2	0.006	0.009	0.004	0.003
F-Test[1]	38.0	23.4	35.3	39.2
Mean of standardised bias[2]	2.51	3.20	1.78	1.60

[1] Degrees of freedom for the F-Test: 41 for men and 40 for women.
[2] Mean standardised bias has been calculated as an unweighted average of all covariates.

Additionally Sianesi (2004) suggests to re-estimate the propensity score on the matched sample (i.e. on participants and matched non-participants) and compare the pseudo-R^2's before and after matching. After matching there should be no systematic differences in the distribution of the covariates between both groups. Therefore, the pseudo-R^2 after matching should be fairly low. As the results from Table 5.5 show, this is true for our estimation. The results of the F-tests (with degrees of freedom in brackets) point in the same direction, indicating a joint significance of all regressors before, but not after matching.

---

[6] Looking at the results in more detail (table B.5) also shows that the matching procedure increases the bias for a few variables. These are in particular categorial dummy variables. A good example is the variable 'professional training' of men in West Germany. The bias before matching for the category 'technical school' has been 1.1% and increases after matching to 2.8%. This increase has to be seen in relation to the high decrease in the other categories of this variable, e.g. the bias for 'industrial training' drops from 31.27% to 0.52%. Hence, it is of less importance. There are also two non-categorial variables for which the matching increases the bias: the bias of 'age' for women in East Germany is increased from 1.4% to 2.5% and the bias for 'rehabilitation attendant' for men in East Germany increases from 0.1% to 0.8%. Since the bias after matching is still fairly low, this is of minor importance, too.

5.3 Implementation of the Matching Estimator 145

Matching Quality for the Sub-Groups and the Regions

Now that we have shown that the matching procedure is able to balance the distribution of the covariates between treated and comparison individuals in the main groups, we have to test this for the sub-groups and the regions, too.

Table 5.6 contains the results for the eleven sub-groups. The first column in the table refers to the MSB before matching and the second column shows the MSB after matching, when matching is done with the estimated 'overall' propensity score as shown in table B.4. This propensity score specification, which we label P_1, has been done separately for the four main groups. However, it is very clear that the matching procedure based on the overall scores is not able to balance the covariates between treated and matched non-treated individuals in the sub-groups. For example, the bias after matching for men in West Germany reaches a level of 13.23% for rehabilitation attendants. Even though this is a reduction compared to the MSB before matching, it is not acceptable. For women in West Germany in this group the bias after matching is 18.69%. In East Germany the bias after matching is not much lower, reaching levels of 13.11% for young men and 15.11% for young women. Even though there are some sub-groups for which the bias is acceptable, the overall matching quality in the sub-groups is not. Hence, alternative strategies are called for.

One way to do so is to re-define the propensity score estimation. Whereas the 'overall' propensity score estimation has only been done separately for men and women in West and East Germany, we estimate in a second step 'group-specific' propensity scores. The basic idea behind that is to account more accurately for variables with varying influences for certain sub-groups. Since we have eleven sub-groups for both gender and regions, we are left with 44 propensity score estimations. The results can be found in tables B.6 to B.13 in appendix B. Based on these 'group-specific' estimations, labelled P_2, we re-run the matching procedure and estimate the MSB once again. It can be seen that the MSB is now clearly lower not only compared to the situation before matching but also compared to the situation when matching on the 'overall' score. This result shows that using the 'overall' score specification has not been fine enough to balance the relevant characteristics between participants and non-participants in the sub-groups. Hence, we will use the 'group-specific' propensity scores for the further analysis in the sub-groups.

Finally, looking at the MSB in the different regions, as depicted in table 5.7, shows rather good results. The MSB after matching is between 2.3 and 6.9% in five out of seven regions. Two exceptions are the clusters IV and V, where the MSB for men after matching is 8.2% (cluster IV) and 10.0% (cluster V). For women, the bias after matching is even higher at 12.2% in cluster IV and 10.6% in cluster V. However, since these are also the clusters with the lowest number of participants, we refrain from a cluster-specific estimation and use the overall specification of the propensity score for further analysis in the clusters.

Table 5.6: Mean Standardised Bias in the Sub-Groups[1,2,3]

	West Germany						East Germany					
	Men			Women			Men			Women		
	Before Matching	After Matching with		Before Matching	After Matching with		Before Matching	After Matching with		Before Matching	After Matching with	
Propensity Score Specification		P_1	P_2		P_1	P_2		P_1	P_2		P_1	P_2
Sub-Groups												
Age (in years)												
<25	10.48	11.53	3.08	12.50	14.37	6.82	14.74	13.11	4.94	13.73	15.11	8.90
25-50	11.30	5.82	2.66	15.56	5.79	2.98	11.91	3.98	2.47	9.84	2.48	1.36
>50	17.82	12.48	5.83	20.48	12.70	6.62	16.79	9.48	2.55	14.98	6.56	1.55
Duration of unemployment												
< 13 weeks	15.71	9.79	4.96	16.18	12.19	4.58	19.05	10.47	4.74	13.78	10.80	4.37
13-52 weeks	12.79	5.89	4.04	16.10	7.51	4.32	12.43	3.45	2.42	11.74	4.03	1.53
> 52 weeks	17.77	6.03	3.06	19.13	7.65	4.18	13.55	7.51	2.00	11.61	3.48	1.69
Without professional experience	14.02	9.50	5.69	15.93	11.49	6.36	12.10	10.43	4.18	12.17	5.51	3.35
Without professional training	14.31	3.99	3.29	16.79	4.68	4.25	11.17	5.68	2.48	11.04	4.42	2.72
With high degree	17.18	10.64	7.52	14.50	9.64	5.77	18.14	12.99	6.10	15.04	12.48	5.64
Rehabilitation attendant	18.13	13.23	8.45	23.96	18.69	16.31	12.88	10.05	4.38	15.87	10.71	5.87
With placement restrictions	19.29	8.92	4.61	26.99	11.37	4.99	15.35	8.22	3.91	18.37	6.84	3.11

Standardised bias before matching calculated as: $100 \cdot (\overline{X}_1 - \overline{X}_0)/\{\sqrt{(V_1(X) + V_0(X))/2}\}$.
Standardised bias after matching calculated as: $100 \cdot (\overline{X}_{1M} - \overline{X}_{0M})/\{\sqrt{(V_{1M}(X) + V_{0M}(X))/2}\}$.
[1] Mean standardised bias has been calculated as an unweighted average of all covariates.
[2] P_1 refers to the 'overall' propensity score estimation in table B.4.
[3] P_2 refers to the 'group-specific' propensity score estimation in tables B.6-B.13.

Table 5.7: Mean Standardised Bias in the Seven Clusters[1]

	Men		Women	
	Before	After	Before	After
Cluster	Matching	Matching	Matching	Matching
Ia	13.19	4.50	14.09	4.16
Ib	13.33	3.47	11.64	2.34
Ic	15.59	6.91	11.79	5.77
II	17.39	3.65	15.71	5.55
III	16.90	4.29	20.30	4.53
IV	16.55	8.21	22.79	12.24
V	14.21	10.00	18.62	10.62

Standardised bias before matching calculated as: $100 \cdot (\overline{X}_1 - \overline{X}_0)/\{\sqrt{(V_1(X) + V_0(X))/2}\}$.
Standardised bias after matching calculated as: $100 \cdot (\overline{X}_{1M} - \overline{X}_{0M})/\{\sqrt{(V_{1M}(X) + V_{0M}(X))/2}\}$.

[1] Mean standardised bias has been calculated as an unweighted average of all covariates.

5.4 Results

An important decision which has to be made in every evaluation is when to measure the programme effects. We have discussed this point in subsection 3.2.5. The empirical analysis should ensure that participants and non-participants are compared in the same economic environment and the same lifecycle position. The literature is dominated by two approaches, either comparing individuals from begin or after the end of programmes. The latter approach is problematic for two reasons. First, since it implies comparison of participants and non-participants in the month(s) after programmes end, very different economic situations may be compared if exits are spread over a longer time period. Second, this approach entails an endogeneity problem of programme exits (Gerfin and Lechner, 2002). A second approach which is predominant in the recent literature (see e.g. Sianesi (2004) or Gerfin and Lechner (2002)) and which is also used here, measures the effects from begin of the programmes. Basically, the policy-relevant question to be answered is if the placement officer should place an unemployed individual in February 2000 in a JCS or not. Therefore comparing both groups from the begin of the programme seems to be a reasonable approach. What should be kept in mind is the possible occurrence of locking-in effects for the group of participants. Tables B.14 to B.17 in appendix B contain the cumulated exit rates for the main and the sub-groups. Most of the participants leave the programmes after one year. In March 2001, around 80% (74%) of the male (female) participants in West Germany have left the programmes. The corresponding numbers are approximately 91% for men and 92% for women in East Germany.[7]

Following van Ours (2004), the net effect of a programme consists of two opposite effects. First, the employment probability of the participants is expected to rise due to positive aspects of the programme. Second, since participants who are involved in the programmes do not have the same time to look for new jobs as non-participants, a reduced search intensity during programmes is expected. Since both effects cannot be disentangled, we only observe the net effect. When interpreting the results the different impacts of the two underlying effects have to be considered. As to the fall in the search intensity, we should expect an initial negative effect from any kind of participation in a programme. However, since we observe the outcome of the individuals until almost three years after programmes start, successful programmes should overcompensate for this initial fall.

5.4.1 Results for the Main Groups

The results from the begin (February 2000) to the end (December 2002) of our observation period for the main and the sub-groups are depicted in figures 5.1 to 5.4. Figure 5.1 contains the results for men in West Germany. The solid line in the graphs describes the monthly employment effect, i.e. the difference in the employment rates between participants and matched non-participants. The graphs for the main group are captioned 'total' in the figures. All of the graphs have one thing in common, namely a large drop in the effects for the first months after programme start. This can be interpreted as the expected locking-in effect, which is more pronounced for men (figure 5.1) and women (figure 5.2) in West Germany than for men (figure 5.3) and women (figure 5.4) in East Germany. To allow a more accurate discussion, we have also put together the results for six selected months in tables B.18 for West Germany and B.19 for East Germany. Five months after programmes have started (in July 2000), the effects for men in West Germany lie around -21.1%. That means that the average employment rate of participating men is about 21% lower in comparison to matched non-participants. Clearly, this strong reduction is expected as nearly all participants are still in the programmes, whereas the non-participants have the chance to search, apply for and find a new job. For the interpretation one has to bear in mind, that although JCS

---

[7] At first sight, this is at odds with our findings in the descriptive analysis, that the programme duration is on average shorter in West Germany. However, the results get clear when looking at the exit rates in the first month, where much more participants leave the programmes in West Germany. Additionally, there is quite a significant variation in the exit rates for the sub-groups, e.g. only 73% of the male participants who are older than 50 years have left the programme in March 2001. This variation has to be taken into account when interpreting the results.

are some kind of employment, they are classified as failures when assessing the re-integration success into regular (unsubsidised) employment. For women in West Germany the result is very similar in that month and amounts to around -20.4%. The situation in East Germany is somewhat different. The effects are here -14.0% for men and -9.4% for women. Compared to the results for West Germany, this reflects the worse labour market situation with fewer employment opportunities. Being locked into the programme does not have as much influence, since the chances of non-participants to find a new job are lower anyway.

The development of the effects is quite different for both regions, too. Whereas in West Germany a relatively steep increase in the employment effects can be found, the development in East Germany is much smoother. For example, in July 2001 the employment effect has risen to -12.5% for men and -11.9% for women in West Germany. Hence, the negative effects are nearly halved. In East Germany, however, the effects lie around -10.9% for men and -7.5% for women.

Looking at the last month of our observation period (December 2002), we do not find a significant programme effect for men in West Germany. That is, the employment chances of participants and matched non-participants do not differ. However, for women in West Germany we find a significant positive effect of 4.6%, which means that participating women have benefited from the programme in terms of employment chances. However, this positive result has to be treated with caution since women in West Germany have been the smallest group, we have lost a considerable share of participants due to the common support requirement and the estimates imply a confidence interval which is close to zero.

For East Germany on the other hand, we find negative employment effects of -2.9% for men and -1.4% for women. This shows that the overall effect of JCS for the participating individuals is dissatisfying. Only for one of the groups, namely women in West Germany, we find a positive employment effect nearly three years after programmes have started, whereas for the other three main groups the effects are negative or insignificant. It seems that the pronounced initial negative (locking-in) effect cannot be overcome during our observation period. Judging by these numbers, JCS have to be rated as unsuccessful regarding their goal to re-integrate individuals into regular (unsubsidised) employment.

5.4.2 Results for the Selected Sub-Groups

Even though JCS do not work for the participants as a whole, they may work for some sub-groups. For instance, one could assume that they are especially effective for the explicit target groups of JCS, like long-term unemployed persons or persons without work experience. As mentioned already, we have

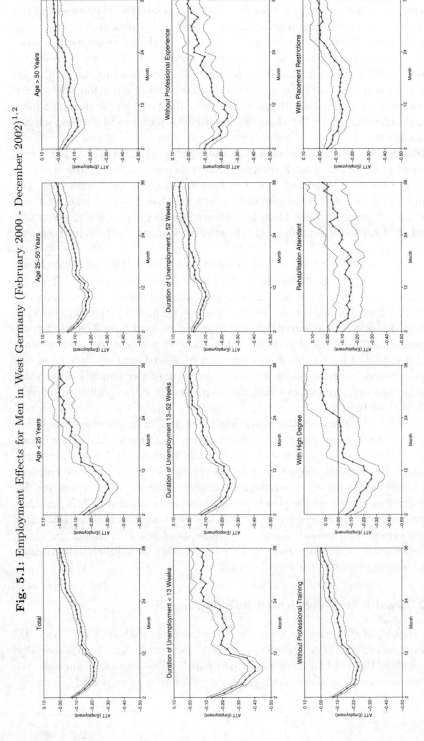

Fig. 5.1: Employment Effects for Men in West Germany (February 2000 - December 2002)[1,2]

[1] Solid line describes the monthly employment effect. Dotted lines are the upper and lower 95% confidence limits.
[2] Month 2 refers to February 2000, month 12 = December 2000, month 24 = December 2001, month 36 = December 2002.

Fig. 5.2: Employment Effects for Women in West Germany (February 2000 - December 2002)[1,2]

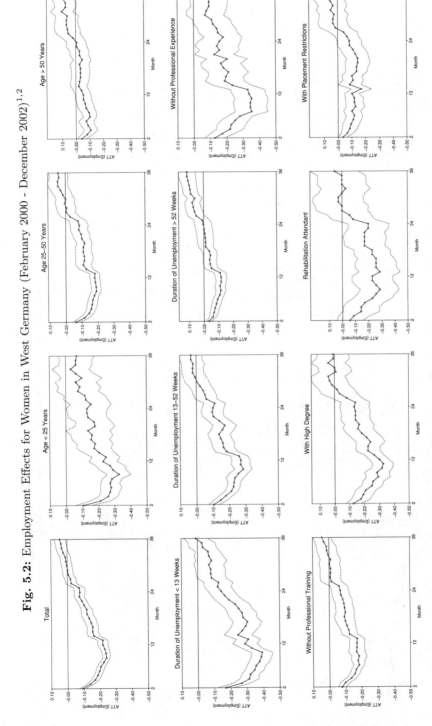

[1] Solid line describes the monthly employment effect. Dotted lines are the upper and lower 95% confidence limits.
[2] Month 2 refers to February 2000, month 12 = December 2000, month 24 = December 2001, month 36 = December 2002.

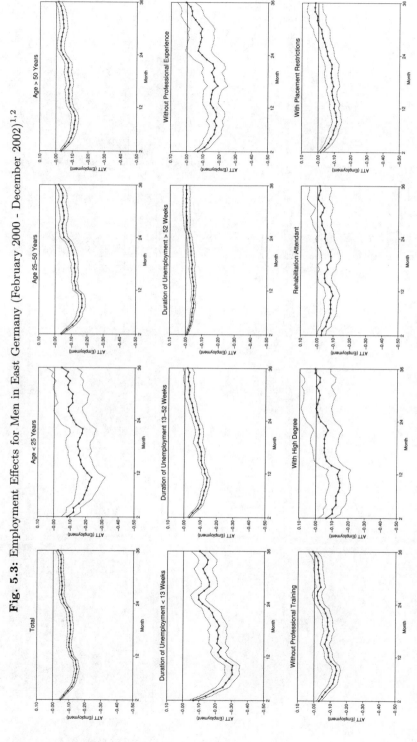

Fig. 5.3: Employment Effects for Men in East Germany (February 2000 - December 2002)[1,2]

[1] Solid line describes the monthly employment effect. Dotted lines are the upper and lower 95% confidence limits.
[2] Month 2 refers to February 2000, month 12 = December 2000, month 24 = December 2001, month 36 = December 2002.

Fig. 5.4: Employment Effects for Women in East Germany (February 2000 - December 2002)[1,2]

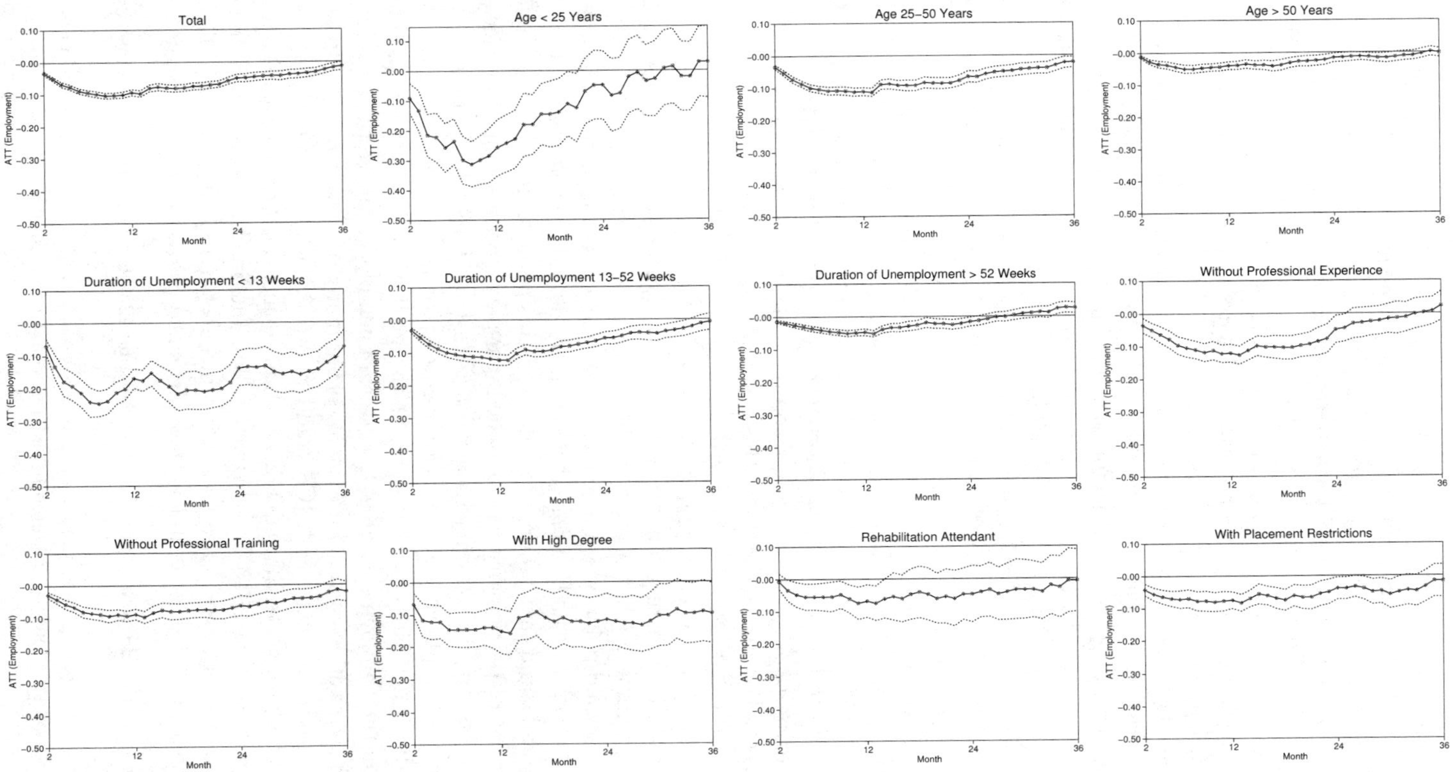

[1] Solid line describes the monthly employment effect. Dotted lines are the upper and lower 95% confidence limits.
[2] Month 2 refers to February 2000, month 12 = December 2000, month 24 = December 2001, month 36 = December 2002.

selected groups according to different age classes[8], unemployment durations[9], persons without work experience, without professional training, with a high degree (college and university graduates), with placement restrictions due to health restraints and rehabilitation attendants. Figures 5.1 to 5.4 and tables B.18 and B.19 contain the results for these groups. To abbreviate the discussion, we concentrate on two main points. First, we will examine the occurrence of locking-in effects and second, we will discuss the results at the end of the observation period (December 2002).

Considering locking-in effects is of interest, since it can be expected that these effects differ for the sub-groups. Good examples are provided by the groups defined by age and unemployment duration. Older unemployed persons have in general fewer labour market opportunities than middle-aged or younger persons. Due to the worse 'outside options' of the non-participants, we expect to find weaker locking-in effects for older participants and stronger effects for the other groups (young and middle-aged persons). The figures support these expectations empirically, independently of gender of region. We will now turn to the three groups defined by the previous unemployment duration. Re-integration into the labour market is generally easier for persons with only a short duration of unemployment ('negative duration dependence'). Therefore, it has to be assumed that short-term unemployed non-participants have a higher probability of receiving a job offer and hence the locking-in effects are larger. The findings support this assumption.

For the other sub-groups the graphs present a similar picture, too. We find the initial fall of the employment effects in the first months after programmes have started and rising tendencies after the majority of participants has left the programmes. The reasons have been discussed already.

The second point we want to discuss are the effects for these sub-groups at the end of our observation period (December 2002). For most of the groups we do not find significant programme effects at this point in time, i.e. the employment rates of participants and matched non-participants do not differ nearly three years after programmes have started. That implies that programmes have neither improved nor worsened the employment chances of participating individuals. However, for some of the groups we find significant differences in the employment rates. Long-term unemployed (more than 52 weeks) men (5.0%) and women (11.3%) in West Germany benefit from participation. These results indicate that JCS could improve the employment chances of this target group. Additionally, high qualified men in West Germany benefit from participation (12.5%), whereas for low qualified persons and individuals without work experience no significant effects can be established. This is somewhat not intuitively understandable, since programmes are designed for

---

[8] Young (below 25 years), middle-aged persons (25-50 years), older persons (over 50 years).

[9] Short-term unemployed persons (up to 13 weeks), mid-term unemployed persons (13-52 weeks), long-term unemployed persons (more than 52 weeks).

persons who are most in need of assistance. Another group who benefits from participation are older women in West Germany, whose employment rate is 12.7% higher than for matched non-participants. This is an encouraging result, because older unemployed persons in particular have only poor opportunities to return to the first labour market. Although for most groups we do not find any enhancement of the employment chances after participation, the results indicate a tendency that programmes are actually only useful for the most-disadvantaged in terms of unemployment duration and age.

Considering the results for the sub-groups in East Germany reveals a somewhat different picture. Focussing on the male groups, we only find a significant negative effect (-10.1%) for participants with a short unemployment duration before programme. As mentioned above, short-term unemployed are expected to return to regular employment easier. Therefore, it may be assumed that participation and the involved locking-in effects harm the re-integration chances of this group more. For all other groups no significant differences in the employment rates can be established. For women in East Germany the results are disappointing as well. Middle-aged (-2.2%) as well as short-term unemployed women (-7.4%) suffer from participation. Another group with clearly negative programme effects in December 2002 are high qualified women (-9.8%). However, there is also one group (long-term unemployed women) for whom we find a small (2.5%) positive programme effect. For the other groups no significant differences can be established. Thus, the above stated hypothesis that programmes are actually only likely to work for the legally defined target groups, can only be supported for long-term unemployed women.

5.4.3 Results for the Regional Clusters

The next point we would like to analyse is the possible effect heterogeneity occurring because of different labour market situations. To do so, the classification of the FEA clusters provides a reasonable framework. Two hypotheses may be formulated. First, it may be the case that JCS work in situations with high labour market imbalances. Second, it may also be stated that JCS work better in prospering regions (when concentrating more explicitly on specific target groups). To check these hypotheses, we analyse the effects in the seven clusters. Table 5.8 contains the employment effects for men and women in six selected months. Once again, we will concentrate our discussion on the locking-in effect (July 2000) and the employment effects at the end of our observation period. Starting with men in East Germany, it can be seen that the highest locking-in effect is measured in districts of cluster Ic (-19.6%), which have the relatively best labour market conditions. For women this can be found, too, even though less pronounced (-10.4% in Ic). The same story extends to West Germany, where men (women) in districts of cluster V have an average employment effect of -33.1% (-30.7%) in July 2000. One might speculate that this is caused by the better 'outside options' of non-participants in these clusters. Thus, participants in clusters with a better labour market environment (Ic and V) experience smaller locking-in effects.

Turning to the results in December 2002 does not allow to extend these findings. Most of the results are insignificant and we do not find that programme participants in clusters with better labour market situations are worse off. In total, we can establish significant differences in the employment levels of participants and matched non-participants for only three groups. The first group are men in districts of cluster Ib, the 'typical' East German labour office. There we find a negative effect of -3.0%. For women in cluster Ib (-1.6%) and Ic (-4.5%) the effects are significantly negative, too. It should be noted that the results do not diverge much from the overall results in West and East Germany. Based on these findings, neither of the two stated hypotheses can be confirmed.

5.4.4 Sensitivity of the Results to Unobserved Heterogeneity

The estimation of treatment effects with matching estimators is based on the CIA. Hence, if both groups differ on unobserved variables which simultaneously affect assignment into treatment and the outcome variable, a 'hidden bias' might arise. It should be clear that matching estimators are not robust against this 'hidden bias'. Since it is impossible to estimate the magnitude of selection bias with non-experimental data, we address this problem with the bounding approach proposed by Rosenbaum (2002) and presented in subsection 3.3. The basic question to be answered is if inference about programme effects may be altered by unobserved factors. In other words, we want to determine how strongly an unmeasured variable must influence the selection process in order to undermine the implications of matching analysis.

Tables B.20 (West-Germany) and B.21 (East-Germany) in the appendix contain the results of the sensitivity analysis for two selected months (July and December 2002) and the examined sub-groups. First of all, the table contains the effects and the results of the Mantel and Haensel (1959) test-statistic for the situation free of hidden bias ($e^\gamma = 1$). A χ^2-value below 3.84 indicates that the treatment effect is not significant. Clearly, a sensitivity analysis for insignificant effects is not meaningful and hence will be omitted. For the significant effects, we gradually increase the level of e^γ until the inference about the treatment effect is changed. In other words, we are assessing the strength unmeasured influences would require in order to change inference about the treatment effect.

The interpretation is straightforward: Taking the effect for men in West Germany in July 2002 as an example, we see that the effect is -3.06% and significant. The critical value of e^γ is between 1.50 and 1.55. A critical value of 1.50 suggests that individuals with the same X-vector differ in their odds of participation by a factor of 1.50, or 50%. It is important to note that these are worst-case scenarios. Hence, a critical value of $e^\gamma = 1.50$ does not mean

Table 5.8: Employment Effects in the Regional Clusters

	Jul 00 Effect	S.E.	Dec 00 Effect	S.E.	Jul 01 Effect	S.E.	Dec 01 Effect	S.E.	Jul 02 Effect	S.E.	Dec 02 Effect	S.E.
Men												
Cluster Ia	**-0.1484**	0.0118	**-0.1095**	0.0113	**-0.0980**	0.0158	**-0.0663**	0.0148	-0.0346	0.0186	-0.0014	0.0187
Cluster Ib	**-0.1477**	0.0074	**-0.1245**	0.0080	**-0.1080**	0.0077	**-0.0656**	0.0086	**-0.0518**	0.0088	**-0.0298**	0.0106
Cluster Ic	**-0.1957**	0.0220	**-0.1615**	0.0245	**-0.1677**	0.0255	**-0.1025**	0.0236	-0.0652	0.0293	-0.0124	0.0298
Cluster II	**-0.1446**	0.0126	**-0.1557**	0.0141	**-0.0723**	0.0169	**-0.0623**	0.0176	-0.0145	0.0172	-0.0033	0.0175
Cluster III	**-0.2340**	0.0137	**-0.1711**	0.0192	**-0.1220**	0.0231	**-0.0818**	0.0210	-0.0377	0.0233	-0.0063	0.0239
Cluster IV	**-0.1646**	0.0381	-0.0732	0.0405	*-0.0732*	0.0552	-0.0427	0.0486	0.0000	0.0529	0.0183	0.0472
Cluster V	**-0.3311**	0.0312	**-0.2669**	0.0315	**-0.2264**	0.0339	**-0.1284**	0.0403	*-0.0912*	0.0363	-0.0507	0.0331
Women												
Cluster Ia	**-0.0815**	0.0075	**-0.0783**	0.0091	**-0.0618**	0.0114	**-0.0511**	0.0105	**-0.0404**	0.0157	-0.0189	0.0149
Cluster Ib	**-0.0990**	0.0059	**-0.0940**	0.0046	**-0.0788**	0.0054	**-0.0537**	0.0058	**-0.0456**	0.0072	*-0.0155*	0.0067
Cluster Ic	**-0.1043**	0.0141	**-0.1329**	0.0171	**-0.0818**	0.0212	**-0.0573**	0.0214	**-0.0593**	0.0200	*-0.0450*	0.0224
Cluster II	**-0.1647**	0.0214	**-0.1909**	0.0185	**-0.1265**	0.0268	**-0.1146**	0.0293	-0.0358	0.0346	-0.0191	0.0292
Cluster III	**-0.1935**	0.0212	**-0.2016**	0.0231	**-0.1210**	0.0272	-0.0565	0.0299	0.0215	0.0301	0.0618	0.0326
Cluster IV	**-0.1972**	0.0639	**-0.1972**	0.0627	-0.0423	0.0817	-0.0845	0.0875	0.1127	0.0943	0.1268	0.0882
Cluster V	**-0.3077**	0.0376	**-0.2582**	0.0387	**-0.1648**	0.0459	-0.0769	0.0505	-0.0055	0.0478	0.0000	0.0470

Bold letters indicate significance on a 1% level, *italic* letters refer to the 5% level, standard errors are bootstrapped with 50 replications.
Results refer to NN matching without replacement and a caliper of 0.02.

that unobserved heterogeneity exists and that there is no effect of treatment on the outcome variable. This result only states that the confidence interval for the effect would include zero if an unobserved variable caused the odds ratio of treatment assignment to differ between treatment and comparison groups by 1.50. Additionally, this variable's effect on the outcome would have to be so strong that it almost perfectly determines the outcome in each pair of matched cases in the data. However, even if there is unobserved heterogeneity to a degree of $e^\gamma = 1.50$ in the group of West German men, inference about the treatment effect would not be changed.

The results are ambivalent and differ between West and East Germany. In West Germany most of the effects for men and women in the sub-groups are insignificant. But for those groups where the effects are significant, even a large influence of unobserved heterogeneity does not have much influence on the inference about treatment effects. The lowest critical value of e^γ can be found for men without professional training in July 2002 and the largest critical values of 1.75-1.80 can be found for high-qualified men (in July and December 2002) as well as for long-term unemployed women in July 2002 and high qualified women in December 2002. Therefore, we can conclude for West Germany that even large amounts of unobserved heterogeneity would not alter the inference about the estimated effects.

In contrast to that the results in East Germany are not so clear-cut. We find that for some of the sub-groups, like older or short-term unemployed men as well as for high qualified women and for women with placement restrictions, inference would change in July 2002 even with small amounts of hidden bias. The critical value of e^γ is somewhere below 1.05, which implies that even small magnitudes of 'hidden bias' would alter the inference. Consequently, interpretation for these sub-populations hinges on this restriction. For the results of the main groups, i.e. men and women, the critical value of e^γ in December 2002 is somewhere between 1.25 and 1.30. So these effects can be viewed as relatively robust to unobserved heterogeneity.

5.5 Conclusion

The aim of this chapter was the evaluation of the re-integration effects of job creation schemes into regular (unsubsidised) employment for the participating individuals in Germany. Special attention was given to the possible occurrence of individual, i.e. group-specific, and regional heterogeneity in the effects. That is we estimated the effects for men and women in West and East Germany ('main groups') as well as for eleven 'sub-groups' and within seven regional clusters.

Due to the non-experimental data used in this analysis the problem of selection bias has to be addressed. Given the very informative dataset, we apply a matching estimator based on the conditional independence assumption. The

5.5 Conclusion

large number of relevant covariates makes exact matching unfeasible. Hence, we use propensity score matching (PSM) for the analysis. When implementing PSM estimators, several decisions have to be made. The estimation of the propensity score is a first and crucial issue and hence we tested several specifications. In the end we decided to use the full specification set of variables. Furthermore, we also tested the sensitivity of the effects with respect to different matching algorithms. It turns out that the results are not sensitive to the algorithm choice and NN matching without replacement (and a caliper of 0.02) is the best choice for our situation. The major goal of PSM is to balance the distribution of covariates across the groups of participants and non-participants. A suitable measure to test this is the standardised bias. It turns out that our 'overall' propensity score, which we have estimated for the 'main groups', was able to balance the distribution in the 'main groups' very well. However, it was not able to balance the distribution accurately in the sub-groups. Thus, we estimated 'group-specific' propensity scores and used these for the analysis in the sub-groups.

The effects are estimated from begin of the programmes in February 2000 until December 2002. Since JCS are usually promoted for twelve months, we find large locking-in effects for all of the groups. The locking-in effects are more pronounced in West Germany and less substantial in East Germany. This may be caused by the better employment opportunities for non-participants in the West.

Regarding the effects at the end of the observation period programmes, we find a significant positive effect only for women in West Germany (4.6%), whereas the effect for men in West Germany is insignificant. For men (-2.9%) and women (-1.4%) in East Germany the effects are significantly negative. Interpretation of the results may be hampered by two issues. First, the number of treated individuals lost due to the common support requirement and second, the matching quality. As already said, the matching quality is very good for the 'main groups' even though for women in West Germany the matching quality was less satisfying. This group was also the one for whom we lost the highest number of individuals in comparison to the other groups due to the common support requirement, advising some caution interpreting the positive effects. Hence, except for women in West Germany, it seems that the initial negative locking-in effect cannot be overcome during the observation period.

For most of the sub-groups we do not find significant effects at all. However, some exceptions have to be noted. Long-term unemployed men (5.0%) and women (12.7%) as well as high qualified men (12.5%) and older women (12.7%) in West Germany benefit from participation. Common support and matching quality are not an issue for the long-term unemployed, but they definitely are for the latter two groups, since we lose nearly 7% of older women and over 14% of high qualified men due to failing common support. Looking additionally at the relatively high remaining bias after matching for these two groups makes an interpretation of their results questionable.

The only sub-group with a positive effect in East Germany are long-term unemployed women (2.5%). In East Germany we find significant negative effects for short-term unemployed men (-10.1%) and women (-7.4%) as well as for women between 25 and 50 years (-2.2%) and for high qualified women (-9.8%). Matching quality is satisfying for all of these five sub-groups. However, for the short-term unemployed persons and women with high degree we lose substantial amounts of individuals due to failure of the common support, indicating that it is problematic to find short-term unemployed individuals and women with high degree who did not participate and have similar characteristics as the participants.

The positive findings for the long-term unemployed persons may indicate that the programmes do work for this problem group of the labour market. However, this result cannot be extended to other problem groups, like individuals with placement restrictions, individuals without work experience or low qualified persons. Even though we would have expected positive effects for these problem groups of the labour market, we did not find any. Our regional analysis did not support any of the hypotheses that JCS either work better in regions with a depressed or prospering labour market situation. The results for the clusters did not diverge much from the overall result in West and East Germany. To some extent the effects reflect the different purpose of JCS in both parts. Whereas they are used as a relief of the labour market in East Germany, they are more tightly addressed to problem groups in the West. The overall picture is rather disappointing since most of the effects are insignificant or negative. That means that participation in programmes did not help individuals to re-integrate into regular (unsubsidised) employment. One notable exception are long-term unemployed men and women in West Germany as well as long-term unemployed women in East Germany. Hence, one policy implication is to address programmes to this problem group more tightly.

6

Microeconometric Evaluation of Job Creation Schemes - Part II: Programme Heterogeneity

6.1 Introduction

In the last chapter we have estimated the employment effects of JCS on the participating individuals. Thereby the focus has been on effect heterogeneity caused by group-specific and regional differences. That is, we have estimated the effects of JCS separately not only for men and women in West and East Germany, but also for specific sub-populations like long-term unemployed individuals or persons with placement restrictions, and for seven regional clusters. The reasoning for that differentiation is based on the very likely assumption, that treatment effects are not homogeneous. Thus, identifying the sources of effect heterogeneity can help to improve programmes in the future. Clearly, any evaluation of a large scale ALMP programme like JCS has to consider differences in the effects with respect to the varying design of the programmes, too. Therefore we focus in this chapter explicitly on programme heterogeneity. We have presented the design of JCS already in section 4.2 and showed that they can be carried out by different implementing institutions from the PUBLIC or NON-COMMERCIAL sector and to a small extent also by PRIVATE BUSINESSES. Additionally they can be started in different sectors of the economy like AGRICULTURE, OFFICE AND SERVICES or COMMUNITY SERVICES. Furthermore, they differ also in the type of promotion an individual receives. Whereas the standard type is REGULAR promotion, in special cases an ENFORCED promotion can be authorised by the local placement officer, which is mainly reflected by a higher subsidy to the implementing institution.

Obviously, these differences may influence the effects. For example, assignment to JCS in the AGRICULTURE sector requires different abilities of the individual than assignment to OFFICE AND SERVICES and clearly, the occupation in these sectors differs, too. Thus, different effects can be expected. Additionally, implementation of programmes varies also between providers which may also be a source for different effects on the employment chances of individuals. Together with the type of promotion, these are three potential sources of effect heterogeneity from which only one has been considered so far in empirical analysis. Hujer, Caliendo, and Thomsen (2004) analysed the effects of JCS with respect to five major programme sectors. We extend their analysis in two directions. First, in addition to the different sectors we also consider further aspects of the programmes like the provider and the type of promotion. Second, due to data limitations it was yet only possible to estimate the effects on the unemployment probability of individuals. We have laid out in section 4.4 that we can now use information of the Employment Statistics Register ('Beschäftigtenstatistik', ESR) which allows us to analyse the effects of JCS on the re-integration chances of participants into regular (unsubsidised) employment. By using this information, we are also able to extend the observation period to nearly three years after programmes start.

We will use the same evaluation approach as in chapter 5, namely propensity score matching, and we consider the first participation of individuals only, too.[1] The rest of this chapter is organised as follows. In section 6.2 we present some facts about programme heterogeneity in the implementation of JCS. As we have presented the dataset and the outcome variable in use already in section 4.4, we start by describing the groups of analysis and provide some selected descriptives for them. Since we have discussed a lot of implementation issues concerning PSM already in the previous chapter, we will not repeat this here. Based on section 5.3.1 we take the plausibility of the CIA as given and use the same matching approach as suggested in section 5.3.3. Hence, we will start the empirical analysis in 6.3 directly by presenting the propensity score estimation, discussing the quality of our matching procedure and some common support issues. Section 6.4 contains the results differentiated by sectors, providers and types of promotion and section 6.5 concludes.

6.2 Groups of Analysis and Selected Descriptives

6.2.1 Groups of Analysis

JCS can be implemented in nine different economic sectors. The categorisation of the sectors was set up in the mid 1980s, and changes due to the German Unification, the further labour market reforms in the 1990s and the general changing situation on the labour market are not reflected. Due to this, several sectors like 'coast protection and land reclamation' are nowadays only of minor importance (see Brinkmann, Caliendo, Jahn, Hujer, and Thomsen (2002) for details). However, four main sectors can be identified: AGRICULTURE, CONSTRUCTION AND INDUSTRY, OFFICE AND SERVICES and COMMUNITY SERVICES. We analyse these four major sectors and summarise

---

[1] Every subsequent participation is treated as an outcome of the first participation.

the remaining sectors in the category OTHER. Figure 6.1 presents the number of participants in the five programme sectors in West and East Germany. To allow a reasonable estimation and interpretation of treatment effects, groups with less than 100 participants are excluded from the analysis. This is relevant for women in West Germany participating either in the sectors AGRICULTURE (41) or CONSTRUCTION AND INDUSTRY (36). Leaving participants in the sector OTHER apart, the majority of men in both regions participate in sectors AGRICULTURE (584 participants in West Germany / 925 in East Germany) and CONSTRUCTION AND INDUSTRY (317/416). The largest share of female participants in both parts can be found in the sector COMMUNITY SERVICES with 503 participants in West Germany and 1,810 participants in East Germany. The smallest share of participants is employed in OFFICE AND SERVICES' occupations. This may on the one hand be due to specific abilities needed for these kinds of job, which most of the participants may not have. On the other hand, this may also be caused by the fact that occupations in this sector are not additional in nature and of value for the society. Since these are the pre-conditions for a promotion of JCS (see the discussion in section 4.2.3) this would explain the relatively low share of participants in this sector. This first glance already shows significant differences in the allocation to the different sectors not only between the regions but also between men and women.

Fig. 6.1: Number of Participants in the Five Sectors

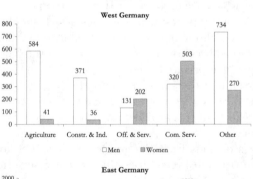

Figure 6.2 additionally differentiates the number of participants in the different sectors by type of promotion and provider. Comparing the shares of participants with regular and enforced promotion (left hand side of the figure) shows notable differences between East and West Germany and reflects the worse situation on the labour market in East Germany. While in West Germany the majority of programmes (over 70%) is implemented as regular promotion, in East Germany the picture is inverted. Here, 68% of the men and 53% of the women are in enforced promotion. Since the major difference between the two types of promotion is a higher subsidy to the implementing institution, it is not surprising that JCS are on average more expensive in East Germany. While the average monthly costs per participant have been 1,419 Euro in West Germany, 1,518 Euro have been spent on average per participant in East Germany in the year 2001 (Bundesanstalt für Arbeit, 2002). The share of regular promotion is highest in the sectors OFFICE AND SERVICES and COMMUNITY SERVICES. In West Germany over 96% of the male participants in the first sector receive regular promotion and 90% of the women. In COMMUNITY SERVICES the numbers are 69% for men and 74% for women. In East Germany the share of participants with regular promotion is much lower than in West Germany (55% / 62% of the men / women in OFFICE AND SERVICES, 61% / 60% in COMMUNITY SERVICES) but still much higher when compared to the other sectors.

The graphs on the right side of figure 6.2 present the numbers of participants differentiated by providers of jobs. As mentioned above, JCS in private businesses are rare (number in brackets). JCS can only be promoted if they support activities which are of value for the society and additional in nature. Furthermore, JCS participants in private businesses should be from special target groups of the labour market and get educational supervision during the programme (see subsection 4.2.3). This leads to the fact that the largest group of participants in private businesses are women in the sector OTHER in East Germany (81), and the smallest group are two male participants in the sector OFFICE AND SERVICES in West Germany. Therefore, we do not analyse the employment effects of this provider and exclude the concerned individuals from the analysis.

What becomes obvious from the graphs is, that JCS are mainly accomplished by NON-COMMERCIAL entities, like friendly societies, charities and non-profit enterprises. Although the institutions from the PUBLIC SECTOR, e.g. adminstration departments of municipalities and towns, also provide a substantial number of occupations, they only dominate the schemes in AGRICULTURE for men in West Germany. The dominance of NON-COMMERCIAL ENTITIES is not surprising, since JCS should stabilise and qualify hard-to-place individuals for later re-integration into regular employment by providing temporary occupations that do not compete with regular jobs. Those regulations are in order to avoid substitution effect and windfall gains and can most likely be met by non-commercial institutions, which have on the one hand a sufficient demand for workers, do not compete with private businesses and could not provide long-run opportunities for comparable employees without the subsidy.

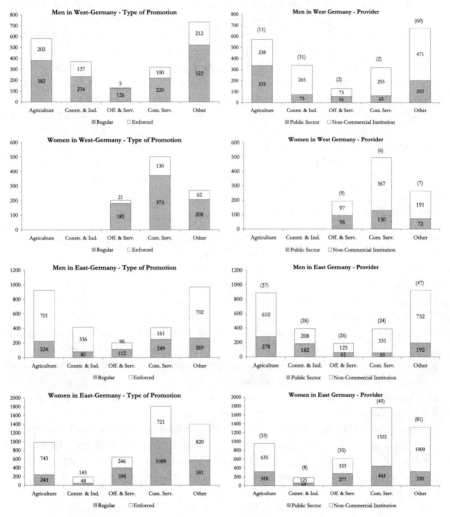

Fig. 6.2: Number of Participants in the Sectors (Differentiated by type of promotion and provider) [a,b]

[a] Left side shows the number of participants in the sectors differentiated by type of promotion (regular and enforced).
[b] Right side shows the number of participants in the sectors differentiated by provider (public sector or non-commercial institution, participants in private sector in brackets).

Let us summarise so far. The occupations between the sectors differ and there are also differences in the implementation of schemes between the two types of providers. Finally, the type of promotion is not homogenous, either. Hence, we expect the employment effects to be heterogeneous, too. The direction of the effect heterogeneity is not clear a-priori. We have discussed already that the occupations in the different sectors differ and also require different abilities from the participants. However, it is a-priori not clear which type of occupation will improve the employment chances of individuals more. The same is true regarding the providers. Finally, also with respect to the third source of possible effect heterogeneity - the type of promotion - different arguments may be thought of. Since the type of promotion indicates a higher degree of 'need for assistance', it can be argued that ENFORCED promotion should lead to better outcomes, since the costs are usually higher and the programme is more intense. On the other hand, it may also be claimed that those individuals have on average worse labour market prospects. Clearly, these presumptions can be confirmed or discarded only by empirical examination as we will do in the following.

6.2.2 Selected Descriptives

Before we do so, let us briefly consider the different characteristics of participants in the five sectors and compare them with the group of non-participants. Tables C.1 to C.4 in the appendix present means and frequencies of relevant variables with differentiation by gender, region and sector. The characteristics are ordered according to the four types of variables as described in section 4.4. In addition, the average programme duration within the sectors is added. With respect to this information, some notable differences are visible. Whereas men in West Germany experience the shortest programmes on average in the sector AGRICULTURE with 261.5 days, their counterparts in this sector in East Germany leave programmes on average after 325.0 days, i.e. approximately two months later. As already noted, only a small fraction of male participants is employed in OFFICE AND SERVICES. Furthermore, the programmes in this sector last the longest time (336.7 days in West Germany/ 332.1 in East Germany). Unfortunately, our data lacks information about the reasons for the different durations. We are unable to identify whether programme duration is determined by the planning of the caseworkers in the first place, or whether better alternatives for the participating individuals are obtained during programmes. For women in East Germany, the average programme duration differs between sectors, too. The participants in CONSTRUCTION AND INDUSTRY leave the programmes on average after 289.5 days, whereas women in OTHER stay in programmes for nearly 341 days. In contrast to that, programme durations for women in West Germany vary hardly. Women in West Germany remain in programmes between 305.1 days (COMMUNITY SERVICES) and 310.7 days (OTHER). Apart from these sectoral differences, it has to be

6.2 Groups of Analysis and Selected Descriptives 167

mentioned that participants in West Germany remain in programmes on average shorter than in East Germany (independently of gender). That may be on the one hand due to better alternatives on the labour market, e.g. regular job opportunities or other ALMP programmes, or on the other hand due to a different acknowledgement of programmes by the participants.

Let us now compare some selected characteristics of participants and non-participants in the different sectors. A first thing to note is that male participants in West Germany are significantly older than non-participants, who are on average 43.2 years in January 2000. It can also be seen, that the age of participants varies considerably between the sectors. Whereas men in CONSTRUCTION AND INDUSTRY and COMMUNITY SERVICES are at the begin of programmes on average about 35 years old, participants in AGRICULTURE are already 39 and in OFFICE AND SERVICES even about 43, which almost equals the age of non-participants. Looking at the results for women in West Germany shows a similar picture. Again non-participants are on average older (43.3 years) than the participants, independently of sectors. In contrast to that, the results for men in East Germany show quite a different picture. Participants are on average clearly older than the non-participants. The youngest participants (approximately 43 years) are employed in COMMUNITY SERVICES and CONSTRUCTION AND INDUSTRY, the oldest in AGRICULTURE (46 years) and OFFICE AND SERVICES (49 years), whereas the non-participants are on average 41.7 years. Women in East Germany are the most homogeneous group with respect to the age of participants and non-participants. Age varies slightly between 43 years (CONSTRUCTION AND INDUSTRY, AGRICULTURE and OTHER) and 45 years (OFFICE AND SERVICES) for participants and is on average 44 years for non-participants. Except for women in West Germany, participants in OFFICE AND SERVICES are the oldest of all sectors. Although the individual's age may be expected to be an important determinant for a possible re-integration into regular employment and therefore shorter programme duration, this expectation is only partly affirmed by the results. There is a tendency that programmes last on average longer if participants are older, but no clear pattern can be revealed. With respect to health restrictions, we find that men without health restrictions are over-represented in the sectors AGRICULTURE and CONSTRUCTION AND INDUSTRY when compared to non-participants. This is intuitively understandable since occupations in these sectors may involve some form of manual labour. The same findings emerge for men and women in East Germany.

It is quite interesting to look at the professional training of individuals in the different sectors. Participants without completed professional training are over-represented in the sectors AGRICULTURE and CONSTRUCTION AND INDUSTRY, whereas individuals with higher degrees are over-represented in the sectors OFFICE AND SERVICES and COMMUNITY SERVICES. Both points are true irrespective of gender and region, even though the first point is more pronounced in West-Germany. We have mentioned already in the descriptive analysis in the last chapter, that the share of individuals without any professional training (and without certificate for secondary education) is rather low in East Germany. Most of the individuals here have at least some formal degree ('industrial training'). Clearly, this has also to be seen in relation to the higher age of participants in East Germany. The professional rank points in the same direction. Men in West Germany who are white-collar workers are over-represented in the OFFICE AND SERVICES sector and unskilled workers are primarily found in AGRICULTURE or CONSTRUCTION AND INDUSTRY. White-collar females in West Germany are remarkably over-represented in OFFICE AND SERVICES and COMMUNITY SERVICES. Taking together, this shows that higher qualified persons are more likely to be found in the sectors OFFICE AND SERVICES and COMMUNITY SERVICES, whereas low-qualified individuals are more likely to be in AGRICULTURE or CONSTRUCTION AND INDUSTRY. It is quite interesting to note that non-participants in West Germany have on average more work experience when compared to the participants. In East Germany on the other hand the situation is much more balanced and no large differences in work experience between participants and non-participants are visible.

These findings confirm two expectations. First, participants and non-participants differ remarkably in their characteristics. Clearly, this has been expected and highlights once again that a simple comparison of treated and non-treated individuals will lead to selection bias. We will address this problem with a matching estimator. Second, the participants in the different sectors have also rather different characteristics, and the estimation has to take this into account properly.

6.3 Implementation of the Propensity Score Matching

In this section, the implementation of the propensity score matching estimator will be discussed. Since we have discussed a lot of technical issues concerning PSM already in the previous chapter, we will not repeat this here. Based on section 5.3.1 we take the plausibility of the CIA as given and use the same matching approach as suggested in section 5.3.3. Therefore we start the discussion directly by presenting the propensity score estimation and discuss the quality of our matching procedure. Once again, we will estimate the effects separately for men and women in West and East Germany.

6.3.1 Propensity Score Estimation

Finding the right propensity score specification in this context is not an easy task. Estimating the propensity score for participation in JCS versus non-participation is not sufficient. To give an example, let us reconsider one finding from the last section. It has been shown that higher qualified individuals are more likely to be found in the sectors OFFICE AND SERVICES and COMMUNITY SERVICES, whereas low-qualified individuals are more likely to be in AGRICULTURE or CONSTRUCTION AND INDUSTRY. Hence, it can be expected that the qualification variable 'professional training' has a different influence on the participation probability in the different sectors. The aim of the matching procedure is to find for each individual in the treatment group a similar individual out of the group of non-participants. If we would estimate only one propensity score (participation vs. non-participation), sector-specific differences like mentioned above would not be regarded and consequently, a poor matching quality could be expected. To avoid this, we estimate binary logit models for every treatment group in the five sectors against the group of non-participants. Thereby we run the estimations separately for men and women in West and East Germany. Since we exclude participating women in West Germany who are in the sectors AGRICULTURE and CONSTRUCTION AND INDUSTRY, this leaves us with 18 logit estimations. At this point one might wonder why we do not use a multinomial probit model, which would reduce the estimation (and documentation) burden significantly. This is due to the fact that the decision process, as described in subsection 4.2.3, is a binary one. In the placement process, the individual is offered a specific job in a measure where a place is available and which fits his characteristics. Thus, we have a binary decision process making a multinomial approach unappropriate.

The results of the binary logit estimations can be found in tables C.5 (Men, West Germany), C.6 (Women, West Germany), C.7 (Men, East Germany) and C.8 (Women, East Germany) in appendix C. A first thing which becomes obvious is that the parameters of the choice estimations do not only diverge with respect to regional and gender-specific differences, but also with respect to sector specific aspects. Clearly, based on the descriptive analysis in the last section nothing else has been expected. For example, married men (0.6680) and women (0.1677) in West Germany have a higher probability to join a programme in the sector COMMUNITY SERVICES than men (-0.2582/not significant) and women (-0.4877) in the East. A good example for sector-specific differences is the individuals' age. Whereas age has a negative impact on the probability for men in West Germany to join CONSTRUCTION AND INDUSTRY (-0.1343), it has a positive effect for them to join OFFICE AND SERVICES (0.3791). Clearly, there are also variables that influence participation probabilities irrespective of gender and region. The number of placement propositions is a fine example as it increases the participation probabilities for men and women in both parts and all sectors. There is a strong tendency for men and women with health restrictions to participate in the sectors OFFICE AND SERVICES or COMMUNITY SERVICES when compared to individuals without health restrictions. This makes sense as it is not very likely for people with health problems to work in the sectors AGRICULTURE or CONSTRUCTION AND INDUSTRY. People with higher qualifications (reference category is without completed professional training and CSE) tend to go in the sectors OFFICE AND SERVICES and COMMUNITY SERVICES, too. For example the coefficient for West German men with college or university degree to join the sector OFFICE AND SERVICES is 1.5608, whereas this characteristic reduces the probability to join AGRICULTURE by a coefficient of -1.2767. The influence of professional rank works in the same direction. Individuals with a higher rank (compared to unskilled workers) are less likely to participate in AGRICULTURE (and to a certain extent also CONSTRUCTION AND INDUSTRY). The coefficients for the occupational groups are as expected. People who come from service professions are also more likely to join sectors OFFICE AND SERVICES and COMMUNITY SERVICES and less likely to join AGRICULTURE and CONSTRUCTION AND INDUSTRY. No clear differences between the sectors can be found for the unemployment duration and the duration of last employment. The latter one decreases the participation probability for all groups in all sectors. The unemployment duration (in three classes: less than 13 weeks (reference), 13-52 weeks and over 52 weeks) has significant influence mainly in East Germany, where it increases the probability for nearly all sectors. Overall it can be stated that sector-specific differences play a major role for the participation probabilities and hence that it was a good choice to estimate the probabilities for the different sectors separately.

6.3.2 Matching Quality and Common Support

Based upon the propensity score estimates and the chosen matching algorithm, we check the matching quality by comparing the standardised bias (SB) before and after matching. Since we do not condition on all the covariates but on the propensity scores, this is a necessary step to see if the matching procedure is able to balance the distribution of the covariates between the group of participants and non-participants. The SB, as suggested by Rosenbaum and Rubin (1985b) and described in subsection 3.2.2, is a convenient way to do so as it assesses the distance in the marginal distributions of the covariates. To abbreviate the documentation, we calculated the means of the SB before and after matching for men and women in West and East Germany for the different sectors as an unweighted average of all variables (mean standardised bias, MSB). The results can be found in table 6.1. Starting with men in West Germany we see that the overall bias before matching is between 14.77% (OTHER) and 23.23% (OFFICE AND SERVICES). The matching procedure is able to achieve a significant reduction in all of the sectors and leads to a MSB after matching between 3.42% and 4.33% for four of the five sectors. The MSB after matching in the sector OFFICE AND SERVICES is still quite high (6.86%). But taking into account that this group is the smallest group of men in West Germany and the enormous reduction compared to the situation before matching, this is acceptable. For women in West Germany, the MSB is reduced from 21.76% to 5.31% in the sector OFFICE AND SERVICES, from 18.11% to 3.07% in the sector COMMUNITY SERVICES and from 15.83% to 5.01% in the sector OTHER. The bias reduction in East Germany is even better, leaving us with a MSB after matching between 2.17% (AGRICULTURE) and 5.72% (OFFICE AND SERVICES) for men and between 1.58% (COMMUNITY SERVICES) and 5.74% (CONSTRUCTION AND INDUSTRY) for women. Overall, these are enormous reductions and show that the matching procedure is able to balance the characteristics in the treatment and the matched control group.

Table 6.1: Mean Standardised Bias Before and After Matching in Programme Sectors[1]

	All Individuals		Promotion REGULAR		Promotion ENFORCED		Provider PUBLIC		Provider NON-COMM.	
	before	after	before	after	before	after	before	after	before	after
West Germany										
Men										
AGRICULTURE	18.88	3.76	19.56	4.33	19.81	5.88	19.07	5.08	18.79	5.97
CONSTRUCTION AND INDUSTRY	22.32	3.70	19.16	5.62	26.81	5.61	–	–	21.18	4.62
OFFICE AND SERVICES	23.23	6.86	23.10	7.01	–	–	–	–	–	–
COMMUNITY SERVICES	17.89	4.33	16.86	6.10	–	–	–	–	17.47	5.65
OTHER	14.77	3.42	14.82	3.16	20.67	6.29	19.05	5.25	15.08	3.48
Women										
AGRICULTURE	–	–	–	–	–	–	–	–	–	–
CONSTRUCTION AND INDUSTRY	–	–	–	–	–	–	–	–	–	–
OFFICE AND SERVICES	21.76	5.31	22.01	6.07	–	–	–	–	–	–
COMMUNITY SERVICES	18.11	3.07	18.34	3.43	22.65	10.48	19.49	7.69	18.28	3.97
OTHER	15.83	5.01	16.63	3.81	–	–	–	–	15.40	5.52
East Germany										
Men										
AGRICULTURE	17.02	2.17	17.53	5.23	17.46	3.18	17.53	5.80	16.86	3.26
CONSTRUCTION AND INDUSTRY	16.65	4.02	–	–	15.73	3.76	18.11	7.98	16.20	5.74
OFFICE AND SERVICES	25.43	5.72	27.60	7.93	–	–	–	–	26.19	7.52
COMMUNITY SERVICES	16.24	4.13	18.29	3.76	17.30	5.17	–	–	16.36	4.97
OTHER	11.55	3.05	17.11	4.01	11.54	3.74	13.44	6.15	11.44	3.52
Women										
AGRICULTURE	18.10	2.14	16.95	5.23	17.92	2.92	17.45	5.27	18.25	3.02
CONSTRUCTION AND INDUSTRY	13.11	5.74	–	–	14.17	6.10	–	–	14.66	8.25
OFFICE AND SERVICES	17.62	3.02	18.18	9.94	17.13	4.70	18.13	9.47	17.50	4.10
COMMUNITY SERVICES	11.81	1.58	13.46	2.37	10.77	3.20	13.86	3.83	11.58	2.05
OTHER	11.03	2.73	13.11	3.68	12.05	2.75	13.77	3.87	10.87	3.31

Standardised bias before matching calculated as: $100 \cdot (\overline{X}_1 - \overline{X}_0) / \left[\sqrt{(V_1(X) + V_0(X))/2}\right]$.

Standardised bias after matching calculated as: $100 \cdot (\overline{X}_{1M} - \overline{X}_{0M}) / \left[\sqrt{(V_{1M}(X) + V_{0M}(X))/2}\right]$.

Mean standardised bias has been calculated as an unweighted average of all covariates.

[1] Groups of less than 100 participants are excluded from estimation.

However, taking the 18 propensity score estimations for the further subgroups (differentiated by type of promotion and implementing institution) was not satisfactory in terms of balancing the covariates. Hence, we additionally estimated propensity scores to be in a specific sector and receive REGULAR or ENFORCED promotion as well as to be in a specific sector with a PUBLIC or NON-COMMERCIAL provider. Thereby we excluded groups with less than 100 observations. The results can be found in table 6.1, too. It can be seen that the finer propensity score specification is able to reduce the MSB after matching for most groups fairly below 6%. However, there are some groups for which the MSB after matching is still quite high. For example, women with enforced promotion in the sector COMMUNITY SERVICES in West Germany have a MSB after matching of 10.48%. This highlights the fact that it is not always possible to find comparable individuals in the group of non-participants and that the matching approach reaches its boundaries in such situations. Fortunately, this is only the case for very few sub-groups but has to be considered when interpreting the results.

A final thing to bear in mind when implementing matching is the region of common support between participants and non-participants. We have discussed this issue at length in subsection 3.2.3. Clearly, matching estimates are only defined over the common support region and treated individuals who fall outside this region have to be discarded. If the share of individuals lost is high, the effects have to be re-interpreted which might cause problems for the explanatory power of the results. Table C.9 in the appendix shows the number of lost treated individuals due to missing common support. It can be seen that we lose nearly none of the treated individuals in the five sectors. For men in West Germany we lose between zero (CONSTRUCTION AND INDUSTRY) and 1.53% (OFFICE AND SERVICES) of all treated individuals, which corresponds to a total loss of ten participants. For women in West Germany we lose seven observations and the numbers in East Germany are even lower with four men and five women. The picture is equally good for the sub-groups defined by different providers and types of promotion.[2] Hence, common support is guaranteed and not a problem for this analysis.

6.4 Results

Our empirical analysis tries to answer the question, if individuals who join a JCS in February 2000 have a higher employment probability compared to individuals who do not enter the programme in February 2000. To do so, we estimate the monthly employment effects from begin of the programme, which leaves us with 35 monthly effects. This ensures that participants and non-participants are compared in the same economic environment and the same individual lifecycle position.[3] Clearly, what has to be kept in mind is the occurrence of locking-in effects. Since participants are involved in the programme, they do not have the same time for job searching activities as non-participants. We have discussed already that the net-effect of each programme can be separated in two opposite effects. On the one hand we have a negative effect due to reduced search intensity and on the other hand we have a positive

---

[2] One exception are women in West Germany participating in COMMUNITY SERVICES with ENFORCED promotion. For this group we lose 14.6% of the observations. This corresponds to the finding regarding the MSB in this group and basically permits a further interpretation of the results in this group.

[3] See subsection 3.2.5 for an extensive discussion on when to measure treatment effects.

effect through the programme itself. The reduced search intensity causes the locking-in effect in the first months after programmes begin. However, since we observe the outcomes for nearly three years after programme begin and the average programme duration is less than one year, a successful programme should overcompensate for this initial fall. To allow a more accurate discussion, we present the results for six selected months only in the following tables. The results over time, i.e. from February 2000 until December 2002, can be found in figures C.1 to C.9 in the appendix. We will start the discussion with the effects in the five different sectors for men and women in West and East Germany. After that, we additionally differentiate by type of promotion and the providers.

6.4.1 Results for the Five Sectors

Let us start with the main effects in the different sectors, which are depicted in table 6.2. The results show that the expected locking-in effects vary considerably not only between the different sectors but also in both regions. Five month after programmes start in July 2000, we find significant negative employment effects for men in West Germany which lie between -15.6% (AGRICULTURE) and -27.2% (COMMUNITY SERVICES). That means, that the average employment rate of male participants in the sector COMMUNITY SERVICES is 27.2% lower compared to matched non-participants. Clearly, this strong reduction is expected as nearly all participants are still in the programmes, whereas non-participants have the chance to search, apply for and find a new job. For women in West Germany, the effects in July 2000 lie between -19.3% (COMMUNITY SERVICES) and -22.9% (OFFICE AND SERVICES). The locking-in effects in East Germany are less pronounced, which may indicate that being locked into the programme does not have as much influence, since the chances of non-participants to find a new job are lower anyway. For men the effects are bounded between -13.3% (COMMUNITY SERVICES) and -19.5% (CONSTRUCTION AND INDUSTRY). The locking-in effects for women in East Germany are even lower and lie between -8.7% (AGRICULTURE) and -12.9% (CONSTRUCTION AND INDUSTRY). Most of the participants leave the programmes after one year. In fact, in March 2001 around 80% (74%) of the male (female) participants in West Germany and approximately 91% (92%) of the male (female) participants in East Germany have left the programmes.[4] Hence, any locking-in effects should start to fade away after that time, which is also reflected by our findings. In July 2001, the effects for all of the groups in both regions have increased, even though they are still significantly negative. The improvement is stronger in West Germany, where the effects for men now lie between -7.7% (AGRICULTURE) and -15.5% (OFFICE AND SERVICES) and for women between -11.3% (COMMUNITY SERVICES) and -12.9% (OTHER). In contrast to that, the improvement in East Germany is smaller

---

[4] See tables B.14 to B.17 in the appendix for details about the exit patterns.

Table 6.2: Employment Effects in the Programme Sectors for Selected Months[1]

		Jul 00	Dec 00	Jul 01	Dec 01	Jul 02	Dec 02
West Germany							
Men							
AGRICULTURE	Effect	**-0.1561**	**-0.0892**	**-0.0772**	-0.0223	-0.0309	0.0086
	S.E.	0.0160	0.0166	0.0202	0.0245	0.0268	0.0256
CONSTRUCTION AND INDUSTRY	Effect	**-0.2318**	**-0.1833**	**-0.1321**	-0.0108	0.0000	0.0243
	S.E.	0.0204	0.0232	0.0300	0.0338	0.0360	0.0330
OFFICE AND SERVICES	Effect	**-0.2016**	**-0.2016**	**-0.1550**	*-0.0853*	*0.0930*	*0.1008*
	S.E.	0.0323	0.0315	0.0384	0.0384	0.0465	0.0486
COMMUNITY SERVICES	Effect	**-0.2722**	**-0.2057**	**-0.1203**	**-0.0886**	-0.0190	-0.0032
	S.E.	0.0317	0.0299	0.0333	0.0332	0.0314	0.0334
OTHER	Effect	**-0.1956**	**-0.1669**	**-0.1094**	**-0.0725**	-0.0027	0.0027
	S.E.	0.0163	0.0187	0.0232	0.0236	0.0246	0.0235
Women							
AGRICULTURE	Effect	–	–	–	–	–	–
	S.E.	–	–	–	–	–	–
CONSTRUCTION AND INDUSTRY	Effect	–	–	–	–	–	–
	S.E.	–	–	–	–	–	–
OFFICE AND SERVICES	Effect	**-0.2289**	**-0.2438**	*-0.1144*	-0.0647	0.0498	0.0796
	S.E.	0.0289	0.0333	0.0480	0.0434	0.0448	0.0482
COMMUNITY SERVICES	Effect	**-0.1932**	**-0.2173**	**-0.1127**	**-0.0865**	-0.0020	0.0362
	S.E.	0.0171	0.0234	0.0270	0.0283	0.0315	0.0273
OTHER	Effect	**-0.2000**	**-0.2185**	**-0.1296**	*-0.0926*	-0.0037	0.0444
	S.E.	0.0249	0.0292	0.0337	0.0391	0.0423	0.0447
East Germany							
Men							
AGRICULTURE	Effect	**-0.1427**	**-0.0984**	**-0.1146**	**-0.0605**	**-0.0714**	-0.0216
	S.E.	0.0123	0.0124	0.0140	0.0148	0.0161	0.0148
CONSTRUCTION AND INDUSTRY	Effect	**-0.1947**	**-0.1370**	**-0.1298**	**-0.0769**	**-0.0841**	*-0.0601*
	S.E.	0.0173	0.0230	0.0237	0.0244	0.0217	0.0238
OFFICE AND SERVICES	Effect	**-0.1343**	**-0.1343**	**-0.1144**	*-0.0746*	-0.0249	0.0199
	S.E.	0.0181	0.0240	0.0334	0.0343	0.0378	0.0360
COMMUNITY SERVICES	Effect	**-0.1327**	**-0.1425**	**-0.1376**	**-0.0860**	-0.0467	-0.0319
	S.E.	0.0218	0.0185	0.0255	0.0253	0.0279	0.0203
OTHER	Effect	**-0.1401**	**-0.1205**	**-0.0989**	**-0.0639**	**-0.0649**	*-0.0340*
	S.E.	0.0105	0.0113	0.0139	0.0138	0.0149	0.0164
Women							
AGRICULTURE	Effect	**-0.0873**	**-0.0782**	**-0.0711**	**-0.0650**	**-0.0376**	-0.0183
	S.E.	0.0084	0.0094	0.0125	0.0126	0.0121	0.0144
CONSTRUCTION AND INDUSTRY	Effect	**-0.1295**	**-0.0984**	**-0.1036**	-0.0207	-0.0415	0.0104
	S.E.	0.0233	0.0229	0.0310	0.0286	0.0320	0.0311
OFFICE AND SERVICES	Effect	**-0.0916**	**-0.0916**	**-0.0652**	**-0.0807**	**-0.0575**	**-0.0497**
	S.E.	0.0102	0.0106	0.0174	0.0173	0.0184	0.0174
COMMUNITY SERVICES	Effect	**-0.0867**	**-0.0912**	**-0.0602**	**-0.0343**	-0.0133	*0.0232*
	S.E.	0.0063	0.0075	0.0107	0.0118	0.0126	0.0111
OTHER	Effect	**-0.1001**	**-0.1023**	**-0.0851**	**-0.0601**	**-0.0572**	**-0.0258**
	S.E.	0.0087	0.0066	0.0105	0.0105	0.0111	0.0131

Bold letters indicate significance on a 1% level, *italic* letters refer to the 5% level, standard errors are bootstrapped with 50 replications.
Results refer to NN matching without replacement and a caliper of 0.02.
[1] Groups of less than 100 participants are excluded from estimation.

but still visible leading to effects for men between -9.9% (OTHER) and -13.8% (COMMUNITY SERVICES) and for women between -6.0% (COMMUNITY SERVICES) and -10.4% (CONSTRUCTION AND INDUSTRY). Even though this is a remarkable development, the crucial question remains, if programme participants have a higher employment rate at the end of our observation period in December 2002. Unfortunately, this is only true for men in West Germany who participate in the sector OFFICE AND SERVICES (10.1%) and for women in East Germany participating in the sector COMMUNITY SERVICES (2.3%). These are the only groups who benefit from participation in terms of a higher employment rate. For all other groups we find insignificant or negative effects. In particular we find negative effects for men in East Germany participating in the sectors CONSTRUCTION AND INDUSTRY (-6.0%) and OTHER (-3.4%) as well as for East German women in OFFICE AND SERVICES (-5.0%) and OTHER (-2.6%). Taken together, the results are rather discouraging and confirm our previous empirical findings. Participation in JCS does not increase the employment chances of individuals in most cases and has therefore to be rated as a failure. What is left to examine is, if we can establish positive effects for the two different types of promotion (REGULAR and ENFORCED) and for the two different providers (PUBLIC and NON-COMMERCIAL). We will do so in the following.

6.4.2 Results for the Sectors and Types of Promotion

Tables 6.3 (West Germany) and 6.4 (East Germany) contain the results in the different sectors differentiated by the type of promotion. As discussed already, there are two types of promotion: REGULAR and ENFORCED. The difference between those types is that the subsidy quota for participants in ENFORCED promotion is usually higher and the duration may be longer. Since this indicates a higher degree of 'need for assistance', it is a priori not clear, what effects are to be expected. On the one hand it may be argued, that ENFORCED promotion may lead to better outcomes, since the costs are usually higher and the programme is more intense. On the other hand, it may also be claimed that those individuals have on average worse labour market prospects. Clearly, these presumptions can only be confirmed or discarded by empirical examination.[5] Thereby, we excluded any groups with less than 100 observations.

Taking the results in July 2000 as an indicator for the magnitude of locking-in effects, an unexpected finding emerges. We would have expected that an ENFORCED promotion corresponds to higher locking-in effects. However, in West Germany, this expectation could only be confirmed for men in AGRICULTURE (-16.7% in regular, -20.5% in enforced promotion). For women in West Germany no strong statements are possible, since we cannot estimate effects for most of the sub-groups due to the small number of observations. In East Germany, the hypothesis is confirmed for two male groups (and rejected for one) and for three female groups (again, rejected for one). However, the differences are not very pronounced and do no not allow a clear confirmation of the hypothesis.

---

[5] Since the characteristics of individuals in REGULAR and ENFORCED differ, we estimated the propensity scores for both types separately.

Table 6.3: Employment Effects in the Programme Sectors differentiated by Types of Promotion - Selected Months (West Germany)[1]

West Germany Men								
Sector	Type of Promotion		Jul 00	Dec 00	Jul 01	Dec 01	Jul 02	Dec 02
AGRICULTURE	Regular	Effect	**-0.1675**	**-0.1414**	**-0.1126**	**-0.0707**	-0.0471	-0.0366
		S.E.	0.0208	0.0233	0.0279	0.0254	0.0278	0.0278
	Enforced	Effect	**-0.2050**	**-0.1550**	*-0.1100*	-0.0400	-0.0400	-0.0050
		S.E.	0.0317	0.0332	0.0461	0.0469	0.0404	0.0382
CONSTR. AND IND.	Regular	Effect	**-0.2607**	**-0.2308**	**-0.1709**	**-0.0940**	-0.0684	-0.0299
		S.E.	0.0370	0.0291	0.0407	0.0360	0.0366	0.0376
	Enforced	Effect	**-0.2482**	**-0.1752**	-0.0803	0.0000	-0.0365	0.0365
		S.E.	0.0397	0.0491	0.0566	0.0543	0.0496	0.0516
OFFICE AND SERVICES	Regular	Effect	**-0.1520**	**-0.1680**	-0.0960	-0.0320	0.0800	*0.1360*
		S.E.	0.0381	0.0373	0.0501	0.0470	0.0643	0.0643
	Enforced	Effect	–	–	–	–	–	–
		S.E.	–	–	–	–	–	–
COMMUNITY SERVICES	Regular	Effect	**-0.2018**	**-0.1881**	-0.0688	-0.0780	0.0183	0.0275
		S.E.	0.0320	0.0357	0.0365	0.0422	0.0396	0.0385
	Enforced	Effect	–	–	–	–	–	–
		S.E.	–	–	–	–	–	–
OTHER	Regular	Effect	**-0.2231**	**-0.1865**	**-0.0981**	-0.0481	-0.0288	-0.0038
		S.E.	0.0199	0.0189	0.0250	0.0326	0.0285	0.0301
	Enforced	Effect	**-0.2115**	**-0.1538**	*-0.0962*	*-0.0913*	-0.0721	-0.0288
		S.E.	0.0344	0.0384	0.0431	0.0410	0.0415	0.0400
Women								
AGRICULTURE	Regular	Effect	–	–	–	–	–	–
		S.E.	–	–	–	–	–	–
	Enforced	Effect	–	–	–	–	–	–
		S.E.	–	–	–	–	–	–
CONSTR. AND IND.	Regular	Effect	–	–	–	–	–	–
		S.E.	–	–	–	–	–	–
	Enforced	Effect	–	–	–	–	–	–
		S.E.	–	–	–	–	–	–
OFFICE AND SERVICES	Regular	Effect	**-0.2067**	**-0.1732**	-0.0726	-0.0112	0.1061	0.1117
		S.E.	0.0300	0.0358	0.0546	0.0570	0.0557	0.0581
	Enforced	Effect	–	–	–	–	–	–
		S.E.	–	–	–	–	–	–
COMMUNITY SERVICES	Regular	Effect	**-0.2183**	**-0.2264**	**-0.1617**	**-0.1321**	-0.0270	-0.0108
		S.E.	0.0237	0.0246	0.0315	0.0327	0.0343	0.0339
	Enforced	Effect	**-0.2252**	**-0.1982**	*-0.1261*	-0.0541	0.0450	*0.1261*
		S.E.	0.0401	0.0407	0.0555	0.0536	0.0572	0.0553
OTHER	Regular	Effect	**-0.2067**	**-0.1875**	**-0.1058**	-0.0144	*0.0817*	*0.1202*
		S.E.	0.0251	0.0356	0.0410	0.0393	0.0404	0.0499
	Enforced	Effect	–	–	–	–	–	–
		S.E.	–	–	–	–	–	–

Bold letters indicate significance on a 1% level, *italic* letters refer to the 5% level.
Standard errors are bootstrapped with 50 replications.
Results refer to NN matching without replacement and a caliper of 0.02.
[1] Groups of less than 100 participants are excluded from estimation.

Let us now look at the effects in more detail, starting with the effects for West Germany. Table 6.3 shows that the positive effect for men in OFFICE AND SERVICES is confirmed and even higher for men in regular promotion. The employment rate of these men is 13.6% higher than the one from the matched non-participants. It is also quite interesting to note that the differentiation between REGULAR and ENFORCED promotion for women in COMMUNITY SERVICES leads to positive effects. The effect for the whole group has

Table 6.4: Employment Effects in the Programme Sectors differentiated by Types of Promotion - Selected Months (East Germany)[1]

East Germany Men								
Sector	Type of Promotion		Jul 00	Dec 00	Jul 01	Dec 01	Jul 02	Dec 02
AGRICULTURE	Regular	Effect	**-0.1384**	**-0.1071**	**-0.1250**	**-0.0804**	**-0.0759**	*-0.0536*
		S.E.	0.0210	0.0221	0.0255	0.0216	0.0269	0.0255
	Enforced	Effect	**-0.1626**	**-0.0927**	**-0.1127**	**-0.0599**	**-0.0728**	-0.0300
		S.E.	0.0113	0.0133	0.0172	0.0167	0.0184	0.0193
CONSTR. AND IND.	Regular	Effect	–	–	–	–	–	–
		S.E.	–	–	–	–	–	–
	Enforced	Effect	**-0.1786**	**-0.1161**	**-0.1280**	**-0.0655**	*-0.0595*	-0.0387
		S.E.	0.0173	0.0217	0.0282	0.0236	0.0303	0.0254
OFFICE AND SERVICES	Regular	Effect	**-0.1182**	**-0.1273**	-0.0636	-0.0273	0.0364	0.0818
		S.E.	0.0331	0.0375	0.0425	0.0463	0.0443	0.0473
	Enforced	Effect	–	–	–	–	–	–
		S.E.	–	–	–	–	–	–
COMMUNITY SERVICES	Regular	Effect	**-0.1573**	**-0.1331**	**-0.1250**	**-0.1331**	**-0.0927**	*-0.0645*
		S.E.	0.0231	0.0243	0.0270	0.0230	0.0285	0.0289
	Enforced	Effect	**-0.1118**	**-0.1242**	*-0.0932*	-0.0311	-0.0062	-0.0559
		S.E.	0.0315	0.0288	0.0397	0.0473	0.0473	0.0451
OTHER	Regular	Effect	**-0.1078**	**-0.0929**	**-0.1190**	**-0.0632**	-0.0335	0.0149
		S.E.	0.0218	0.0209	0.0295	0.0247	0.0302	0.0233
	Enforced	Effect	**-0.1439**	**-0.1254**	**-0.0954**	**-0.0670**	**-0.0570**	-0.0157
		S.E.	0.0143	0.0147	0.0213	0.0163	0.0186	0.0161
Women								
AGRICULTURE	Regular	Effect	**-0.0785**	**-0.0579**	*-0.0579*	**-0.0620**	-0.0496	-0.0165
		S.E.	0.0181	0.0199	0.0248	0.0226	0.0291	0.0261
	Enforced	Effect	**-0.0861**	**-0.0888**	**-0.0848**	**-0.0740**	**-0.0458**	*-0.0350*
		S.E.	0.0099	0.0122	0.0135	0.0132	0.0142	0.0139
CONSTR. AND IND.	Regular	Effect	–	–	–	–	–	–
		S.E.	–	–	–	–	–	–
	Enforced	Effect	**-0.1103**	**-0.0966**	*-0.0759*	-0.0483	-0.0483	-0.0552
		S.E.	0.0320	0.0270	0.0334	0.0379	0.0360	0.0334
OFFICE AND SERVICES	Regular	Effect	**-0.0852**	**-0.0877**	**-0.0602**	**-0.0576**	-0.0326	-0.0251
		S.E.	0.0159	0.0168	0.0226	0.0224	0.0255	0.0241
	Enforced	Effect	**-0.1423**	**-0.1301**	**-0.0772**	*-0.0569*	-0.0447	-0.0163
		S.E.	0.0240	0.0212	0.0278	0.0256	0.0290	0.0299
COMMUNITY SERVICES	Regular	Effect	**-0.0808**	**-0.0927**	**-0.0459**	**-0.0331**	-0.0165	0.0294
		S.E.	0.0078	0.0097	0.0137	0.0127	0.0147	0.0151
	Enforced	Effect	**-0.0847**	**-0.0889**	**-0.0569**	-0.0139	0.0056	0.0250
		S.E.	0.0112	0.0114	0.0127	0.0169	0.0207	0.0178
OTHER	Regular	Effect	**-0.0794**	**-0.0967**	**-0.0846**	**-0.0829**	**-0.0535**	-0.0328
		S.E.	0.0112	0.0112	0.0182	0.0185	0.0191	0.0220
	Enforced	Effect	**-0.0732**	**-0.0610**	**-0.0646**	**-0.0415**	-0.0268	-0.0024
		S.E.	0.0117	0.0101	0.0147	0.0119	0.0154	0.0145

Bold letters indicate significance on a 1% level, *italic* letters refer to the 5% level. Standard errors are bootstrapped with 50 replications.
Results refer to NN matching without replacement and a caliper of 0.02.
[1] Groups of less than 100 participants are excluded from estimation.

been positive but insignificant, and is now 12.6% for ENFORCED promotion and insignificant for women in REGULAR promotion. However, what should be kept in mind is that the MSB for this group after matching was quite high and we additionally lost a significant share of participants due to missing common support. Hence, the interpretation of the results for this group is strongly restricted. Positive effects could not be established for any of the groups in East Germany (table 6.4). In contrary, we find negative effects for men in AGRI-

CULTURE (-5.4%) and COMMUNITY SERVICES (-6.5%) who receive REGULAR promotion. For women we find only one significant effect, namely -3.5% for participants in ENFORCED promotion in AGRICULTURE. Hence, we can give no clear recommendation on which type of promotion should be preferred. There are only two groups with positive effects anyway. For the first group (men in OFFICE AND SERVICES in West Germany) we can only estimate the effects of REGULAR promotion, since the number of participants in ENFORCED promotion is too small. For the second group (women in COMMUNITY SERVICES), the findings should not be over-emphasised since the matching indicators (MSB and number of treated individuals lost due to common support) are not favourable. However, for most of the groups participation in JCS has no effect at all.

6.4.3 Results for the Sectors and Providers

Tables 6.5 (West Germany) and 6.6 (East Germany) contain the results in the programme sectors differentiated by the provider. We have presented already that there are three types of providers, namely institutions from the PUBLIC sector, NON-COMMERCIAL organisations and PRIVATE businesses. Since the number of participants in PRIVATE businesses is very small, we had to exclude this group from the analysis. Additionally, especially in West Germany the differentiation between providers leads to group classes below 100 observations, such that we can estimate the effects only for three female and six male groups. In East Germany this is not so problematic and we exclude only three out of 20 groups.

Turning to the results in West Germany shows, that there are no clear differences with respect to locking-in effects in the first months. For example men in AGRICULTURE in the PUBLIC SECTOR have an effect of -19.8% in July 2000, whereas those participating in a programme provided by a NON-COMMERCIAL institution have an effect of -18.5% in the same month. The same relation also holds for participants in the sector OTHER. For women in COMMUNITY SERVICES on the other hand the relation is the other way around, with -19.8% in the PUBLIC SECTOR and -21.0% in the NON-COMMERCIAL sector. One year later in July 2001, that is nearly four months after most of the participants have left the programmes, the effects are still significantly negative for all of the groups ranging for men from -9.8% (OTHER provided by NON-COMMERCIAL institution) to -15.9% (OTHER provided by PUBLIC institution) and for women from -11.6% (COMMUNITY SERVICES, NON-COMMERCIAL provider) to -14.3% (COMMUNITY SERVICES, PUBLIC provider). After that point in time, the effects start to move against zero, which leads to no significant effects at all in December 2002. That means, that participation in JCS neither harms nor helps individuals in terms of a higher employment rate in December 2002.

The situation in East Germany is different but unfortunately not better. The locking-in effects are much smaller and range from -12.5% (AGRICULTURE,

Table 6.5: Employment Effects in the Programme Sectors for the Two Types of Providers - Selected Months (West Germany)[1]

West Germany Men Sector	Provider		Jul 00	Dec 00	Jul 01	Dec 01	Jul 02	Dec 02
AGRICULTURE	Public	Effect	**-0.1976**	**-0.1108**	**-0.1138**	*-0.0659*	-0.0449	-0.0120
		S.E.	0.0228	0.0218	0.0239	0.0258	0.0297	0.0228
	Non-Commercial	Effect	**-0.1849**	**-0.1681**	*-0.0840*	*-0.0378*	0.0168	0.0294
		S.E.	0.0316	0.0308	0.0337	0.0373	0.0363	0.0325
CONSTR. AND IND.	Public	Effect	–	–	–	–	–	–
		S.E.	–	–	–	–	–	–
	Non-Commercial	Effect	**-0.1932**	**-0.1818**	**-0.1023**	-0.0379	-0.0455	-0.0076
		S.E.	0.0274	0.0264	0.0365	0.0328	0.0356	0.0363
OFFICE AND SERVICES	Public	Effect	–	–	–	–	–	–
		S.E.	–	–	–	–	–	–
	Non-Commercial	Effect	–	–	–	–	–	–
		S.E.	–	–	–	–	–	–
COMMUNITY SERVICES	Public	Effect	–	–	–	–	–	–
		S.E.	–	–	–	–	–	–
	Non-Commercial	Effect	**-0.2283**	**-0.2165**	**-0.1496**	**-0.1024**	-0.0472	0.0197
		S.E.	0.0302	0.0329	0.0380	0.0373	0.0383	0.0362
OTHER	Public	Effect	**-0.2189**	**-0.1990**	**-0.1592**	**-0.1343**	*-0.0945*	-0.0348
		S.E.	0.0365	0.0360	0.0377	0.0366	0.0377	0.0359
	Non-Commercial	Effect	**-0.2047**	**-0.1599**	**-0.0981**	**-0.0661**	-0.0235	0.0043
		S.E.	0.0215	0.0263	0.0252	0.0256	0.0297	0.0309
Women								
AGRICULTURE	Public	Effect	–	–	–	–	–	–
		S.E.	–	–	–	–	–	–
	Non-Commercial	Effect	–	–	–	–	–	–
		S.E.	–	–	–	–	–	–
CONSTR. AND IND.	Public	Effect	–	–	–	–	–	–
		S.E.	–	–	–	–	–	–
	Non-Commercial	Effect	–	–	–	–	–	–
		S.E.	–	–	–	–	–	–
OFFICE AND SERVICES	Public	Effect	–	–	–	–	–	–
		S.E.	–	–	–	–	–	–
	Non-Commercial	Effect	–	–	–	–	–	–
		S.E.	–	–	–	–	–	–
COMMUNITY SERVICES	Public	Effect	**-0.1984**	**-0.1984**	**-0.1429**	-0.0635	-0.0079	-0.0079
		S.E.	0.0411	0.0395	0.0446	0.0484	0.0593	0.0564
	Non-Commercial	Effect	**-0.2099**	**-0.2431**	**-0.1160**	**-0.0939**	0.0138	0.0442
		S.E.	0.0200	0.0247	0.0297	0.0326	0.0304	0.0318
OTHER	Public	Effect	–	–	–	–	–	–
		S.E.	–	–	–	–	–	–
	Non-Commercial	Effect	**-0.1937**	**-0.2304**	**-0.1257**	-0.0785	0.0000	0.0105
		S.E.	0.0249	0.0355	0.0424	0.0430	0.0455	0.0454

Bold letters indicate significance on a 1% level, *italic* letters refer to the 5% level. Standard errors are bootstrapped with 50 replications.
Results refer to NN matching without replacement and a caliper of 0.02.
[1] Groups of less than 100 participants are excluded from estimation.

NON-COMMERCIAL provider) to -18.3% (CONSTRUCTION AND INDUSTRY, NON-COMMERCIAL provider) for men and -8.2% (AGRICULTURE, PUBLIC provider) to -11.6% (CONSTRUCTION AND INDUSTRY, NON-COMMERCIAL provider) for women. In July 2001 the effects are, similar to West Germany, still significantly negative for most of the groups, but on a slightly lower level. There is also a further improvement in the following months leading to insignificant effects in December 2002. However, we find significant negative effects for men in the sector AGRICULTURE provided by NON-COMMERCIAL

Table 6.6: Employment Effects in the Programme Sectors for the Two Types of Providers - Selected Months (East Germany) [1]

Sector	Provider		Jul 00	Dec 00	Jul 01	Dec 01	Jul 02	Dec 02
East Germany								
Men								
AGRICULTURE	Public	Effect	**-0.1475**	**-0.1079**	**-0.1403**	**-0.0827**	-0.0432	-0.0180
		S.E.	0.0222	0.0201	0.0260	0.0196	0.0229	0.0243
	Non-Comm.	Effect	**-0.1246**	**-0.0902**	**-0.0918**	**-0.0689**	**-0.0754**	**-0.0525**
		S.E.	0.0141	0.0133	0.0176	0.0158	0.0153	0.0141
CONSTR. AND IND.	Public	Effect	**-0.1556**	**-0.1667**	**-0.1000**	-0.0667	-0.0500	-0.0611
		S.E.	0.0290	0.0261	0.0377	0.0393	0.0326	0.0319
	Non-Comm.	Effect	**-0.1827**	**-0.1154**	**-0.1538**	**-0.0913**	*-0.0721*	-0.0433
		S.E.	0.0289	0.0287	0.0368	0.0307	0.0358	0.0286
OFFICE AND SERVICES	Public	Effect	–	–	–	–	–	–
		S.E.	–	–	–	–	–	–
	Non-Comm.	Effect	**-0.1290**	**-0.1048**	**-0.1290**	-0.0645	0.0161	0.0484
		S.E.	0.0354	0.0325	0.0393	0.0373	0.0519	0.0453
COMMUNITY SERVICES	Public	Effect	–	–	–	–	–	–
		S.E.	–	–	–	–	–	–
	Non-Comm.	Effect	**-0.1524**	**-0.1494**	**-0.1128**	**-0.0976**	*-0.0488*	-0.0122
		S.E.	0.0221	0.0178	0.0246	0.0274	0.0209	0.0268
OTHER	Public	Effect	**-0.1719**	**-0.0990**	**-0.1146**	**-0.0990**	-0.0573	-0.0260
		S.E.	0.0286	0.0273	0.0338	0.0312	0.0338	0.0299
	Non-Comm.	Effect	**-0.1434**	**-0.1298**	**-0.0943**	**-0.0464**	**-0.0464**	-0.0055
		S.E.	0.0144	0.0106	0.0156	0.0178	0.0167	0.0139
Women								
AGRICULTURE	Public	Effect	**-0.0818**	**-0.0881**	**-0.0597**	**-0.0723**	-0.0377	-0.0314
		S.E.	0.0155	0.0161	0.0217	0.0170	0.0213	0.0204
	Non-Comm.	Effect	**-0.0866**	**-0.0677**	**-0.0772**	**-0.0409**	-0.0252	-0.0142
		S.E.	0.0116	0.0091	0.0171	0.0153	0.0187	0.0157
CONSTR. AND IND.	Public	Effect	–	–	–	–	–	–
		S.E.	–	–	–	–	–	–
	Non-Comm.	Effect	**-0.1157**	*-0.0579*	-0.0579	0.0165	-0.0165	0.0165
		S.E.	0.0292	0.0274	0.0357	0.0375	0.0375	0.0373
OFFICE AND SERVICES	Public	Effect	**-0.0939**	**-0.0903**	*-0.0614*	*-0.0614*	*-0.0578*	-0.0181
		S.E.	0.0135	0.0169	0.0283	0.0252	0.0270	0.0271
	Non-Comm.	Effect	**-0.1145**	**-0.1205**	**-0.0663**	*-0.0512*	-0.0120	-0.0181
		S.E.	0.0171	0.0164	0.0245	0.0219	0.0265	0.0227
COMMUNITY SERVICES	Public	Effect	**-0.0880**	**-0.1129**	**-0.0745**	*-0.0474*	-0.0451	-0.0316
		S.E.	0.0121	0.0134	0.0219	0.0232	0.0272	0.0250
	Non-Comm.	Effect	**-0.0984**	**-0.1037**	**-0.0689**	**-0.0386**	-0.0182	0.0144
		S.E.	0.0081	0.0092	0.0127	0.0132	0.0119	0.0137
OTHER	Public	Effect	**-0.1000**	**-0.0938**	**-0.0688**	*-0.0531*	-0.0313	0.0000
		S.E.	0.0163	0.0168	0.0212	0.0231	0.0234	0.0204
	Non-Comm.	Effect	**-0.1032**	**-0.0942**	**-0.0862**	**-0.0581**	**-0.0481**	*-0.0381*
		S.E.	0.0091	0.0096	0.0132	0.0133	0.0153	0.0153

Bold letters indicate significance on a 1% level, *italic* letters refer to the 5% level. Standard errors are bootstrapped with 50 replications.
Results refer to NN matching without replacement and a caliper of 0.02.
[1] Groups of less than 100 participants are excluded from estimation.

institutions (-5.3%) and for women in OTHER provided by NON-COMMERCIAL institutions (-3.8%). That means, that participation in JCS either harms or does not influence the participants in East Germany in terms of a higher employment rate in December 2002.

6.5 Conclusions

Previous empirical evaluations of job creation schemes in Germany have focused on effect heterogeneity caused by group-specific or regional differences and so has our analysis in chapter 5. In contrast to that we focussed in this chapter explicitly on effect heterogeneity caused by differences in the implementation of programmes. Job creation schemes can be implemented in different sectors of the economy (e.g. AGRICULTURE, CONSTRUCTION AND INDUSTRY or OFFICE AND SERVICES), by different providers (for example PUBLIC or NON-COMMERCIAL INSTITUTIONS) and there are also two types of promotion. These are three potential sources from which only one has been considered so far by Hujer, Caliendo, and Thomsen (2004) who analysed the effects of job creation schemes with respect to sectoral heterogeneity. Identifying the sources of effect heterogeneity can help to improve programmes in the future. We have discussed that the direction of the effect heterogeneity is a-priori not clear. Different arguments may be thought of and can be confirmed or discarded only by empirical examination as was done in this chapter.

We were able to evaluate the employment effects of participants for nearly three years after programmes have started. The analysis was based on the dataset described in section 4.4 and has been done separately for men and women in West and East Germany and additionally differentiated by sectors, providers and types of promotion. Although we find positive employment effects for some groups, i.e. men in West Germany assigned to programmes in OFFICE AND SERVICES, and women in East Germany in COMMUNITY SERVICES, for all other groups the programmes do not have any effect or even harm the employment chances of the participants. These findings are consistent with our results in chapter 5 and confirm that job creation schemes are overall not able to improve the re-integration probability into the first labour market for participating unemployed persons.

7

Conclusions and Outlook

The aim of this book was twofold: In the first part of the book we wanted to give some practical guidance for researchers who want to evaluate active labour market programmes (or other measures) and have to decide between different available non-experimental estimators. Thereby we concentrated on (propensity score) matching and discussed several issues arising during its implementation. We used this knowledge in the second part of the book to evaluate the employment effects of JCS for the participating individuals in Germany.

In the first chapter we presented an overview of the most relevant microeconometric evaluation methods and gave researchers some guidance on how to choose between different approaches. The discussion in this chapter has shown that each non-experimental estimation strategy relies on identifying assumptions and has to be justified case-by-case. Clearly, in an ideal world, the evaluator is already involved at early stages of the programme design and has influence on the data collected for later evaluation. In that case, one can make sure to collect those data needed to justify either the unconfoundedness assumption or to create an instrument (or an exclusion restriction) that allows to use IV methods or selection models. If the evaluator is instead faced with an ongoing programme, he carefully has to assess which identification strategy works for the situation at hand, taking the design of the programme, the selection process, and the available data into account. With matching one tries to construct a 'comparable' control group, selection models try to model the selection decision completely and IV methods focus on finding a good instrument. As Smith (2004) notes, matching methods make no sense without rich data, IV methods make no sense without a good instrument, and finally, longitudinal methods make no sense when selection into treatment depends on transitory rather than permanent shocks.

Chapter 2 than focussed on the matching approach. We have presented several alternative matching estimators and also have shown, that asymptotically all approaches should yield the same results. However, we have highlighted that in small samples the choice can be important. All matching estimators contrast the outcome of a treated individual with the outcome of comparison group members. The presented estimators differ not only in the way the neighbourhood for each treated individual is defined and the common support problem is handled, but also with respect to the weights given to these neighbours. Usually a trade-off between bias and variance arises. We have shown that there is no clear winner for all situations and that the choice of the estimator crucially depends on the situation at hand. Pragmatically, it seems sensible to try a number of approaches. Should they give similar results, the choice may be unimportant. Should the results differ, further investigation may be needed in order to reveal more about the source of the disparity. Finally, we have also presented the benefits which can be achieved by combining matching with other methods, e.g. to take time-invariant unobservable factors into account or to exploit the relation between covariates and outcomes.

In chapter 3 we have focussed on some practical issues when implementing propensity score matching. Our discussion has made clear that the researcher faces a lot of decisions during the implementation. The first step of implementation is the estimation of the propensity score. As to that we have discussed not only the choice of the model but also the choice of the variables to be included in the model. Second, our discussion has emphasised that treatment effects can only be estimated in the region of common support and that testing the overlap in the propensity score distribution of participants and non-participants is a pre-condition for applying matching estimators. The third choice, namely the choice between different matching algorithms usually involves a trade-off between bias and variance and has been discussed extensively, too. Since the main goal of the matching procedure is to balance the distribution of covariates in the treatment and control group, one has to check in a fourth step if that goal was achieved. We presented several procedures to do so. Finally, one has to estimate standard errors and to decide when to measure the effects. A last step of matching analysis is to test the sensitivity of the results with respect to 'hidden bias'. We have presented an approach (Rosenbaum bounds) that allows the researcher to determine how strongly an unmeasured variable must influence the selection process in order to undermine the implications of matching analysis.

Based on the methodological discussion in chapters 1 to 3, part II of the book was concerned with the evaluation of the employment effects of JCS on the participating individuals in Germany.

In chapter 4 we have presented the institutional setup of labour market policies in Germany in general and of JCS in particular. We have shown that microeconometric evaluation of JCS in Germany was hampered for a long time by the absence of suitable data. The earlier evaluation studies of JCS mainly concentrated on the East German labour market and were based on survey data, either the labour market monitor of East Germany or the one of Sachsen-Anhalt. The relatively small groups of participants did not allow to take adequately into account effect heterogeneity. The presentation of the dataset we used for the empirical analysis made clear, that this is not a problem for this study, since we could draw on a dataset containing all entries in JCS in February 2000.

In chapter 5 we started the actual empirical analysis. The aim of this chapter was the evaluation of the re-integration effects of JCS into regular (unsubsidised) employment for the participating individuals in Germany and special attention was given to the possible occurrence of individual, i.e. group-specific, and regional heterogeneity in the effects. That is we estimated the effects for men and women in West and East Germany ('main groups') as well as for eleven 'sub-groups' and within seven regional clusters. Given the very informative dataset, we applied a propensity score matching estimator and discussed several issues concerning its implementation. The effects have been estimated from begin of the programmes in February 2000 until December 2002. Since JCS are usually promoted for twelve months, we find large locking-in effects for all of the groups. The locking-in effects are more pronounced in West Germany and less substantial in East Germany. This may be caused by the better employment opportunities for non-participants in the West. Regarding the effects for the 'main groups' at the end of the observation period, we find a significant positive effect only for women in West Germany (4.6%). However, a relatively bad matching quality and a limited common support advise to use some caution when interpreting the results for this group. The effects for men in West Germany were insignificant and for men (-2.9%) and women (-1.4%) in East Germany the effects were significantly negative. Hence, except for women in West Germany, it seems that the initial negative locking-in effect could not be overcome during our observation period. For most of the sub-groups we do not find significant effects at all. However, some exceptions are worth noting: Long-term unemployed men (5.0%) and women (12.7%) in West Germany and long-term unemployed women (2.5%) in East Germany benefit from participation, whereas for all other groups we either find negative or insignificant effects. The positive findings for the long-term unemployed persons may indicate that the programmes do work for this problem group of the labour market. However, this result cannot be extended to other problem groups, like individuals with placement restrictions, individuals without work experience or low qualified persons. Even though we would have expected positive effects for these problem groups of the labour market, we did not find any. Our regional analysis did not support any of the hypotheses, that JCS work better either in regions with a depressed or prospering labour market situation. The results for the clusters did not diverge much from the overall result in West and East Germany. To some extent the effects reflect the different purpose of JCS in both parts. Whereas they are used as a relief of the tense labour market situation in East Germany, they are more tightly addressed to problem groups in the West. The overall picture is rather disappointing since most of the effects are insignificant or negative. Hence, participation in programmes did not help individuals to re-integrate into regular (unsubsidised) employment. One notable exception are the results for long-term unemployed. Hence, one policy implication is to address programmes to this problem group more tightly.

In contrast to chapter 5, we focussed in chapter 6 explicitly on effect heterogeneity caused by differences in the implementation of programmes. JCS can be implemented in different sectors of the economy (e.g. AGRICULTURE, CONSTRUCTION AND INDUSTRY or OFFICE AND SERVICES), by different providers (for example PUBLIC or NON-COMMERCIAL INSTITUTIONS) and there are also two types of promotion. These are three potential sources of effect heterogeneity, from which only one has been considered so far (sectoral heterogeneity). The effects have been estimated separately for men and women in West and East Germany and were additionally differentiated by sectors, providers and types of promotion. Although we find positive employment effects for some groups, i.e. men in West Germany assigned to programmes in Office and Services and women in East Germany in Community Services, for all other groups the programmes do not have any effect or even harm the employment chances of the participants. These findings are consistent with our results in chapter 5 and confirm that JCS are overall not able to improve the re-integration probability into the first labour market for participating unemployed persons.

Taken together the results are rather disappointing. Participation in JCS does not help the majority of participants to increase their employment chances significantly. Even worse, it harms some of the analysed sub-groups. The possible reasons for that are manifold. First, we found large locking-in effects for all of the groups. Clearly, the effects start to fade away after the majority of participants have left the programme, but they cannot be overcome during our observation period. Since we were able to use information on the outcome variable for nearly three years after programme begin (and two years after programme end for most of the participants), this finding cannot be due to a 'too short' observation period. Hence, one suggestion for future programme design is to reduce the duration of JCS. If the programme is supposed to increase the 'employability' of participants, it might be sufficient to run them for a shorter time. This brings us to the second point which concerns missing 'qualificational' elements. Even though participants in JCS are allowed to take some form of practical training during the participation, it is not very common and participants do not get a formal degree. Clearly, this is a shortcoming and lowers also the appreciation of the programmes by possible employees. This may also be a cause for the often cited 'stigma-effects', which further reduces the possible benefits of a participation in JCS. Our analysis has also shown that these 'sigma-effects' might be over-emphasised, since a clear orientation of JCS to problem groups of the labour market could only be found in West Germany. In East Germany programmes are still used as a relief for the tense labour market situation. This is the fourth point to take into account for future programme design. We found that JCS have positive effects for long-term unemployed men and women in West Germany and long-term unemployed women in East Germany. Hence, it may be beneficial to address programmes in the future more tightly to this problem group of the labour market. Obviously, this should come together with a further reduction of the number of participants (especially in East Germany). If programmes are more specifically tailored to the needs of this (or other) problem group(s), it may enhance their efficiency. In this sense JCS could be a programme for those individuals who belong to a specific problem group of the labour market and do not fit the criteria for other programmes.

Assuming that the reforms would be in place and would lead to positive effects for the participating individuals, a next step to do would be to analyse the effects of JCS on the macroeconomic level and to conduct a cost-benefit analysis, i.e. to compare the individual benefits (in terms of higher employment rates) with the associated costs. We have refrained from doing so here, since the effects have been negative already on the individual level.

A

Additional Material to Chapter 4

A Additional Material to Chapter 4

Fig. A.1: Job Seeker Rate in Germany (Monthly Average), 1999[1]

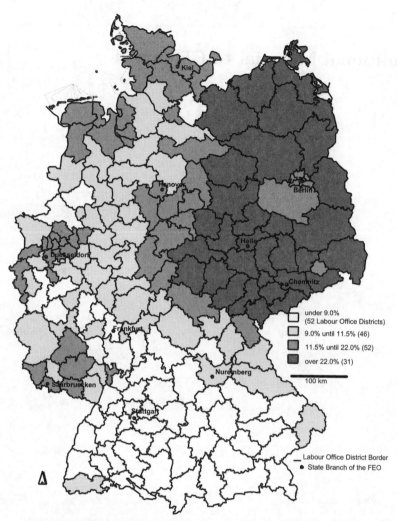

[1] The job seeker rate is defined as the unemployment rate extended by the rate of people participating in ALMP measures.

Source: Hujer, Blien, Caliendo, and Zeiss (2002)

Fig. A.2: Relation Between Job Creation Schemes and Vocational Training Measures, 1999[1]

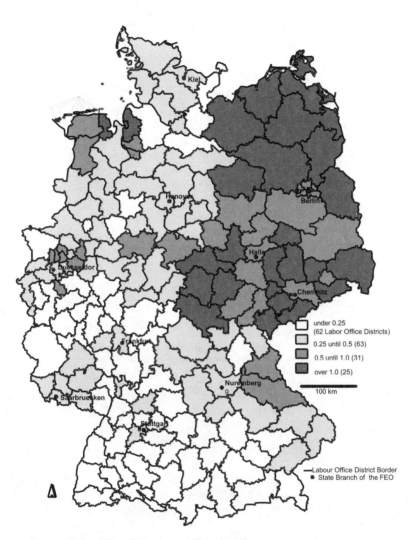

Source: Hujer, Blien, Caliendo, and Zeiss (2002)

B

Additional Material to Chapter 5

Table B.1: Selected Descriptives for the Main Groups

	West Germany				East Germany			
	Men		Women		Men		Women	
Variable	Part.	Non-Part.	Part.	Non-Part.	Part.	Non-Part.	Part.	Non-Part.
	Means							
Programme duration	278.04		304.88		318.78		333.27	
Socio-Demographic Variables								
Age	37.21	43.22	37.82	43.33	44.51	41.73	43.86	44.01
Married	0.35	0.52	0.40	0.63	0.54	0.48	0.68	0.64
Number of children	0.43	0.41	0.58	0.58	0.40	0.36	0.79	0.67
Duration last employment	19.31	72.08	25.00	64.12	24.12	55.51	31.10	63.44
Number of placement propositions	7.70	3.60	6.87	2.99	6.06	3.01	5.42	2.77
Last contact to job center	2.48	2.54	2.53	2.40	2.54	2.79	2.59	2.78
Rehabilitation attendant	0.05	0.06	0.04	0.03	0.07	0.07	0.03	0.05
Placement restrictions	0.17	0.22	0.14	0.18	0.13	0.16	0.07	0.12
	Frequencies in %							
Health restrictions								
No health restrictions	74.30	68.23	78.23	73.29	76.57	74.99	85.08	79.55
Acc. DoR,[1] 80% and over	2.29	1.26	2.85	0.79	0.55	0.47	0.44	0.28
Acc. DoR, 50% to under 80%	6.17	5.87	5.04	3.93	3.49	2.44	1.95	1.63
Acc. DoR, 30% to under 50%	0.47	0.37	0.76	0.26	1.27	0.65	0.70	0.45
Acc. DoR, 30% to under 50%, no equalis.[2]	2.76	4.74	1.71	3.52	1.47	1.74	0.71	1.16
Other health restrictions	14.02	19.54	11.41	18.20	16.66	19.71	11.12	16.94
Qualification Variables								
Professional training								
Without compl. prof. training, no CSE[3]	26.03	15.48	7.98	10.64	8.72	6.01	3.54	4.91
Without compl. prof. training, with CSE	36.59	33.64	37.26	39.30	19.90	17.09	18.73	20.94
Industrial training	29.35	44.25	32.79	41.62	60.23	68.57	62.74	66.03
Full-time vocational school	0.75	1.05	2.57	2.22	0.65	0.56	1.99	1.14
Technical school	2.06	2.22	5.51	2.82	5.51	3.63	9.22	4.86
Polytechnic	1.82	1.25	5.42	0.97	1.20	1.09	1.05	0.49
College, university	3.41	2.12	8.46	2.44	3.80	3.05	2.74	1.63
Occupational group								
Plant cultivation, breeding, fishery	8.69	3.72	2.00	1.75	6.77	5.35	7.27	5.18
Mining, mineral extraction	0.23	0.62	0.00	0.02	0.14	0.27	0.00	0.05
Manufacturing	52.10	47.71	14.64	23.53	52.43	52.82	18.67	19.73
Technical professions	2.85	5.34	1.90	2.08	6.91	5.97	5.20	3.18
Service professions	33.64	40.71	79.56	71.16	32.97	32.67	68.60	70.34
Other professions	2.48	0.12	1.90	0.06	0.79	0.04	0.26	0.02
Professional rank								
Unskilled Worker	31.96	24.25	13.78	17.05	30.47	21.51	24.97	20.55
Skilled Worker	7.10	15.29	3.71	5.71	20.01	29.40	14.18	15.96
White-collar worker, simple occupations	5.05	7.24	18.54	18.45	4.92	4.20	10.55	9.13
White-collar worker, advanced occupations	3.69	4.71	9.41	4.35	1.68	2.01	1.83	1.85
Other	52.20	48.52	54.56	54.45	42.92	42.87	48.48	52.50
Qualification (with work experience)	87.24	92.56	84.89	92.56	89.98	89.16	90.11	89.62
Career Variables								
Duration of unemployment (in weeks)								
<13	26.07	27.66	22.53	22.09	19.77	33.96	11.42	16.27
13-52	34.77	31.54	38.31	35.75	42.68	35.29	39.13	34.84
>52	39.16	40.79	39.16	42.16	37.55	30.75	49.45	48.89
Programme before unemployment								
No further education or programme	71.45	89.95	66.83	91.14	52.84	82.92	42.72	72.15
Further education compl., cont. education	9.77	6.97	12.36	7.38	14.16	8.74	23.54	16.65
Further education compl., voc. adjustment	1.07	0.48	0.57	0.25	5.57	2.90	4.77	3.07
Job-preparative measure	0.05	0.05	0.57	0.04	0.21	0.14	0.08	0.12
Job creation scheme	16.92	1.56	18.54	0.79	26.44	4.56	28.58	7.62
Rehabilitation measure	0.75	0.98	1.14	0.41	0.79	0.74	0.32	0.39

[1] DoR = degree of restriction
[2] People with accepted degree of restriction, but no equalisation to other persons with the same DoR.
[3] CSE = Certificate for secondary education

B Additional Material to Chapter 5   195

Table B.2: Selected Descriptives for Clusters Ia-Ic

Variable	Cluster Ia[1]				Cluster Ib[2]				Cluster Ic[3]			
	Men		Women		Men		Women		Men		Women	
	Part.	Non-Part.	Part.	Non-Part.	Part.	Non-Part.	Part.	Non-Part.	Part.	Non-Part.	Part.	Non-Part.
No. Of Observations	696	14,349	1,232	17,439	1829	42,029	3,234	49,807	324	6,820	490	7,738
	Means											
Programme duration (in days)	336.41		345.15		315.25		333.19		295.21		304.91	
Age	43.57	41.65	42.86	44.22	45.34	41.80	44.26	43.99	43.51	41.34	44.65	43.51
Married	0.54	0.49	0.69	0.66	0.56	0.48	0.67	0.64	0.48	0.48	0.73	0.65
Duration of employment (in months)	22.45	59.36	27.68	63.83	25.50	54.81	33.37	63.42	20.46	49.97	25.81	61.06
Number of placement propositions	5.09	2.41	4.83	2.17	6.32	3.10	5.50	2.86	7.23	3.76	6.34	3.50
Placement restraints	0.10	0.16	0.06	0.11	0.14	0.16	0.07	0.12	0.18	0.16	0.13	0.12
	Frequencies in %											
No health restrictions	79.74	75.40	87.58	79.49	76.05	74.83	85.06	79.69	70.06	74.72	80.00	79.04
Without professional training	24.57	21.08	21.10	23.56	28.81	23.94	21.83	26.43	31.17	22.42	25.10	27.20
With high degree	1.87	2.06	1.95	1.08	4.48	3.21	2.97	1.78	3.40	3.26	3.06	1.50
With work experience	89.94	87.22	89.04	87.68	91.09	89.63	90.82	90.09	87.96	89.91	90.61	90.51
Duration of unemployment												
less than 13	19.54	33.02	9.90	13.98	19.63	33.52	11.47	16.66	18.21	39.91	13.88	18.92
between 13 and 52	40.09	34.10	36.44	33.47	44.29	35.90	39.89	35.10	40.43	33.30	40.00	36.52
more than 52 weeks	40.37	32.88	53.65	52.55	36.09	30.58	48.64	48.24	41.36	26.79	46.12	44.56
No ALMP participation before unemp.	52.01	83.46	43.83	72.93	54.02	82.79	42.08	71.99	44.14	81.48	40.61	68.80

[1] Cluster Ia contains the five East German labour office districts with the worst labour market conditions.
[2] Cluster Ib contains 23 East German labour office districts with bad labour market conditions.
[3] Cluster Ic contains the five East German labour office districts with the best labour market conditions in relation to the other East German labour office districts, but is also characterised by a high unemployment and low labour market dynamics.

Table B.3: Selected Descriptives for Clusters II-V

Variable	Cluster II[1] Men Part.	Non-Part.	Cluster II[1] Women Part.	Non-Part.	Cluster III[2] Men Part.	Non-Part.	Cluster III[2] Women Part.	Non-Part.	Cluster IV[3] Men Part.	Non-Part.	Cluster IV[3] Women Part.	Non-Part.	Cluster V[4] Men Part.	Non-Part.	Cluster V[4] Women Part.	Non-Part.
No. Of Observations	902	19,090	422	13,236	820	16,424	418	13,957	184	3,709	81	2937	309	6,462	210	5,625
									Means							
Programme duration (in days)	285.98		319.39		276.57		298.14		276.03		314.77		275.72		293.74	
Age	37.43	43.43	38.17	43.58	35.90	42.54	36.75	42.67	37.39	45.18	36.46	46.04	39.97	42.94	39.99	43.40
Married	0.36	0.50	0.39	0.59	0.34	0.51	0.39	0.65	0.32	0.55	0.35	0.63	0.36	0.55	0.45	0.67
Duration of employment (in months)	18.84	74.59	23.40	62.63	19.54	67.82	22.64	61.22	17.17	84.57	24.10	80.22	21.98	66.14	32.97	68.38
Number of placement propositions	7.40	3.49	6.71	2.92	7.17	3.54	6.41	2.96	8.98	4.16	9.28	3.49	8.27	3.61	6.66	2.91
Placement restraints	0.13	0.20	0.15	0.17	0.18	0.22	0.12	0.17	0.19	0.22	0.19	0.21	0.20	0.22	0.16	0.19
							Frequencies in %									
No health restrictions	77.83	69.42	76.54	74.33	74.02	67.71	82.06	74.33	73.37	68.51	74.07	69.73	68.61	67.95	75.71	71.50
Without professional training	66.30	50.82	47.87	48.39	61.71	45.70	44.26	46.98	59.78	52.33	41.98	55.06	53.07	44.27	41.43	51.80
With high degree	3.33	2.49	6.40	2.83	2.93	1.67	8.85	2.11	4.89	4.02	11.11	3.10	4.85	2.23	9.05	2.29
With work experience	84.37	91.03	80.81	90.90	86.22	92.38	83.97	92.53	88.59	95.39	90.12	95.51	93.85	95.51	89.05	94.77
Duration of unemployment																
less than 13	21.95	21.61	19.67	19.08	28.41	30.39	22.97	22.48	28.26	25.88	24.69	21.93	32.04	39.86	24.76	26.65
between 13 and 52	36.03	33.06	36.73	34.85	35.85	30.99	40.43	36.08	31.52	33.22	39.51	35.10	30.74	29.20	39.05	36.76
more than 52 weeks	42.02	45.33	43.60	46.06	35.73	38.62	36.60	41.45	40.22	40.90	35.80	42.97	37.22	30.93	36.19	36.59
No ALMP participation before unemp.	72.28	89.08	68.72	90.22	66.71	88.96	62.20	90.50	80.43	93.53	76.54	93.80	75.73	92.43	67.62	91.93

[1] Cluster II contains 20 West German labour office districts dominated by large cities and the East German labour office district of Dresden.
[2] Cluster III contains 63 West German labour office districts characterised by rural elements, medium-sized industry and average unemployment.
[3] Cluster IV contains 10 West German labour office districts with good labour market prospects.
[4] Cluster V contains the 47 West German labour office districts with the best labour market prospects.

Table B.4: Estimation Results of the Logit-Models for the Propensity Score

| | West Germany | | | | East Germany | | | |
| | Men | | Women | | Men | | Women | |
Variable	Coeff.	S.E.	Coeff.	S.E.	Coeff.	S.E.	Coeff.	S.E.
Constant	**-1.1739**	0.2731	**-3.1254**	0.4533	**-5.7880**	0.3659	**-8.0021**	0.3944
Socio-Demographic Variables								
Age	**-0.0599**	0.0145	-0.0067	0.0235	**0.0901**	0.0141	**0.1702**	0.0136
Age^2	*0.0004*	0.0002	-0.0003	0.0003	**-0.0008**	0.0002	**-0.0019**	0.0002
Married	**-0.1676**	0.0612	**-0.4483**	0.0761	**0.2683**	0.0506	**0.1145**	0.0344
Number of children	*0.0653*	0.0281	-0.0183	0.0439	-0.0335	0.0266	-0.0238	0.0184
German	**0.4402**	0.0683	*0.2825*	0.1211	**0.6284**	0.1966	**0.7082**	0.2432
Health restrictions								
No health restrictions	Ref.		Ref.		Ref.		Ref.	
Acc. DoR^1, 80% and over	**0.9160**	0.1826	**1.3404**	0.2578	*0.5491*	0.2758	**1.1375**	0.2442
Acc. DoR, 50% to under 80%	**0.8052**	0.1267	**0.6433**	0.1978	**0.4991**	0.1270	**0.6032**	0.1242
Acc. DoR, 30% to under 50%	**1.1190**	0.3658	**1.9871**	0.4246	**0.5691**	0.1925	**0.7999**	0.1954
Acc. DoR, 30% to under 50%, no equalis.^{2}	0.2757	0.1570	0.0651	0.2685	-0.0708	0.1721	-0.0725	0.1826
Other health restrictions	-0.0472	0.0892	-0.0751	0.1390	**-0.1918**	0.0716	*-0.1422*	0.0608
Qualification Variables								
Professional training								
Without compl. prof. training, no CSE^3	Ref.		Ref.		Ref.		Ref.	
Without compl. prof. training, with CSE	**-0.3364**	0.0622	0.2294	0.1334	0.1015	0.0823	**0.3428**	0.0865
Industrial training	**-0.6738**	0.0692	-0.0808	0.1399	*-0.1777*	0.0748	**0.3315**	0.0820
Full-time vocational school	**-0.7639**	0.2685	-0.0734	0.2432	-0.3223	0.2594	**0.8588**	0.1384
Technical school	-0.0987	0.1756	**0.7183**	0.1927	0.2227	0.1231	**1.0166**	0.0977
Polytechnic	0.3534	0.2009	**1.4983**	0.2144	-0.0135	0.2058	**1.0388**	0.1794
College, university	0.2399	0.1577	**1.0221**	0.1869	0.0810	0.1354	**0.9004**	0.1272
Occupational group								
Plant cultivation, breeding, fishery	*0.2222*	0.0927	0.2628	0.2501	0.0092	0.0828	**0.2370**	0.0670
Mining, mineral extraction	-0.5605	0.4657			-0.7494	0.5154		
Manufacturing	Ref.		Ref.		Ref.		Ref.	
Technical professions	**-0.5810**	0.1544	-0.1609	0.2605	-0.1954	0.0999	**0.2149**	0.0819
Service professions	**-0.3077**	0.0544	**0.3167**	0.0995	**-0.1739**	0.0478	0.0127	0.0406
Other professions	0.1023	0.1533	0.3933	0.2628	**-1.1891**	0.2170	**-1.2092**	0.2860
Professional rank								
Unskilled worker	Ref.		Ref.		Ref.		Ref.	
Skilled worker	**-0.5499**	0.0982	-0.1637	0.1944	**-0.1811**	0.0597	0.0657	0.0525
White-collar worker, simple occupations	0.0163	0.1152	0.1490	0.1256	0.1809	0.1067	**0.2197**	0.0605
White-collar worker, advanced occupations	0.0877	0.1536	**0.5131**	0.1624	-0.2838	0.1662	-0.0404	0.1215
Other	0.0112	0.0563	0.1512	0.1054	0.0345	0.0528	*0.1004*	0.0437
Qualification (with work experience)	**-0.3397**	0.0745	**-0.3139**	0.1017	**-0.2279**	0.0695	*-0.1175*	0.0527
Career Variables								
Duration of last employment (months)	**-0.0046**	0.0005	**-0.0033**	0.0007	**-0.0038**	0.0004	**-0.0028**	0.0003
Duration of unemployment (weeks)								
Up to 13 weeks	Ref.		Ref.		Ref.		Ref.	
Between 13 and 52 weeks	**0.2055**	0.0616	0.0698	0.0889	**0.4673**	0.0561	**0.2509**	0.0511
More than 52 weeks	**0.3087**	0.0678	0.0888	0.0974	**0.4498**	0.0599	**0.1694**	0.0509
Number of placement propositions	**0.0494**	0.0028	**0.0530**	0.0042	**0.0610**	0.0030	**0.0919**	0.0031
Last contact to job center (weeks)	-0.0013	0.0125	0.0520	0.0177	**-0.1204**	0.0114	**-0.0644**	0.0085
Rehabilitation attendant	-0.1533	0.1185	0.0696	0.2039	**0.2958**	0.0939	0.1535	0.1024
Placement restrictions	**-0.3396**	0.0989	-0.2654	0.1546	**-0.3164**	0.0870	**-0.3000**	0.0825
Programme before unemployment								
No further education or programme	Ref.		Ref.		Ref.		Ref.	
Further education compl., cont. education	**0.2292**	0.0801	**0.5301**	0.1043	**0.4830**	0.0628	**0.5263**	0.0422
Further education compl., voc. adjustment	**0.6479**	0.2286	0.4613	0.4466	**0.6545**	0.0893	**0.5634**	0.0746
Job-preparative measure	-0.4764	1.0285	**2.6387**	0.5245	**1.1431**	0.4289	0.3364	0.5250
Job creation scheme	**2.1463**	0.0777	**3.0671**	0.1141	**1.7272**	0.0546	**1.5382**	0.0418
Rehabilitation measure	-0.0929	0.2706	**0.9368**	0.3406	0.4232	0.2273	0.3780	0.2720
Regional Context Variables^4								
Cluster Ia					-0.1040	0.1291	0.1421	0.1238
Cluster Ib					*-0.3077*	0.1248	-0.0242	0.1210
Cluster Ic					*-0.2838*	0.1361	-0.1841	0.1292
Cluster II	**-0.2225**	0.0730	**-0.5666**	0.0960	Ref.		Ref.	
Cluster III	*-0.1841*	0.0722	**-0.4601**	0.0917				
Cluster IV	-0.0080	0.1002	**-0.4530**	0.1423				
Cluster V	Ref.		Ref.					

Bold letters indicate significance at the 1% level. *Italic* letters refer to the 5% level.
[1] DoR = degree of restriction.
[2] People with accepted degree of restriction, but no equalisation to other persons with the same DoR.
[3] CSE = Certificate for secondary education
[4] Cluster according to the classification as described in table 4.6.

Table B.5: Standardised Bias Main Groups - Before and After Matching

	West Germany				East Germany			
	Men		Women		Men		Women	
	Before	After	Before	After	Before	After	Before	After
Socio-Demographic Variables								
Age	48.64	4.22	47.62	5.64	22.84	1.09	1.37	2.49
Married	34.17	6.28	48.47	8.16	11.29	0.89	6.98	0.47
Number of children	2.25	1.11	0.75	0.58	5.32	1.32	12.20	1.26
German	8.19	1.30	13.97	3.27	6.98	1.84	6.29	0.69
Health restrictions								
No health restrictions	13.44	5.27	11.55	5.31	3.69	0.81	14.55	3.24
Acc. DoR,[1] 80% and over	7.83	0.33	15.47	1.96	1.14	0.90	2.70	0.89
Acc. DoR, 50% to under 80%	1.25	1.82	5.34	2.59	6.16	0.19	2.35	1.27
Acc. DoR, 30% to under 50%	1.59	3.97	6.97	4.10	6.32	0.90	3.29	1.81
Acc. DoR, 30% to under 50%, no equalis.[2]	10.46	3.62	11.36	4.99	2.14	1.16	4.59	0.98
Other health restrictions	14.80	2.89	19.22	1.26	7.92	0.73	16.81	4.76
Qualification Variables								
Professional training								
Without compl. prof. training, no CSE[3]	26.22	4.05	9.12	2.59	10.39	1.79	6.82	1.65
Without compl. prof. training, with CSE	6.19	1.57	4.18	5.01	7.25	0.77	5.55	3.22
Industrial training	31.27	0.52	18.34	4.99	17.50	0.70	6.87	1.64
Full-time vocational school	3.20	1.13	2.26	2.45	1.15	3.79	6.81	0.84
Technical school	1.10	2.77	13.50	0.00	9.02	1.19	17.06	2.10
Polytechnic	4.68	1.09	25.51	2.48	1.01	0.96	6.48	1.52
College, university	7.86	1.06	26.76	2.88	4.11	2.02	7.60	0.84
Occupational group								
Plant cultivation, breeding, fishery	20.69	1.52	1.79	0.00	5.98	0.00	8.63	1.32
Mining, mineral extraction	5.95	2.17	0.00		3.04	3.51	0.00	
Manufacturing	8.80	0.09	22.79	5.31	0.78	0.07	2.72	0.66
Technical professions	12.59	0.00	1.27	4.83	3.80	1.73	10.10	0.09
Service professions	14.66	1.30	19.54	5.92	0.63	0.87	3.86	0.00
Other professions	3.97	1.48	3.52	0.75	15.85	0.38	13.43	1.79
Professional rank								
Unskilled worker	17.22	2.52	9.01	2.04	20.54	1.92	10.55	1.14
Skilled worker	26.18	6.56	9.45	3.09	21.91	6.40	4.98	3.54
White-collar worker, simple occupations	9.13	1.06	0.20	4.66	3.46	0.80	4.75	3.04
White-collar worker, advanced occupations	5.06	3.14	20.09	4.58	2.52	1.65	0.21	1.21
Other	7.36	1.51	0.22	3.89	0.10	4.00	8.05	3.58
Qualification (with work experience)	17.71	0.70	24.41	3.89	2.68	1.69	1.65	0.13
Career Variables								
Duration of last employment (months)	57.08	6.26	51.99	9.34	36.23	0.77	37.47	1.44
Duration of unemployment (weeks)								
Up to 13 weeks	3.58	2.92	1.07	1.45	32.44	8.44	14.09	1.45
Between 13 and 52 weeks	6.85	3.83	5.31	2.93	15.20	2.42	8.89	0.08
More than 52 weeks	3.34	1.16	6.12	4.21	14.38	4.22	1.13	0.84
Number of placement propositions	59.16	4.74	60.13	0.50	57.97	1.79	64.89	0.04
Last contact to job center (weeks)	2.55	0.38	6.04	2.77	12.16	1.35	9.21	0.19
Rehabilitation attendant	4.65	0.43	5.74	2.17	0.11	0.78	7.83	2.49
Placement restrictions	12.85	4.28	9.46	6.48	7.56	1.49	15.11	2.32
Programme before unemployment								
No further education or programme	48.23	2.85	62.49	2.96	68.03	0.62	62.35	0.48
Further education compl., cont. education	10.11	5.34	16.75	2.45	17.08	4.98	17.26	4.67
Further education compl., voc. adjustment	6.73	3.36	5.04	1.36	13.31	3.74	8.75	0.56
Job-preparative measure	0.15	0.00	9.67	2.42	1.52	0.73	1.37	0.00
Job creation scheme	54.99	9.35	62.93	2.47	63.39	5.84	56.58	3.69
Rehabilitation measure	2.55	0.00	8.39	1.78	0.56	1.49	1.27	0.00
Regional Context Variables[4]								
Cluster Ia					3.94	0.48	3.98	2.39
Cluster Ib					4.83	0.21	1.84	2.56
Cluster Ic					1.78	0.76	1.29	1.20
Cluster II	2.13	2.31	3.41	1.51	0.71	0.88	3.24	1.31
Cluster III	2.21	0.78	2.11	0.21				
Cluster IV	0.67	2.06	3.23	0.39				
Cluster V	0.61	0.54	9.15	1.78				
Mean (unweighted average)	13.85	2.46	15.36	3.14	11.84	1.81	10.93	1.56

[1] DoR = degree of restriction.
[2] People with accepted degree of restriction, but no equalisation to other persons with the same DoR.
[3] CSE = Certificate for secondary education
[4] Cluster according to the classification as described in table 4.6

Table B.6: Estimation Results of the Logit-Models for the Propensity Score in the Sub-Groups - Men West Germany I

Variable	Age (in years) < 25	25 – 50	> 50	Duration of unemployment (in weeks) < 13	13 – 52	> 52
Constant	19.2224	-5.7829	-43.6753	2.3490	-0.9859	-3.4319
Socio-Demographic Variables						
Age	-1.8352	0.1360	1.5942	-0.2917	-0.0934	0.1343
Age²	0.0390	-0.0016	-0.0156	0.0037	0.0011	-0.0022
Married	0.0387	-0.1907	-0.0389	-0.3043	-0.2107	-0.0299
Number of children	0.0755	0.0670	-0.0547	-0.0546	0.1534	0.0400
German	0.3141	0.4163	-0.0853	0.2950	0.6700	0.3684
Health restrictions						
No health restrictions	Ref.	Ref.	Ref.	Ref.	Ref.	Ref.
Acc. DoR,[1] 80% and over	1.0806	0.9859	0.3597	0.9387	0.9420	0.7115
Acc. DoR, 50% to under 80%	0.4628	1.0383	0.5372	1.3338	0.7209	0.6035
Acc. DoR, 30% to under 50%	–	1.0690	1.2877	2.3474	0.5596	0.7528
Acc. DoR, 30% to under 50%, no equalis.[2]	–	0.4891	0.0615	0.3307	-0.1961	0.4390
Other health restrictions	-0.1973	-0.0143	-0.0312	0.1780	-0.1468	-0.1283
Qualification Variables						
Professional training						
Without compl. prof. training, no CSE[3]	Ref.	Ref.	Ref.	Ref.	Ref.	Ref.
Without compl. prof. training, with CSE	-0.5419	-0.2922	0.2171	-0.4920	-0.3925	-0.1748
Industrial training	-2.0355	-0.3749	0.1957	-1.1871	-0.6633	-0.2282
Full-time vocational school	–	-0.3774	-0.5766	-1.2116	-0.7420	-0.4562
Technical school	–	0.0424	0.7335	-0.0948	0.1104	-0.2446
Polytechnic	–	0.5685	0.5298	0.4920	0.4158	0.3810
College, university	–	0.2700	1.2210	-0.0349	0.3025	0.5130
Occupational group						
Plant cultivation, breeding, fishery	-0.0987	0.3032	0.5068	0.2226	0.3178	0.2409
Mining, mineral extraction	–	-0.1519	–	-0.7839	-0.6409	-0.4042
Manufacturing	Ref.	Ref.	Ref.	Ref.	Ref.	Ref.
Technical professions	-0.4096	-0.7000	-0.2693	-0.7573	-0.9581	-0.2679
Service professions	-0.4072	-0.2785	-0.4416	-0.3740	-0.2886	-0.3318
Other professions	-0.3725	-0.2442	-1.7136	-0.0160	-0.0163	-0.1265
Professional rank						
Unskilled worker	Ref.	Ref.	Ref.	Ref.	Ref.	Ref.
Skilled worker	-0.9983	-0.4245	-0.6198	-0.9986	-0.2304	-0.3017
White-collar worker, simple occupations	0.1994	-0.0252	-0.2276	0.2774	0.0200	-0.1964
White-collar worker, advanced occupations	1.4763	0.1528	-0.5604	0.5580	0.4167	-0.4424
Other	0.3160	-0.1803	-0.5193	0.4531	-0.1286	-0.3765
Qualification (with work experience)	-0.3040	-0.3060	0.4182	-0.4217	-0.1755	-0.3806
Career Variables						
Duration of last employment (months)	-0.0136	-0.0026	-0.0045	-0.0086	-0.0051	-0.0041
Duration of unemployment (weeks)						
Up to 13 weeks	Ref.	Ref.	Ref.	n./i.	n./i.	n./i.
Between 13 and 52 weeks	-0.1889	0.5711	0.0003	n./i.	n./i.	n./i.
More than 52 weeks	0.7101	0.8123	-0.7455	n./i.	n./i.	n./i.
Number of placement propositions	0.0609	0.0455	0.0849	0.0621	0.0498	0.0376
Last contact to job center (weeks)	-0.1044	-0.0096	0.0725	0.0318	-0.0229	0.0003
Rehabilitation attendant	0.4729	-0.3167	0.0499	0.2402	0.0078	-0.4055
Placement restrictions	-0.0452	-0.3239	-0.4378	-0.1962	-0.2365	-0.4780
Programme before unemployment						
No further education or programme	Ref.	Ref.	Ref.	Ref.	Ref.	Ref.
Further education compl., cont. education	-0.4245	0.3309	0.1782	0.3135	0.2797	0.1148
Further education compl., voc. adjustment	1.2458	0.1891	1.2807	1.3713	0.3546	0.3810
Job-preparative measure	-0.5547	–	–	-0.1050	–	–
Job creation scheme	1.6855	2.1406	2.0873	4.2424	2.3059	1.2748
Rehabilitation measure	-0.7142	0.0161	–	0.0412	-0.0784	-0.3715
Regional Context Variables[4]						
Cluster II	0.4709	-0.4021	-0.3371	-0.0959	-0.1140	-0.5906
Cluster III	0.6413	-0.4360	-0.2342	-0.0462	-0.0800	-0.5332
Cluster IV	0.9096	-0.2057	-0.1870	0.1493	-0.1115	-0.1169
Cluster V	Ref.	Ref.	Ref.	Ref.	Ref.	Ref.

Bold letters indicate significance at the 1% level. *Italic* letters refer to the 5% level.
[1] DoR = degree of restriction
[2] People with accepted degree of restriction, but no equalisation to other persons with the same DoR.
[3] CSE = Certificate for secondary education
[4] Cluster according to the classification as described in table 4.6.
  n./i.: not included in the estimation
  – no observations in relevant sub-group

Table B.7: Estimation Results of the Logit-Models for the Propensity Score in the Sub-Groups - Men West Germany II

Variable	without professional experience	without professional training	with high degree	with placement restrictions	rehabilitation attendants
Constant	0.9086	0.4978	**-9.5336**	-1.7075	-0.2817
Socio-Demographic Variables					
Age	-0.1705	-0.1449	0.2487	0.0604	-0.0089
Age^2	*0.0014*	**0.0014**	*-0.0029*	*-0.0011*	-0.0003
Married	0.0442	*-0.1602*	-0.0856	-0.2144	-0.0380
Number of children	0.1014	**0.0976**	0.0294	0.0570	-0.1511
German	0.0465	**0.4157**	0.1720	0.3481	0.0846
Health restrictions					
No health restrictions	Ref.	Ref.	Ref.	Ref.	Ref.
Acc. DoR,[1] 80% and over	0.5442	**1.0216**	0.9161	-0.5085	–
Acc. DoR, 50% to under 80%	*1.0699*	**0.7344**	1.1354	-0.5368	-0.3366
Acc. DoR, 30% to under 50%	**3.0225**	0.7656	–	–	0.4220
Acc. DoR, 30% to under 50%, no equalis.[2]	0.4056	0.0593	–	**-1.2335**	*-0.8671*
Other health restrictions	-0.1985	-0.1524	0.8832	**-1.4093**	**-1.3746**
Qualification Variables					
Professional training					
Without compl. prof. training, no CSE[3]	Ref.	n./i.	n./i.	Ref.	Ref.
Without compl. prof. training, with CSE	-0.2807	n./i.	n./i.	-0.1272	-0.0945
Industrial training	**-1.1182**	n./i.	n./i.	-0.2994	0.0491
Full-time vocational school	-0.9716	n./i.	n./i.	-0.7384	0.9032
Technical school	-1.4109	n./i.	n./i.	0.4007	0.6162
Polytechnic	0.1760	n./i.	n./i.	1.0165	
College, university	0.1697	n./i.	n./i.	-0.0780	
Occupational group					
Plant cultivation, breeding, fishery	0.2699	0.1700	1.0698	0.0848	0.5692
Mining, mineral extraction	*1.6121*	-0.3894			
Manufacturing	Ref.	Ref.	Ref.	Ref.	Ref.
Technical professions	-0.3647	-0.4265	-0.6653	-0.9056	-0.1689
Service professions	-0.1020	**-0.3708**	0.3496	**-0.3566**	-0.0619
Other professions	-0.0556	0.0605		*-0.7632*	-0.4286
Professional rank					
Unskilled worker	Ref.	Ref.	Ref.	Ref.	Ref.
Skilled worker	-0.5143	-0.2760	1.5238	-0.2729	-0.4078
White-collar worker, simple occupations	0.6075	-0.3988	*2.2911*	0.0401	0.0609
White-collar worker, advanced occupations	**1.2666**	0.0212	1.7898	-0.2111	-0.1126
Other	0.2073	-0.0628	1.5540	-0.2594	-0.2908
Qualification (with work experience)	n./i.	**-0.3672**	-0.5405	-0.1547	-0.1053
Career Variables					
Duration of last employment (months)	-0.0010	**-0.0048**	-0.0090	**-0.0045**	-0.0031
Duration of unemployment (weeks)					
Up to 13 weeks	Ref.	Ref.	Ref.	Ref.	Ref.
Between 13 and 52 weeks	-0.2072	0.0588	0.4053	-0.2131	-0.3252
More than 52 weeks	**0.5780**	**0.3454**	0.1206	**-0.4451**	-0.5193
Number of placement propositions	0.0690	0.0518	0.0614	0.0645	0.0466
Last contact to job center (weeks)	-0.0422	**-0.0733**	*0.1003*	0.0030	0.0195
Rehabilitation attendant	-0.1064	**-0.4860**	–	-0.2406	n./i.
Placement restrictions	-0.3973	-0.1973	-0.7783	n./i.	-0.4808
Programme before unemployment					
No further education or programme	Ref.	Ref.	Ref.	Ref.	Ref.
Further education compl., cont. education	-0.0664	0.0688	0.4433	0.3985	*0.8633*
Further education compl., voc. adjustment	–	0.5829	1.1214	-0.1987	0.9562
Job-preparative measure	–	-0.6492	–	–	–
Job creation scheme	**2.0412**	**1.9736**	**1.8373**	**2.4849**	**2.3799**
Rehabilitation measure	0.6798	0.1987		-0.4136	0.1933
Regional Context Variables[4]					
Cluster II	0.2019	-0.0203	*-0.6513*	**-0.5914**	*-0.7510*
Cluster III	0.2807	-0.0732	-0.5448	**-0.4404**	-0.5817
Cluster IV	0.5891	0.0923	-0.3586	-0.0153	0.1469
Cluster V	Ref.	Ref.	Ref.	Ref.	Ref.

Bold letters indicate significance at the 1% level. *Italic* letters refer to the 5% level.
[1] DoR = degree of restriction
[2] People with accepted degree of restriction, but no equalisation to other persons with the same DoR.
[3] CSE = Certificate for secondary education
[4] Cluster according to the classification as described in table 4.6.
 n./i.: not included in the estimation
 – no observations in relevant sub-group

Table B.8: Estimation Results of the Logit-Models for the Propensity Score in the Sub-Groups - Women West Germany I

Variable	Age (in years)			Duration of unemployment (in weeks)		
	< 25	25 – 50	> 50	< 13	13 – 52	> 52
Constant	10.6581	**-8.3547**	**-111.2167**	0.4324	**-3.0753**	**-5.4332**
Socio-Demographic Variables						
Age	-0.9888	0.1986	4.0834	-0.2434	-0.0167	0.1365
Age²	0.0184	**-0.0025**	**-0.0391**	0.0028	0.0000	**-0.0022**
Married	0.0682	**-0.4735**	**-0.5664**	-0.1794	**-0.4042**	**-0.6957**
Number of children	-0.4780	0.0040	0.0783	-0.0192	-0.0923	0.0570
German	-0.0050	*0.3723*	0.0165	*0.6553*	0.2276	0.0420
Health restrictions						
No health restrictions Ref.	Ref.	Ref.	Ref.	Ref.	Ref.	Ref.
Acc. DoR,¹ 80% and over	**2.7825**	**1.0247**	*1.5175*	**2.3472**	**1.7269**	0.4078
Acc. DoR, 50% to under 80%	1.1635	**0.7403**	0.1760	**1.2239**	**1.1856**	-0.0672
Acc. DoR, 30% to under 50%	–	**2.3281**	1.5630	–	**2.8976**	**1.6529**
Acc. DoR, 30% to under 50%, no equalis.²	–	-0.1657	0.1916	0.3533	-0.0053	-0.2535
Other health restrictions	*0.8537*	-0.1975	-0.1662	0.2427	-0.0573	-0.4034
Qualification Variables						
Professional training						
Without compl. prof. training, no CSE³	Ref.	Ref.	Ref.	Ref.	Ref.	Ref.
Without compl. prof. training, with CSE	-0.3774	**0.4798**	0.8822	-0.3195	*0.5371*	*0.4642*
Industrial training	**-1.4577**	0.3404	0.8080	**-0.7530**	0.0681	*0.4573*
Full-time vocational school	-0.9174	0.4283	0.1838	-1.1125	0.6597	-0.0711
Technical school	0.2209	**1.1432**	0.6720	0.3616	**0.9725**	**1.0278**
Polytechnic	–	**1.9700**	-0.3876	**1.4877**	**1.9094**	**1.5600**
College, university	–	**1.3733**	1.8171	0.6445	**1.6323**	**1.0214**
Occupational group						
Plant cultivation, breeding, fishery	-0.0887	0.5032	–	0.1859	0.5561	0.0688
Mining, mineral extraction	–	–	–	–	–	–
Manufacturing	Ref.	Ref.	Ref.	Ref.	Ref.	Ref.
Technical professions	–	-0.4370	**1.5068**	-0.5651	-0.4894	0.1601
Service professions	-0.1598	**0.3727**	0.4405	0.3184	*0.3582*	0.2795
Other professions	-0.2963	-0.3291	-0.2078	0.1840	0.2846	0.6185
Professional rank						
Unskilled worker						
Skilled worker	-0.2388	-0.0937	0.1499	-0.1956	-0.5207	0.3060
White-collar worker, simple occupations	-0.0900	0.1429	0.3606	-0.0495	0.0177	*0.4173*
White-collar worker, advanced occupations	0.1511	**0.5721**	-0.0164	0.2167	**0.7560**	0.3429
Other	0.2885	0.0635	0.0051	**0.6741**	-0.2617	0.0718
Qualification (with work experience)	**-0.5454**	-0.2078	0.4637	-0.3787	*-0.3687*	-0.0452
Career Variables						
Duration of last employment (months)	-0.0093	**-0.0025**	-0.0031	*-0.0043*	**-0.0035**	**-0.0032**
Duration of unemployment (weeks)						
Up to 13 weeks	Ref.	Ref.	Ref.	n./i.	n./i.	n./i.
Between 13 and 52 weeks	-0.1991	**0.3435**	-0.4244	n./i.	n./i.	n./i.
More than 52 weeks	0.3524	**0.4721**	-0.7664	n./i.	n./i.	n./i.
Number of placement propositions	**0.0681**	**0.0463**	**0.0869**	**0.0640**	**0.0515**	**0.0487**
Last contact to job center (weeks)	0.0315	*0.0434*	*0.0881*	0.0768	0.0094	**0.0634**
Rehabilitation attendant	0.7018	0.0410	-0.0673	0.1821	0.3201	0.1098
Placement restrictions	**-1.1975**	-0.0114	-0.3778	-0.1668	*-0.5457*	0.0226
Programme before unemployment						
No further education or programme	Ref.	Ref.	Ref.	Ref.	Ref.	Ref.
Further education compl., cont. education	0.4239	**0.4862**	**1.0261**	0.3843	**0.7124**	**0.4974**
Further education compl., voc. adjustment	–	0.5851	0.7044	0.6198	–	0.9691
Job-preparative measure	**2.5023**	–	–	-819.9959	**3.1897**	1.6544
Job creation scheme	**2.9243**	**3.0119**	**3.0391**	**5.4260**	**3.4163**	**2.4785**
Rehabilitation measure	0.6365	*0.8368*	**2.5011**	0.4511	**1.3511**	0.6461
Regional Context Variables⁴						
Cluster II	-0.4451	**-0.5437**	**-0.8248**	*-0.5455*	**-0.5534**	**-0.7261**
Cluster III	0.0718	**-0.5353**	**-0.6931**	-0.2462	**-0.3816**	**-0.7440**
Cluster IV	-0.1442	-0.2686	**-1.6149**	-0.2292	*-0.5048*	**-0.6171**
Cluster V	Ref.	Ref.	Ref.	Ref.	Ref.	Ref.

Bold letters indicate significance at the 1% level. *Italic* letters refer to the 5% level.
¹ DoR = degree of restriction
² People with accepted degree of restriction, but no equalisation to other persons with the same DoR.
³ CSE = Certificate for secondary education
⁴ Cluster according to the classification as described in table 4.6.
n./i.: not included in the estimation
– no observations in relevant sub-group

Table B.9: Estimation Results of the Logit-Models for the Propensity Score in the Sub-Groups - Women West Germany II

Variable	without professional experience	without professional training	with high degree	with placement restrictions	rehabilitation attendants
Constant	-0.7924	-0.8437	-29.6931	-3.9176	-1.8893
Socio-Demographic Variables					
Age	-0.1003	-0.0851	0.5346	0.0602	0.1097
Age^2	0.0007	0.0005	**-0.0065**	-0.0014	-0.0020
Married	-0.2893	**-0.3669**	-0.3609	-0.0755	-0.0295
Number of children	-0.2055	*-0.1465*	-0.0897	-0.0077	-0.8314
German	-0.1205	*0.2934*	0.5950	*1.8635*	0.8757
Health restrictions					
No health restrictions	Ref.	Ref.	Ref.	Ref.	Ref.
Acc. DoR,[1] 80% and over	**1.7312**	**1.2836**	0.7704	–	-2.2439
Acc. DoR, 50% to under 80%	*1.2989*	0.6874	*1.7456*	-0.5676	*-1.7208*
Acc. DoR, 30% to under 50%	–	**1.9682**	–	0.8967	–
Acc. DoR, 30% to under 50%, no equalis.[2]	0.1477	-0.3593	1.0516	-0.7913	*-2.3093*
Other health restrictions	0.3157	-0.1738	0.5230	**-1.5582**	**-2.4023**
Qualification Variables					
Professional training					
Without compl. prof. training, no CSE[3]	Ref.	n./i.	n./i.	Ref.	Ref.
Without compl. prof. training, with CSE	0.3371	n./i.	n./i.	*0.7987*	0.4518
Industrial training	-0.7344	n./i.	n./i.	0.5703	0.3333
Full-time vocational school	-0.2524	n./i.	n./i.	0.3579	-0.5076
Technical school	0.2984	n./i.	n./i.	*1.4259*	0.2133
Polytechnic	**1.6320**	n./i.	n./i.	**2.4725**	**3.4128**
College, university	*1.1050*	n./i.	n./i.	1.3604	–
Occupational group					
Plant cultivation, breeding, fishery	0.3226	0.2196	**16.6621**	-0.4686	–
Mining, mineral extraction	–	–	–	–	–
Manufacturing	Ref.	Ref.	Ref.	Ref.	Ref.
Technical professions	-0.2706	0.7829	**15.5258**	-0.0637	–
Service professions	0.5290	0.2270	**16.8791**	-0.0840	0.1029
Other professions	0.5474	0.2886		-0.4072	-0.9081
Professional rank					
Unskilled worker	Ref.	Ref.	Ref.	Ref.	Ref.
Skilled worker	0.4922	-0.3179	-0.6125	0.0818	0.5353
White-collar worker, simple occupations	-0.1878	-0.0422	0.2123	0.4694	0.8302
White-collar worker, advanced occupations	-0.0541	**0.9614**	0.3728	-0.1237	–
Other	0.1383	0.0706	-0.0854	-0.4823	-0.4042
Qualification (with work experience)	n./i.	**-0.5000**	-0.3792	-0.4411	-0.5030
Career Variables					
Duration of last employment (months)	-0.0071	-0.0044	-0.0024	*-0.0045*	-0.0017
Duration of unemployment (weeks)					
Up to 13 weeks	Ref.	Ref.	Ref.	Ref.	Ref.
Between 13 and 52 weeks	-0.1168	-0.0510	*0.5476*	-0.2695	-0.0044
More than 52 weeks	-0.1482	-0.0150	-0.0285	-0.4715	-0.0536
Number of placement propositions	**0.0586**	**0.0523**	**0.0560**	**0.0642**	0.0460
Last contact to job center (weeks)	0.0087	0.0311	-0.0234	*0.0900*	0.0028
Rehabilitation attendant	0.1244	0.1092	-0.3284	0.0425	n./i.
Placement restrictions	-0.3234	-0.2301	-0.3499	n./i.	-0.1923
Programme before unemployment					
No further education or programme	Ref.	Ref.	Ref.	Ref.	Ref.
Further education compl., cont. education	-0.4605	**0.5548**	0.1119	**0.9273**	-0.2455
Further education compl., voc. adjustment	–	–	0.7592	–	–
Job-preparative measure	2.3640	**2.4653**	–	–	–
Job creation scheme	**3.3938**	**2.9377**	**2.1688**	**2.9205**	**1.8661**
Rehabilitation measure	1.0536	-0.6581	–	0.7394	0.7531
Regional Context Variables[4]					
Cluster II	-0.4169	**-0.4691**	**-1.0564**	*-0.6045*	-0.8996
Cluster III	-0.2347	**-0.4339**	-0.2327	**-0.7750**	*-0.9586*
Cluster IV	-0.4429	*-0.4885*	-0.5266	-0.4691	-0.5157
Cluster V	Ref.	Ref.	Ref.	Ref.	Ref.

Bold letters indicate significance at the 1% level. *Italic* letters refer to the 5% level.
[1] DoR = degree of restriction
[2] People with accepted degree of restriction, but no equalisation to other persons with the same DoR.
[3] CSE = Certificate for secondary education
[4] Cluster according to the classification as described in table 4.6.
n./i.: not included in the estimation
– no observations in relevant sub-group

Table B.10: Estimation Results of the Logit-Models for the Propensity Score in the Sub-Groups - Men East Germany I

Variable	Age (in years) < 25	25 − 50	> 50	Duration of unemployment (in weeks) < 13	13 − 52	> 52
Constant	13.5732	-3.8391	-238.8922	-4.6606	-5.0998	-5.9168
Socio-Demographic Variables						
Age	-1.3078	-0.1093	8.7264	0.0004	0.0582	0.1591
Age²	0.0269	0.0019	-0.0805	0.0006	-0.0004	**-0.0020**
Married	-0.7581	*0.1677*	**0.3589**	0.1231	**0.2653**	**0.3925**
Number of children	0.4678	0.0403	-0.0139	-0.0360	0.0105	-0.0526
German	0.7945	**0.6642**	-0.0440	*1.2625*	**0.8085**	0.4366
Health restrictions						
No health restrictions	Ref.	Ref.	Ref.	Ref.	Ref.	Ref.
Acc. DoR,[1] 80% and over	**2.0207**	0.4226	-0.5481	0.7920	0.7132	-0.1608
Acc. DoR, 50% to under 80%	1.0831	**0.7806**	-0.1421	**1.1226**	0.6530	-0.1127
Acc. DoR, 30% to under 50%	−	*0.5689*	0.3587	*1.2752*	**0.8724**	-0.4211
Acc. DoR, 30% to under 50%, no equalis.[2]	1.4045	-0.0536	-0.1966	0.0610	0.2227	-0.5038
Other health restrictions	-0.0501	-0.1892	**-0.3627**	0.0924	-0.1932	**-0.4426**
Qualification Variables						
Professional training						
Without compl. prof. training, no CSE[3]	Ref.	Ref.	Ref.	Ref.	Ref.	Ref.
Without compl. prof. training, with CSE	*-0.4693*	0.1439	0.2663	0.2528	-0.0694	0.1208
Industrial training	**-1.1019**	0.0584	-0.1078	**-0.5481**	-0.1769	-0.0439
Full-time vocational school	−	-0.3119	-0.0837	−	-0.0996	0.0365
Technical school	−	**0.6144**	0.1356	0.1006	0.1804	0.2924
Polytechnic	−	0.2415	-0.1202	-0.6210	-0.0402	0.1120
College, university	−	*0.4300*	-0.0309	-0.5415	0.0256	0.1630
Occupational group						
Plant cultivation, breeding, fishery	0.5612	0.0186	-0.1539	-0.1815	0.0397	0.1972
Mining, mineral extraction		-0.1001	-1.9224		-0.4306	-1.0655
Manufacturing	Ref.	Ref.	Ref.	Ref.	Ref.	Ref.
Technical professions	-0.2571	-0.1353	*-0.3047*	0.3015	-0.2498	*-0.3399*
Service professions	*-0.4135*	-0.1146	**-0.3372**	0.0487	**-0.2009**	**-0.2181**
Other professions	**-1.2800**	**-1.5919**	**-1.1671**	-0.6607	**-1.4277**	**-1.1442**
Professional rank						
Skilled worker	Ref.	Ref.	Ref.	Ref.	Ref.	Ref.
Unskilled worker	**-1.0221**	*-0.2042*	0.0183	**-0.7317**	-0.0751	0.1281
White-collar worker, simple occupations	-0.3466	*0.4242*	0.2383	-0.1909	0.2921	-0.0490
White-collar worker, advanced occupations	−	0.0066	0.0183	-0.3269	0.1229	*-0.6612*
Other	-0.3301	0.0354	-0.1418	0.0580	-0.0641	*-0.1765*
Qualification (with work experience)	-0.2366	-0.1033	0.3674	**-0.6192**	-0.0605	-0.1601
Career Variables						
Duration of last employment (months)	0.0015	-0.0026	-0.0040	-0.0061	-0.0050	-0.0036
Duration of unemployment (weeks)						
Up to 13 weeks	Ref.	Ref.	Ref.	n./i.	n./i.	n./i.
Between 13 and 52 weeks	*0.3105*	**0.6115**	0.3536	n./i.	n./i.	n./i.
More than 52 weeks	**1.6580**	**0.8118**	0.0397	n./i.	n./i.	n./i.
Number of placement propositions	**0.0721**	**0.0524**	0.0862	**0.0866**	**0.0545**	**0.0443**
Last contact to job center (weeks)	**-0.1381**	**-0.0826**	-0.1497	-0.0516	**-0.1692**	**-0.0922**
Rehabilitation attendant	*0.7648*	0.1537	0.0510	*0.6042*	**0.4438**	0.0091
Placement restrictions	-0.3430	-0.2176	**-0.4122**	-0.3513	*-0.3078*	-0.2586
Programme before unemployment						
No further education or programme	Ref.	Ref.	Ref.	Ref.	Ref.	Ref.
Further education compl., cont. education	0.3034	**0.4296**	**0.7066**	**0.6629**	**0.6407**	0.1706
Further education compl., voc. adjustment	**0.9493**	**0.6714**	**0.6153**	**1.7828**	**0.6016**	0.0241
Job-preparative measure	0.3428	*1.9199*	−	**1.9154**	*1.2044*	−
Job creation scheme	**2.0412**	**1.7266**	**1.5890**	**3.9594**	**1.5704**	**0.7989**
Rehabilitation measure	-0.3730	*0.5346*	0.2735	0.0433	*0.7342*	-0.0621
Regional Context Variables[4]						
Cluster Ia	**-1.4758**	**0.6616**	0.1526	**-0.7304**	0.0398	0.2545
Cluster Ib	**-1.7657**	0.4260	-0.0174	**-0.9478**	-0.1171	0.0321
Cluster Ic	**-1.3678**	*0.5218*	-0.1565	**-1.1962**	-0.1465	0.3036
Cluster II	Ref.	Ref.	Ref.	Ref.	Ref.	Ref.

Bold letters indicate significance at the 1% level. *Italic* letters refer to the 5% level.
[1] DoR = degree of restriction
[2] People with accepted degree of restriction, but no equalisation to other persons with the same DoR.
[3] CSE = Certificate for secondary education
[4] Cluster according to the classification as described in table 4.6.
 n./i.: not included in the estimation
 − no observations in relevant sub-group

Table B.11: Estimation Results of the Logit-Models for the Propensity Score in the Sub-Groups - Men East Germany II

Variable	without professional experience	without professional training	with high degree	with placement restrictions	reha-bilitation attendants
Constant	-2.6827	-2.1066	-13.9979	-4.3694	-1.4614
Socio-Demographic Variables					
Age	0.0149	-0.0554	0.5344	0.0617	-0.0120
Age^2	-0.0003	0.0008	-0.0059	-0.0008	0.0001
Married	**0.5086**	**0.3101**	*0.4893*	**0.3837**	0.2902
Number of children	-0.0482	-0.0173	-0.1173	-0.0683	0.0532
German	1.3789	**0.9481**	-0.2896	0.8685	–
Health restrictions					
No health restrictions	Ref.	Ref.	Ref.	Ref.	Ref.
Acc. DoR,[1] 80% and over	1.0344	0.2325	2.2346	–	–
Acc. DoR, 50% to under 80%	0.4732	**0.7160**	0.8734	-0.0690	-0.0707
Acc. DoR, 30% to under 50%	–	0.1333	0.8755	-0.0067	-0.2961
Acc. DoR, 30% to under 50%, no equalis.[2]	0.1653	0.1666	1.2159	-0.7772	-0.8062
Other health restrictions	-0.0002	-0.1197	-0.0451	-0.6473	-0.6332
Qualification Variables					
Professional training					
Without compl. prof. training, no CSE[3]	Ref.	n./i.	n./i.	Ref.	Ref.
Without compl. prof. training, with CSE	-0.4111	n./i.	n./i.	0.0710	-0.2495
Industrial training	**-0.6138**	n./i.	n./i.	-0.0142	-0.0820
Full-time vocational school	–	n./i.	n./i.	0.1636	0.7135
Technical school	-1.0304	n./i.	n./i.	-0.7370	–
Polytechnic	–	n./i.	n./i.	-1.0257	–
College, university	0.0510	n./i.	n./i.	-0.3160	–
Occupational group					
Plant cultivation, breeding, fishery	0.0487	0.1625	-0.6454	*0.4980*	*0.6934*
Mining, mineral extraction	–	-0.0618	–	0.3790	–
Manufacturing	Ref.	Ref.	Ref.	Ref.	Ref.
Technical professions	-0.0494	-0.0833	*-1.1475*	0.3676	0.6047
Service professions	*-0.3113*	*-0.2137*	-0.5346	0.0167	0.0848
Other professions	*-0.9041*	-1.0285	–	-1.1446	-1.4704
Professional rank					
Unskilled worker	Ref.	Ref.	Ref.	Ref.	Ref.
Skilled worker	*-0.4685*	-0.1313	0.3422	-0.3090	-0.4500
White-collar worker, simple occupations	0.9869	0.1547	0.5327	**0.9444**	0.8930
White-collar worker, advanced occupations	0.1593	-0.3857	0.0620	-0.3722	0.6932
Other	-0.1220	-0.1544	0.2880	*-0.3282*	-0.1348
Qualification (with work experience)	n./i.	-0.1547	-0.1399	-0.2143	*-0.3903*
Career Variables					
Duration of last employment (months)	0.0003	-0.0037	-0.0070	-0.0040	-0.0019
Duration of unemployment (weeks)					
Up to 13 weeks	Ref.	Ref.	Ref.	Ref.	Ref.
Between 13 and 52 weeks	0.0992	0.1483	0.2481	-0.0066	0.0180
More than 52 weeks	*0.4405*	0.2620	0.0058	*-0.3274*	-0.4262
Number of placement propositions	**0.0511**	**0.0719**	0.0513	0.0494	0.0605
Last contact to job center (weeks)	**-0.1620**	**-0.1904**	*-0.1175*	-0.1693	-0.1544
Rehabilitation attendant	0.6629	0.2319	–	0.3212	n./i.
Placement restrictions	-0.2742	*-0.3244*	-0.8725	n./i.	0.0884
Programme before unemployment					
No further education or programme	Ref.	Ref.	Ref.	Ref.	Ref.
Further education compl., cont. education	0.3408	0.1444	**0.9407**	**0.7741**	0.3133
Further education compl., voc. adjustment	**1.0850**	0.5512	0.9213	*0.5275*	-0.2150
Job-preparative measure	0.7811	0.3456	–	1.6120	*1.7065*
Job creation scheme	**1.7503**	**1.3481**	**2.8638**	**1.4924**	**1.6557**
Rehabilitation measure	0.1776	-1.2114	–	0.4731	0.0411
Regional Context Variables[4]					
Cluster Ia	**-1.6941**	**-0.7788**	-0.2336	0.0172	-0.3128
Cluster Ib	**-1.6751**	**-0.9016**	-0.2253	0.2081	-0.1557
Cluster Ic	**-1.4147**	**-0.7590**	-0.5282	0.3785	-0.2369
Cluster II	Ref.	Ref.	Ref.	Ref.	Ref.

Bold letters indicate significance at the 1% level. *Italic* letters refer to the 5% level.
[1] DoR = degree of restriction
[2] People with accepted degree of restriction, but no equalisation to other persons with the same DoR.
[3] CSE = Certificate for secondary education
[4] Cluster according to the classification as described in table 4.6.
  n./i.: not included in the estimation
  – no observations in relevant sub-group

Table B.12: Estimation Results of the Logit-Models for the Propensity Score in the Sub-Groups - Women East Germany I

Variable	Age (in years) < 25	25 − 50	> 50	Duration of unemployment (in weeks) < 13	13 − 52	> 52
Constant	17.7318	**-6.8356**	**-193.6120**	**-3.2206**	**-7.0740**	**-8.5335**
Socio-Demographic Variables						
Age	-1.8032	0.0627	7.0812	-0.0510	0.1202	0.2325
Age^2	0.0422	-0.0005	**-0.0659**	*0.0010*	**-0.0012**	**-0.0028**
Married	-0.4856	*0.0951*	*0.1752*	0.0791	**0.1675**	0.0804
Number of children	-0.0545	0.0358	0.0457	*0.1532*	-0.0525	-0.0364
German	–	0.6531	0.7526		0.5631	0.5473
Health restrictions						
No health restrictions	Ref.	Ref.	Ref.	Ref.	Ref.	Ref.
Acc. DoR,[1] 80% and over	**2.3752**	**1.2911**	0.5872	**2.4498**	**1.1125**	0.5178
Acc. DoR, 50% to under 80%	0.9588	**0.7686**	0.4074	**1.1643**	**0.5591**	*0.4365*
Acc. DoR, 30% to under 50%	–	**0.8518**	0.8819	**1.7537**	*0.6653*	0.4529
Acc. DoR, 30% to under 50%, no equalis.[2]	–	0.0766	-0.1752	0.8221	0.0490	-0.3667
Other health restrictions	-0.4905	-0.0983	-0.1709	0.2286	*-0.2675*	-0.1379
Qualification Variables						
Professional training						
Without compl. prof. training, no CSE[3]	Ref.	Ref.	Ref.	Ref.	Ref.	Ref.
Without compl. prof. training, with CSE	0.5163	**0.4664**	0.0627	0.0845	**0.5611**	*0.2601*
Industrial training	-0.4776	**0.5198**	0.1293	-0.2206	**0.5461**	**0.3229**
Full-time vocational school	0.4411	**0.9846**	0.7855	0.3846	**0.9961**	**0.8186**
Technical school	**1.7244**	**1.3458**	0.5129	0.6271	**1.3441**	**0.8768**
Polytechnic	1.5520	**1.1298**	0.8068	0.1935	**1.1729**	**1.1698**
College, university	–	**1.0438**	0.9729	0.5516	**1.1738**	**0.7909**
Occupational group						
Plant cultivation, breeding, fishery	0.0411	**0.2728**	0.2139	0.3062	**0.3404**	**0.2647**
Mining, mineral extraction	–	–	–	–	–	–
Manufacturing	Ref.	Ref.	Ref.	Ref.	Ref.	Ref.
Technical professions	-0.1679	0.1046	0.4442	0.1127	0.1113	**0.3947**
Service professions	-0.2629	0.0338	-0.0386	0.1645	0.0766	-0.0181
Other professions	-0.9534	**-1.9742**	-0.8607	-0.9207	**-1.2207**	**-1.2045**
Professional rank						
Unskilled worker	Ref.	Ref.	Ref.	Ref.	Ref.	Ref.
Skilled worker	-0.3429	0.0617	0.1272	**-0.5552**	*0.1967*	0.1086
White-collar worker, simple occupations	0.2204	**0.3024**	0.1466	-0.0892	**0.4050**	0.1047
White-collar worker, advanced occupations	–	0.0703	-0.0759	-0.5541	*0.4131*	-0.2570
Other	-0.1266	0.0721	-0.0040	**-0.5101**	0.2321	-0.0286
Qualification (with work experience)	-0.0505	-0.0922	-0.1479	*-0.3112*	0.0349	-0.1475
Career Variables						
Duration of last employment (months)	-0.0091	**-0.0027**	**-0.0019**	**-0.0031**	**-0.0039**	**-0.0023**
Duration of unemployment (weeks)						
Up to 13 weeks	Ref.	Ref.	Ref.	n./i.	n./i.	n./i.
Between 13 and 52 weeks	-0.0076	**0.3714**	0.0088	n./i.	n./i.	n./i.
More than 52 weeks	**0.9603**	**0.4699**	-0.4272	n./i.	n./i.	n./i.
Number of placement propositions	*0.0463*	**0.0812**	0.1470	0.1249	0.0967	0.0751
Last contact to job center (weeks)	-0.0470	**-0.0321**	-0.1242	0.1295	-0.1181	-0.0548
Rehabilitation attendant	0.4309	0.0131	*0.3754*	0.4448	0.2081	0.0394
Placement restrictions	-0.5051	**-0.2756**	*-0.3492*	*-0.5941*	-0.1164	**-0.4019**
Programme before unemployment						
No further education or programme	Ref.	Ref.	Ref.	Ref.	Ref.	Ref.
Further education compl., cont. education	0.6073	**0.4789**	0.6793	**0.7308**	**0.6856**	0.3857
Further education compl., voc. adjustment	0.0705	**0.3888**	0.9768	1.0508	0.2022	**0.6921**
Job-preparative measure	0.6113	0.1246	–	–	-0.1151	0.7818
Job creation scheme	**2.4487**	**1.3360**	**1.8564**	**3.6862**	**1.5546**	**1.1226**
Rehabilitation measure	*1.3329*	0.3973	–	0.7026	0.4286	0.2434
Regional Context Variables[4]						
Cluster Ia	**-1.8211**	**0.6168**	0.0610	-0.2409	-0.0343	*0.4612*
Cluster Ib	**-2.2639**	*0.4156*	-0.0167	-0.4144	-0.2372	0.3262
Cluster Ic	**-2.1955**	0.1994	-0.0874	-0.5274	*-0.4106*	0.1912
Cluster II	Ref.	Ref.	Ref.	Ref.	Ref.	Ref.

Bold letters indicate significance at the 1% level. *Italic* letters refer to the 5% level.
[1] DoR = degree of restriction
[2] People with accepted degree of restriction, but no equalisation to other persons with the same DoR.
[3] CSE = Certificate for secondary education
[4] Cluster according to the classification as described in table 4.6.
n./i.: not included in the estimation
– no observations in relevant sub-group

Table B.13: Estimation Results of the Logit-Models for the Propensity Score in the Sub-Groups - Women East Germany II

Variable	without professional experience	without professional training	with high degree	with placement restrictions	reha-bilitation attendants
Constant	-5.4542	-4.6508	-8.6957	-5.9015	*-3.4940*
Socio-Demographic Variables					
Age	0.1079	0.0797	0.1823	0.1325	0.0479
Age^2	*-0.0012*	**-0.0009**	-0.0018	**-0.0016**	-0.0004
Married	**0.3683**	0.0945	-0.1812	**0.5260**	0.3322
Number of children	-0.0219	-0.0394	0.0164	-0.1138	-0.1086
German	0.7561	0.8813	0.8858	0.2362	
Health restrictions					
No health restrictions	Ref.	Ref.	Ref.	Ref.	Ref.
Acc. DoR,[1] 80% and over	1.0744	0.7035	0.4408	–	–
Acc. DoR, 50% to under 80%	0.6111	-0.0186	0.8891	**-0.7914**	*-1.4326*
Acc. DoR, 30% to under 50%	1.0275	**1.2322**	–	-0.5929	-0.2376
Acc. DoR, 30% to under 50%, no equalis.[2]	-0.2475	-0.4625	–	**-1.4669**	*-1.5368*
Other health restrictions	-0.2220	**-0.3287**	0.3565	**-1.4201**	**-1.4582**
Qualification Variables					
Professional training					
Without compl. prof. training, no CSE[3]	Ref.	n./i.	n./i.	Ref.	Ref.
Without compl. prof. training, with CSE	0.2847	n./i.	n./i.	0.6162	0.5223
Industrial training	-0.0254	n./i.	n./i.	**1.0380**	0.7740
Full-time vocational school	-0.4208	n./i.	n./i.	*1.1518*	1.5601
Technical school	*0.8702*	n./i.	n./i.	**1.6763**	0.9645
Polytechnic	1.0921	n./i.	n./i.	1.4532	–
College, University	0.3168	n./i.	n./i.	**1.7580**	*2.0844*
Occupational group					
Plant cultivation, breeding, fishery	0.2822	0.2184	1.6802	-0.0783	0.4605
Mining, mineral extraction	–	–	–	–	–
Manufacturing	Ref.	Ref.	Ref.	Ref.	Ref.
Technical professions	-0.1591	0.3228	0.3352	0.6039	1.1130
Service professions	0.0212	-0.0885	0.6437	0.1047	0.1787
Other professions	-0.5124	-0.8312	–	**-1.1029**	*-1.1534*
Professional rank					
Unskilled worker	Ref.	Ref.	Ref.	Ref.	Ref.
Skilled worker	0.0958	0.2160	*-1.0991*	0.1689	0.4266
White-collar worker, simple occupations	0.1484	**0.3840**	-0.5329	0.3767	*0.8961*
White-collar worker, advanced occupations	-0.0432	0.2284	-0.7680	0.7158	0.6756
Other	0.2369	0.0512	-0.4387	-0.0977	-0.1914
Qualification (with work experience)	n./i.	**-0.2728**	0.1613	-0.0730	0.0118
Career Variables					
Duration of last employment (months)	-0.0019	**-0.0029**	-0.0044	**-0.0030**	*-0.0036*
Duration of unemployment (weeks)					
Up to 13 weeks	Ref.	Ref.	Ref.	Ref.	Ref.
Between 13 and 52 weeks	-0.1255	0.0718	*0.4839*	0.0806	-0.1973
More than 52 weeks	0.0708	-0.0147	0.2173	-0.2595	-0.4276
Number of placement propositions	**0.1023**	0.0959	0.0983	**0.1177**	**0.1030**
Last contact to job center (weeks)	-0.0201	-0.1739	-0.0326	-0.0845	-0.2311
Rehabilitation attendant	0.0278	0.3001	0.6570	**0.3679**	n./i.
Placement restrictions	-0.3118	**-0.5766**	-0.0860	n./i.	0.0799
Programme before unemployment					
No further education or programme	Ref.	Ref.	Ref.	Ref.	Ref.
Further education compl., cont. education	**0.4726**	**0.4857**	0.7813	**0.5584**	0.2770
Further education compl., voc. adjustment	*0.6610*	**0.4891**	0.6469	0.5412	0.2049
Job-preparative measure	0.4889	0.0680	–	–	–
Job creation scheme	**1.5513**	**1.2749**	**1.6621**	**1.5575**	**1.3785**
Rehabilitation measure	*0.9370*	0.4775	–	-0.2402	0.5243
Regional Context Variables[4]					
Cluster Ia	**-1.1810**	*-0.4112*	0.6802	-0.3686	-0.1445
Cluster Ib	**-1.2800**	**-0.6813**	0.2196	-0.4145	0.1129
Cluster Ic	**-1.2981**	**-0.7156**	0.6707	-0.0070	0.3546
Cluster II	Ref.	Ref.	Ref.	Ref.	Ref.

Bold letters indicate significance at the 1% level. *Italic* letters refer to the 5% level.
[1] DoR = degree of restriction
[2] People with accepted degree of restriction, but no equalisation to other persons with the same DoR.
[3] CSE = Certificate for secondary education
[4] Cluster according to the classification as described in table 4.6.
n./i.: not included in the estimation
– no observations in relevant sub-group

Table B.14: Cumulated Exit Rates in Main and Sub-Groups - Men in West Germany (cumulated frequencies)

Month	Total	< 25 years	25-50 years	> 50 years	< 13 weeks unemployed	13-52 weeks unemployed	< 52 weeks unemployed	w.o. prof. exper.	w.o. prof. train.	with high degree	rehabil. attend.	with placement restraints
Mar 00	2.06	2.62	2.02	1.45	2.33	2.02	1.91	2.56	2.01	0.00	4.50	2.26
Apr 00	3.88	4.37	4.11	2.32	3.94	4.03	3.70	4.03	4.25	1.79	5.41	4.52
May 00	5.89	6.33	6.51	2.90	6.81	5.11	5.97	7.33	6.49	3.57	7.21	5.93
Jun 00	8.97	11.35	8.90	6.09	10.22	8.87	8.23	10.99	10.22	4.46	8.11	8.47
Jul 00	11.59	13.76	11.82	7.83	12.90	11.56	10.74	13.19	13.06	6.25	9.01	12.15
Aug 00	16.50	18.34	16.90	12.46	16.67	16.80	16.11	17.22	18.58	8.04	15.32	16.95
Sep 00	19.30	23.80	19.07	14.20	20.43	19.89	18.02	20.51	21.87	8.93	16.22	17.80
Oct 00	23.60	32.53	22.44	16.23	26.70	23.52	21.60	23.81	27.24	9.82	21.62	22.60
Nov 00	29.30	39.52	28.35	19.42	32.44	29.97	26.61	32.23	33.28	12.50	25.23	27.12
Dec 00	33.22	43.45	31.56	26.09	40.14	33.06	28.76	35.53	37.31	16.07	27.93	31.64
Jan 01	37.57	47.60	35.98	30.43	45.34	37.10	32.82	39.56	41.57	17.86	32.43	36.44
Feb 01	67.71	73.36	68.59	56.81	72.22	67.34	65.00	68.50	69.85	61.61	61.26	64.12
Mar 01	79.77	80.13	81.45	72.75	80.82	79.84	79.00	80.22	81.19	78.57	73.87	78.81
Apr 01	80.65	81.00	82.35	73.62	82.26	80.51	79.71	81.68	82.46	78.57	75.68	79.66
May 01	81.87	84.28	82.87	74.78	84.23	81.85	80.31	82.78	84.10	79.46	76.58	79.94
Jun 01	83.36	86.03	84.22	76.52	86.20	82.93	81.86	85.35	85.30	80.36	78.38	81.07
Jul 01	85.00	88.21	85.64	78.26	87.10	84.95	83.65	87.18	87.01	81.25	81.08	82.77
Aug 01	85.84	89.30	86.39	79.13	88.17	85.62	84.49	87.55	87.99	82.14	81.98	83.33
Sep 01	87.15	91.27	87.51	80.29	89.61	87.10	85.56	89.38	89.18	83.04	81.98	84.75
Oct 01	88.36	93.23	88.41	81.74	91.40	88.17	86.52	90.11	90.30	83.93	83.78	85.88
Nov 01	89.30	94.76	89.38	81.74	92.11	89.38	87.35	90.48	91.27	84.82	86.49	87.57
Dec 01	90.09	95.41	90.13	82.90	92.65	90.19	88.31	92.31	92.09	87.50	86.49	87.85
Jan 02	91.26	96.29	91.32	84.35	93.19	91.26	89.98	92.67	92.99	87.50	86.49	89.27
Feb 02	97.48	98.69	97.46	95.94	96.77	97.98	97.49	98.53	98.13	95.54	96.40	96.61
Mar 02	98.41	98.91	98.43	97.68	97.85	98.66	98.57	98.53	98.73	98.21	96.40	97.46
Apr 02	98.46	98.91	98.50	97.68	98.03	98.66	98.57	98.53	98.73	98.21	96.40	97.46
May 02	98.74	99.56	98.73	97.68	98.57	98.92	98.69	98.53	99.10	98.21	97.30	97.74
Jun 02	98.83	99.56	98.80	97.97	98.75	98.92	98.81	98.53	99.25	98.21	97.30	98.31
Jul 02	98.97	99.56	98.95	98.26	98.75	99.06	99.05	98.53	99.40	98.21	98.20	98.59
Aug 02	99.07	99.56	99.03	98.55	98.92	99.19	99.05	98.90	99.40	98.21	99.10	99.15
Sep 02	99.07	99.56	99.03	98.55	98.92	99.19	99.05	98.90	99.40	98.21	99.10	99.15
Oct 02	99.07	99.56	99.03	98.55	98.92	99.19	99.05	98.90	99.40	98.21	99.10	99.15
Nov 02	99.07	99.56	99.03	98.55	98.92	99.19	99.05	98.90	99.40	98.21	99.10	99.15
Dec 02	99.30	99.78	99.25	98.84	99.46	99.46	99.05	98.90	99.48	99.11	99.10	99.15

Table B.15: Cumulated Exit Rates in Main and Sub-Groups - Women in West Germany (cumulated frequencies)

Month	Total	< 25 years	25-50 years	> 50 years	< 13 weeks unemployed	13-52 weeks unemployed	< 52 weeks unemployed	w.o. prof. exper.	w.o. prof. train.	with high degree	rehabil. attend.	with placement restraints
Mar 00	1.43	1.10	1.55	1.24	0.84	1.49	1.70	0.63	2.52	0.00	4.55	3.38
Apr 00	2.76	3.30	2.40	3.73	3.38	2.23	2.91	2.52	4.41	0.00	6.82	6.76
May 00	3.80	3.85	3.24	6.21	4.22	3.23	4.13	2.52	5.25	0.00	6.82	8.78
Jun 00	5.61	5.49	4.94	8.70	7.17	4.96	5.34	4.40	7.35	0.68	6.82	9.46
Jul 00	7.22	7.69	6.21	11.18	8.86	6.20	7.28	5.66	9.66	2.74	6.82	10.81
Aug 00	11.22	12.09	9.59	17.39	13.08	10.92	10.44	10.06	12.82	6.85	11.36	13.51
Sep 00	15.21	20.88	12.41	21.12	19.83	13.90	13.83	15.09	17.44	12.33	11.36	15.54
Oct 00	17.02	23.63	14.10	22.36	21.52	16.87	14.56	16.35	19.96	15.07	13.64	18.24
Nov 00	21.10	29.67	17.91	25.47	25.74	21.59	17.96	22.01	24.79	16.44	20.45	24.32
Dec 00	24.33	33.52	21.30	27.33	29.54	25.81	19.90	25.16	28.36	20.55	22.73	26.35
Jan 01	27.38	35.71	24.54	30.43	32.49	28.29	23.54	28.93	30.46	23.29	22.73	28.38
Feb 01	61.60	60.99	61.07	64.60	61.60	61.54	61.65	62.26	61.55	60.27	65.91	64.19
Mar 01	73.38	71.98	73.34	75.16	75.53	71.96	73.54	75.47	72.69	76.71	70.45	71.62
Apr 01	74.05	73.63	73.91	75.16	76.37	72.95	73.79	75.47	73.95	76.71	75.00	72.97
May 01	75.00	76.37	74.47	75.78	78.48	73.70	74.27	77.36	75.00	77.40	75.00	72.97
Jun 01	76.05	77.47	75.32	77.64	79.32	75.43	74.76	77.99	76.26	77.40	75.00	74.32
Jul 01	76.81	79.67	75.88	77.64	80.59	76.18	75.24	79.25	77.52	77.40	77.27	75.00
Aug 01	77.66	81.32	76.73	77.64	81.01	77.17	76.21	79.25	78.36	78.08	77.27	75.00
Sep 01	78.90	85.16	77.29	78.88	82.28	78.41	77.43	81.13	80.25	78.77	79.55	79.05
Oct 01	80.23	87.91	77.86	81.99	84.39	79.90	78.16	83.65	81.93	80.14	84.09	79.05
Nov 01	81.18	89.01	78.70	83.23	85.23	80.89	79.13	84.91	83.19	80.14	84.09	80.41
Dec 01	81.94	89.56	79.55	83.85	86.08	81.39	80.10	84.91	84.03	80.82	84.09	81.08
Jan 02	83.56	91.76	81.10	85.09	87.76	82.63	82.04	86.79	85.92	81.51	84.09	82.43
Feb 02	95.63	96.15	95.20	96.89	96.62	96.28	94.42	94.34	97.06	91.78	95.45	95.95
Mar 02	97.91	97.25	97.88	98.76	97.05	98.51	97.82	98.11	97.90	97.26	97.73	99.32
Apr 02	98.00	97.25	98.03	98.76	97.05	98.51	98.06	98.11	98.11	97.26	97.73	99.32
May 02	98.10	97.80	98.03	98.76	97.05	98.76	98.06	98.74	98.32	97.26	97.73	99.32
Jun 02	98.10	97.80	98.03	98.76	97.05	98.76	98.06	98.74	98.32	97.26	97.73	99.32
Jul 02	98.29	97.80	98.31	98.76	97.47	99.01	98.30	98.74	98.32	97.26	97.73	99.32
Aug 02	98.38	97.80	98.45	98.76	97.47	99.01	98.30	98.74	98.53	97.26	97.73	99.32
Sep 02	98.48	97.80	98.59	98.76	97.47	99.26	98.30	98.74	98.74	97.26	97.73	99.32
Oct 02	98.67	98.35	98.59	99.38	97.47	99.26	98.79	98.74	98.74	97.26	97.73	99.32
Nov 02	98.76	98.35	98.73	99.38	97.89	99.26	98.79	98.74	98.95	97.95	97.73	99.32
Dec 02	98.95	99.45	98.73	99.38	98.31	99.50	98.79	99.37	99.37	97.95	97.73	99.32

Table B.16: Cumulated Exit Rates in Main and Sub-Groups - Men in East Germany (cumulated frequencies)

Month	Total	< 25 years	25-50 years	> 50 years	< 13 weeks unem- ployed	13-52 weeks unem- ployed	< 52 weeks unem- ployed	w.o. prof. exper.	w.o. prof. train.	with high degree	rehabil. attend.	with place- ment re- straints
Mar 00	0.51	1.67	0.32	0.54	1.21	0.32	0.36	1.02	0.48	0.00	0.92	0.25
Apr 00	1.30	3.33	1.08	1.17	2.25	1.12	1.00	2.05	1.43	0.68	1.83	1.52
May 00	3.04	6.25	3.18	2.16	6.06	2.56	2.00	4.78	3.46	0.68	4.59	2.54
Jun 00	4.38	7.92	4.65	3.23	8.13	4.09	2.73	6.83	5.50	0.68	5.50	3.55
Jul 00	6.02	13.75	6.24	4.04	10.33	6.01	3.92	9.56	7.89	1.37	6.42	4.57
Aug 00	9.51	20.42	8.91	8.00	16.09	9.13	6.47	12.97	10.27	4.11	7.80	7.11
Sep 00	12.31	23.33	11.65	10.87	18.34	13.06	8.29	15.70	13.14	7.53	9.17	8.63
Oct 00	16.35	30.42	16.61	12.94	25.43	16.99	10.84	20.48	19.24	7.53	14.22	14.21
Nov 00	19.46	34.17	19.99	15.54	29.07	19.63	14.21	25.26	22.70	10.27	16.51	16.24
Dec 00	21.89	41.67	22.22	17.16	33.39	21.96	15.76	27.99	25.93	10.27	20.64	19.29
Jan 01	23.53	44.58	23.49	19.05	35.29	23.48	17.40	29.69	28.08	11.64	21.10	20.56
Feb 01	66.93	72.50	67.54	64.87	70.93	67.39	64.30	66.55	63.80	69.86	63.30	64.47
Mar 01	90.60	91.67	91.79	88.68	92.04	88.70	91.99	91.47	91.64	82.88	89.45	88.07
Apr 01	90.80	92.08	91.98	88.86	92.21	89.02	92.08	91.47	91.76	82.88	89.45	88.07
May 01	91.28	92.92	92.49	89.22	92.73	89.50	92.53	92.15	92.00	83.56	89.45	88.07
Jun 01	91.69	92.92	92.93	89.67	92.91	90.14	92.81	92.15	92.47	83.56	90.37	88.83
Jul 01	91.93	93.33	93.13	89.94	93.25	90.46	93.08	92.49	92.83	84.25	90.37	89.09
Aug 01	92.20	93.75	93.38	90.21	93.25	90.87	93.17	92.83	92.95	84.93	91.74	89.59
Sep 01	92.44	94.17	93.70	90.30	93.77	91.19	93.17	93.86	93.07	84.93	92.66	90.10
Oct 01	92.68	95.00	93.83	90.57	94.12	91.35	93.44	94.20	93.43	84.93	92.66	90.61
Nov 01	92.99	96.25	94.08	90.75	94.81	91.59	93.62	94.88	93.79	84.93	93.58	91.62
Dec 01	93.23	96.67	94.33	90.93	94.98	91.91	93.81	95.22	94.15	85.62	94.04	91.88
Jan 02	93.40	97.50	94.53	90.93	95.33	92.07	93.90	95.56	94.38	85.62	94.04	91.88
Feb 02	97.64	99.17	98.22	96.50	97.92	96.88	98.36	98.63	97.73	95.21	96.33	96.19
Mar 02	99.76	99.58	99.75	99.82	100.00	99.52	99.91	99.66	99.76	100.00	99.08	99.24
Apr 02	99.76	99.58	99.75	99.82	100.00	99.52	99.91	99.66	99.76	100.00	99.08	99.24
May 02	99.76	99.58	99.75	99.82	100.00	99.52	99.91	99.66	99.76	100.00	99.08	99.24
Jun 02	99.76	99.58	99.75	99.82	100.00	99.52	99.91	99.66	99.76	100.00	99.08	99.24
Jul 02	99.79	100.00	99.75	99.82	100.00	99.60	99.91	99.66	99.88	100.00	99.08	99.49
Aug 02	99.79	100.00	99.75	99.82	100.00	99.60	99.91	99.66	99.88	100.00	99.08	99.49
Sep 02	99.79	100.00	99.75	99.82	100.00	99.60	99.91	99.66	99.88	100.00	99.08	99.49
Oct 02	99.83	100.00	99.81	99.82	100.00	99.68	100.00	99.66	99.88	100.00	99.08	99.49
Nov 02	99.86	100.00	99.87	99.82	100.00	99.68	100.00	99.66	100.00	100.00	99.08	99.49
Dec 02	99.86	100.00	99.87	99.82	100.00	99.68	100.00	99.66	100.00	100.00	99.08	99.49

210   B Additional Material to Chapter 5

Table B.17: Cumulated Exit Rates in Main and Sub-Groups - Women in East Germany (cumulated frequencies)

Month	Total	< 25 years	25-50 years	> 50 years	< 13 weeks unemployed	13-52 weeks unemployed	< 52 weeks unemployed	w.o. prof. exper.	w.o. prof. train.	with high degree	rehabil. attend.	with placement restraints
Mar 00	0.81	0.68	0.84	0.78	1.22	0.86	0.68	0.40	0.80	1.05	1.28	1.60
Apr 00	1.33	0.68	1.41	1.23	1.74	1.68	0.96	1.20	1.25	2.62	3.21	2.66
May 00	2.26	3.38	2.24	2.20	3.83	2.59	1.65	2.21	2.41	3.14	3.85	3.46
Jun 00	3.02	4.05	3.02	2.91	5.22	3.50	2.13	2.81	3.21	3.14	3.85	3.99
Jul 00	3.69	4.05	3.77	3.50	5.74	4.47	2.61	3.41	3.75	5.24	6.41	5.85
Aug 00	6.43	6.76	6.37	6.54	9.57	6.70	5.50	5.42	6.69	7.33	9.62	10.37
Sep 00	8.18	10.14	7.96	8.48	12.87	8.32	6.99	6.83	8.74	8.38	10.26	11.97
Oct 00	9.85	14.86	9.58	9.97	18.26	9.85	7.91	9.44	10.17	8.90	10.90	13.03
Nov 00	12.39	16.89	11.82	13.20	21.39	12.28	10.40	12.05	12.13	9.95	11.54	15.43
Dec 00	13.94	20.95	13.32	14.63	23.65	14.16	11.53	14.66	14.01	10.47	11.54	15.43
Jan 01	15.49	22.97	15.20	15.40	26.09	15.58	12.97	16.47	15.61	12.57	12.18	16.49
Feb 01	67.37	64.86	66.31	69.90	67.48	66.45	68.07	65.86	65.03	67.02	58.97	65.43
Mar 01	92.17	85.81	92.34	92.43	89.74	90.96	93.69	93.17	93.58	85.34	88.46	91.22
Apr 01	92.35	86.49	92.55	92.49	90.09	91.17	93.82	93.57	93.76	85.34	89.10	91.49
May 01	92.65	86.49	92.94	92.62	90.26	91.73	93.94	94.38	94.11	85.34	89.10	91.76
Jun 01	92.89	87.16	93.18	92.82	90.96	91.78	94.22	94.78	94.38	85.34	89.74	92.02
Jul 01	93.15	89.86	93.33	93.07	91.48	92.08	94.38	95.38	94.65	85.34	90.38	92.29
Aug 01	93.41	91.22	93.51	93.40	91.83	92.49	94.50	95.78	95.09	85.34	90.38	92.29
Sep 01	93.57	92.57	93.66	93.46	92.00	92.64	94.66	95.78	95.36	85.34	91.67	92.82
Oct 01	93.78	93.92	93.84	93.66	92.35	92.99	94.74	95.78	95.45	85.86	91.67	92.82
Nov 01	93.94	95.27	93.99	93.72	92.87	93.10	94.86	96.18	95.81	85.86	91.67	92.82
Dec 01	94.06	95.27	94.17	93.72	92.87	93.25	94.98	96.39	95.99	86.39	91.67	93.09
Jan 02	94.08	95.27	94.17	93.79	93.04	93.25	94.98	96.39	96.07	86.39	91.67	93.09
Feb 02	97.97	98.65	98.08	97.67	97.04	97.77	98.35	98.59	98.93	94.76	94.87	97.61
Mar 02	99.72	100.00	99.67	99.81	99.48	99.75	99.76	100.00	99.82	98.95	99.36	99.47
Apr 02	99.76	100.00	99.67	99.94	99.65	99.75	99.80	100.00	100.00	98.95	100.00	99.73
May 02	99.82	100.00	99.76	99.94	99.83	99.83	99.84	100.00	100.00	98.95	100.00	99.73
Jun 02	99.82	100.00	99.76	99.94	99.83	99.80	99.84	100.00	100.00	98.95	100.00	99.73
Jul 02	99.82	100.00	99.76	99.94	99.83	99.80	99.84	100.00	100.00	98.95	100.00	99.73
Aug 02	99.84	100.00	99.79	99.94	99.83	99.85	99.84	100.00	100.00	99.48	100.00	99.73
Sep 02	99.86	100.00	99.82	99.94	99.83	99.88	99.88	100.00	100.00	100.00	100.00	100.00
Oct 02	99.88	100.00	99.85	99.94	99.83	99.85	99.92	100.00	100.00	100.00	100.00	100.00
Nov 02	99.88	100.00	99.85	99.94	99.83	99.85	99.92	100.00	100.00	100.00	100.00	100.00
Dec 02	99.90	100.00	99.88	99.94	99.83	99.90	99.92	100.00	100.00	100.00	100.00	100.00

Table B.18: Employment Effects in the Sub-Groups in West Germany

Men	Jul 00		Dec 00		Jul 01		Dec 01		Jul 02		Dec 02	
Group	Effect	S.E.	Effect	S.E.	Effect	S.E.	Effect	S.E.	Effect	S.E.	Effect	S.E.
Total	**-0.2110**	0.0098	**-0.1653**	0.0101	**-0.1253**	0.0119	**-0.0763**	0.0120	*-0.0306*	0.0136	-0.0019	0.0121
Age (in years)												
<25	**-0.2880**	0.0257	**-0.2258**	0.0275	**-0.1014**	0.0235	-0.0276	0.0326	-0.0046	0.0320	-0.0276	0.0326
25-50	**-0.1709**	0.0114	**-0.1566**	0.0124	**-0.1069**	0.0134	**-0.0715**	0.0140	-0.0211	0.0183	0.0151	0.0160
>50	**-0.1250**	0.0218	**-0.0843**	0.0196	**-0.0698**	0.0238	-0.0378	0.0230	0.0203	0.0224	0.0262	0.0216
Duration of unemployment												
< 13 weeks	**-0.3705**	0.0218	**-0.2500**	0.0286	**-0.2136**	0.0282	*-0.0818*	0.0350	-0.0705	0.0307	-0.0477	0.0299
13-52 weeks	**-0.2292**	0.0183	**-0.2125**	0.0183	**-0.1014**	0.0196	**-0.0736**	0.0181	-0.0194	0.0187	-0.0097	0.0182
> 52 weeks	**-0.0707**	0.0104	**-0.0814**	0.0123	*-0.0275*	0.0169	-0.0096	0.0172	*0.0443*	0.0179	**0.0503**	0.0170
Without professional experience	**-0.1862**	0.0244	**-0.2267**	0.0341	**-0.1174**	0.0397	-0.0364	0.0341	-0.0364	0.0354	-0.0040	0.0333
Without professional training	**-0.2153**	0.0118	**-0.1752**	0.0143	**-0.1065**	0.0182	**-0.0664**	0.0163	**-0.0486**	0.0147	-0.0046	0.0121
With high degree	**-0.1771**	0.0444	**-0.2083**	0.0585	*-0.0313*	0.0712	-0.0104	0.0761	*0.1354*	0.0683	*0.1250*	0.0626
With placement restrictions	**-0.1166**	0.0242	**-0.1319**	0.0240	**-0.1411**	0.0293	*-0.0644*	0.0274	-0.0215	0.0283	0.0153	0.0265
Rehabilitation attendant	**-0.1500**	0.0448	**-0.1600**	0.0404	**-0.1600**	0.0463	-0.1000	0.0552	-0.0400	0.0567	0.0300	0.0653

Women	Jul 00		Dec 00		Jul 01		Dec 01		Jul 02		Dec 02	
Group	Effect	S.E.	Effect	S.E.	Effect	S.E.	Effect	S.E.	Effect	S.E.	Effect	S.E.
Total	**-0.2041**	0.0123	**-0.2163**	0.0165	**-0.1194**	0.0186	**-0.0765**	0.0167	0.0082	0.0163	*0.0459*	0.0180
Age (in years)												
<25	**-0.2716**	0.0299	**-0.2284**	0.0444	*-0.1358*	0.0696	*-0.1296*	0.0662	-0.0988	0.0642	-0.0679	0.0555
25-50	**-0.1674**	0.0154	**-0.1795**	0.0153	**-0.1101**	0.0248	**-0.0860**	0.0284	0.0166	0.0296	0.0452	0.0303
>50	-0.1000	0.0244	-0.0533	0.0283	-0.0267	0.0349	-0.0067	0.0360	**0.1000**	0.0416	**0.1267**	0.0433
Duration of unemployment												
< 13 weeks	**-0.3545**	0.0292	**-0.2857**	0.0377	**-0.2698**	0.0452	**-0.1429**	0.0405	-0.0847	0.0491	0.0106	0.0371
13-52 weeks	**-0.2274**	0.0195	**-0.2712**	0.0285	**-0.1589**	0.0353	**-0.1014**	0.0339	0.0082	0.0365	0.0329	0.0347
> 52 weeks	**-0.0925**	0.0162	**-0.1175**	0.0202	-0.0125	0.0257	0.0025	0.0298	**0.0875**	0.0253	**0.1125**	0.0299
Without professional experience	**-0.2813**	0.0380	**-0.3359**	0.0523	**-0.1641**	0.0624	*-0.1563*	0.0663	-0.0781	0.0610	-0.0703	0.0567
Without professional training	**-0.1834**	0.0170	**-0.1700**	0.0245	**-0.0984**	0.0291	*-0.0671*	0.0272	-0.0089	0.0318	0.0425	0.0286
With high degree	**-0.2583**	0.0346	**-0.3000**	0.0334	**-0.1583**	0.0518	**-0.1333**	0.0504	0.0417	0.0573	0.0083	0.0532
With placement restrictions	**-0.1197**	0.0307	**-0.1026**	0.0270	**-0.1453**	0.0455	-0.0855	0.0453	0.0513	0.0519	0.1026	0.0541
Rehabilitation attendant	**-0.2286**	0.0747	**-0.2286**	0.0780	*-0.1714*	0.0772	*-0.2000*	0.0792	0.0000	0.0901	0.0571	0.0949

Bold letters indicate significance on a 1% level, *italic* letters refer to the 5% level, standard errors are bootstrapped with 50 replications.
Results refer to NN matching without replacement and a caliper of 0.02.

Table B.19: Employment Effects in the Sub-Groups in East Germany

Men	Jul 00		Dec 00		Jul 01		Dec 01		Jul 02		Dec 02	
Group	Effect	S.E.	Effect	S.E.	Effect	S.E.	Effect	S.E.	Effect	S.E.	Effect	S.E.
Total	**-0.1399**	0.0075	**-0.1167**	0.0073	**-0.1088**	0.0095	**-0.0657**	0.0080	**-0.0482**	0.0076	**-0.0287**	0.0079
Age (in years)												
<25	**-0.1921**	0.0310	**-0.2096**	0.0339	**-0.1485**	0.0395	**-0.1179**	0.0449	-0.0873	0.0480	-0.0437	0.0476
25-50	**-0.1541**	0.0100	**-0.1268**	0.0095	**-0.1127**	0.0130	**-0.0522**	0.0120	**-0.0439**	0.0125	-0.0185	0.0116
>50	**-0.1099**	0.0107	**-0.0885**	0.0102	**-0.0764**	0.0120	**-0.0428**	0.0097	**-0.0447**	0.0121	-0.0130	0.0100
Duration of unemployment												
< 13 weeks	**-0.2869**	0.0223	**-0.2313**	0.0228	**-0.2227**	0.0262	**-0.1199**	0.0233	**-0.1328**	0.0263	**-0.1006**	0.0274
13-52 weeks	**-0.1195**	0.0101	**-0.1276**	0.0098	**-0.0829**	0.0148	**-0.0715**	0.0114	*-0.0309*	0.0151	-0.0163	0.0146
> 52 weeks	**-0.0410**	0.0056	**-0.0492**	0.0065	**-0.0364**	0.0092	*-0.0219*	0.0087	-0.0009	0.0114	-0.0018	0.0104
Without professional experience	**-0.1730**	0.0206	**-0.1626**	0.0258	**-0.1661**	0.0326	*-0.0934*	0.0381	-0.0727	0.0402	0.0069	0.0284
Without professional training	**-0.1234**	0.0131	**-0.0874**	0.0126	**-0.0814**	0.0158	*-0.0335*	0.0142	-0.0275	0.0143	0.0120	0.0143
With high degree	**-0.1250**	0.0325	**-0.1324**	0.0351	-0.0515	0.0433	-0.0294	0.0451	-0.0147	0.0463	0.0074	0.0484
With placement restrictions	**-0.0970**	0.0148	**-0.0970**	0.0141	**-0.0809**	0.0206	**-0.0566**	0.0205	0.0000	0.0259	0.0189	0.0221
Rehabilitation attendant	**-0.0837**	0.0179	**-0.0884**	0.0201	**-0.0837**	0.0287	**-0.0465**	0.0284	-0.0419	0.0275	-0.0140	0.0328

Women	Jul 00		Dec 00		Jul 01		Dec 01		Jul 02		Dec 02	
Group	Effect	S.E.	Effect	S.E.	Effect	S.E.	Effect	S.E.	Effect	S.E.	Effect	S.E.
Total	**-0.0937**	0.0042	**-0.0931**	0.0049	**-0.0750**	0.0056	**-0.0499**	0.0059	**-0.0376**	0.0070	*-0.0135*	0.0067
Age (in years)												
<25	**-0.2361**	0.0390	**-0.2569**	0.0478	**-0.2065**	0.0573	-0.0486	0.0584	0.0069	0.0638	0.0278	0.0608
25-50	**-0.1037**	0.0055	**-0.1106**	0.0063	**-0.0837**	0.0087	**-0.0654**	0.0089	**-0.0420**	0.0089	**-0.0219**	0.0082
>50	**-0.0500**	0.0064	**-0.0398**	0.0061	**-0.0317**	0.0078	*-0.0169*	0.0071	-0.0142	0.0077	-0.0020	0.0069
Duration of unemployment												
< 13 weeks	**-0.2413**	0.0228	**-0.1694**	0.0154	**-0.2065**	0.0299	**-0.1392**	0.0274	**-0.1601**	0.0290	**-0.0742**	0.0260
13-52 weeks	**-0.1049**	0.0077	**-0.1228**	0.0085	**-0.0825**	0.0091	**-0.0565**	0.0094	**-0.0362**	0.0107	-0.0076	0.0127
> 52 weeks	**-0.0402**	0.0041	**-0.0470**	0.0052	*-0.0185*	0.0077	*-0.0165*	0.0070	0.0100	0.0082	**0.0245**	0.0081
Without professional experience	**-0.1043**	0.0143	**-0.1207**	0.0141	**-0.1043**	0.0184	*-0.0491*	0.0214	-0.0143	0.0249	0.0225	0.0224
Without professional training	**-0.0851**	0.0086	**-0.0887**	0.0084	**-0.0762**	0.0117	**-0.0636**	0.0159	**-0.0421**	0.0143	-0.0215	0.0154
With high degree	**-0.1463**	0.0278	**-0.1524**	0.0353	**-0.1098**	0.0421	**-0.1159**	0.0413	*-0.1037*	0.0486	*-0.0976*	0.0475
With placement restrictions	**-0.0691**	0.0141	**-0.0746**	0.0132	**-0.0608**	0.0169	*-0.0987*	0.0173	*-0.0497*	0.0238	-0.0166	0.0254
Rehabilitation attendant	*-0.0541*	0.0217	**-0.0676**	0.0257	-0.0473	0.0411	-0.0473	0.0445	-0.0338	0.0442	-0.0068	0.0488

Bold letters indicate significance on a 1% level, *italic* letters refer to the 5% level, standard errors are bootstrapped with 50 replications.
Results refer to NN matching without replacement and a caliper of 0.02.

Table B.20: Sensitivity Analysis for Unobserved Heterogeneity - West Germany

West Germany		Men				
		July 2002			December 2002	
Group	Effect	Q-MH for $exp(y)=1$	Critical value for $exp(y)$	Effect	Q-MH for $exp(y)=1$	Critical value for $exp(y)$
Total	*-0.0306*	5.35	1.50-1.55	-0.0019	n.s	n.s.
Age (in years)						
<25	-0.0046	n.s	n.s	-0.0276	n.s	n.s
25-50	-0.0211	n.s	n.s	0.0151	n.s	n.s
>50	0.0203	n.s	n.s	0.0262	n.s	n.s
Duration of unemployment						
< 13 weeks	*-0.0705*	4.82	1.55-1.60	-0.0477	n.s	n.s
13-52 weeks	-0.0194	n.s	n.s	-0.0097	n.s	n.s
> 52 weeks	*0.0443*	6.06	1.65-1.70	**0.0503**	8.19	1.65-1.70
Without professional experience	-0.0364	n.s	n.s	-0.0040	n.s	n.s
Without professional training	**-0.0486**	8.44	1.40-1.45	-0.0046	n.s	n.s
With high degree	*0.1354*	3.97	1.75-1.80	*0.1250*	3.54	1.75-1.80
With placement restrictions	-0.0215	n.s	n.s	0.0153	n.s	n.s
Rehabilitation attendant	-0.0400	n.s	n.s	0.0300	n.s	n.s
		Women				
Total	0.0082	n.s	n.s	*0.0459*	4.80	1.75-1.80
Age (in years)						
<25	-0.0988	n.s	n.s	-0.0679	n.s	n.s
25-50	0.0166	n.s	n.s	0.0452	n.s	n.s
>50	**0.1000**	4.73	1.65-1.70	**0.1267**	7.40	1.75-1.80
Duration of unemployment						
< 13 weeks	-0.0847	n.s	n.s	0.0106	n.s	n.s
13-52 weeks	0.0082	n.s	n.s	0.0329	n.s	n.s
> 52 weeks	**0.0875**	8.24	1.75-1.80	**0.1125**	13.26	1.80-18.5
Without professional experience	-0.0781	n.s	n.s	-0.0703	n.s	n.s
Without professional training	-0.0089	n.s	n.s	0.0425	n.s	n.s
With high degree	0.0417	n.s	n.s	0.0083	n.s	n.s
With placement restrictions	0.0513	n.s	n.s	0.1026	n.s	n.s
Rehabilitation attendant	0.0000	n.s	n.s	0.0571	n.s	n.s

Table B.21: Sensitivity Analysis for Unobserved Heterogeneity - East Germany

East Germany		Men				
		July 2002			December 2002	
Group	Effect	Q-MH for $\exp(y)=1$	Critical value for $exp(y)$	Effect	Q-MH for $\exp(y)=1$	Critical value for $exp(y)$
Total	**-0.0482**	31.23	1.15-1.20	**-0.0287**	12.11	1.25-1.30
Age (in years)						
<25	-0.0873	4.56	1.20-1.25	-0.0437	n.s	n.s
25-50	**-0.0439**	12.46	1.20-1.25	-0.0185	n.s	n.s
>50	**-0.0447**	16.11	1.00-1.05	-0.0130	n.s	n.s
Duration of unemployment						
< 13 weeks	**-0.1328**	24.79	1.00-1.05	**-0.1006**	15.25	1.05-1.10
13-52 weeks	*-0.0309*	5.16	1.25-1.30	-0.0163	n.s	n.s
> 52 weeks	-0.0009	n.s	n.s	-0.0018	n.s	n.s
Without professional experience	-0.0727	n.s	n.s	0.0069	n.s	n.s
Without professional training	-0.0275	n.s	n.s	0.0120	n.s	n.s
With high degree	-0.0147	n.s	n.s	0.0074	n.s	n.s
With placement restrictions	0.0000	n.s	n.s	0.0189	n.s	n.s
Rehabilitation attendant	-0.0419	n.s	n.s	-0.0140	n.s	n.s
		Women				
Total	**-0.0376**	33.02	1.25-1.30	*-0.0135*	12.11	1.25-1.30
Age (in years)						
<25	0.0069	n.s	n.s	0.0278	n.s	n.s
25-50	**-0.0420**	23.64	1.30-1.35	**-0.0219**	6.20	1.40-1.45
>50	-0.0142	n.s	n.s	-0.0020	n.s	n.s
Duration of unemployment						
< 13 weeks	**-0.1601**	30.64	1.00-1.05	**-0.0742**	7.56	1.15-1.20
13-52 weeks	**-0.0362**	11.01	1.25-1.30	-0.0076	n.s	n.s
> 52 weeks	0.0100	n.s	n.s	**0.0245**	9.74	1.60-1.65
Without professional experience	-0.0143	n.s	n.s	0.0225	n.s	n.s
Without professional training	**-0.0421**	10.20	1.10-1.15	-0.0215	n.s	n.s
With high degree	*-0.1037*	5.95	1.00-1.05	*-0.0976*	5.08	1.00-1.05
With placement restrictions	*-0.0497*	4.11	1.00-1.05	-0.0166	n.s	n.s
Rehabilitation attendant	-0.0338	n.s	n.s	-0.0068	n.s	n.s

Fig. B.1: Common Support for Men in West Germany (Main and Sub-Groups)[1]

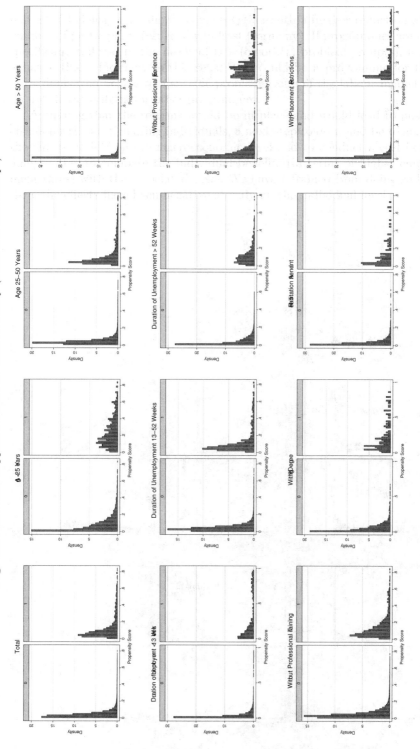

[1] The left side of the graphs refers to non-participants ($D=0$), the right side to participants ($D=1$) in each group.

Fig. B.2: Common Support for Women in West Germany (Main and Sub-Groups)[1]

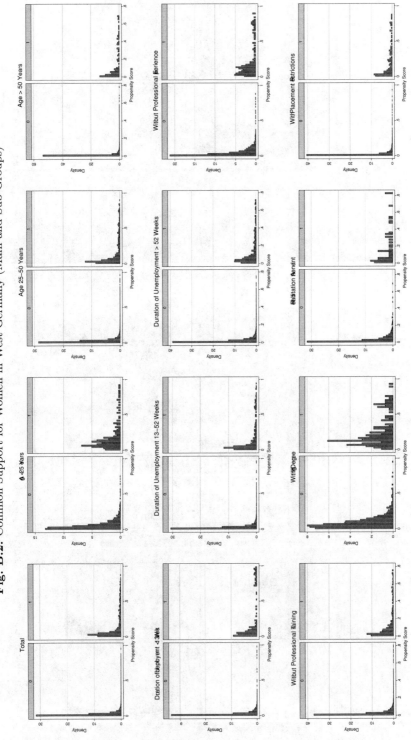

[1] The left side of the graphs refers to non-participants ($D = 0$), the right side to participants ($D = 1$) in each group.

Fig. B.3: Common Support for Men in East Germany (Main and Sub-Groups)[1]

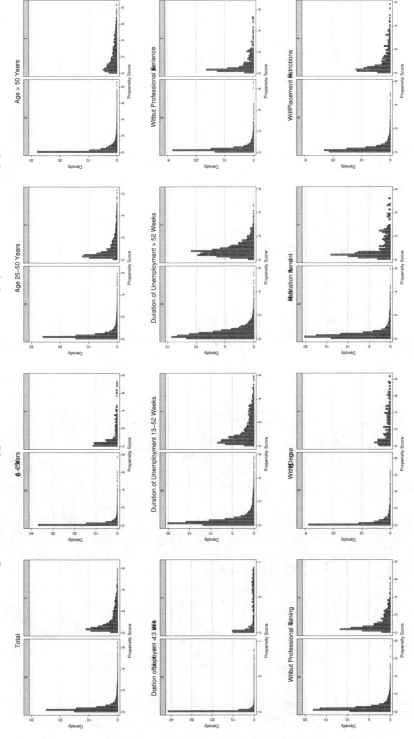

[1] The left side of the graphs refers to non-participants ($D=0$), the right side to participants ($D=1$) in each group.

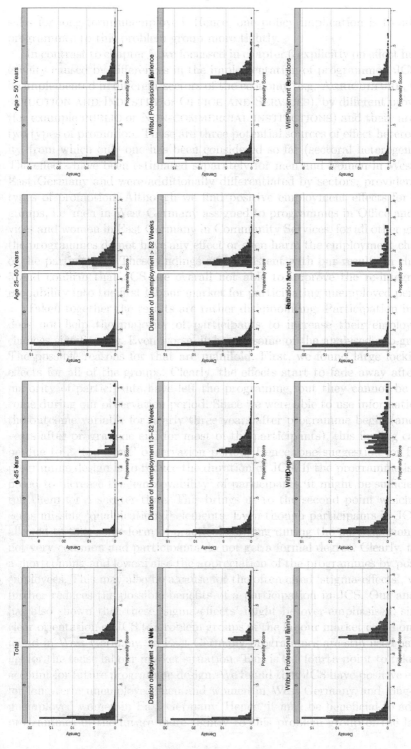

Fig. B.4: Common Support for Women in East Germany (Main and Sub-Groups)[1]

[1] The left side of the graphs refers to non-participants ($D = 0$), the right side to participants ($D = 1$) in each group.

C

Additional Material to Chapter 6

220   C Additional Material to Chapter 6

Table C.1: Selected Descriptives for Men in West Germany

Variables	Non-part.	Agricul.	Constr. and Industry	Office and Services	Comm. Services	Other
Number of observations	44095	584	371	131	320	734
Programme Duration (in days)		261.5	279.1	336.7	285.2	277.1
Socio-Demographic Variables						
Age	43.22	39.02	35.01	42.65	34.98	36.88
Married	0.52	0.37	0.37	0.38	0.30	0.34
Number of children	0.41	0.51	0.44	0.41	0.38	0.39
Health restrictions						
No health restrictions	0.68	0.74	0.81	0.58	0.76	0.74
Acc. DoR,[1] 80% and over	0.01	0.02	0.01	0.07	0.02	0.02
Acc. DoR, 50% to under 80%	0.06	0.05	0.03	0.15	0.07	0.06
Acc. DoR, 30% to under 50%	0.00	0.01	0.00	0.02	0.01	0.00
Acc. DoR, 30% to under 50%, no equalis.[2]	0.05	0.03	0.03	0.06	0.02	0.02
Other health restrictions	0.20	0.15	0.12	0.12	0.12	0.15
Rehabilitation attendant	0.06	0.05	0.06	0.11	0.06	0.04
Placement restrictions	0.22	0.16	0.14	0.22	0.16	0.18
Qualification Variables						
Professional Training						
Without compl. prof. training, no CSE[3]	0.15	0.34	0.31	0.07	0.18	0.24
Without compl. prof. training, with CSE	0.34	0.36	0.44	0.15	0.34	0.38
Industrial training	0.44	0.27	0.24	0.47	0.30	0.31
Full-time vocational school	0.01	0.00	0.01	0.02	0.02	0.01
Technical school	0.02	0.01	0.00	0.10	0.04	0.01
Polytechnic	0.01	0.00	0.00	0.07	0.05	0.01
College, university	0.02	0.01	0.00	0.14	0.08	0.03
Occupational group						
Plant cultivation, breeding, fishery	0.04	0.17	0.08	0.04	0.03	0.06
Mining, mineral extraction	0.01	0.00	0.01	0.00	0.00	0.00
Manufacturing	0.48	0.52	0.67	0.17	0.41	0.56
Technical professions	0.05	0.01	0.02	0.17	0.03	0.03
Service professions	0.41	0.28	0.20	0.63	0.50	0.33
Other professions	0.02	0.02	0.03	0.00	0.03	0.03
Professional Rank						
Unskilled worker	0.24	0.45	0.39	0.11	0.18	0.28
Skilled worker	0.15	0.06	0.07	0.05	0.07	0.09
White-collar worker, simple occupations	0.07	0.02	0.03	0.14	0.09	0.05
White-collar worker, advanced occupations	0.05	0.01	0.01	0.19	0.06	0.03
Other	0.49	0.46	0.51	0.50	0.59	0.55
Qualification (with work experience)	0.93	0.92	0.88	0.84	0.84	0.85
Career Variables						
Duration last employment	72.08	16.71	18.57	27.14	18.97	20.51
Duration of unemployment						
< 13	0.28	0.22	0.28	0.18	0.30	0.28
13 − 52	0.32	0.33	0.37	0.31	0.38	0.34
> 52	0.41	0.45	0.35	0.51	0.32	0.38
Number of placement propositions	3.60	8.17	6.87	9.23	7.08	7.74
Last contact to job center	2.54	2.27	2.38	2.97	2.49	2.61
Programme before unemployment						
No further education or programme	0.90	0.69	0.66	0.66	0.78	0.74
Further education compl., cont. education	0.07	0.10	0.11	0.14	0.09	0.09
Further education compl., voc. adjustment	0.00	0.02	0.01	0.01	0.00	0.01
Job-preparative measure	0.00	0.00	0.00	0.00	0.00	0.00
Job creation scheme	0.02	0.19	0.21	0.16	0.13	0.15
Rehabilitation measure	0.01	0.01	0.01	0.03	0.00	0.01
Regional Context Variables						
Cluster II	0.40	0.37	0.61	0.31	0.23	0.37
Cluster III	0.37	0.47	0.28	0.39	0.39	0.36
Cluster IV	0.08	0.06	0.02	0.07	0.16	0.11
Cluster V	0.15	0.10	0.08	0.23	0.23	0.16

[1] DoR = degree of restriction
[2] People with accepted degree of restriction, but no equalisation to other persons with the same DoR.
[3] CSE = Certificate for secondary education

Table C.2: Selected Descriptives for Women in West Germany

Variables	Non-part.	Agricul.	Constr. and Industry	Office and Services	Comm. Services	Other
Number of observations	34227			202	503	270
Programme Duration (in days)				307.2	305.1	310.7
Socio-Demographic Variables						
Age	43.33			39.93	38.00	36.92
Married	0.63			0.50	0.40	0.36
Number of children	0.58			0.62	0.65	0.47
Health restrictions						
No health restrictions	0.73			0.76	0.79	0.79
Acc. DoR,[1] 80% and over	0.01			0.03	0.03	0.03
Acc. DoR, 50% to under 80%	0.04			0.09	0.03	0.06
Acc. DoR, 30% to under 50%	0.00			0.01	0.01	0.01
Acc. DoR, 30% to under 50%, no equalis.[2]	0.04			0.01	0.02	0.01
Other health restrictions	0.18			0.08	0.12	0.11
Rehabilitation attendant	0.03			0.05	0.04	0.05
Placement restrictions	0.18			0.16	0.13	0.13
Qualification Variables						
Professional Training						
Without compl. prof. training, no CSE[3]	0.11			0.01	0.08	0.11
Without compl. prof. training, with CSE	0.39			0.29	0.37	0.41
Industrial training	0.42			0.46	0.29	0.30
Full-time vocational school	0.02			0.03	0.03	0.02
Technical school	0.03			0.03	0.08	0.03
Polytechnic	0.01			0.04	0.07	0.04
College, university	0.02			0.13	0.07	0.08
Occupational group						
Plant cultivation, breeding, fishery	0.02			0.00	0.01	0.03
Mining, mineral extraction	0.00			0.00	0.00	0.00
Manufacturing	0.24			0.03	0.10	0.26
Technical professions	0.02			0.05	0.00	0.03
Service professions	0.71			0.89	0.88	0.66
Other professions	0.01			0.03	0.01	0.02
Professional Rank						
Unskilled worker	0.17			0.05	0.15	0.15
Skilled worker	0.06			0.03	0.03	0.04
White-collar worker, simple occupations	0.18			0.27	0.20	0.13
White-collar worker, advanced occupations	0.04			0.08	0.12	0.07
Other	0.54			0.56	0.50	0.61
Qualification (with work experience)	0.93			0.84	0.86	0.85
Career Variables						
Duration last employment	64.12			32.98	24.82	21.09
Duration of unemployment						
< 13	0.22			0.23	0.20	0.25
13 − 52	0.36			0.39	0.40	0.36
> 52	0.42			0.38	0.39	0.40
Number of placement propositions	2.99			8.08	6.42	6.80
Last contact to job center	2.40			2.57	2.69	2.29
Programme before unemployment						
No further education or programme	0.91			0.57	0.67	0.74
Further education compl., cont. education	0.07			0.20	0.11	0.10
Further education compl., voc. adjustment	0.00			0.01	0.00	0.01
Job-preparative measure	0.00			0.00	0.01	0.00
Job creation scheme	0.01			0.18	0.20	0.15
Rehabilitation measure	0.00			0.03	0.01	0.01
Regional Context Variables						
Cluster II	0.34			0.23	0.35	0.34
Cluster III	0.41			0.47	0.38	0.38
Cluster IV	0.09			0.06	0.08	0.08
Cluster V	0.16			0.23	0.18	0.20

[1] DoR = degree of restriction
[2] People with accepted degree of restriction, but no equalisation to other persons with the same DoR.
[3] CSE = Certificate for secondary education

Table C.3: Selected Descriptives for Men in East Germany

Variables	NON-PART.	AGRICUL.	CONSTR. AND INDUSTRY	OFFICE AND SERVICES	COMM. SERVICES	OTHER
Number of observations	64788	925	416	202	410	971
Programme Duration (in days)		325.0	273.5	332.1	324.3	327.1
Socio-Demographic Variables						
Age	41.73	46.02	43.13	48.87	42.83	43.47
Married	0.48	0.54	0.51	0.73	0.58	0.50
Number of children	0.36	0.42	0.45	0.40	0.40	0.37
Health restrictions						
No health restrictions	0.75	0.79	0.81	0.75	0.69	0.77
Acc. DoR,[1] 80% and over	0.00	0.01	0.00	0.01	0.01	0.01
Acc. DoR, 50% to under 80%	0.02	0.02	0.02	0.08	0.06	0.04
Acc. DoR, 30% to under 50%	0.01	0.01	0.01	0.02	0.03	0.01
Acc. DoR, 30% to under 50%, no equalis.[2]	0.02	0.02	0.01	0.03	0.02	0.01
Other health restrictions	0.20	0.17	0.15	0.11	0.20	0.17
Rehabilitation attendant	0.07	0.05	0.05	0.07	0.15	0.08
Placement restrictions	0.16	0.11	0.09	0.14	0.20	0.14
Qualification Variables						
Professional Training						
Without compl. prof. training, no CSE[3]	0.06	0.13	0.09	0.02	0.04	0.07
Without compl. prof. training, with CSE	0.17	0.19	0.19	0.11	0.18	0.24
Industrial training	0.69	0.64	0.70	0.41	0.60	0.57
Full-time vocational school	0.01	0.00	0.00	0.01	0.01	0.01
Technical school	0.04	0.02	0.01	0.26	0.07	0.06
Polytechnic	0.01	0.00	0.00	0.05	0.02	0.01
College, university	0.03	0.01	0.00	0.14	0.08	0.04
Occupational group						
Plant cultivation, breeding, fishery	0.05	0.13	0.06	0.03	0.02	0.04
Mining, mineral extraction	0.00	0.00	0.00	0.00	0.00	0.00
Manufacturing	0.53	0.56	0.72	0.13	0.42	0.53
Technical professions	0.06	0.03	0.02	0.34	0.09	0.06
Service professions	0.33	0.27	0.20	0.50	0.46	0.35
Other professions	0.03	0.01	0.00	0.00	0.01	0.01
Professional Rank						
Unskilled worker	0.22	0.38	0.34	0.15	0.22	0.28
Skilled worker	0.29	0.20	0.23	0.15	0.21	0.19
White-collar worker, simple occupations	0.04	0.02	0.02	0.18	0.07	0.06
White-collar worker, advanced occupations	0.02	0.01	0.01	0.05	0.04	0.01
Other	0.43	0.39	0.40	0.47	0.45	0.46
Qualification (with work experience)	0.89	0.93	0.92	0.91	0.84	0.89
Career Variables						
Duration last employment	55.51	25.38	19.53	28.04	18.35	26.52
Duration of unemployment						
< 13	0.34	0.18	0.20	0.19	0.23	0.20
13 − 52	0.35	0.38	0.42	0.47	0.48	0.44
> 52	0.31	0.44	0.38	0.34	0.29	0.36
Number of placement propositions	3.01	5.41	6.86	7.08	6.35	6.01
Last contact to job center	2.79	2.59	2.41	2.71	2.65	2.47
Programme before unemployment						
No further education or programme	0.83	0.49	0.51	0.46	0.49	0.60
Further education compl., cont. education	0.09	0.13	0.15	0.28	0.13	0.12
Further education compl., voc. adjustment	0.03	0.06	0.06	0.04	0.06	0.04
Job-preparative measure	0.00	0.00	0.00	0.00	0.01	0.00
Job creation scheme	0.05	0.32	0.26	0.21	0.29	0.22
Rehabilitation measure	0.01	0.00	0.00	0.02	0.01	0.01
Regional Context Variables						
Cluster Ia	0.22	0.35	0.15	0.24	0.11	0.22
Cluster Ib	0.65	0.52	0.62	0.68	0.74	0.66
Cluster Ic	0.11	0.12	0.20	0.08	0.12	0.07
Cluster II	0.02	0.00	0.03	0.00	0.02	0.05

[1] DoR = degree of restriction
[2] People with accepted degree of restriction, but no equalisation to other persons with the same DoR.
[3] CSE = Certificate for secondary education

Table C.4: Selected Descriptives for Women in East Germany

Variables	Non-part.	Agricul.	Constr. and Industry	Office and Services	Comm. Services	Other
Number of observations	76512	986	193	645	1810	1401
Programme Duration (in days)		322.2	289.5	337.9	336.6	340.7
Socio-Demographic Variables						
Age	44.01	43.37	43.09	45.23	44.27	43.16
Married	0.64	0.67	0.65	0.75	0.70	0.62
Number of children	0.67	0.89	0.87	0.74	0.75	0.80
Health restrictions						
No health restrictions	0.80	0.90	0.87	0.84	0.83	0.85
Acc. DoR,[1] 80% and over	0.00	0.00	0.01	0.00	0.01	0.01
Acc. DoR, 50% to under 80%	0.02	0.01	0.00	0.04	0.02	0.02
Acc. DoR, 30% to under 50%	0.00	0.00	0.01	0.01	0.01	0.01
Acc. DoR, 30% to under 50%, no equalis.[2]	0.01	0.00	0.00	0.01	0.01	0.00
Other health restrictions	0.17	0.09	0.12	0.10	0.12	0.12
Rehabilitation attendant	0.05	0.01	0.03	0.03	0.04	0.03
Placement restrictions	0.12	0.04	0.06	0.07	0.10	0.08
Qualification Variables						
Professional Training						
Without compl. prof. training, no CSE[3]	0.05	0.09	0.10	0.00	0.01	0.03
Without compl. prof. training, with CSE	0.21	0.23	0.17	0.12	0.18	0.20
Industrial training	0.66	0.64	0.69	0.62	0.63	0.61
Full-time vocational school	0.01	0.01	0.01	0.02	0.03	0.02
Technical school	0.05	0.02	0.02	0.14	0.12	0.10
Polytechnic	0.00	0.01	0.00	0.03	0.01	0.01
College, university	0.02	0.01	0.00	0.06	0.02	0.03
Occupational group						
Plant cultivation, breeding, fishery	0.05	0.20	0.16	0.02	0.03	0.05
Mining, mineral extraction	0.00	0.00	0.00	0.00	0.00	0.00
Manufacturing	0.20	0.31	0.30	0.03	0.14	0.22
Technical professions	0.03	0.03	0.03	0.10	0.04	0.07
Service professions	0.70	0.46	0.52	0.84	0.79	0.66
Other professions	0.02	0.00	0.00	0.00	0.00	0.00
Professional Rank						
Unskilled worker	0.21	0.40	0.41	0.12	0.21	0.23
Skilled worker	0.16	0.11	0.15	0.16	0.16	0.14
White-collar worker, simple occupations	0.09	0.02	0.04	0.15	0.13	0.12
White-collar worker, advanced occupations	0.02	0.01	0.00	0.04	0.02	0.02
Other	0.53	0.46	0.39	0.53	0.48	0.49
Qualification (with work experience)	0.90	0.91	0.93	0.92	0.90	0.89
Career Variables						
Duration last employment	63.44	25.10	24.89	37.54	33.54	30.07
Duration of unemployment						
< 13	0.16	0.10	0.17	0.13	0.10	0.13
13 − 52	0.35	0.33	0.37	0.42	0.42	0.39
> 52	0.49	0.58	0.46	0.45	0.48	0.48
Number of placement propositions	2.77	4.67	5.40	6.10	5.57	5.44
Last contact to job center	2.78	2.57	2.45	2.54	2.58	2.65
Programme before unemployment						
No further education or programme	0.72	0.42	0.49	0.34	0.42	0.47
Further education compl., cont. education	0.17	0.19	0.16	0.34	0.25	0.22
Further education compl., voc. adjustment	0.03	0.05	0.07	0.05	0.05	0.04
Job-preparative measure	0.00	0.00	0.00	0.00	0.00	0.00
Job creation scheme	0.08	0.33	0.28	0.27	0.28	0.27
Rehabilitation measure	0.00	0.00	0.00	0.00	0.00	0.00
Regional Context Variables						
Cluster Ia	0.23	0.35	0.30	0.17	0.19	0.27
Cluster Ib	0.65	0.53	0.60	0.69	0.70	0.64
Cluster Ic	0.10	0.12	0.09	0.13	0.10	0.07
Cluster II	0.02	0.00	0.02	0.01	0.02	0.02

[1] DoR = degree of restriction
[2] People with accepted degree of restriction, but no equalisation to other persons with the same DoR.
[3] CSE = Certificate for secondary education

Table C.5: Estimation Results of the Logit-Models for the Propensity Score for Men in West Germany

Variables	Agricul.	Constr. and Industry	Office and Services	Comm. Services	Other
Constant	**-4.5090**	**-2.0459**	**-14.7072**	**-1.9766**	**-1.4588**
Socio-Demographic Variables					
Age	0.0296	**-0.1343**	**0.3791**	**-0.1129**	**-0.0903**
Age^2	-0.0004	**0.0012**	**-0.0046**	0.0008	**0.0008**
Married	-0.1962	**0.2334**	**-0.2226**	**-0.2582**	*-0.2198*
Number of children	0.0821	0.0138	0.0544	0.1037	0.0470
German	**0.4813**	**0.7739**	**0.3909**	*0.3824*	*0.2198*
Health restrictions					
No health restrictions	Ref.	Ref.	Ref.	Ref.	Ref.
Acc. DoR,[1] 80% and over	**1.0175**	-0.1815	**2.6592**	*0.9154*	**0.8374**
Acc. DoR, 50% to under 80%	**0.6903**	-0.2525	**2.1295**	**1.0849**	**0.7921**
Acc. DoR, 30% to under 50%	*1.2822*	–	**2.2650**	*1.6448*	**1.0191**
Acc. DoR, 30% to under 50%, no equalis.[2]	0.4658	-0.1619	**1.5272**	0.2676	-0.0430
Other health restrictions	0.0007	*-0.5748*	0.3054	-0.0625	0.0104
Qualification Variables					
Professional training					
Without compl. prof. training, no CSE[3]	Ref.	Ref.	Ref.	Ref.	Ref.
Without compl. prof. training, with CSE	**-0.4973**	-0.2519	0.0767	-0.1785	*-0.2244*
Industrial training	**-0.8328**	**-0.9076**	**0.7825**	*-0.4150*	**-0.6079**
Full-time vocational school	**-2.2360**	-0.7638	0.5245	0.1831	**-0.8342**
Technical school	**-0.6101**	**-1.9566**	**1.8069**	*0.8077*	**-0.3926**
Polytechnic	**-1.1617**	**-1.2058**	**1.5514**	**1.5481**	0.2834
College, University	**-1.2767**	**-1.6570**	**1.5608**	**1.1832**	0.3560
Occupational group					
Plant cultivation, breeding, fishery	**0.7547**	-0.2927	0.5320	-0.5022	-0.2250
Mining, mineral extraction	-0.1697	-0.2687	–	–	**-1.0362**
Manufacturing	Ref.	Ref.	Ref.	Ref.	Ref.
Technical professions	**-1.1560**	**-0.3301**	**1.1658**	**-0.9419**	**-0.6920**
Service professions	**-0.3911**	**-0.9058**	**0.8755**	0.2073	**-0.3893**
Other professions	0.1087	-0.0414	–	0.0509	0.1483
Professional rank					
Unskilled worker	Ref.	Ref.	Ref.	Ref.	Ref.
Skilled worker	**-0.9516**	**-0.6308**	-0.1782	**-0.2041**	**-0.2274**
White-collar worker, simple occupations	**-0.9201**	**-0.3070**	**0.9784**	**0.7277**	0.1837
White-collar worker, advanced occupations	-0.4016	**-0.9263**	**1.2236**	*0.6425*	0.2038
Other	**-0.3683**	-0.1285	0.4315	**0.5479**	0.1596
Qualification (with work experience)	-0.1010	-0.0272	**-0.6922**	*-0.3797*	**-0.5170**
Career Variables					
Duration of last employment (months)	**-0.0060**	**-0.0037**	**-0.0045**	**-0.0042**	**-0.0042**
Duration of unemployment (weeks)					
Up to 13 weeks	Ref.	Ref.	Ref.	Ref.	Ref.
Between 13 and 52 weeks	**0.3618**	0.1339	0.1228	0.1566	0.0478
More than 52 weeks	**0.4661**	0.1087	0.2744	0.1279	0.1306
Number of placement propositions	**0.0488**	**0.0390**	**0.0548**	**0.0422**	**0.0509**
Last contact to job center (weeks)	**-0.0868**	-0.0427	**0.1005**	0.0370	*0.0481*
Rehabilitation attendant	-0.1213	0.3637	0.0981	0.0664	**-0.6723**
Placement restrictions	**-0.5594**	0.1139	**-0.9824**	-0.2758	-0.0975
Programme before unemployment					
No further education or programme	Ref.	Ref.	Ref.	Ref.	Ref.
Further education compl., cont. education	0.2545	**0.4914**	0.3483	0.0440	0.1234
Further education compl., voc. adjustment	*0.7916*	**1.3185**	0.0651	–	**0.7083**
Job-preparative measure	–	–	–	–	**0.4281**
Job creation scheme	**1.8566**	**2.3925**	**2.2831**	**2.1205**	**2.1139**
Rehabilitation measure	-0.3244	-0.3238	0.2913	-1.3737	0.2296
Regional Context Variables[4]					
Cluster II	0.0350	**0.8558**	**-1.0783**	**-1.2007**	**-0.3589**
Cluster III	*0.3023*	0.0440	**-0.6491**	**-0.5698**	*-0.2780*
Cluster IV	-0.0778	**-0.5322**	*-0.9304*	0.0819	0.1881
Cluster V	Ref.	Ref.	Ref.	Ref.	Ref.
Number of Observations	44657	44283	43097	43907	44829
Log-Likelihood	-2641.6	-1788.1	-690.5	-1630.7	-3325.6
Adj. R-2	0.151	0.166	0.224	0.139	0.112
F-Test	942.6	711.1	399.1	526.1	841.3

Bold letters indicate significance at the 1% level. *Italic* letters refer to the 5% level.
[1] DoR = degree of restriction
[2] People with accepted degree of restriction, but no equalisation to other persons with the same DoR.
[3] CSE = Certificate for secondary education
[4] Cluster according to the classification as described in table 4.6.
– no observations in relevant sub-group

Table C.6: Estimation Results of the Logit-Models for the Propensity Score for Women in West Germany

Variables	AGRICUL.	CONSTR. AND INDUSTRY	OFFICE AND SERVICES	COMM. SERVICES	OTHER
Constant			-10.8847	-4.0484	-2.8853
Socio-Demographic Variables					
Age			*0.1432*	-0.0184	-0.0337
Age^2			**-0.0020**	-0.0001	0.0000
Married			-0.0555	**-0.4877**	**-0.5266**
Number of children			-0.0584	0.0991	-0.1484
German			0.2172	0.2534	0.0660
Health restrictions					
No health restrictions			Ref.	Ref.	Ref.
Acc. DoR,[1] 80% and over			**1.6533**	**1.2490**	**1.1843**
Acc. DoR, 50% to under 80%			**1.2609**	0.1901	*0.8155*
Acc. DoR, 30% to under 50%			**2.6829**	*1.6893*	**1.9266**
Acc. DoR, 30% to under 50%, no equalis.[2]			-0.1754	0.0613	-0.1396
Other health restrictions			-0.5043	0.0392	-0.1831
Qualification Variables					
Professional training					
Without compl. prof. training, no CSE[3]			Ref.	Ref.	Ref.
Without compl. prof. training, with CSE			*1.4281*	0.2030	0.1662
Industrial training			*1.4096*	-0.1961	-0.1883
Full-time vocational school			1.2480	0.0993	-0.3989
Technical school			1.2967	**1.0363**	0.2617
Polytechnic			**1.9382**	**1.7607**	**1.0906**
College, University			**2.6014**	**0.7199**	**0.9856**
Occupational group					
Plant cultivation, breeding, fishery			–	-0.3153	0.1718
Mining, mineral extraction			–	–	–
Manufacturing			Ref.	Ref.	Ref.
Technical professions			**2.1652**	*-1.5239*	-0.2572
Service professions			**1.7365**	**0.7999**	*-0.3822*
Other professions			**2.7255**	0.3314	-0.2270
Professional rank					
Unskilled worker			Ref.	Ref.	Ref.
Skilled worker			0.3798	-0.3085	-0.1599
White-collar worker, simple occupations			**0.9857**	0.0576	-0.0256
White-collar worker, advanced occupations			0.6057	**0.6116**	0.5002
Other			0.6401	-0.0642	*0.3818*
Qualification (with work experience)			**-0.5613**	*-0.2914*	-0.2246
Career Variables					
Duration of last employment (months)			-0.0011	-0.0036	-0.0052
Duration of unemployment (weeks)					
Up to 13 weeks			Ref.	Ref.	Ref.
Between 13 and 52 weeks			-0.0406	0.1764	-0.0637
More than 52 weeks			-0.1897	0.1289	0.0470
Number of placement propositions			0.0639	0.0405	0.0519
Last contact to job center (weeks)			0.0715	0.0868	-0.0107
Rehabilitation attendant			-0.2866	0.0587	0.4787
Placement restrictions			-0.2261	-0.2235	-0.4517
Programme before unemployment					
No further education or programme			Ref.	Ref.	Ref.
Further education compl., cont. education			**1.0745**	**0.4635**	0.1449
Further education compl., voc. adjustment			0.8883	0.2137	0.7757
Job-preparative measure			–	**3.0067**	1.9089
Job creation scheme			**3.2762**	**3.0801**	**2.6577**
Rehabilitation measure			**2.4833**	0.4374	0.1713
Regional Context Variables[4]					
Cluster II			**-1.1530**	**-0.4614**	**-0.4831**
Cluster III			*-0.4413*	**-0.4805**	**-0.4413**
Cluster IV			**-0.9771**	-0.3191	-0.3983
Cluster V			Ref.	Ref.	Ref.
Number of Observations			33808	34722	34489
Log-Likelihood			-978.6	-2155.6	-1366.9
Adj. R^2			0.208	0.180	0.134
F-Test			514.1	947.4	423.0

Bold letters indicate significance at the 1% level. *Italic* letters refer to the 5% level.
[1] DoR = degree of restriction
[2] People with accepted degree of restriction, but no equalisation to other persons with the same DoR.
[3] CSE = Certificate for secondary education
[4] Cluster according to the classification as described in table 4.6.
  – no observations in relevant sub-group

Table C.7: Estimation Results of the Logit-Models for the Propensity Score for Men in East Germany

Variables	AGRICUL.	CONSTR. AND INDUSTRY	OFFICE AND SERVICES	COMM. SERVICES	OTHER
Constant	**-8.2748**	**-9.5586**	**-13.5752**	**-7.7192**	**-5.8072**
Socio-Demographic Variables					
Age	**0.1404**	**0.1422**	**0.2537**	0.0405	*0.0536*
Age^2	**-0.0012**	**-0.0015**	**-0.0027**	-0.0006	-0.0005
Married	*0.1750*	**0.2778**	**0.7052**	**0.6680**	0.1540
Number of children	-0.0003	-0.0185	-0.0923	-0.1112	-0.0355
German	*0.9722*	0.9294	–	0.4182	0.2826
Health restrictions					
No health restrictions	Ref.	Ref.	Ref.	Ref.	Ref.
Acc. DoR,[1] 80% and over	0.7313	–	1.0624	0.9844	0.3286
Acc. DoR, 50% to under 80%	0.1230	0.3058	**1.2961**	**0.7323**	*0.4997*
Acc. DoR, 30% to under 50%	-0.0321	*0.9936*	0.8507	**0.9713**	0.5456
Acc. DoR, 30% to under 50%, no equalis.[2]	0.1819	-0.1677	0.6446	0.1971	-0.6727
Other health restrictions	-0.1835	-0.0607	-0.3975	-0.1103	-0.2133
Qualification Variables					
Professional training					
Without compl. prof. training, no CSE[3]	Ref.	Ref.	Ref.	Ref.	Ref.
Without compl. prof. training, with CSE	-0.1993	0.0082	0.7288	0.5236	*0.3536*
Industrial training	**-0.4028**	-0.0537	0.6616	0.4050	-0.1207
Full-time vocational school	*-1.1763*	–	0.7572	0.9366	-0.0298
Technical school	**-0.7256**	**-0.9740**	**1.9463**	**1.0078**	*0.4512*
Polytechnic	**-1.2676**	-0.5647	*1.2524*	**1.2241**	0.1479
College, University	**-1.0406**	*-2.3433*	**1.5007**	**1.2085**	0.3227
Occupational group					
Plant cultivation, breeding, fishery	**0.4311**	*-0.4405*	0.7232	*-0.6927*	*-0.4147*
Mining, mineral extraction	-0.2213	–	–	–	-0.9264
Manufacturing	Ref.	Ref.	Ref.	Ref.	Ref.
Technical professions	*-0.5769*	**-0.7692**	**2.0272**	-0.0203	-0.3332
Service professions	**-0.3614**	**-0.8173**	**1.5137**	**0.3114**	-0.1208
Other professions	**-0.8095**	-2.5447	–	*-1.1155*	**-1.1386**
Professional rank					
Unskilled worker	Ref.	Ref.	Ref.	Ref.	Ref.
Skilled worker	**-0.2621**	-0.1943	0.0823	0.1961	*-0.2162*
White-collar worker, simple occupations	*-0.5796*	-0.0050	**0.8196**	**0.6719**	*0.3583*
White-collar worker, advanced occupations	**-0.4724**	0.0520	0.1988	**0.8298**	*-0.6402*
Other	-0.0491	-0.0736	0.1469	*0.3534*	0.0624
Qualification (with work experience)	0.0340	0.0726	*-0.5968*	**-0.5560**	*-0.2526*
Career Variables					
Duration of last employment (months)	**-0.0033**	**-0.0046**	**-0.0047**	**-0.0058**	**-0.0032**
Duration of unemployment (weeks)					
Up to 13 weeks	Ref.	Ref.	Ref.	Ref.	Ref.
Between 13 and 52 weeks	**0.4516**	**0.5849**	0.2067	0.2123	**0.4993**
More than 52 weeks	**0.6017**	**0.6374**	-0.1582	-0.1864	**0.4252**
Number of placement propositions	**0.0478**	**0.0563**	**0.0865**	**0.0599**	**0.0619**
Last contact to job center (weeks)	**-0.1348**	**-0.1612**	*-0.0797*	*-0.0580*	**-0.1404**
Rehabilitation attendant	-0.0539	0.1741	0.1138	**0.8264**	0.2646
Placement restrictions	*-0.3779*	**-0.6037**	-0.3717	-0.1578	-0.2246
Programme before unemployment					
No further education or programme	Ref.	Ref.	Ref.	Ref.	Ref.
Further education compl., cont. education	**0.5840**	**0.5980**	**1.1618**	**0.5393**	0.2033
Further education compl., voc. adjustment	**0.7988**	**0.7730**	0.2532	**1.0237**	*0.3476*
Job-preparative measure	–	**2.0179**	–	**2.0594**	0.0596
Job creation scheme	**1.7722**	**1.7151**	**1.6850**	**2.2508**	**1.4818**
Rehabilitation measure	–	0.3156	*1.4364*	0.2399	*0.6264*
Regional Context Variables[4]					
Cluster Ia	Ref.	Ref.	Ref.	Ref.	Ref.
Cluster Ib	**-0.7175**	*0.2881*	-0.3000	**0.6637**	-0.0922
Cluster Ic	**-0.4215**	**0.9103**	**-0.7914**	**0.5424**	**-0.6073**
Cluster II	**-1.8884**	**0.8778**	–	**0.6829**	**0.7615**
Number of Observations	65143	64363	60196	65020	65759
Log-Likelihood	-4171.0	-2196.1	-1050.4	-2154.7	-4612.0
Adj. R-2	0.141	0.126	0.223	0.133	0.088
F-Test	1365.7	631.7	604.1	662.5	886.0

Bold letters indicate significance at the 1% level. *Italic* letters refer to the 5% level.
[1] DoR = degree of restriction
[2] People with accepted degree of restriction, but no equalisation to other persons with the same DoR.
[3] CSE = Certificate for secondary education
[4] Cluster according to the classification as described in table 4.6.
– no observations in relevant sub-group

Table C.8: Estimation Results of the Logit-Models for the Propensity Score for Women in East Germany

Variables	AGRICUL.	CONSTR. AND INDUSTRY	OFFICE AND SERVICES	COMM. SERVICES	OTHER
Constant	**-8.3115**	**-7.3101**	**-17.9453**	**-11.0899**	**-7.4834**
Socio-Demographic Variables					
Age	**0.1646**	0.1095	**0.2713**	**0.1896**	**0.1357**
Age^2	**-0.0019**	-0.0012	**-0.0030**	**-0.0021**	**-0.0016**
Married	*0.1734*	0.0965	**0.3118**	**0.1677**	-0.0951
Number of children	-0.0079	0.0391	-0.0247	-0.0443	-0.0068
German	**1.2282**	0.1296	**0.9727**	*0.9592*	0.2932
Health restrictions					
No health restrictions	Ref.	Ref.	Ref.	Ref.	Ref.
Acc. DoR,[1] 80% and over	0.5151	**1.3060**	0.4847	**1.2810**	**1.3117**
Acc. DoR, 50% to under 80%	-0.4661	–	**1.4311**	**0.5698**	*0.5660*
Acc. DoR, 30% to under 50%	-0.0995	0.6024	*1.0580*	**0.9809**	*0.7660*
Acc. DoR, 30% to under 50%, no equalis.[2]	-0.4257	–	-0.1513	0.3423	-0.7409
Other health restrictions	**-0.3801**	-0.0696	0.0203	-0.1429	-0.0935
Qualification Variables					
Professional training					
Without compl. prof. training, no CSE[3]	Ref.	Ref.	Ref.	Ref.	Ref.
Without compl. prof. training, with CSE	-0.1973	**-0.7454**	**2.8098**	**1.1480**	**0.4957**
Industrial training	*-0.2955*	*-0.4954*	**3.1291**	**1.1850**	*0.3712*
Full-time vocational school	-0.1436	-0.5663	**3.5078**	**1.9609**	**0.7458**
Technical school	**-1.0249**	-1.0713	**3.8222**	**2.0607**	**1.1572**
Polytechnic	0.1174	–	**4.2966**	**1.8746**	*0.8370*
College, University	-0.6146	–	**4.1203**	**1.6008**	**1.1025**
Occupational group					
Plant cultivation, breeding, fishery	**0.7666**	*0.5567*	**0.8609**	-0.4426	*-0.3304*
Mining, mineral extraction	–	–	–	–	–
Manufacturing	Ref.	Ref.	Ref.	Ref.	Ref.
Technical professions	-0.1984	-0.0814	**2.1028**	-0.0027	*0.3317*
Service professions	**-0.6008**	**-0.4644**	**1.7419**	**0.4004**	**-0.2090**
Other professions	*-2.1141*	–	–	**-0.8522**	*-0.9722*
Professional rank					
Unskilled worker	Ref.	Ref.	Ref.	Ref.	Ref.
Skilled worker	**-0.3874**	-0.3283	**0.7162**	**0.2401**	0.1468
White-collar worker, simple occupations	**-1.1101**	-0.7485	**0.8690**	**0.3714**	**0.5205**
White-collar worker, advanced occupations	-0.6226	–	**0.7576**	0.0554	-0.0237
Other	-0.0863	*-0.4287*	**0.6151**	0.1320	**0.2311**
Qualification (with work experience)	-0.0233	0.2537	0.0397	*-0.1753*	*-0.2035*
Career Variables					
Duration of last employment (months)	**-0.0038**	*-0.0036*	-0.0018	-0.0025	**-0.0032**
Duration of unemployment (weeks)					
Up to 13 weeks	Ref.	Ref.	Ref.	Ref.	Ref.
Between 13 and 52 weeks	0.1846	-0.1683	0.0900	**0.4047**	0.1262
More than 52 weeks	**0.4296**	-0.3131	-0.1725	*0.2016*	0.0354
Number of placement propositions	**0.0720**	**0.0945**	**0.0871**	**0.0844**	**0.0883**
Last contact to job center (weeks)	**-0.0903**	**-0.1270**	**-0.0665**	**-0.0624**	**-0.0412**
Rehabilitation attendant	-0.3401	0.4405	0.1995	*0.3138*	0.0668
Placement restrictions	-0.3940	-0.3174	**-0.6241**	-0.1234	-0.2779
Programme before unemployment					
No further education or programme	Ref.	Ref.	Ref.	Ref.	Ref.
Further education compl., cont. education	**0.3164**	0.1885	**1.0771**	**0.6341**	**0.3466**
Further education compl., voc. adjustment	**0.7365**	**0.8097**	**0.8346**	**0.5587**	*0.3103*
Job-preparative measure	0.7493	–	–	1.1397	–
Job creation scheme	**1.3215**	**1.1128**	**2.0433**	**1.6684**	**1.4558**
Rehabilitation measure	0.7830	–	0.5727	0.4027	0.1661
Regional Context Variables[4]					
Cluster Ia	Ref.	Ref.	Ref.	Ref.	Ref.
Cluster Ib	**-0.6175**	*-0.3887*	0.1607	**0.1800**	**-0.3009**
Cluster Ic	**-0.4307**	*-0.5747*	*0.2994*	-0.0548	**-0.8413**
Cluster II	**-2.9446**	-0.2383	-0.6426	**0.4739**	-0.0499
Number of Observations	77456	70413	75868	78280	77777
Log-Likelihood	-4602.3	-1224.2	-3112.0	-7635.1	-6387.1
Adj. R-2	0.129	0.080	0.163	0.113	0.089
F-Test	1360.2	214.3	1210.6	1944.0	1257.2

Bold letters indicate significance at the 1% level. *Italic* letters refer to the 5% level.
[1] DoR = degree of restriction
[2] People with accepted degree of restriction, but no equalisation to other persons with the same DoR.
[3] CSE = Certificate for secondary education
[4] Cluster according to the classification as described in table 4.6.
– no observations in relevant sub-group

Table C.9: Number of Treated Individuals Lost Due to Common Support[1]

	Agriculture			Construction and Industry			Office and Services			Community Services			Other		
	Before Matching	After Matching	Lost in %	Before Matching	After Matching	Lost in %	Before Matching	After Matching	Lost in %	Before Matching	After Matching	Lost in %	Before Matching	After Matching	Lost in %
West Germany - Men	584	583	0.17	371	371	0.00	131	129	1.53	320	316	1.25	734	731	0.41
Provider															
Public	335	334	0.30	–	–	–	–	–	–	–	–	–	203	201	0.99
Non-Commercial	238	238	0.00	265	264	0.38	–	–	–	255	254	0.39	471	469	0.42
Type of Promotion															
Regular	382	382	0.00	234	234	0.00	126	125	0.79	220	218	0.91	522	520	0.38
Enforced	202	200	0.99	137	137	0.00	–	–	–	–	–	–	212	208	1.89
West Germany - Women	–	–	–	–	–	–	202	201	0.50	503	497	1.19	270	270	0.00
Provider															
Public	–	–	–	–	–	–	–	–	–	130	126	3.08	–	–	–
Non-Commercial	–	–	–	–	–	–	–	–	–	367	362	1.36	191	191	0.00
Type of Promotion															
Regular	–	–	–	–	–	–	181	179	1.10	373	371	0.54	208	208	0.00
Enforced	–	–	–	–	–	–	–	–	–	130	111	14.62	–	–	–
East Germany - Men	925	925	0.00	416	416	0.00	202	201	0.50	410	407	0.73	971	971	0.00
Provider															
Public	278	278	0.00	182	180	1.10	125	124	0.80	331	328	0.91	192	192	0.00
Non-Commercial	610	610	0.00	208	208	0.00	–	–	–	–	–	–	732	732	0.00
Type of Promotion															
Regular	224	224	0.00	336	336	0.00	112	110	1.79	249	248	0.40	269	269	0.00
Enforced	701	701	0.00	193	193	0.00	–	–	–	161	161	0.00	702	702	0.00
East Germany - Women	986	985	0.10	–	–	–	645	644	0.16	1810	1810	0.00	1401	1398	0.21
Provider															
Public	318	318	0.00	–	–	–	277	277	0.00	443	443	0.00	320	320	0.00
Non-Commercial	635	635	0.00	121	121	0.00	333	332	0.30	1322	1321	0.08	1000	998	0.20
Type of Promotion															
Regular	243	242	0.41	–	–	–	399	399	0.00	1089	1089	0.00	581	579	0.34
Enforced	743	743	0.00	145	145	0.00	246	246	0.00	721	720	0.14	820	820	0.00

[1] Results refer to a NN matching without replacement and a caliper of 0.02. – Groups with less than 100 participants are omitted.

C Additional Material to Chapter 6 229

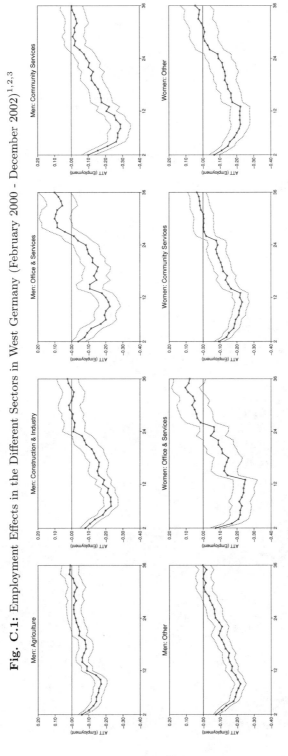

Fig. C.1: Employment Effects in the Different Sectors in West Germany (February 2000 - December 2002)[1,2,3]

[1] Solid line describes the monthly employment effect. Dotted lines are the upper and lower 95% confidence limits.
[2] Month 2 refers to February 2000, month 12 = December 2000, month 24 = December 2001, month 36 = December 2002.
[3] Effects for groups with less than 100 participants are omitted.

230 C Additional Material to Chapter 6

Fig. C.2: Employment Effects in the Different Sectors in East Germany (February 2000 - December 2002)[1,2,3]

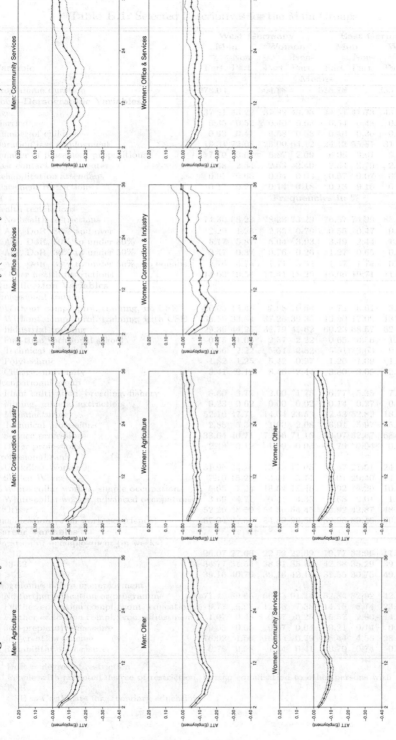

[1] Solid line describes the monthly employment effect. Dotted lines are the upper and lower 95% confidence limits.
[2] Month 2 refers to February 2000, month 12 = December 2000, month 24 = December 2001, month 36 = December 2002.
[3] Effects for groups with less than 100 participants are omitted.

C Additional Material to Chapter 6   231

Fig. C.3: Employment Effects for Men in the Different Sectors and by Type of Promotion in West Germany (February 2000 - December 2002)[1,2,3]

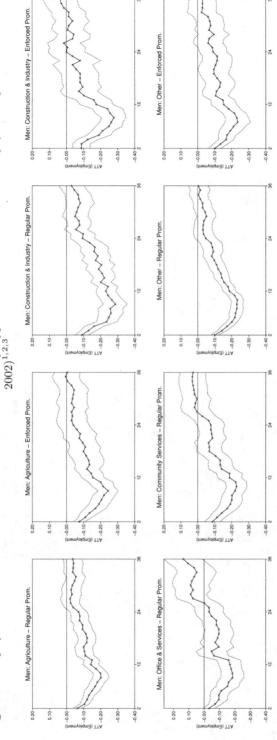

[1] Solid line describes the monthly employment effect. Dotted lines are the upper and lower 95% confidence limits.
[2] Month 2 refers to February 2000, month 12 = December 2000, month 24 = December 2001, month 36 = December 2002.
[3] Effects for groups with less than 100 participants are omitted.

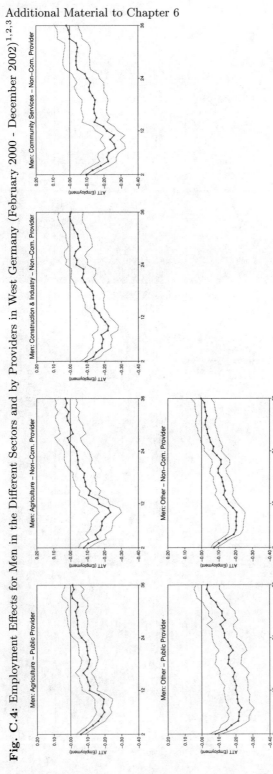

Fig. C.4: Employment Effects for Men in the Different Sectors and by Providers in West Germany (February 2000 - December 2002)[1,2,3]

[1] Solid line describes the monthly employment effect. Dotted lines are the upper and lower 95% confidence limits.
[2] Month 2 refers to February 2000, month 12 = December 2000, month 24 = December 2001, month 36 = December 2002.
[3] Effects for groups with less than 100 participants are omitted.

Fig. C.5: Employment Effects for Women in the Different Sectors by Type of Promotion and Providers in West Germany (February 2000 − December 2002)[1,2,3]

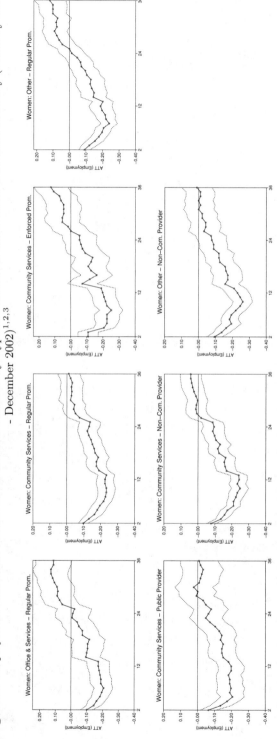

[1] Solid line describes the monthly employment effect. Dotted lines are the upper and lower 95% confidence limits.
[2] Month 2 refers to February 2000, month 12 = December 2000, month 24 = December 2001, month 36 = December 2002.
[3] Effects for groups with less than 100 participants are omitted.

234 C Additional Material to Chapter 6

Fig. C.6: Employment Effects for Men in the Different Sectors by Type of Promotion in East Germany (February 2000 - December 2002)[1,2,3]

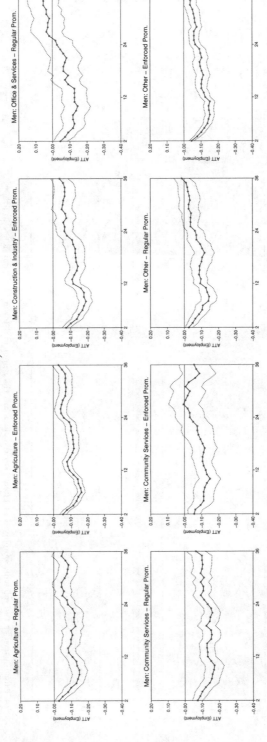

[1] Solid line describes the monthly employment effect. Dotted lines are the upper and lower 95% confidence limits.
[2] Month 2 refers to February 2000, month 12 = December 2000, month 24 = December 2001, month 36 = December 2002.
[3] Effects for groups with less than 100 participants are omitted.

C Additional Material to Chapter 6 235

Fig. C.7: Employment Effects for Men in the Different Sectors by Providers in East Germany (February 2000 - December 2002)[1,2,3]

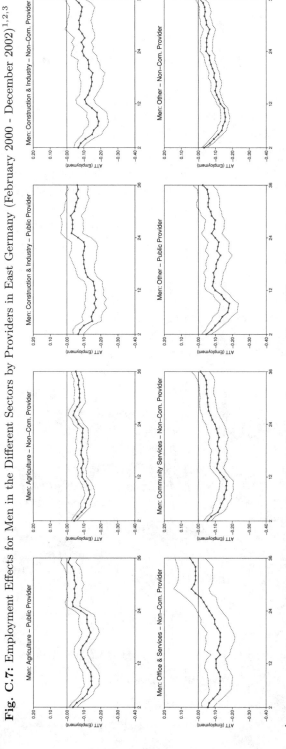

[1] Solid line describes the monthly employment effect. Dotted lines are the upper and lower 95% confidence limits.
[2] Month 2 refers to February 2000, month 12 = December 2000, month 24 = December 2001, month 36 = December 2002.
[3] Effects for groups with less than 100 participants are omitted.

236 C Additional Material to Chapter 6

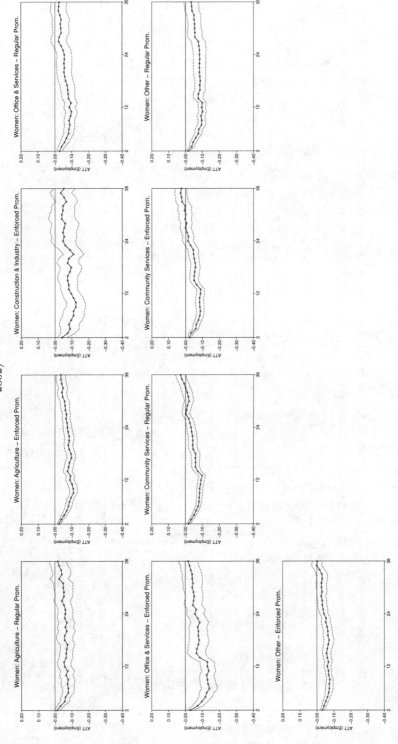

Fig. C.8: Employment Effects for Women in the Different Sectors by Type of Promotion in East Germany (February 2000 - December 2002)[1,2,3]

[1] Solid line describes the monthly employment effect. Dotted lines are the upper and lower 95% confidence limits.
[2] Month 2 refers to February 2000, month 12 = December 2000, month 24 = December 2001, month 36 = December 2002.
[3] Effects for groups with less than 100 participants are omitted.

C Additional Material to Chapter 6 237

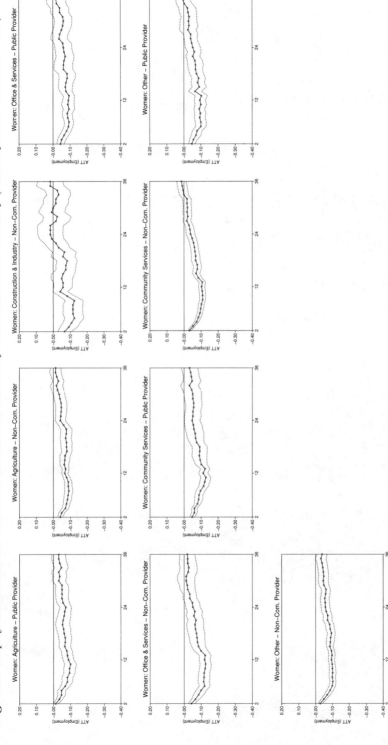

Fig. C.9: Employment Effects for Women in the Different Sectors by Providers in East Germany (February 2000 - December 2002)[1,2,3]

[1] Solid line describes the monthly employment effect. Dotted lines are the upper and lower 95% confidence limits.
[2] Month 2 refers to February 2000, month 12 = December 2000, month 24 = December 2001, month 36 = December 2002.
[3] Effects for groups with less than 100 participants are omitted.

List of Tables

1	Spending on Labour Market Policies for Selected European Countries	2
2.1	Kernel Functions	51
2.2	Trade-Offs in Terms of Bias and Efficiency	66
3.1	Implementation of Propensity Score Matching	94
4.1	Some Key Figures of the German Labour Market, 1997-2003	102
4.2	Spending on Labour Market Policies, 1997-2003	106
4.3	Microeconometric Evaluations of Job Creation Schemes in East Germany	116
4.4	Macroeconomic Evaluations of Labour Market Policies in Germany	117
4.5	Data Sources and Attributes	120
4.6	Classification of Labour Office Districts in Germany	122
5.1	Number of Observations in Main and Sub-Groups	130
5.2	Hit-Rates and Pseudo-R^2 for Different Propensity Score Specifications	136
5.3	The Effects in the Main Groups for Different Matching Algorithms	140
5.4	Number of Treated Individuals Lost Due to Common Support Requirement	142
5.5	Some Quality Indicators	144
5.6	Mean Standardised Bias in the Sub-Groups	146
5.7	Mean Standardised Bias in the Seven Clusters	147
5.8	Employment Effects in the Regional Clusters	157
6.1	Mean Standardised Bias Before and After Matching in Programme Sectors	171

6.2	Employment Effects in the Programme Sectors for Selected Months	174
6.3	Employment Effects - Sectors and Type of Promotion - West Germany	176
6.4	Employment Effects - Sectors and Type of Promotion - East Germany	177
6.5	Employment Effects - Sectors and Providers - West Germany	179
6.6	Employment Effects - Sectors and Providers - East Germany	180
B.1	Selected Descriptives for the Main Groups	194
B.2	Selected Descriptives for Clusters Ia-Ic	195
B.3	Selected Descriptives for Clusters II-V	196
B.4	Estimation Results of the Logit-Models for the Propensity Score	197
B.5	Standardised Bias Main Groups - Before and After Matching	198
B.6	Propensity Score Logit Models for Men in West Germany, Sub-Groups Part I	199
B.7	Propensity Score Logit Models for Men in West Germany, Sub-Groups Part II	200
B.8	Propensity Score Logit Models for Women in West Germany, Sub-Groups Part I	201
B.9	Propensity Score Logit Models for Women in West Germany, Sub-Groups Part II	202
B.10	Propensity Score Logit Models for Men in East Germany, Sub-Groups Part I	203
B.11	Propensity Score Logit Models for Men in East Germany, Sub-Groups Part II	204
B.12	Propensity Score Logit Models for Women in East Germany, Sub-Groups Part I	205
B.13	Propensity Score Logit Models for Women in East Germany, Sub-Groups Part II	206
B.14	Cumulated Exit Rates in Main and Sub-Groups - Men in West Germany	207
B.15	Cumulated Exit Rates in Main and Sub-Groups - Women in West Germany	208
B.16	Cumulated Exit Rates in Main and Sub-Groups - Men in East Germany	209
B.17	Cumulated Exit Rates in Main and Sub-Groups - Women in East Germany	210
B.18	Employment Effects in the Sub-Groups in West Germany	211
B.19	Employment Effects in the Sub-Groups in East Germany	212
B.20	Sensitivity Analysis for Unobserved Heterogeneity - West Germany	213
B.21	Sensitivity Analysis for Unobserved Heterogeneity - East Germany	214

C.1 Selected Descriptives for Men in West Germany 220
C.2 Selected Descriptives for Women in West Germany 221
C.3 Selected Descriptives for Men in East Germany 222
C.4 Selected Descriptives for Women in East Germany............ 223
C.5 Propensity Score Logit-Models for Men in West Germany 224
C.6 Propensity Score Logit-Models for Women in West Germany... 225
C.7 Propensity Score Logit-Models for Men in East Germany...... 226
C.8 Propensity Score Logit-Models for Women in East Germany ... 227
C.9 Number of Treated Individuals Lost Due to Common Support . 228

List of Figures

1.1 Relationship between Hypoth. (Counterfactual) Population and Observed Data 19
1.2 Ashenfelter's Dip 22
1.3 Common Support in Matching and Regression Analysis 37
1.4 Alternative Evaluation Estimators 42

2.1 Different Matching Estimators 65

3.1 Implementing Propensity Score Matching.................... 72
3.2 The Common Support Problem 82

4.1 Entries in and Spending on VT and Subsidised Employment in West Germany... 108
4.2 Entries in and Spending on VT and Subsidised Employment in East Germany 108
4.3 Data Availability 123

5.1 Employment Effects for Men in West Germany (Feb. 2000 - Dec. 2002)... 150
5.2 Employment Effects for Women in West Germany (Feb. 2000 - Dec. 2002) 151
5.3 Employment Effects for Men in East Germany (Feb. 2000 - Dec. 2002)... 152
5.4 Employment Effects for Women in West Germany (Feb. 2000 - Dec. 2002) 153

6.1 Number of Participants in the Five Sectors 163
6.2 Number of Participants (Sectors, Provider, Type of Promotion) 165

A.1 Job Seeker Rate in Germany (Monthly Average), 1999 190

A.2 Relation Between Job Creation Schemes and Vocational Training Measures, 1999.................................191

B.1 Common Support for Men in West Germany (Main and Sub-Groups)...215
B.2 Common Support for Women in West Germany (Main and Sub-Groups)...216
B.3 Common Support for Men in East Germany (Main and Sub-Groups)...217
B.4 Common Support for Women in East Germany (Main and Sub-Groups)...218

C.1 Employment Effects - Sectors - West Germany 229
C.2 Employment Effects - Sectors - East Germany 230
C.3 Employment Effects - Type of Promotion - Men in West Germany..231
C.4 Employment Effects - Providers - Men in West Germany 232
C.5 Employment Effects - Type of Prom. and Providers - Women in West Germany..233
C.6 Employment Effects - Type of Promotion - Men in East Germany..234
C.7 Employment Effects - Providers - Men in East Germany.......235
C.8 Employment Effects - Type of Promotion - Women in East Germany..236
C.9 Employment Effects - Providers - Women in East Germany 237

References

AAKVIK, A. (2001): "Bounding a Matching Estimator: The Case of a Norwegian Training Program," *Oxford Bulletin of Economics and Statistics*, 63(1), 115–143.

ABADIE, A., D. DRUKKER, J. LEBER HERR, AND G. W. IMBENS (2004): "Implementing Matching Estimators for Average Treatment Effects in STATA," *The Stata Journal*, 4(3), 290–311.

ABADIE, A., AND G. IMBENS (2004): "Large Sample Properties of Matching Estimators for Average Treatment Effects," Working Paper, Harvard University.

ABBRING, J., AND G. VAN DEN BERG (2003): "The Nonparametric Identification of Treatment Effects in Duration Models," *Econometrica*, 71(5), 1491–1517.

ANGRIST, J. (1998): "Estimating the Labor Market Impact of Voluntary Military Sevice using Social Security Data on Military Applicants," *Econometrica*, 66(2), 249–288.

ANGRIST, J., AND J. HAHN (2004): "When to Control for Covariates? Panel-Asymptotic Results for Estimates of Treatment Effects," *The Review of Economics and Statistics*, 86(1), 58–72.

ANGRIST, J. D., G. W. IMBENS, AND D. B. RUBIN (1996): "Identification of Causal Effects Using Instrumental Variables," *Journal of the American Statistical Association*, 91(434), 444–472.

ANGRIST, J. D., AND D. LAVY (1999): "Using Maimodis' Rule to Estimate the Effect of Class Size on Scholastic Achievement," *Quarterly Journal of Economics*, 114(2), 533–575.

ASHENFELTER, O. (1978): "Estimating the Effects of Training Programs on Earnings," *Review of Economics and Statistics*, 60(1), 47–57.

ASHENFELTER, O., AND D. CARD (1985): "Using the Longitudinal Structure of Earnings to Estimate the Effect of Training Programs," *The Review of Economics and Statistics*, 67(4), 648–660.

AUGURZKY, B., AND C. SCHMIDT (2000a): "The Evaluation of Community-Based Interventions: A Monte Carlo Study," Discussion Paper No. 333, University of Heidelberg, Department of Economics.

——— (2000b): "The Propensity Score: A Means to An End," Working Paper, University of Heidelberg.

BARNOW, B., G. CAIN, AND A. GOLDBERGER (1980): "Issues in the Analysis of Selectivity Bias," in *Evaluation Studies Vol.5*, ed. by E. Stromsdorfer, and G. Farkas, pp. 290–317. Sage Publications.

BEHRMAN, J., Y. CHENG, AND P. TODD (2004): "Evaluating Preschool Programs when Length of Exposure to the Program Varies: A Nonparametric Approach," *Review of Economics and Statistics*, 86(1), 108–132.

BERGEMANN, A., B. FITZENBERGER, B. SCHULTZ, AND S. SPECKESSER (2000): "Multiple Active Labor Market Policy Participation in East Germany: An Assesment of Outcomes," *Konjunkturpolitik*, 51, 195–243.

BERGEMANN, A., B. FITZENBERGER, AND S. SPECKESSER (2001): "Evaluating the Employment Effects of Public Sector Sponsored Training in East Germany: Conditional Difference-in-Differences and Ashenfelters's Dip," Discussion Paper, University of Mannheim.

BERGEMANN, A., AND B. SCHULTZ (2000): "Effizienz von Qualifizierungs- und Arbeitsbeschaffungsmaßnahmen in Ostdeutschland," *Wirtschaft im Wandel*, 6(9), 243–253.

BIJWAARD, G., AND G. RIDDER (2004): "Correcting for Selective Compliance in a Re-employment Bonus Experiment," *Journal of Econometrics*, forthcoming.

BJÖRKLUND, A., AND R. MOFFIT (1987): "Estimation of Wage Gains and Welfare Gains in Self-Selection Models," *Review of Economics and Statistics*, 69(1), 42–49.

BLACK, D., AND J. SMITH (2004): "How Robust is the Evidence on the Effects of the College Quality? Evidence from Matching," *Journal of Econometrics*, 121(1), 99–124.

BLIEN, U., L. BLUME, A. EICKELPASCH, G. GEPPERT, V. MAIERHOFER, AND W. WOLF (2003): "Die Entwicklung der ostdeutschen Regionen," *Beiträge zur Arbeitsmarkt- und Berufsforschung*, 267.

BLIEN, U., F. HIRSCHENAUER, M. ARENDT, H. J. BRAUN, D.-M. GUNST, S. KILCIOGLU, H. KLEINSCHMIDT, M. MUSATI, H. ROSS, D. VOLLKOMMER, AND J. WEIN (2004): "Typisierung von Bezirken der Agenturen der Arbeit," *Zeitschrift für Arbeitsmarktforschung*, 37(2), 146–175.

BLUNDELL, R., AND M. COSTA DIAS (2000): "Evaluation Methods for Non-Experimental Data," *Fiscal Studies*, 21(4), 427–468.

——— (2002): "Alternative Approaches to Evaluation in Empirical Microeconomics," *Portuguese Economic Journal*, 1, 91–115.

BLUNDELL, R., L. DEARDEN, AND B. SIANESI (2005): "Evaluating the Impact of Education on Earnings in the UK: Models, Methods and Results from the NCDS," *Journal of the Royal Statistical Society, Series A*, 168(3), 473–512.

BOARDMAN, A., D. GREENBERG, A. VINING, AND D. WEIMER (2001): *Cost-Benefit Analysis: Concepts and Practice*. Prentice Hall, New York.

BOUND, J., D. JAEGER, AND R. BAKER (1995): "Problems with Instrumental Variables Estimation when the Correlation between the Instruments and the Endogenous Explanatory Variable is Weak," *Journal of the American Statistical Association*, 90(430), 443–450.

BRAND, J., AND C. HALABY (2003): "Regression and Matching Estimates of the Effects of Elite College Attendance on Career Outcomes," Working Paper, University of Wisconsin, Madison.

BREIMAN, L., J. FRIEDMAN, R. OLSEN, AND C. STONE (1984): *Classification and Regression Trees*. Wadsworth International Group, Belmont.

BRINKMANN, C. (1999): "Controlling and Evaluation of Employment Promotion and the Employment Services in Germany," *IAB Labour Market Research Topics*, 36.

BRINKMANN, C., M. CALIENDO, E. JAHN, R. HUJER, AND S. THOMSEN (2002): "Dreifache Heterogenität von ABM und SAM und der Arbeitslosigkeitsstaus der Teilnehmer sechs Monate nach Programm-Ende - Erste deskriptive Befunde," Werkstattbericht 18/2002, IAB, Nuremberg.

BRODATY, T., B. CREPON, AND D. FOUGERE (2001): "Using Matching Estimators to Evaluate Alternative Youth Employment Programs: Evidence from France, 1986-1988," in *Econometric Evaluation of Labour Market Policies*, ed. by M. Lechner, and F. Pfeiffer, pp. 85–123. Physica-Verlag.

BROWNSTONE, D., AND R. VALLETTA (2001): "The Bootstrap and Multiple Imputations: Harnessing Increased Computing Power for Improved Statistical Tests," *Journal of Economic Perspectives*, 15(4), 129–141.

BRYSON, A. (2002): "The Union Membership Wage Premium: An Analysis Using Propensity Score Matching," Discussion Paper No. 530, Centre for Economic Performance, London.

BRYSON, A., R. DORSETT, AND S. PURDON (2002): "The Use of Propensity Score Matching in the Evaluation of Labour Market Policies," Working Paper No. 4, Department for Work and Pensions.

BÜTTNER, T., AND H. PREY (1998): "Does Active Labour-Market Policy Affect Structural Unemployment? An Empirical Investigation for West German Regions, 1986-1993," *Zeitschrift für Wirtschafts- und Sozialwissenschaften*, 118, 389–413.

Bundesanstalt für Arbeit (2002): *Arbeitsmarkt 2001 – Amtliche Nachrichten der Bundesanstalt für Arbeit* 50. Jahrgang, Nürnberg.

BUNDESANSTALT FÜR ARBEIT (2002): *Daten zu den Eingliederungsbilanzen 2001.* Nürnberg.

——— (various issues): *Arbeitsmarkt.* Nürnberg.

Bundesministerium für Wirtschaft und Arbeit (2003): "Moderne Dienstleistungen am Arbeitsmarkt," Bericht der Kommission zum Abbau der Arbeitslosigkeit und zur Umstrukturierung der Bundesanstalt für Arbeit.

BURTLESS, G. (1995): "The Case for Randomized Field Trials in Economic and Policy Research," *Journal of Economic Perspectives*, 9(2), 63–84.

BURTLESS, G., AND L. ORR (1986): "Are Classical Experiments Needed for Manpower Policy?," *The Journal of Human Resources*, 21(4), 606–640.

CALIENDO, M., T. HAGEN, AND R. HUJER (2004): "Makroökonomische Evaluation auf Basis von Regionaldaten," in *Hartz-Gesetze - Methodische Ansätze zu einer Evaluierung*, ed. by T. Hagen, and A. Spermann, pp. 84–97. Nomos-Verlag.

CALIENDO, M., AND R. HUJER (2004a): "Finanzielle Anreize für Arbeitgeber: Kapital für Arbeit und Lohnkostenzuschüsse," in *Hartz-Gesetze - Methodische Ansätze zu einer Evaluierung*, ed. by T. Hagen, and A. Spermann, pp. 203–214. Nomos-Verlag.

——— (2004b): "Reform von ABM und SAM," in *Hartz-Gesetze - Methodische Ansätze zu einer Evaluierung*, ed. by T. Hagen, and A. Spermann, pp. 215–226. Nomos-Verlag.

CALIENDO, M., R. HUJER, AND S. THOMSEN (2003): "Evaluation der Netto-Effekte von ABM in Deutschland - Ein Matching-Ansatz mit Berücksichtigung von regionalen und individuellen Unterschieden," Werkstattbericht 2/2003, IAB, Nuremberg.

CALIENDO, M., AND E. JAHN (2004): "Verbleibsquote ein Controlling-Indikator für den Eingliederungserfolg von ABM!?," *Zeitschrift für Evaluation*, 2(1), 51–69.

CALMFORS, L. (1994): "Active Labour Market Policy and Unemployment - A Framework for the Analysis of Crucial Design Features," *OECD Economic Studies*, 22, 7–47.

CALMFORS, L., A. FORSLUND, AND M. HEMSTRÖM (2002): "Does Active Labour Market Policy Work? Lessons From The Swedish Experience," CESifo Working Paper No. 675(4), CESifo.

CALMFORS, L., AND P. SKEDINGER (1995): "Does Active Labour-Market Policy Increase Employment? Theoretical Considerations and Some Empirical Evidence from Sweden," *Oxford Review of Economic Policy*, 11(1), 91–109.

CARD, D. (2000): "Reforming the Financial Incentives of the Welfare System," Discussion Paper No. 172, IZA, Bonn.

COCHRANE, W., AND S. CHAMBERS (1965): "The Planning of Observational Studies of Human Populations," *Journal of the Royal Statistical Society, Series A*, 128(2), 234–266.

COCHRANE, W., AND D. RUBIN (1973): "Controlling Bias in Observational Studies," *Sankyha*, 35(4), 417–446.

DANN, S., A. KIRCHMANN, A. SPERMAN, AND J. VOLKERT (2001): "Das Einstiegsgeld - eine zielgruppenorientierte negative Einkommensteuer: Konzeption, Umsetzung und eine erste Zwischenbilanz nach 15 Monaten in Baden-Württemberg," Discussion Paper, Institut für Angewandte Wirtschaftsforschung.

DAVIES, R., AND S. KIM (2003): "Matching and the Estimated Impact of Interlisting," Discussion Paper in Finance No. 2001-11, ISMA Centre, Reading.

DAVIES, R., AND S. KIM (2004): "Matching and the Estimated Impact of Interlisting," Working Paper, University of Reading.

DAWID, A. (1979): "Conditional Independence in Statistical Theory," *Journal of the Royal Statistical Society, Series B*, 41(1), 1–31.

DEHEJIA, R. (2005): "Practical Propensity Score Matching," *Journal of Econometrics*, 125, 255–264.

DEHEJIA, R. H., AND S. WAHBA (1999): "Causal Effects in Nonexperimental Studies: Reevaluating the Evaluation of Training Programs," *Journal of the American Statistical Association*, 94(448), 1053–1062.

——— (2002): "Propensity Score Matching Methods for Nonexperimental Causal Studies," *The Review of Economics and Statistics*, 84(1), 151–161.

DINARDO, J., AND J. TOBIAS (2001): "Nonparametric Density and Regression Estimation," *Journal of Economic Perspectives*, 15(4), 11–28.

DIPRETE, T., AND M. GANGL (2004): "Assessing Bias in the Estimation of Causal Effects: Rosenbaum Bounds on Matching Estimators and Instrumental Variables Estimation with Imperfect Instruments," Working Paper, WZB.

DOLTON, P., AND D. O'NEILL (1996): "Unemployment Duration and the Restart Effect: Some Experimental Evidence," *Economic Journal*, 106(435), 387–400.

EICHLER, M., AND M. LECHNER (2002): "An Evaluation of Public Sector Sponsored Continuous Vocational Training Programs in the East German State of Sachsen Anhalt," *Labour Economics*, 9(2), 143–186.

EUROPEAN COMMISSION (2001): "The EU Economy - 2000 Review," Report, European Comission.

FAN, J. (1993): "Local Linear Regression Smoothers and Their Minimax Efficiencies," *The Annals of Statistics*, 21(1), 196–216.

FAY, R. (1996): "Enhancing the Effectiveness of Active Labor Market Policies: Evidence from Programme Evaluations in OECD Countries," Labour Market and Social Policy Occasional Papers, OECD.

FERTIG, M., J. KLUVE, AND C. SCHMIDT (2004): "Evaluation der Umsetzung der Vorschläge der Hartz-Kommission zur Arbeitsmarktpolitik - Erstellung einer Vorstudie," Gutachten erstellt für das Bundesministerium für Wirtschaft und Arbeit (BMWA), RWI, Essen.

FERTIG, M., AND C. SCHMIDT (2000): "Discretionary Measures of Active Labour Market Policy - The German Employment Promotion Reform in Perspective," Working Paper, University of Heidelberg.

FISHER, R. (1935): *Design of Experiments*. Hafner, New York.

FITZENBERGER, B., AND R. HUJER (2002): "Stand und Perspektiven der Evaluation der Aktiven Arbeitsmarktpolitik in Deutschland," *Perspektiven der Wirtschaftspolitik*, 3(2), 139–158.

FITZENBERGER, B., AND S. SPECKESSER (2000): "Zur wissenschaftlichen Evaluation der Aktiven Arbeitsmarktpolitik in Deutschland," *Mitteilungen aus der Arbeitsmarkt und Berufsforschung, Schwerpunktheft: Erfolgskontrolle aktiver Arbeitsmarktpolitik*, 3, 532–549.

FORSLUND, A., AND A. KRUEGER (1994): "An Evaluation of the Swedish Active Labor Market Policy: New and Received Wisdom," Working Paper No. 4802, NBER.

FRAKER, T., AND R. MAYNARD (1987): "The adequacy of comparison group designs for evaluations of employment-related programs," *Journal of Human Resources*, 22(2), 194–227.

FREDRIKSSON, P., AND P. JOHANSSON (2004): "Dynamic Treatment Assignment - The Consequences for Evaluations Using Observational Data," Discussion Paper No. 1062, IZA.

FRÖLICH, M. (2002): *Programme Evaluation and Treatment Choice*. Springer, Lecture Notes in Economics and Mathematical Systems.

——— (2004a): "Finite-Sample Properties of Propensity-Score Matching and Weighting Estimators," *The Review of Economics and Statistics*, 86(1), 77–90.

——— (2004b): "Matching Estimators and Optimal Bandwidth Choice," Discussion Paper, Department of Economics, University of St. Gallen.

——— (2004c): "A Note on the Role of the Propensity Score for Estimating Average Treatment Effects," *Econometric Reviews*, 23(2), 167–174.

GALDO, J. (2004): "Evaluating the Performance of Non-Experimental Estimators: Evidence from a Randomized UI Program," Working Paper, Centre for Policy Research, Toronto.

GERFIN, M., AND M. LECHNER (2002): "A Microeconometric Evaluation of the Active Labour Market Policy in Switzerland," *The Economic Journal*, 112(482), 854–893.

GREENE, W. H. (2003): *Econometric Analysis*. New York University, New York.

HAGEN, T. (2003a): "Do Fixed-Term Contracts Increase the Long-Term Employment Opportunities of the Unemployed?," Discussion Paper 03-49, ZEW.

——— (2003b): "Three Approaches to the Evaluation of Active Labour Market Policy in East Germany Using Regional Data," Discussion Paper 03-27, ZEW.

HAGEN, T., AND A. SPERMANN (2004): *Hartz-Gesetze - Methodische Ansätze zu einer Evaluierung*. Nomos-Verlag, Baden-Baden.

HAGEN, T., AND V. STEINER (2000): *Von der Finanzierung der Arbeitslosigkeit zur Förderung von Arbeit - Analysen und Empfehlungen zur Arbeitsmarktpolitik in Deutschland*. Nomos Verlagsgesellschaft, Baden-Baden.

HAHN, J. (1998): "On the Role of the Propensity Score in Efficient Semiparametric Estimation of Average Treatment Effects," *Econometrica*, 66(2), 315–331.

HAHN, J., P. TODD, AND W. VAN DER KLAAUW (1999): "Evaluating the Effect of an Antidiscrimination Law Using a Regression-Discontinuity Design," Working Paper No. 7131, NBER.

——— (2001): "Identification and Estimation of Treatment Effects with a Regression-Discontinuity Design," *Econometrica*, 69(1), 201–209.

HAM, J., X. LI, AND P. REAGAN (2003): "Propensity Score Matching, a Distance-Based Measure of Migration, and the Wage Growth of Young Men," Working Paper, Department of Economics, Ohio State University.

HÜBLER, O. (1997): "Evaluation beschäftigungspolitischer Maßnahmen in Ostdeutschland," *Jahrbücher für Nationalökonomie und Statistik*, 216, 21–44.

HECKMAN, J. (1978): "Dummy Endogenous Variables in a Simultaneous Equation System," *Econometrica*, 46, 931–959.

——— (1979): "Sample Selection Bias as a Specification Error," *Econometrica*, 47(1), 153–161.

——— (1997): "Instrumental Variables - A Study of the Implicit Behavioral Assumptions Used in Making Program Evaluations," *The Journal of Human Resources*, 32(3), 441–462.

HECKMAN, J. (2001): "Micro Data, Heterogeneity, and the Evaluation of Public Policy: Nobel Lecture," *Journal of Political Economy*, 109(4), 673–748.

References

HECKMAN, J., AND J. HOTZ (1989): "Choosing Among Alternative Nonexperimental Methods for Estimating the Impact of Social Programs: The Case of Manpower Training," *Journal of the American Statistical Association*, 84(408), 862–874.

HECKMAN, J., H. ICHIMURA, J. SMITH, AND P. TODD (1996): "Sources of Selection Bias in Evaluating Social Programs: An Interpretation of Conventional Measures and Evidence on the Effectiveness of Matching as a Program Evaluation Method," *Proceedings of the National Academy of Sciences of the United States of America*, 93(23), 13416–13420.

―――― (1998): "Characterizing Selection Bias Using Experimental Data," *Econometrica*, 66(5), 1017–1098.

HECKMAN, J., H. ICHIMURA, AND P. TODD (1997): "Matching as an Econometric Evaluation Estimator: Evidence from Evaluating a Job Training Programme," *Review of Economic Studies*, 64(4), 605–654.

―――― (1998): "Matching as an Econometric Evaluation Estimator," *Review of Economic Studies*, 65(2), 261–294.

HECKMAN, J., R. LALONDE, AND J. SMITH (1999): "The Economics and Econometrics of Active Labor Market Programs," in *Handbook of Labor Economics Vol.III*, ed. by O. Ashenfelter, and D. Card, pp. 1865–2097. Elsevier, Amsterdam.

HECKMAN, J., AND R. ROBB (1985a): "Alternative Methods for Evaluating the Impact of Interventions - An Overview," *Journal of Econometrics*, 30(1-2), 239–267.

―――― (1985b): "Alternative Models for Evaluating the Impact of Interventions," in *Longitudinal Analysis of Labor Market Data*, ed. by J. Heckman, and B. Singer, pp. 156–245. Cambridge University Press.

HECKMAN, J., AND J. SMITH (1995): "Assessing the Case for Social Experiments," *Journal of Economic Perspectives*, 9(2), 85–110.

―――― (1998): "Evaluating the Welfare State," in *Econometrics and Economic Theory in the 20th Century: The Ragnar Frisch Centennial*, ed. by S. Strom, pp. 241–318. Cambridge University Press.

―――― (1999): "he Pre-Program Earnings Dip and the Determinants of Participation in a Social Program: Implications for Simple Program Evaluation Strategies," *Economic Journal*, 109(457), 313–348.

HECKMAN, J., AND E. VYTLACIL (2001): "Policy-Relevant Treatment Effects," *American Economic Review*, 91(2), 107–111.

HECKMAN, J. J., J. SMITH, AND N. CLEMENTS (1997): "Making the Most out of Programme Evaluations and Social Experiments: Accounting for Heterogeneity in Programme Impacts," *The Review of Economic Studies*, 64(4), 487–535.

HIRANO, K., AND G. IMBENS (2002): "Estimation of Causal Effects using Propensity Score Weighting: An Application to Data on Right Heart Catherization," *Health Services & Outcomes Research Methodology*, 2(3-4), 259–278.

HIRANO, K., G. IMBENS, AND G. RIDDER (2003): "Efficient Estimation of Average Treatment Effects using the Estimated Propensity Score," *Econometrica*, 71(4), 1161–1189.

HITT, L., AND F. FREI (2002): "Do Better Customers Utilize Electronic Distribution Channels? The Case of PC Banking," *Management Science*, 48, No. 6, 732–748.

HOLLAND, P. (1986): "Statistics and Causal Inference," *Journal of the American Statistical Association*, 81(396), 945–960.

HUI, S., AND J. SMITH (2002): "The Labor Market Impacts of Adult Education and Training in Canada," Report Prepared for Human Resources Development Canada.

HUJER, R., U. BLIEN, M. CALIENDO, AND C. ZEISS (2002): "Macroeconometric Evaluation of Active Labour Market Policies in Germany - A Dynamic Panel Approach Using Regional Data," Discussion Paper No. 616, IZA.

——— (2005): "Macroeconometric Evaluation of Active Labour Market Policies in Germany - A Dynamic Panel Approach Using Regional Data," in *Regions, Europe and the Labour Market. Recent Problems and Developments*, ed. by F. Carloeo, and S. Destefanis. forthcoming, Physica Verlag.

HUJER, R., AND M. CALIENDO (2001): "Evaluation of Active Labour Market Policy - Methodological Concepts and Empirical Estimates," in *Soziale Sicherung in einer dynamischen Gesellschaft*, ed. by I. Becker, N. Ott, and G. Rolf, pp. 583–617. Campus-Verlag.

——— (2003): "Lohnsubventionen in Deutschland - Wie sieht eine optimale Evaluierungsstrategie aus?," *Quarterly Journal of Economic Research - Vierteljahreshefte zur Wirtschaftsforschung*, 72(1), 109–123.

HUJER, R., M. CALIENDO, AND D. RADIC (2001a): "Estimating the Effects of Wage Subsidies on the Labour Demand in West Germany Using the IAB Establishment Panel," *ifo-Studien*, 47(2), 163–199.

——— (2001b): "Nobody Knows...How Do Different Evaluation Estimators Perform in a Simulated Labour Market Experiment?," Working Paper, J.W.Goethe-University, Frankfurt.

——— (2004): "Methods and Limitations of Evaluation and Impact Research," in *The Foundations of Evaluation and Impact Research (CEDEFOP Reference Series 58)*, ed. by P. Descy, and M. Tessaring, pp. 131–190. Office for Official Publications of the European Communities.

HUJER, R., M. CALIENDO, AND S. THOMSEN (2004): "New Evidence on the Effects of Job Creation Schemes in Germany - A Matching Approach with Threefold Heterogeneity," *Research in Economics*, 58(4), 257–302.

HUJER, R., AND D. RADIC (2005): "Evaluating the Impacts of Subsidies on Innovation Activities in Germany," *Scottish Journal of Political Economy*, forthcoming.

HUJER, R., AND M. WELLNER (2000a): "Berufliche Weiterbildung und individuelle Arbeitslosigkeitsdauer in West- und Ostdeutschland: Eine mikroökonometrische Analyse," *Mitteilungen aus der Arbeitsmarkt- und Berufsforschung*, 33(3), 405–420.

─────── (2000b): "The Effects of Public Sector Sponsored Training on Individual Employment Performance in East Germany," Discussion Paper No. 141, IZA.

HUJER, R., AND C. ZEISS (2003): "Macroeconomic Impacts of ALMP on the Matching Process in West Germany," Working Paper No. 915, IZA.

IMBENS, G. (2000): "The Role of the Propensity Score in Estimating Dose-Response Functions," *Biometrika*, 87(3), 706–710.

─────── (2004): "Nonparametric Estimation of Average Treatment Effects under Exogeneity: A Review," *The Review of Economics and Statistics*, 86(1), 4–29.

IMBENS, G., AND J. ANGRIST (1994): "Identification and Estimation of Local Average Treatment Effects," *Econometrica*, 62(2), 467–475.

JACKMAN, R., C. PISSARIDES, AND S. SAVOURI (1990): "Labour Market Policies and Unemployment in the OECD," *Economic Policy*, 5, 450–490.

KRAUS, F., P. PUHANI, AND V. STEINER (2000): "Do Public Works Programs Work? Some Unpleasant Results from the East German Experience," in *Research in Labour Economics*, ed. by S. Polachek. JAI Press.

LALONDE, R. (1986): "Evaluating the Econometric Evaluations of Training Programs with Experimental Data," *The American Economic Review*, 76(4), 604–620.

LAYARD, R., S. NICKELL, AND R. JACKMAN (1991): *Unemployment - Macroeconomic Performance and the Labour Market*. Oxford University Press, New York.

LECHNER, M. (1998): "Mikroökonometrische Evaluationsstudien: Anmerkungen zu Theorie und Praxis," in *Qualifikation, Weiterbildung und Arbeitsmarkterfolg. ZEW-Wirtschaftsanalysen Band 31*, ed. by F. Pfeiffer, and W. Pohlmeier. Nomos-Verlag.

─────── (1999): "Earnings and Employment Effects of Continuous Off-the-Job Training in East Germany After Unification," *Journal of Business Economic Statistics*, 17(1), 74–90.

─────── (2000a): "An Evaluation of Public Sector Sponsored Continuous Vocational Training Programs in East Germany," *Journal of Human Resources*, 35(2), 347–375.

——— (2000b): "A Note on the Common Support Problem in Applied Evaluation Studies," Discussion Paper, SIAW.

——— (2001): "Identification and estimation of causal effects of multiple treatments under the conditional independence assumption," in *Econometric Evaluation of Labour Market Policies*, ed. by M. Lechner, and F. Pfeiffer, pp. 1–18. Physica-Verlag, Heidelberg.

——— (2002a): "Programme Heterogeneity and Propensity Score Matching: An Application to the Evaluation of Active Labor Market Policies," *The Review of Economics and Statistics*, 84(2), 205–220.

——— (2002b): "Some practical issues in the evaluation of heterogenous labour market programmes by matching methods," *Journal of the Royal Statistical Society, A*, 165, 59–82.

——— (2004): "Sequential Matching Estimation of Dynamic Causal Models," Discussion Paper, No. 1042, IZA.

LECHNER, M., AND R. MIQUEL (2002): "Identification of Effects of Dynamic Treatments by Sequential Conditional Independence Assumptions," Working Paper, SIAW.

LEUVEN, E., AND B. SIANESI (2003): "PSMATCH2: Stata Module to Perform Full Mahalanobis and Propensity Score Matching, Common Support Graphing, and Covariate Imbalance Testing," Software, http://ideas.repec.org/c/boc/bocode/s432001.html.

MANSKI, C. (1997): "The Mixing Problem in Programme Evaluation," *The Review of Economic Studies*, 64(4), 537–553.

MANSKI, C. (2000): "Using Studies of Treatment Response to Inform Treatment Choice in Heterogeneous Populations," Technical Working Paper, No. 263, NBER.

MANTEL, N., AND W. HAENSZEL (1959): "Statistical Aspects of the Analysis of Data from Retrospective Studies of Disease," *Journal of the National Cancer Institute*, 22(4), 719–748.

MARTIN, J. (1998): "What Works Among Active Labour Market Polices: Evidence From OECD Countries' Experience," Occasional Papers, OECD.

MARTIN, P., AND D. GRUBB (2001): "What works and for whom: A review of OECD countries experiences with active labour market policies," *Swedish Economic Policy Review*, 8, 9–56.

NAVARRO-LOZANO, S. (2002): "Matching, Selection and the Propensity Score: Evidence from Training in Mexico," Working Paper, University of Chicago.

NEYMAN, J. (1935): "Statistical Problems in Agricultural Experiments," *The Journal of the Royal Statistical Society*, 2(2), 107–180.

OECD (1991): *Employment Outlook*. Paris.

――― (1993): *Employment Outlook*. Paris.
――― (1994): *The OECD Jobs Study*. OECD, Paris.
――― (1999): *Employment Outlook*. Paris.
――― (2002): *Employment Outlook*. Paris.
――― (2004): *Employment Outlook*. Paris.
PAGAN, A., AND A. ULLAH (1999): *Nonparametric Econometrics*. Cambridge University Press, Cambridge.
PANNENBERG, M., AND J. SCHWARZE (1998): "Labor Market Slack and the Wage curve," *Economics letters*, 58(3), 351–354.
PERKINS, S. M., W. TU, M. G. UNDERHILL, X. ZHOU, AND M. D. MURRAY (2000): "The Use of Propensity Scores in Pharmacoepidemiologic Research," *Pharmacoepidemiology and Drug Safety*, 9(2), 93–101.
PREY, H. (1999): *Wirkungen staatlicher Qualifizierungsmaßnahmen. Eine empirische Untersuchung für die Bundesrepublik Deutschland*. Paul Haupt-Verlag, Bern, Stuttgart, Wien.
PUHANI, P. (1998): "Advantage through Training? A Microeconometric Evaluation of the Employment Effects of Active Labour Market Programmes in Poland," Discussion Paper No. 98-25, ZEW.
PUHANI, P. A. (2000): "The Heckman Correction for Sample Selection and Its Critique," *Journal of Economic Surveys*, 14(1), 53–68.
QUANDT, R. (1972): "Methods for Estimating Switching Regressions," *Journal of the American Statistical Association*, 67(338), 306–310.
――― (1988): *The Economics of Disequilibrium*. Basil Blackwell, Oxford.
ROSENBAUM, P., AND D. RUBIN (1983): "The Central Role of the Propensity Score in Observational Studies for Causal Effects," *Biometrika*, 70(1), 41–50.
――― (1985a): "The Bias due to Incomplete Matching," *Bioemetrics*, 41(1), 103–116.
――― (1985b): "Constructing a Control Group Using Multivariate Matched Sampling Methods that Incorporate the Propensity Score," *The American Statistican*, 39(1), 33–38.
ROSENBAUM, P. R. (2002): *Observational Studies*. Springer, New York.
ROY, A. (1951): "Some Thoughts on the Distribution of Earnings," *Oxford Economic Papers*, 3(2), 135–145.
RUBIN, D. (1973): "The Use of Matching and Regression Adjustment to Remove Bias in Observational Studies," *Biometrics*, 29(1), 185–203.
――― (1974): "Estimating Causal Effects to Treatments in Randomised and Non-randomised Studies," *Journal of Educational Psychology*, 66, 688–701.
――― (1977): "Assignment to Treatment Group on the Basis of a Covariate," *Journal of Educational Studies*, 2, 1–26.

―――― (1979): "Using Multivariate Matched Sampling and Regression Adjustment to Control Bias in Observational Studies," *Journal of the American Statistical Association*, 74(366), 318–328.

―――― (1980): "Comment on Basu, D. - Randomization Analysis of Experimental Data: The Fisher Randomization Test," *Journal of the American Statistical Association*, 75(371), 591–593.

RUBIN, D. B., AND N. THOMAS (1996): "Matching Using Estimated Propensity Scores: Relating Theory to Practice," *Biometrics*, 52(1), 249–264.

SCHMID, G., S. SPECKESSER, AND C. HILBERT (2000): "Does Active Labour Market Policy Matter? An Aggregate Impact Analysis for Germany," in *Labour Market Policy and Unemployment. Evaluation of Active Measures in France, Germany, The Netherlands, Spain and Sweden*, pp. 2–41. Edward Elgar.

SCHMIDT, C. (1999): "Knowing What Works - The Case for Rigorous Program Evaluation," Discussion Paper No. 77, IZA.

SEIFERT, B., AND T. GASSER (1996): "Finite-Sample Variance of Local Polynomials: Analysis and Solutions," *Journal of American Statistical Association*, 91(433), 267–275.

―――― (2000): "Data Adaptive Ridging in Local Ploynomial Regression," *Journal of Computational and Graphical Statistics*, 9(2), 338–360.

SELL, S. (1998): "Entwicklung und Reform des Arbeitsförderungsgesetzes als Anpassung des Sozialrechts an flexible Erwerbsformen," *Mitteilungen aus der Arbeitsmarkt und Berufsforschung*, 3, 532–549.

SIANESI, B. (2001): "An Evaluation of the Active Labour Market Programmes in Sweden," Working Paper No. 2001:5, IFAU - Office of Labour Market Policy Evaluation.

―――― (2004): "An Evaluation of the Active Labour Market Programmes in Sweden," *The Review of Economics and Statistics*, 86(1), 133–155.

SILVERMAN, B. (1986): *Density Estimation for Statistics and Data Analysis*. Chapman & Hall, London.

SMITH, H. (1997): "Matching with Multiple Controls to Estimate Treatment Effects in Observational Studies," *Sociological Methodology*, 27, 325–353.

SMITH, J. (2000a): "A Critical Survey of Empirical Methods for Evaluating Active Labor Market Policies," *Schweizerische Zeitschrift für Volkswirtschaft und Statistik*, 136(3), 1–22.

―――― (2000b): "Evaluating Active Labour Market Policies: Lessons from North America," *Mitteilungen aus der Arbeitsmarkt und Berufsforschung*, 3, 345–356.

―――― (2004): "Evaluating Local Development Policies: Theory and Practice," Working Paper, University of Maryland.

SMITH, J., AND P. TODD (2005): "Does Matching Overcome LaLonde's Critique of Nonexperimental Estimators?," *Journal of Econometrics*, 125(1-2), 305–353.

STAAT, M. (1997): *Empirische Evaluation von Fortbildung und Umschulung - Schriftenreihe des ZEW 21*. Nomos Verlagsgesellschaft, Baden-Baden.

STEIGER, H. (2004): "Is Less More? A Look at Nonparticipation in Swiss Active Labour Market Programmes," Working Paper, University of St.Gallen.

STEINER, V., AND F. KRAUS (1995): "Haben Teilnehmer an Arbeitsbeschaffungsmaßnahmen in Ostdeutschland bessere Wiederbeschäftigungschancen als Arbeitslose?," in *Mikroökonomik des Arbeitsmarktes*, ed. by L. Bellmann, and V. Steiner, pp. 387–423. IAB - Beiträge zur Arbeitsmarkt- und Berufsforschung 192.

STEINER, V., E. WOLF, J. EGELN, M. ALMUS, H. SCHRUMPF, AND P. FELDOTTO (1998): *Strukturanalyse der Arbeitsmarktentwicklung in den neuen Bundesländern*. Nomos Verlagsgesellschaft, Baden-Baden.

VAN DEN BERG, G. (2001): "Duration Models: Specification, Identification, and Multiple Durations," in *Handbook of Econometrics*, ed. by J. Heckman, and E. Leamer, vol. 5, chap. 55, pp. 3381–3462. North-Holland.

VAN OURS, J. (2004): "The Locking-in Effect of Subsidized Jobs," *Journal of Comparative Economics*, 32(1), 37–52.

VYTLACIL, E. (2002): "Independence, Monotonicity and Latent Index Models: An Equivalence Result," *Econometrica*, 70(1), 331–341.

ZHAO, Z. (2000): "Data Issues of Using Matching Methods to Estimate Treatment Effects: An Illustration with NSW Data Set," Working Paper, China Centre for Economic Research.

——— (2004): "Using Matching to Estimate Treatment Effects: Data Requirements, Matching Metrics, and Monte Carlo Evidence," *The Review of Economics and Statistics*, 86(1), 91–107.

Lecture Notes in Economics and Mathematical Systems

For information about Vols. 1–475
please contact your bookseller or Springer-Verlag

Vol. 476: R. Demel, Fiscal Policy, Public Debt and the Term Structure of Interest Rates. X, 279 pages. 1999.

Vol. 477: M. Théra, R. Tichatschke (Eds.), Ill-posed Variational Problems and Regularization Techniques. VIII, 274 pages. 1999.

Vol. 478: S. Hartmann, Project Scheduling under Limited Resources. XII, 221 pages. 1999.

Vol. 479: L. v. Thadden, Money, Inflation, and Capital Formation. IX, 192 pages. 1999.

Vol. 480: M. Grazia Speranza, P. Stähly (Eds.), New Trends in Distribution Logistics. X, 336 pages. 1999.

Vol. 481: V. H. Nguyen, J. J. Strodiot, P. Tossings (Eds.). Optimation. IX, 498 pages. 2000.

Vol. 482: W. B. Zhang, A Theory of International Trade. XI, 192 pages. 2000.

Vol. 483: M. Königstein, Equity, Efficiency and Evolutionary Stability in Bargaining Games with Joint Production. XII, 197 pages. 2000.

Vol. 484: D. D. Gatti, M. Gallegati, A. Kirman, Interaction and Market Structure. VI, 298 pages. 2000.

Vol. 485: A. Garnaev, Search Games and Other Applications of Game Theory. VIII, 145 pages. 2000.

Vol. 486: M. Neugart, Nonlinear Labor Market Dynamics. X, 175 pages. 2000.

Vol. 487: Y. Y. Haimes, R. E. Steuer (Eds.), Research and Practice in Multiple Criteria Decision Making. XVII, 553 pages. 2000.

Vol. 488: B. Schmolck, Ommitted Variable Tests and Dynamic Specification. X, 144 pages. 2000.

Vol. 489: T. Steger, Transitional Dynamics and Economic Growth in Developing Countries. VIII, 151 pages. 2000.

Vol. 490: S. Minner, Strategic Safety Stocks in Supply Chains. XI, 214 pages. 2000.

Vol. 491: M. Ehrgott, Multicriteria Optimization. VIII, 242 pages. 2000.

Vol. 492: T. Phan Huy, Constraint Propagation in Flexible Manufacturing. IX, 258 pages. 2000.

Vol. 493: J. Zhu, Modular Pricing of Options. X, 170 pages. 2000.

Vol. 494: D. Franzen, Design of Master Agreements for OTC Derivatives. VIII, 175 pages. 2001.

Vol. 495: I. Konnov, Combined Relaxation Methods for Variational Inequalities. XI, 181 pages. 2001.

Vol. 496: P. Weiß, Unemployment in Open Economies. XII, 226 pages. 2001.

Vol. 497: J. Inkmann, Conditional Moment Estimation of Nonlinear Equation Systems. VIII, 214 pages. 2001.

Vol. 498: M. Reutter, A Macroeconomic Model of West German Unemployment. X, 125 pages. 2001.

Vol. 499: A. Casajus, Focal Points in Framed Games. XI, 131 pages. 2001.

Vol. 500: F. Nardini, Technical Progress and Economic Growth. XVII, 191 pages. 2001.

Vol. 501: M. Fleischmann, Quantitative Models for Reverse Logistics. XI, 181 pages. 2001.

Vol. 502: N. Hadjisavvas, J. E. Martínez-Legaz, J.-P. Penot (Eds.), Generalized Convexity and Generalized Monotonicity. IX, 410 pages. 2001.

Vol. 503: A. Kirman, J.-B. Zimmermann (Eds.), Economics with Heterogenous Interacting Agents. VII, 343 pages. 2001.

Vol. 504: P.-Y. Moix (Ed.), The Measurement of Market Risk. XI, 272 pages. 2001.

Vol. 505: S. Voß, J. R. Daduna (Eds.), Computer-Aided Scheduling of Public Transport. XI, 466 pages. 2001.

Vol. 506: B. P. Kellerhals, Financial Pricing Models in Con-tinuous Time and Kalman Filtering. XIV, 247 pages. 2001.

Vol. 507: M. Koksalan, S. Zionts, Multiple Criteria Decision Making in the New Millenium. XII, 481 pages. 2001.

Vol. 508: K. Neumann, C. Schwindt, J. Zimmermann, Project Scheduling with Time Windows and Scarce Resources. XI, 335 pages. 2002.

Vol. 509: D. Hornung, Investment, R&D, and Long-Run Growth. XVI, 194 pages. 2002.

Vol. 510: A. S. Tangian, Constructing and Applying Objective Functions. XII, 582 pages. 2002.

Vol. 511: M. Külpmann, Stock Market Overreaction and Fundamental Valuation. IX, 198 pages. 2002.

Vol. 512: W.-B. Zhang, An Economic Theory of Cities.XI, 220 pages. 2002.

Vol. 513: K. Marti, Stochastic Optimization Techniques. VIII, 364 pages. 2002.

Vol. 514: S. Wang, Y. Xia, Portfolio and Asset Pricing. XII, 200 pages. 2002.

Vol. 515: G. Heisig, Planning Stability in Material Requirements Planning System. XII, 264 pages. 2002.

Vol. 516: B. Schmid, Pricing Credit Linked Financial Instruments. X, 246 pages. 2002.

Vol. 517: H. I. Meinhardt, Cooperative Decision Making in Common Pool Situations. VIII, 205 pages. 2002.

Vol. 518: S. Napel, Bilateral Bargaining. VIII, 188 pages. 2002.

Vol. 519: A. Klose, G. Speranza, L. N. Van Wassenhove (Eds.), Quantitative Approaches to Distribution Logistics and Supply Chain Management. XIII, 421 pages. 2002.

Vol. 520: B. Glaser, Efficiency versus Sustainability in Dynamic Decision Making. IX, 252 pages. 2002.

Vol. 521: R. Cowan, N. Jonard (Eds.), Heterogenous Agents, Interactions and Economic Performance. XIV, 339 pages. 2003.

Vol. 522: C. Neff, Corporate Finance, Innovation, and Strategic Competition. IX, 218 pages. 2003.

Vol. 523: W.-B. Zhang, A Theory of Interregional Dynamics. XI, 231 pages. 2003.

Vol. 524: M. Frölich, Programme Evaluation and Treatment Choise. VIII, 191 pages. 2003.

Vol. 525: S. Spinler, Capacity Reservation for Capital-Intensive Technologies. XVI, 139 pages. 2003.

Vol. 526: C. F. Daganzo, A Theory of Supply Chains. VIII, 123 pages. 2003.

Vol. 527: C. E. Metz, Information Dissemination in Currency Crises. XI, 231 pages. 2003.

Vol. 528: R. Stolletz, Performance Analysis and Optimization of Inbound Call Centers. X, 219 pages. 2003.

Vol. 529: W. Krabs, S. W. Pickl, Analysis, Controllability and Optimization of Time-Discrete Systems and Dynamical Games. XII, 187 pages. 2003.

Vol. 530: R. Wapler, Unemployment, Market Structure and Growth. XXVII, 207 pages. 2003.

Vol. 531: M. Gallegati, A. Kirman, M. Marsili (Eds.), The Complex Dynamics of Economic Interaction. XV, 402 pages, 2004.

Vol. 532: K. Marti, Y. Ermoliev, G. Pflug (Eds.), Dynamic Stochastic Optimization. VIII, 336 pages. 2004.

Vol. 533: G. Dudek, Collaborative Planning in Supply Chains. X, 234 pages. 2004.

Vol. 534: M. Runkel, Environmental and Resource Policy for Consumer Durables. X, 197 pages. 2004.

Vol. 535: X. Gandibleux, M. Sevaux, K. Sörensen, V. T'kindt (Eds.), Metaheuristics for Multiobjective Optimisation. IX, 249 pages. 2004.

Vol. 536: R. Brüggemann, Model Reduction Methods for Vector Autoregressive Processes. X, 218 pages. 2004.

Vol. 537: A. Esser, Pricing in (In)Complete Markets. XI, 122 pages, 2004.

Vol. 538: S. Kokot, The Econometrics of Sequential Trade Models. XI, 193 pages. 2004.

Vol. 539: N. Hautsch, Modelling Irregularly Spaced Financial Data. XII, 291 pages. 2004.

Vol. 540: H. Kraft, Optimal Portfolios with Stochastic Interest Rates and Defaultable Assets. X, 173 pages. 2004.

Vol. 541: G.-y. Chen, X. Huang, X. Yang, Vector Optimization. X, 306 pages. 2005.

Vol. 542: J. Lingens, Union Wage Bargaining and Economic Growth. XIII, 199 pages. 2004.

Vol. 543: C. Benkert, Default Risk in Bond and Credit Derivatives Markets. IX, 135 pages. 2004.

Vol. 544: B. Fleischmann, A. Klose, Distribution Logistics. X, 284 pages. 2004.

Vol. 545: R. Hafner, Stochastic Implied Volatility. XI, 229 pages. 2004.

Vol. 546: D. Quadt, Lot-Sizing and Scheduling for Flexible Flow Lines. XVIII, 227 pages. 2004.

Vol. 547: M. Wildi, Signal Extraction. XI, 279 pages. 2005.

Vol. 548: D. Kuhn, Generalized Bounds for Convex Multistage Stochastic Programs. XI, 190 pages. 2005.

Vol. 549: G. N. Krieg, Kanban-Controlled Manufacturing Systems. IX, 236 pages. 2005.

Vol. 550: T. Lux, S. Reitz, E. Samanidou, Nonlinear Dynamics and Heterogeneous Interacting Agents. XIII, 327 pages. 2005.

Vol. 551: J. Leskow, M. Puchet Anyul, L. F. Punzo, New Tools of Economic Dynamics. XIX, 392 pages. 2005.

Vol. 552: C. Suerie, Time Continuity in Discrete Time Models. XVIII, 229 pages. 2005.

Vol. 553: B. Mönch, Strategic Trading in Illiquid Markets. XIII, 116 pages. 2005.

Vol. 554: R. Foellmi, Consumption Structure and Macroeconomics. IX, 152 pages. 2005.

Vol. 555: J. Wenzelburger, Learning in Economic Systems with Expectations Feedback (planned) 2005.

Vol. 556: R. Branzei, D. Dimitrov, S. Tijs, Models in Cooperative Game Theory. VIII, 135 pages. 2005.

Vol. 557: S. Barbaro, Equity and Efficiency Considerations of Public Higer Education. XII, 128 pages. 2005.

Vol. 558: M. Faliva, M. G. Zoia, Topics in Dynamic Model Analysis. X, 144 pages. 2005.

Vol. 559: M. Schulmerich, Real Options Valuation. XVI, 357 pages. 2005.

Vol. 560: A. von Schemde, Index and Stability in Bimatrix Games. X, 151 pages. 2005.

Vol. 561: H. Bobzin, Principles of Network Economics. XX, 390 pages. 2006.

Vol. 562: T. Langenberg, Standardization and Expectations. IX, 132 pages. 2006.

Vol. 563: A. Seeger (Ed.), Recent Advances in Optimization. XI, 455 pages. 2006.

Vol. 564: P. Mathieu, B. Beaufils, O. Brandouy (Eds.), Artificial Economics. XIII, 237 pages. 2005.

Vol. 565: W. Lemke, Term Structure Modeling and Estimation in a State Space Framework. IX, 224 pages. 2006.

Vol. 566: M. Genser, A Structural Framework for the Pricing of Corporate Securities. XIX, 176 pages. 2006.

Vol. 567: A. Namatame, T. Kaizouji, Y. Aruga (Eds.), The Complex Networks of Economic Interactions. XI, 343 pages. 2006.

Vol. 568: M. Caliendo, Microeconometric Evaluation of Labour Market Policies. XVII, 258 pages. 2006.

Vol. 569: L. Neubecker, Strategic Competition in Oligopolies with Fluctuating Demand. IX, 233 pages. 2006.

Vol. 570: J. Woo, The Political Economy of Fiscal Policy. X, 169 pages. 2006.

Vol. 571: T. Herwig, Market Conform Valuation of Options. VIII, 104 pages. 2006.

Printing and Binding: Strauss GmbH, Mörlenbach